Studying Interpersonal Interaction

THE GUILFORD COMMUNICATION SERIES

Studying

Interpersonal

Interaction

EDITED BY

Barbara M. Montgomery, PhD
Steve Duck, PhD

THE GUILFORD PRESS
New York   London

© 1991 The Guilford Press
A Division of Guilford Publications, Inc.
72 Spring Street, New York, NY 10012

Printed in the United States of America

This book is printed on acid-free paper.

Last digit is print number: 9 8 7 6 5 4 3 2

Library of Congress Cataloging-in-Publication Data

Studying interpersonal interaction / edited by Barbara M. Montgomery, Steve Duck.
   346 p.   cm. — (Guilford communication series)
   Includes bibliographical references and index.
   ISBN 0-89862-312-X   ISBN 0-89862-290-5 (pbk)
   1. Social interaction.   2. Interpersonal communication.
  I. Montgomery, Barbara M. II. Duck, Steve. III. Series.
  HM131.S833 1991
  302—dc20   90-20933
                                              CIP

Contributors

Roger Bakeman, PhD, Department of Psychology, Georgia State University, University Plaza, Atlanta, GA 30303

Leslie A. Baxter, PhD, Department of Rhetoric and Communication, University of California, Davis, CA 95616

Arthur P. Bochner, PhD, Department of Communication, University of South Florida, Tampa, FL 33620

Rosalie Burnett, DPhil, Centre for Criminological Research, University of Oxford, Oxford, England OX2 6LH

Joseph N. Cappella, PhD, Annenberg School of Communication, University of Pennsylvania, Philadelphia, PA 19104

Kenneth N. Cissna, PhD, Department of Communication, University of South Florida, Tampa, FL 33620

William R. Cupach, PhD, Department of Communication, Illinois State University, Normal, IL 61761-6901

Steve Duck, PhD, Department of Communication Studies, University of Iowa, 151 Communication Studies Building, Iowa City, IA 52242

Michael G. Garko, PhD, Department of Communication, University of South Florida, Tampa, FL 33620

Michael E. Holmes, MS, Department of Communication, Purdue University, West Lafayette, IN 47907

Lawrence A. Hosman, PhD, Department of Speech Communication, University of Southern Mississippi, Southern Station Box 5131, Hattiesburg, MS 39406-5131

DEBORAH A. KASHY, MA, Department of Psychology, University of Connecticut, Storrs, CT   06269-1020

DAVID A. KENNY, PhD, Department of Psychology, University of Connecticut, Storrs, CT   06269-1020

GEORGE J. McCALL, PhD, Department of Sociology, University of Missouri, 8001 Natural Bridge Road, St. Louis, MO   63121

SANDRA METTS, PhD, Department of Communication, Illinois State University, Normal, IL   61767-6901

BARBARA M. MONTGOMERY, PhD, Department of Communication, University of New Hampshire, Durham, NH   03824

MARSHALL SCOTT POOLE, PhD, Department of Speech Communication, University of Minnesota, Minneapolis, MN   55455

CARL A. RIDLEY, PhD, Division of Family Studies, School of Family and Consumer Resources, University of Arizona, Tucson, AZ   85721

BARRY H. SCHNEIDER, PhD, Child Study Centre, University of Ottawa, 120 University, Ottawa, Ontario, Canada   K1N 6N5

ALAN L. SILLARS, PhD, Department of Interpersonal Communication, University of Montana, Missoula, MT   59812

J. L. SIMMONS, PhD, Department of Sociology, University of Missouri, 8001 Natural Bridge Road, St. Louis, MO   63121

SUSAN SPRECHER, PhD, Department of Sociology, Illinois State University, Normal, IL   61761-6901

CATHERINE A. SURRA, PhD, Department of Human Ecology, Division of Child Development and Family Relationships, Mary Gearing Hall, University of Texas at Austin, Austin, TX   78712-1097

CHARLES H. TARDY, PhD, Department of Speech Communication, University of Southern Mississippi, Southern Station Box 5131, Hattiesburg, MS   39406-5131

KAREN TRACY, PhD, Department of Communication, University of Colorado, Campus Box 270, Boulder, CO   80309

REBECCA WARNER, PhD, Department of Psychology, University of New Hampshire, Durham, NH   03824

Contents

PART IV: CONCLUSION

Preface

Learning to do good research is a continuous educational experience. It begins for each of us in different ways: with an elementary school science project or a beginning sociology lecture or a Statistics I course. But it never ends. No matter whether we are working on our fifth or our fiftieth research project, experienced researchers know that there is always much more to learn.

This book is intended for those among us who still enjoy learning, especially about ways to study human interaction in interpersonal settings like families, acquaintanceships, friendships, and romantic partnerships. The book offers a comprehensive, critical examination of current research methods in the study of human social behavior. Graduate students and advanced undergraduates will find the book to be a thorough, sophisticated, yet easy to read text for research-oriented courses. Active scholars will find the book to be an invaluable reference for mustering arguments both for and against using particular methods in particular situations.

This is not a how-to book. Chapter authors consistently direct readers to other sources for specific, step-by-step, technical information. Rather, each chapter presents the conceptual rationale underlying a particular approach to data generation or data analysis, relates in general how the approach works, and describes those research purposes that the approach addresses particularly well and those that it does not.

A special feature of the book is the illustrative reference in each chapter to a sample research problem: an "argumentative" exchange that occurs between a hypothetical couple, Michael and Cathy Stone, in the presence of their friends, the Millers. Each chapter author worked with the same transcription, which appears immediately after this preface, to develop applications, illustrate controversial issues, and describe the potential of the particular method under discussion. The result is that readers can compare methods across chapters with reference to the same research context.

Other themes emerge from the chapters as well. There is a marked vitality to the discussions that reflects an energetic development of new methodological approaches to the study of interaction and a reinvigorating fine-tuning of established methods. A thoughtful and reasonable tone also pervades the chapters. No soapbox diatribes are to be found in these pages. The authors explicitly renounce the "law of the hammer," which encourages researchers to hit their investigative problems over and over again with the same methods. Instead, the chapters speak in one voice as they encourage rational methodological choices and an awareness of the theoretical bases of such choices. The underlying assumption is that all approaches are reasonable ones, depending upon one's research purposes. Authors straightforwardly recount both the advantages and disadvantages, the benefits and costs, for each method. The result is a thoughtful and provocative set of chapters that is as useful to the junior researcher as to the seasoned veteran as both make choices about how best to study the questions that concern them.

Part I sets this theme of making reasonable choices by considering the assumptions that researchers must make about the nature of social interaction in order to study it. Steve Duck and Barbara Montgomery begin this section by noting that good research demands rigorously crafted investigative analyses aimed at (1) formulating a research problem in such a way as to make it accessible to study and (2) analyzing the data to provide appropriate answers to the questions posed. The authors examine the relationship between these two analytic processes of problem formulation and data analysis, arguing that each necessarily influences the other and that each carries significant assumptions about the very nature of social interaction. Duck and Montgomery describe many specific links among interaction itself (i.e., "substance"), theory, and method—links that are often overlooked in the research process. They conclude by noting that a competent researcher recognizes that the choice of a methodological approach also implicates choices of certain conceptualizations of interaction phenomena (and the exclusion of others) and certain theoretical assumptions (and the exclusion of others).

In Chapter 2 Art Bochner, Ken Cissna, and Michael Garko carry the theme of research choices further when they consider the many paradigms or perspectives that reflect ways of thinking about interpersonal interaction and in which researchers can anchor their studies. The authors describe in detail perspectives based on control (e.g., compliance gaining, social cognition, and that of constructivists), coordination (e.g., coorientation, coordinated management of meaning) and contextualized interaction (e.g., the interactional view and radical constructivists). Bochner, Cissna, and Garko review, albeit briefly, the world view, vocabulary, research interests, methodologies, and analytic procedures associated with each perspective.

They conclude by arguing that the choice of a perspective should not be made on the basis of any reality-testing criterion, but rather on the basis of the perspective's usefulness. That is, which perspective best accommodates the researcher's goals?

In Chapter 3 Cathy Surra and Carl Ridley contrast information about interaction gained from different sources that are traditionally described as "subjective" (i.e., participants) or "objective" (i.e., peers and observers). The authors argue persuasively that differences among these sources in the way they view interaction reflect differences in the magnitude of their behavioral and cognitive interdependence with the interactants. With this observation as a frame of reference, Surra and Ridley review a considerable body of research that points to systematic and patterned differences among participants', peers' and observers' assessments of the same interactions. The products of this review are a comprehensive list of factors that uniquely shape interaction assessments and, equally important, a description of the research goals, purposes, and conditions that should prompt the choice of a particular data source.

George McCall and J. L. Simmons tackle the problem of choosing levels and units of analysis in Chapter 4. As backdrop to this methodological issue, the authors explicate the multiple layers of meaning inherent in interaction and linked to the hierarchical roles that interactants occupy at individual, dyadic, and group levels of analysis of social organization. The authors call particular attention to what a researcher can "see" by studying an interaction: glimpses of collective action, role construction, and behavioral tactics for accommodating multiple social roles. In their analysis, McCall and Simmons identify and discuss some of the dilemmas of both single- and multiple-level analyses, and they argue that while multiple-level analyses present problems, single-level analyses are *inherently* flawed because they ignore social contexts.

Becky Warner, in Chapter 5, discusses the many ways that time can be incorporated into interaction research. She notes that time can be conceptualized as a resource, suggesting questions about the rewards and costs associated with time allocation, about activities of varying time durations, and about synchronization with other activities. The researcher also can focus on time as it is perceived by interactants, as in the example of time urgency. Warner discusses a number of methodological issues involving time, including time sampling, the role of time as an independent and as a dependent variable, and the nature of time series data. She also reviews two major tracks in the research literature that incorporate time: one that focuses on cycles and one that focuses on sequences. Researchers in both tracks ask the same three basic questions: (1) How is interaction behavior structured over time? (2) How do partners influence each other's behaviors through time? (3) How are the structure and predictability of interaction over time associated with relationship quality? As an in-depth review, Warner's chapter contributes significantly to the development of a language for talking about temporal issues in interaction research.

In Chapter 6 Joe Cappella draws attention to mutual adaptation, stressing that it is an essential defining characteristic of interpersonal communication, that it involves a pervasive set of interaction behaviors, that it exists in even the earliest instances of human interaction between infant and parent, and that it covaries with important relational and individual conditions. Cappella points out that measuring adaptation patterns typically is accomplished through codings, ratings, participant judgments, and observer judgments; and he contrasts these techniques for their precision, efficiency, and utility. Cappella's chapter extends well beyond analytic comparison, however, when he argues that researchers should search for ways to transform results gained from one measurement frame to another. He contends that no one frame is superior to another and that each contributes important but relatively esoteric information about interaction. Cappella suggests some possible avenues for pursuing transformation methods, and he describes a number of both practical and theoretical benefits for initiating such a pursuit.

Part II examines a variety of procedures for gathering interaction data. For instance, in Chapter 7 Roz Burnett details methods for collecting and using accounts and narratives. She notes that employing such subjective explanations and narratives of experience broadens the range of potential data sources from the more traditional forms of self-reported information to letters, books, diaries, stories, and even dialogue. Burnett illustrates how such accounts can provide information about both the content or topics of interaction (e.g., who does which household chores, as well as when, where, and how well) and the processes of interaction (e.g., how meanings are negotiated, how marital roles evolve). Her comprehensive examination of the benefits and the problems associated with account data makes an important contribution to the ongoing dialogue about promising ways of learning about social interaction.

Steve Duck continues that dialogue in Chapter 8 as he describes the use of self-report logs or diaries to produce data about day-to-day interaction events. Two extensive examples, the Rochester Interaction Record and the Iowa Communication Record, illustrate the advantages and some few disadvantages of diary methods. Duck goes further, though, to encourage a mindful consideration of some fairly "radical" but perhaps not obvious assumptions that accompany diary methods, namely, that interpretations of an experience can meaningfully change over time; that relationships exist not only in how partners interact, but also in what they think about their interaction; and that differences among participants' reports are significant sources of information about interaction, not merely error or bias.

In Chapter 9, Sandra Metts, Sue Sprecher, and Bill Cupach describe potential ways for using retrospective self-reports of interactants' experiences, perceptions, feelings, and sense-makings. The authors succinctly review a variety of research designs and data collection procedures particularly well suited for studies of interpersonal interaction. They also discuss at length the advantages—both practical and theoretical—and the disadvantages associated with retrospective self-report data. Throughout, Metts, Sprecher, and Cupach provide multiple examples from the literature. Particularly helpful are their extended illustrations anchored to the common research problem used in this text. The authors demonstrate how self-reports would be particularly effective for studying perceived causes of the conflict that occurs between the hypothetical couple, their management strategies, and the relational impact of the conflict episode on their relationship.

In Chapter 10 Karen Tracy describes five different ways in which discourse is commonly used as data. These include (1) ethnomethodological or conversational analysis, (2) formal/structural approaches that extend the methods of linguistics, (3) culturally focused approaches that link discourse to cultural group membership, (4) discourse-processing analysis that tests theories about text comprehension and production, and (5) discourse and identity approaches that examine associations between discourse characteristics and social outcomes. Tracy's descriptions are enhanced with multiple examples drawn from the discourse literature and from the sample research problem used in this text. Throughout the chapter, she contrasts the different approaches to assessing discourse data along a fixed set of characteristics so that the comparisons are clear and crisp. And she ends the chapter with a description of a new discourse methodology, the laboratory case study, that opens up new possibilities for understanding interaction by focusing on its continuous text.

Chapter 11 by Alan Sillars provides a detailed, in-depth analysis of observational methods. Even those who are most active in the domain of observational research will benefit from an attentive reading of this chapter. After recounting the particular suitability of observational methods for capturing the "in process" nature of interaction, Sillars contrasts the usefulness of observing natural, staged, and simulated interactions, and of using direct, audio-, and video-recording procedures. He provides helpful guidelines for subject, event, and behavioral sampling and for dealing with reactivity to observation.

In Chapter 12, Charles Tardy and Lawrence Hosman examine experimental approaches to studying interaction. After succinctly reviewing the vocabulary and purposes of experiments, the authors consider what distinguishes a good experiment from a bad one, especially in light of current criticisms that experimental methods are artificial, rest on impoverished ontological assumptions, and produce results that lack ecological validity. They convincingly argue that as experimental approaches have matured, direct steps have been taken to address these problems. The authors end the chapter with an extended discussion of how experimental methods could be applied to the research problem represented by the hypothetical couple, the Stones.

Part III highlights relatively new and newly rediscovered methods for analyzing interaction data (we assume that readers are already familiar with traditional regression and mean-differences approaches to data analysis). The chapters present key considerations in deciding to use particular analytic techniques and direct readers to numerous sources for exemplars and for detailed instruction in the step-by-step application of each method.

The section begins with Chapter 13, in which Leslie Baxter examines content analytic methods. Baxter contrasts "manifest" approaches, which describe surface-level interaction content, with "interpretive" approaches, which seek to represent the underlying meanings of content. She focuses primarily on the latter, arguing that interpretive approaches are more complex and challenging to the researcher, especially with regard to reliability and validity issues. Using a set of semantic structures to suggest the varied questions a researcher might pursue through content analysis, Baxter describes five different content analytic options: domain analysis, taxonomic analysis, componential analysis, thematic analysis, and sequential analysis. Her explication is all the richer for the many research examples she provides.

Roger Bakeman details in Chapter 14 two useful methods for analyzing categorical data like those resulting from counting and coding interaction behaviors. The first of these is a simple, and thus all the more elegant, procedure that casts data into 2×2 tables to assess sequential associations or transitions. Bakeman describes a number of well-known and not so well-known statistics for testing the significance of these sequential transitions. Along the way he addresses the issues of sampling and dyadic and sequential interdependence, and his treatment is a fitting complement to the discussion presented by Kenny and Kashy in Chapter 15. The second procedure Bakeman describes is log-linear analysis. Readers will find Bakeman's explanations and examples to be clear and most understandable as he applies log-linear methods to the common researcher problem used in this book.

In Chapter 15 Dave Kenny and Deborah Kashy focus on methods for analyzing data that demonstrate between-dyad interdependence, that is, interdependence in partners' scores that shows up across a sample of dyads. Most researchers know such interdependence as a statistical annoyance, something to be avoided through design manipulations or, worse, by throwing away half of the data. Kenny and Kashy take a different position by treating interdependence not as a problem but as an "opportunity to learn" about the essence of interpersonal relationships. The authors review a series of procedures for measuring interdependence and for dealing constructively with its presence. Highlighted among these is an explication of the Social Relations Model, developed by Kenny and used to decompose interdependence into three distinct types—individual, dyadic, and occasion-specific.

Longitudinal analysis is the theme developed by Michael Holmes and Scott Poole in Chapter 16. These authors describe two quite different but useful procedures for examining time-ordered observations of interaction. The first is traditional time series analysis, which allows the researcher to answer questions about patterns and order in continuous data, developmental trends, cycles, interdependence through time between two variables, and the impact of interventions on a time series. The second is phasic analysis, which punctuates interaction codes into units larger than individual acts or interacts. Phasic analysis allows the researcher to test different models of development, to describe different structural properties of longitudinal interaction (like cycles, repetitions, transitions), and to identify factors that influence development. Using the sample research problem posed in this text, Holmes and Poole lead the reader through an extensive but straightforward illustration of how to conduct a phasic analysis.

In Chapter 17, Barry Schneider describes the problems associated with drawing substantive conclusions about interaction from studies that vary widely in methodologies, sample sizes, quality, effect sizes, and findings. He offers detailed examples of literature reviews that point up their subjectivity and idiosyncratic approaches. To solve these problems, Schneider suggests a number of both qualitative and quantitative techniques, including rigorous attention to the purpose of the review, the sampling of studies, the development of classification schemes, and the use of statistical, meta-analytic techniques.

The book concludes with Chapter 18, in which Barbara Montgomery and Steve Duck argue for methodological pluralism over ethnocentrism. The authors encourage researchers with different and seemingly incommensurate perspectives on interpersonal interaction to engage in an open dialogue in which participants get beyond perspective-exalting monologues to meaningful exchanges that advance understanding about interaction. The authors describe a number of information coordination devices that would facilitate such exchanges among representatives of different perspectives, and they point to examples from the literature and from this text that illustrate the substantive benefits of such exchanges.

We would like to thank Chris Brenneman at the University of Iowa and Kathy Simoneau and Cindy Farrell at the University of New Hampshire for their sterling assistance with the editing chores that go along with preparing a manuscript for print.

BARBARA M. MONTGOMERY
University of New Hampshire

STEVE DUCK
University of Iowa

The Sample Research Problem

The following transcription, produced from a videotaped recording that was part of study of marital communication (Montgomery, 1980), was provided to each contributing author of this text for analysis. Names and some identifying particulars have been changed to protect participants' identities.

Michael and Cathy Stone, who have been married for 5 years, begin an argument in front of the Millers (James and Holly), their dinner guests and long-term friends. The argument is about how to fairly share in getting household tasks done. The following is an excerpt from the argument.*

Holly Miller has just asked how the Stones manage to entertain so graciously when both of them work full-time.

01 CATHY: We can entertain because I do it all!
02 MICHAEL: She's right about the dinner. You wouldn't want to eat my
             cooking—so:: I just don't cook.
                                              [
03 CATHY: You don't cook, you don't
             clean, you don't do laundry!
04 MICHAEL: Come on—that's not fair.
                                       [
05 CATHY: Especially this summer. With a full load at
             work it's a lot of work and the thing that really bothers me is
             that you don't notice when things need to be done! You
             either, you choose to ignore these things, don't you.
             (pause)

---

*Each numbered segment can be considered a turn at talk; overlapping turns are indicated by square brackets ([) placed where the overlap begins; brief pauses within turns are marked with a dash; longer pauses of approximately one second or longer are indicated by (pause); termination marks (? ! .) indicate intonation patterns; the colon (:) indicates prolongation of the preceding syllable, the more colons (:::), the longer the prolongation.

06 MICHAEL: Like the cat box?
                    |
07 CATHY: The dishes really bother me.
08 MICHAEL: I do occasionally do them—but not enough.
09 CATHY: I don't know—we've talked about this before and over the
             course of our marriage it used to bother me more, the
             housework, I think we've gotten a little looser on them—
             maybe not but
             (pause)
10 MICHAEL: Sometimes I think about how I'd do them more often prob-
             ably if you weren't around.
11 CATHY: You mean like if you weren't married to me you might do
             them more often!
12 MICHAEL: Yeah, I may be forced to do them. But you know generally
             I'm not too conscious of these things also. I mean I don't
             have, I don't think in terms of that I should empty the
             garbage again or do that stuff
                                        |
13 CATHY: You mean you just don't think!

Studying Interpersonal Interaction

PART I

ISSUES IN THE STUDY OF INTERPERSONAL INTERACTION

Chapter 1

The Interdependence among Interaction Substance, Theory, and Methods

STEVE DUCK
BARBARA M. MONTGOMERY

Someone recently explained that you're always falling when you're riding a unicycle. The trick is to be constantly balancing one force against another, countering one pull with an opposing motion, and adjusting the wheel under you so that you get where you're going by sustaining and controlling the fall. Doing interaction research seems to be a lot like this. The social scientific environment threatens a serious upending to researchers by pulling them in different directions with competing investigative perspectives, each with its own obstacle course of epistemological and methodological imperatives and semantic rigamarole. Just as the unicyclist counters a fall by a constant juggling of forces, so researchers must vigilantly adapt to the turbulent conditions for investigating interpersonal interaction by matching methods of inquiry to theoretical views, fitting procedures to research questions, and coordinating conclusions from different studies using diverse methodologies.

If we are successful, then a state of exquisitely disciplined imbalance that propels us forward is achieved. Present research goals are met while, simultaneously, progress is made toward future innovations in conceptualization and methodology. Achieving such an imbalance requires risk and rigor. The rigor emerges from implementing a carefully crafted plan of investigative analysis, and the risk arises from an openness to new and different ideas, methods, and perspectives. This chapter—indeed, this book—is about both of these processes.

Risk and Rigor in the Study of Interaction

Researchers planning an investigative program face many difficult choices that require careful, informed analysis. Some scholars typically talk of analysis and mean simply data manipulation. That is, for those scholars, *analysis* refers to working out the forms of data description and/or testing that would be the most appropriate, given the study's purposes. Researchers know that some techniques do some sorts of work and others do different sorts. They know also that care must be taken not to violate a technique's statistical assumptions in applying it to the data. Such analysis is, by its nature, usually carried out during the study.

Another sort of analysis, too infrequently discussed but at least as important, concerns researchers' attempts to formulate a research problem in such a way as to make it accessible to scientific study. In this sense, scholars do considerable analytic work *before* undertaking any particular study. Such work and thinking are essential to ensure that our efforts will be meaningful within the social scientific community. However, the issues involved in this sort of analysis are rarely considered as routinely as are those involved in selecting appropriate statistical tests. Nevertheless, we believe that they are as important and deserve a place here. In short, we draw the start of the process of studying interpersonal interaction at the stage *before* specific design of a particular study itself.

For this reason, one of our interests in this chapter and in this book is in the relationship between these two sorts of analyses, namely, problem formulation and data manipulation. In a way, we are urging researchers to pay as much attention to the medium as to the message and to extend the sorts of thinking that have been done so effectively by those writers who explore the rhetoric of inquiry (Nelson, Megill, & McCloskey, 1987; Prelli, 1989). They focus on the uses and effects of language, the style of argument, and the form of expression of ideas as influences on the structure and even the contents of those ideas. We likewise urge researchers to attend to the effects of the structure and style of our research methods on the form and content of that research.

In brief, we contend that study design and data manipulation techniques will always have built into them assumptions about problem formulation—often unspoken and unarticulated—about one key issue: What constitutes meaningful information about interaction? Today, these assumptions revolve about such issues as the comparative advantages of interpretive and objectivist approaches, the value of participant, peer, and observer perspectives, and the appropriate social unit—individual, dyad, or group—to study.

Assumptions about the very nature of the questions that can be answered through research about interaction are embedded in every methodological approach. To use a questionnaire is implicitly to credit subjects with insight into the processes that we seek to study (Harvey, Hendrick, & Tucker, 1988). To leave questions about talk off a self-report form assessing social participation (Wheeler & Nezlek, 1977) is implicitly to relegate talk to a mere catalytic medium for the transmission and enunciation of internal cognition or thought processes. To employ time series analysis (see Chapters 14 and 16) is to adopt implicitly a model of the universe founded on change rather than stability. To conduct a reliability check on any form of measurement is to subscribe to a model that implies universal stability in the relevant phenomenon, as researchers did for many years in relation to children's early friendships—before they realized that the phenomenon itself is inherently unstable!

Such assumptions are just as important for researchers to analyze as are the frequently pondered assumptions about the structure of data that are built into statistical tests and regularly form the substance of journal reviewers' comments. Partly what we mean here is simply that all of a researcher's tools and approaches are shaped for particular purposes: one does not saw with a screwdriver or hammer with a wrench. More than this, however, we argue by analogy that *to reach for* a wrench rather than a screwdriver is already to act as if the problem has a certain structure. We wish to emphasize that the value of a particular method can be assessed not only in relation to its purposes but also in relation to the assumptions that go with it or are built into it.

Extending this idea, we would also point out that when a researcher approaches a particular topic (such as, say, relationship dissolution) and has it in mind to apply a particular theory (such as, say, Exchange Theory), he or she should be aware of a converse of the above points. Most general theories of human behavior were not crafted specifically to apply to the range of topics to which they are now applied. Why does this matter? Because in approaching a topic, a researcher, as argued above, brings in an implicit conceptualization of the topic as he or she "tools up" for its study. If a Grand Theory does not specify its conceptualization of a particular topic and how the theory should be applied to that conceptualization, then each researcher has to rely on his or her own "theorette" about the nature of the topic. In ways that are probably not going to be made explicit by each researcher, these "theorettes" may differ from one researcher to another. For example, one researcher may assume that relationship dissolution is an event to be simply predicted; another may assume that the event is a product of extended and linked processes that need to be understood as a chain of events, each with its own causal connections. Yet each researcher may use the same Grand Theory irrespective of these differences. For instance, both "simple-event approaches" and "linked-event approaches" have been used to discuss divorce from the perspective of Exchange Theory (see Moles & Levinger, 1979; Orbuch, in press).

Such implicit and unannounced differences between research approaches actually make comparison of the different efforts much more difficult and meretricious than might at first appear to be the case. The point is that similarity of theoretical approach does not guarantee equivalency in the conceptualization of the problem. We must look deeper.

We also want to emphasize the close relationship between logical analysis of a research problem and operational or statistical analysis of it. The more closely a scholar's methods resemble the assumptions of his or her guiding theory, the better he or she will address the problem. Also, the more closely the mathematical operations in a statistical procedure model the psychological, communicative, or behavioral operations that we believe our subjects demonstrate, the more confident we can be that the statistical operations both capture and model the psychological or behavioral realities of the world that we study. For instance, if one's data manipulations sum together a subject's responses on different scales, it behooves one to think carefully whether the subject's psychological processees also actually perform summation in like fashion or perhaps take more adventurous and complex algorithmic turns.

With such goals in mind, the following section discusses some of the close relationships between theory, method, and substance in the analysis of social interaction.

Links between Substance, Theory, and Method

It is not new to suggest that our theories influence our methodological choices. Indeed, authors habitually explicate and justify their methods in terms of theory. By this they mean that theory directs choices of methods or that methods can be placed in terms of a given theory. However, we should look deeper and see that methods often have built-in "theorettes" about phenomena (Duck, in press) that were *not* explicated by their authors or users nor always carefully considered by reviewers.

LINKS BETWEEN THEORY AND SUBSTANCE

In order to measure, one must measure something. The choice about exactly what should be measured, however, is usually made implicitly to be consistent with some theoretical "story" that the researcher has in mind. For example, research on courtship progress often assumes that relationship development is based on route planning and, thus, that trajectories underlie the process—trajectories from lesser involvement to greater intimacy. While such theoretical assumptions are a necessary part of the research process, they are significantly constraining. Having made a trajectory assumption, for instance, researchers are likely to assume that "the relationship" that develops does so by keeping a constant form and moving through different scenery or stages. They are not inclined to explore the possibility that relationships are developed by deep-order transformations—as insects grow from egg to larva to pupa to adult—or the possibility that relationships grow from the resolution of dialectic tensions, each resolution essentially creating a new style or form for the relationship.

The trajectory work also assumes that the driving forces for relationship growth are to be found in the heads of the partners or in the negotiations that they carry out between them about such cranial content. This assumption constrains researchers from exploring the influences of social forces, network members, social norms, time, situation, or environment. Thus, the choice of trajectories as the prevailing theoretical "story" of relationship development limits the research to measuring linear processes in terms of products created by the relationship partners.

Some researchers argue that they avoid the shackles of such theoretical assumptions by adopting a descriptive approach to research. Unfortunately, this argument only begs the question. *Descriptive data are not inherently atheoretical,* since the items chosen to be included in the description are themselves selected from a range of possible items (known and unknown) while others are excluded. For example, to focus on a child's play behavior at school excludes, implicitly, the role of the home environment on play, the scholastic experience on play, and the parent–child relationship on play; one also implicitly excludes personality variables that are not measured, and one treats play as one item in the child's life separate from other factors. Other ways of studying play may implicitly or explicitly include some of these other factors and therefore would implicate a different "theorette" about the role of play in the child's life. In this vein, Hinde (1989) has urged researchers to look instead for commonalities across these different spheres of a child's life.

The point is that inquiry is never innocent. It does not bring information to a blank slate. The vocabularies, interests, thinking patterns, and methodological choices that we bring to a research problem become a part of the solution as well.

LINKS BETWEEN METHOD AND THEORY

We see the unforeseen implications of the tie between method and theory quite clearly in investigations of the question of whether personality similarity increases the likelihood that two persons will get along well. Are two similar people more likely to become fast friends than two dissimilar people? This question has a long and venerable history and has generated much heat and only a little light. The reason for both energy products comes down to the fact that different researchers measured personality and similarity, as well as "getting on well in relationships," in different ways (Duck, 1977, Chapter 6). Some assessed liking, some used marital satisfaction, and some dating choice; some evaluated similarity in terms of the difference between total scores on personality tests of extraversion–introversion, some in terms of specific agreements on particular questions in a large multidimensional test, and some according to profile similarity on such tests. Finally, the range of different sorts of personality tests was legion.

Despite such important differences, scholars insisted on comparing studies as if those differences did not exist or did not matter. In other words, reviewers did not attend to the different "theorettes" about phenomena that were *built in* to the different methods used. Also, they acted as if any measure of similarity was as good as any other, they did not relate similarity to the stage of a relationship that had been reached by the partners when the assessments were done.

But such differences do matter. Consider this: if I as a researcher believe that the existence of similarity is what creates satisfactory relationships, whether the two partners are aware of it or not, then I may be happy to measure similarity in a way that is inaccessible to partners (e.g., absolute total similarity score summed across all items on a personality test). Further, if I believe that total amounts of such similarity are all that is important, then I will sum them without reference to the particular answers that each person gives to particular questions. On the other hand, if I believe that in real life it is important for relationships that two persons know that they are similar, then I am likely to measure similarity on a test that describes everyday behaviors that partners can really see each other perform or perhaps on a test that assesses attitudes that they admit to having discussed. I am also likely to assess similarity by means of a close comparison of particular answers to particular questions without paying any attention to the overall similarity score as a blind total.

Furthermore, if I assume that relationships develop and that development is based on different layers of similarity (superficial similarity at first—in terms of broad, unsubtle dimensions, such as extraversion—and then similarity at more refined and obscure levels later, such as the specific constructs that a person uses to understand another's psychology), then I will set about my research in a way that allows me to test for *layers* of similarity as well as for the simple existence of total similarity scores. I might also design my measures in such a way as to get at the ways in which people gain access to different layers of one another's personalities at different times in real-life communication (for example, by including both measures of large-frame political attitude questions and measures of the details of personal life and measuring them at different stages in the relationship's development). As Neimeyer and Mitchell (1988) have shown, such assumptions about layers of similarity do give a much better handle on this particular issue.

The general point is that the choice to measure particular aspects of social interaction is based on the researcher's conceptualization of the phenomenon—the geography of its important elements and those parts felt to be unimportant. The assumption of the essence of the phenomenon manifests itself in assumptions about the relationships between variables, and although these relationships are often part of the researcher's explicit theory about the phenomena, they may also be hidden in the measures and methods that the researcher uses or in the nonexplicit "theorette" conceptualizing the phenomenon yet not spelled out in the full theory itself.

Just as theoretical assumptions (both explicit and implicit) influence methods, so too do methods influence theory and reflect inbuilt researcher "theorettes". For instance, the chosen types of measures influence the kinds of explanations that will be offered. Consider the area of social support, a field of research that has experienced remarkable growth in recent years (Duck, 1990; Gottlieb, 1987; Hobfoll, 1988; Hobfoll & Stokes, 1988; Sarason, Sarason, & Pierce, 1990). Such research shows, by and large, that a person with more friends and more intimate relationships survives the vicissitudes of life more efficiently and for a longer period than does someone without such support. Naturally, a great deal of research has been devoted to exploring this phenomenon. Explanations have ranged from the psychological, (that is, personality characteristics of persons with large social networks (I. G. Sarason, B. R. Sarason, Shearin, & Pierce, 1987) to the communicative, (that is, the ways in which persons choose to comfort and cheer up others (Barbee, 1990; Burleson, 1990). One explanation is that a person receives social support or believes social support to exist or not as a function of personality factors (Pierce, B. R. Sarason, & I. G. Sarason, 1990). In other words, people are responsible, in some sense, for the amount of support that they receive or can extract from others (Conn & McQuinn, 1989). As Heller (1989) has argued, however, it is quite possible that researchers who reach this conclusion do so because they ask people about their social support in a way that is very similar to the ways we ask them about personality, or indeed builds personality-trait assumptions into the question. For example, the answer to the question, Who accepts you totally, including your worst and best points? is used by Sarason et al. (1987) to assess the amount of support that a person feels he or she can command. It does, however, seem to be based on the idea that the person can conceive of trust in a way rather similar to that embodied in some personality test (e.g., the Interpersonal Style Inventory [Lorr, Youniss, & Huba, 1986] measures an individual's characteristic ways of relating to other on 15 scores in five areas, including "trusting," "tolerance," and "help-seeking"). In both cases a personality variable is almost built into the structure of the question, and thus any explanation of social support *as* a personality variable, if it relies on such questions alone, is clearly derived from the *method* used to assess it.

Perhaps an even more insidious characteristic of this hidden connection between theoretical assumptions and methods involves the fact that the two are often not synchronized in their development. For instance, one may have a stated developmental view of the phenomenon but fail to actually assess it developmentally. A second example is the recent calls for a dyadic view of relationships, a theoretical perspective that treats the couple as the unit of interest. Whether the emphasis is on behavioral exchanges or on the more general, systemic characteristics that the couple possesses *as a couple,* attention is on the dyad itself as a unit, rather than on the two separate individuals in the dyad. In this connection, Hinde (1981) pointed out that certain relational constructs are *emergent,* that is, they are not created by one individual but emerge from the interrelationship of two persons, as, for example, similarity cannot be a simple property of one person, but only of two persons relative to one another. Such a dyadic view implicitly claims that researchers should focus on change in relationships, especially as it is mediated by communication, negotiation, discovery, and compromise.

As theoretically seductive as this dyadic notion has been for many, the methodological consummation of the idea has been far from satisfying because new methods have not proliferated at the same rate as the new theoretical perspective or else because researchers have failed to see that they are working at an individual level to explain essentially dyadic action. To explain dyadic development and dyadic issues, most theoretical work still persists in providing individual-based explanations often founded in individual psychological characteristics (Duck, 1990). While these new methods obviously have their place in the grand scheme of things, they cannot satisfy that place by claiming to explain dyadic action while also "theorette-ically" adopting an individual means of assessing it. Their driving Grand Theory treats dyadic action as something over and above the two individuals in the pair; the "theorette," by contrast, treats the dyad as meaningfully composed of two individuals acting *on* each other rather than *together with* each other. Therefore, researchers either have been forced to reframe their innovative research questions into more mundane forms that can be addressed with mainstream individually-focused methods or, even worse, have used the old methods to provide answers to the new questions, thus violating a host of relevant theoretical and methodological, rather than purely statistical, assumptions (see Kenny, 1988, for detailed examples).

The ideal solution to this kind of problem is the creation of new methods that are compatible with the new theoretical assumptions. This is what is happening to extend the dyadic perspective (see Kenny, 1988, and Kenny & Kashy, Chapter 15, this volume). Yet development of new methods is slow and widespread adoption is even slower. In the meantime, researchers cannot be excused for rushing into research programs with inappropriate, outdated methods, such as measurement of individual characteristics duly compared in a vacuum without attention to the ways in which they arise in emergent form out of interaction. Similarity, as assessed by comparison of two individuals' psychological profiles, is not the same thing as the similarities that the two persons see in themselves and can discover by joint action.

The purpose of interaction research is to change the knowledge base, ideally by increasing it. Accomplishing this goal, however, often brings obsolescence to the very methods used to achieve it. With new knowledge come new questions and the need for new methodologies to address them. For example, researchers do not need more refined and inscrutable measures of similarity of the kinds that are inaccessible to subjects in real life; rather, they need to devote more time first to developing theoretical approaches to the processes that subjects must use to detect and use similarity. Then they must attend to developing methods that access the similarities perceived and acted upon by subjects in their real lives. The reverse is also true: new methodologies suggest new, substantive, interesting questions about interaction. Thus, data analytic techniques and problem formulations are linked in an evolving system. Pragmatically, this means that researchers must not only keep up with emerging ideas about interaction; they also must constantly be involved in reexamining, readjusting, and retooling their methods.

LINKS BETWEEN METHOD AND SUBSTANCE

Researchers have long been aware that the very act of investigating is itself able to affect what is being investigated. What one finds during interaction research is, at least partially, a function of the way in which one chooses to find it. Methodology influences substance. Subjects, for instance, often know that they are the objects of study, and this awareness itself has an impact on the things that they do and say in the research setting. Aware or suspicious subjects are more likely to speculate about the researcher's "true" purpose and to react, either intentionally or unintentionally, by adapting their responses (Orne, 1962; Rosenthal, 1965).

Further, the range of possible responses and behavior is often limited in interaction studies. Self-report surveys ask only a small sample of the questions that might be asked about interaction, and they impose restrictions on the form and the extensiveness of subjects' answers, as well as giving subjects cues as to the usual range of response by setting options and marking endpoints. Observation studies occur in the social context of the research setting, which may well alter the range of behaviors that a subject is willing or prepared to exhibit. As a result, subjects may feel inhibited because of a concern for social appropriateness or they may feel empowered to violate social norms because being in a scientific experiment legitimates unusual behavior (see Orne & Holland, 1968). Additionally, characteristics of the researcher, like physical and social attractiveness, sex, style, and research expectations, are also likely to affect results (Rosenthal & Rosnow, 1969).

These types of influences have been responded to, primarily, in two very different ways. The first has been to erect stronger boundaries between the phenomena and the ways in which we study them, with the goal of reducing and/or controlling the opportunities for methods to contaminate substance. Thus, it is common for investigations to include multiple reliability checks on coders, manipulation checks, control conditions, and instruments that assess social desirability and demand characteristics. All of these tactics are initiated in the name of reducing the bias and increasing the objectivity of the researchers' methods.

In sharp contrast, the second response to the fact that methodology influences substance eschews attempts at objectivity. Rather, this approach endeavors to transcend the boundary between substance and method by assuming a recursive relationship between the researcher and the re-searched. Both are seen to interact to construct knowledge. This "radical constructivist" perspective (see Chapter 2) has many variations, but all affirm the inherent subjective quality of research. Feminist scholarship, for instance, regularly makes this very point.

Despite the apparent incommensurability of these two approaches (but see Chapter 18), researchers associated with each share a core of three critical conclusions about the links between method and substance (noted below). The quality of their scholarship—no matter whether it be objective or subjective in nature—depends upon accommodating these presumptions in their work.

The first conclusion is that *objectivity in interaction research is impossible.* While researchers might differ about whether objectivity is a myth or an ideal, most would agree that it is unobtainable because of inherent confounding conditions in interaction research. Researchers, as behaving, thinking, feeling human beings, study other humans behaving, thinking, and feeling. Further, it takes interaction to study interaction; that is, interaction is both research method and research substance.

Second, as a consequence of the first conclusion, *researchers are responsible for acknowledging, assessing, and accommodating the subjectivity (i.e., "bias" or "social constructions") inherent in the research endeavor.* Since it is futile to adopt a goal to eradicate subjectivity, researchers must actively seek to reconcile its influence with their other purposes. For some, this means identifying and actively constraining confounding sources of bias as much as is reasonably possible. In the spirit of Campbell and Stanley (1963), these researchers employ creative unobtrusive procedures and sound investigative designs. For others, this means deliberately adopting a subjective stance in relation to what they study and thus consciously incorporating personal reactions, intuitions, and empathies into the research process. As an example, Dobris and White (1990) discuss the benefits and limitations of their perceptions as white feminist women interpreting the communication of black feminist women.

Third, *rigorously planned and executed research leads to superior knowledge about interaction*. Research is rigorous to the extent that it holds to the standards for excellence appropriate for the perspective in which it is grounded. All viable research approaches have methodological standards, both qualitative or quantitative (see Rosengren, 1989). Indeed, the remainder of this book documents the many and varied criterion systems that define good research. It is the researcher's responsibility to be well informed, current, and competent in meeting the standards of the particular approach that he or she chooses.

Conclusion

With such thoughts and goals in mind, the authors of the rest of this book lay out the range of methods available to researchers and consider their advantages and drawbacks in clarifying the dynamics between Michael and Cathy Stone, the participants in the sample interaction chosen as the "sample research problem" of this text. Choice between methods is not simply a question of evaluating the pros and cons considered in each of the chapters but of asking oneself the following question: What are the pros and cons of this method in light of (1) my purposes, (2) my conceptualization of the phenomenon, and (3) my stated theory?

In short, a method is never good or bad in and of itself but only in relation to some goal. Achievement of the goal requires the researcher to balance out the pushes and pulls of "theorettes" conflicting with theory, theories competing between themselves, and empirical constraints—to achieve, like the unicyclist, that state of exquisitely disciplined imbalance that makes forward motion possible. Both researcher and unicyclist are essentially in a predicament, solvable by application of developed skills and expertise; a unicyclist has only so far to fall, but a researcher is placed on a potentially more satisfying and essentially less painful seat.

References

Barbee, A. P. (1990). Interactive coping: The cheering up process in close relationships. In S. W. Duck, *Personal relationships and social support* (R. Cohen Silver, Ed.; pp. 46–65). London: Sage.

Burleson, B. R. (1990). Comforting as social support: Relational consequences of supportive behaviors. In S. W. Duck, *Personal relationships and social support* (R. Cohen Silver, Ed.; pp. 66–82). London: Sage.

Campbell, D. T., & Stanley, J. C. (1963). *Experimental and quasi-experimental designs for research*. Chicago: Rand McNally.

Conn, M. K., & McQuinn, R. D. (1989). Loneliness and aspect of social support networks. *Journal of Social and Personal Relationships, 6,* 359–372.

Dobris, C., & White, C. (1990). *Identity discourse: Rhetorical implications for feminist theory and methodology*. Paper presented at the Eastern Communication Association Convention, Philadelphia.

Duck, S. W. (1977). *The study of acquaintance*. Teakfields/Saxon House: Farnborough, UK.

Duck, S. W. (1990). Relationships as unfinished business: Out of the frying pan and into the 1990s. *Journal of Social and Personal Relationships, 7,* 5–29.

Duck, S. W. (in press). The role of theory in relationship loss. In T. L. Orbuch (Ed.), *Relationship loss*. New York: Springer.

Gottlieb, B. H. (1987). *Marshalling social support*. Newbury Park: SAGE.

Harvey, J. H., Hendrick, S. S., & Tucker, K. (1988). Self-report methods in studying personal relationships. In S. W. Duck, D. F. Hay, S. E. Hobfoll, W. Ickes, & B. Montgomery (Eds.), *Handbook of personal relationships* (pp. 99–113). Chichester, UK: Wiley.

Heller, K. (1989, May). The structure of supportive ties among elderly women. Paper presented at the Second International Network on Personal Relationships Conference, Iowa City.

Hinde, R. A. (1981). The bases of a science of interpersonal relationships. In S. W. Duck & R. Gilmour (Eds.), *Personal relationships: 1. Studying personal relationships* (pp. 1–22). London: Academic Press.

Hinde, R. A. (1989, May). *Personality and relationships*. Paper presented at the Second International Network on Personal Relationships Conference, Iowa City.

Hobfoll, S. E. (1988). Overview of section on Community and Clinical. In S. W. Duck, D. F. Hay, S. E. Hobfoll, W. Ickes, & B. Montgomery (Eds.), *Handbook of personal relationships* (pp. 487–495). Chichester, UK: Wiley.

Hobfoll, S. E., & Stokes, J. P. (1988). The process and mechanics of social support. In S. W. Duck, D. F. Hay, S. E. Hobfoll, W. Ickes, & B. Montgomery (Eds.), *Handbook of personal relationships* (pp. 497–517). Chichester, UK: Wiley.

Kenny, D. A. (1988). The analysis of data from two-person relationships. In S. W. Duck, D. F. Hay, S. E. Hobfoll, W. Ickes, & B. Montgomery (Eds.), *Handbook of personal relationships* (pp. 57–77). Chichester, UK: Wiley.

Lorr, M., Youniss, R., & Huba, G. (1986). *The Interpersonal Style Inventory*. Los Angeles: Western Psychology Series.

Moles, O., & Levinger, G. (1979). *Divorce and separation*. New York: Basic Books.

Neimeyer, R. A., & Mitchell, K. A. (1988). Similarity and attraction: A longitudinal study. *Journal of Social and Personal Relationships, 5,* 131–148.

Nelson, J. S., Megill, A., & McCloskey, D. N. (1987). *The Rhetoric of the human sciences.* Madison: University of Wisconsin Press.

Orbuch, T. L. (Ed.). (in press). *Relationship loss.* New York: Springer.

Orne, M. T. (1962). On the social psychology of the psychological experiment. *American Psychologist, 17,* 776–783.

Orne, M. T., & Holland, C. H. (1968). On the ecological validity of laboratory deceptions. *International Journal of Psychiatry, 6,* 282–293.

Pierce, G., Sarason, B. R., & Sarason, I. G. (1990). Integrating social support perspectives: Working models, personal relationships and situational factors. In S. W. Duck, *Personal relationships and social support* (R. Cohen Silver, Ed.; pp. 173–189). London: Sage.

Prelli, L. (1989). *A rhetoric of science: Inventing scientific discourse.* Columbia, SC: University of South Carolina Press.

Rosengren, K. E. (1989). Paradigms lost and regained. In B. Dervin, L. Grossberg, B. O'Keefe, & E. Wartella (Eds.), *Rethinking communication: Vol. 1. Paradigm issues* (pp. 21–39). Newbury Park, CA: Sage.

Rosenthal, R. (1965). The volunteer subject. *Human Relations, 18,* 389–406.

Rosenthal, R., & Rosnow, R. L. (1969). *Artifact in behavioral research.* New York: Academic Press.

Sarason, B. R., Sarason, I. G. & Pierce, G. R. (1990). *Social support: A transactional view.* New York: Wiley.

Sarason, I. G., Sarason, B. R., Shearin, E. N., & Pierce, G. R. (1987). A brief measure of social support: Practical and theoretical implications.

Wheeler, L., & Nezlek, J. (1977). Sex differences in social participation. *Journal of Personality and Social Psychology, 35,* 742–754.

Chapter 2

Optional Metaphors
for Studying Interaction

ARTHUR P. BOCHNER
KENNETH N. CISSNA
MICHAEL G. GARKO

Interpersonal communication is an intoxicating subject that never satiates one's curiosity about the perplexing dilemmas of social life. For many of us, the inspiration for studying interpersonal communication originated in the history of our own personal relationships. We were drawn to interpersonal studies because we wanted to understand, explain, or improve our friendships, marriages, families, and other long-term relationships. At one time or another, most of us have paused to consider how (or why) some people are drawn together, some stay together, and some pull apart. Of course, the lure of research on interpersonal communication is not confined to the intellectual or cognitive realm of experience; its enchantment also is emotional (Ellis, in press). Indeed, one of the main appeals of this subject is its obvious relevance and importance to our emotional lives. Human life is largely a conversation among friends, lovers, and colleagues, and interpersonal communication seems crucial to its outcome.

As teachers and mentors we have observed that the enthusiasm and excitement experienced by new students of our subject is matched only by the frustration they feel as they try to become conversant about the literature and to master the methodological skills required to conduct and analyze research. Students are surprised to learn that interpersonal communication is not a single, unified field of study. There are no rigorous definitions that limit the scope of the field, no texts that definitively articulate its foundations, and little agreement among scholars about which concepts, theories, and methods offer the most promise for unifying the field. Instead of finding a confined field of discourse associated with a single discipline, the new student confronts an open-ended and unspecified universe of discourse that cuts across virtually all of the disciplines concerned with social behavior or human interaction. Moreover, the new student finds that scholars in different disciplines often use vastly different terms to describe the same things whereas scholars in the same discipline sometimes use identical terms to describe vastly different things.

The new student's frustration may be further exacerbated by the discovery of numerous camps or "paradigm-groups," each of which appears to express strong opinions and convincing arguments about the one right way to think about and investigate this subject. Each of these perspectives offers a somewhat different worldview, framed by a different set of terms, expressed in a different vocabulary, oriented toward a different set of research problems, and addressed by different methodological and analytical procedures. Initially, the new student may be innocently exposed to these multiple perspectives without being asked to express a preference. But as time passes, the student is usually expected to form an attachment to one of these worldviews, to stand up and be counted as a "relationalist," an "interactionist," a "behaviorist," a "cognitivist," a "constructivist" or a "culturalist" (to name some prominent sects). There is much at stake in this choice, because normally the perspective one chooses to embrace is assumed to be superior to competing perspectives, which means that it should provide a truer, more accurate, and more literal representation of the essence or nature of interpersonal communication.

Those who push one perspective over others invariably end up defending their choice by making reference to the "essence of man," the "nature of communication," or "the core of reality" (e.g., Delia, 1977; Pearce, 1988). For some writers, human interaction is essentially about meanings and interpretations, whereas others claim it is essentially about behavior and information processing. Some authors see the nature of social life as a drama, others see it as a story, others as a game, and still others as a machine. Each of these different ways of expressing human nature or the "essence of human communication" is intended to provide a correct, or true, description of the way things really are—that is, a description that fits or is faithful to reality (see Rorty, 1979, 1982, 1989).

Unfortunately, "reality" does not speak and thus cannot provide any criteria by which to arbitrate disagreements about the superiority of different ways of talking about or describing human nature. The vocabularies that describe or conceptualize our subject can only be compared with one another, not with something outside or beyond them called "facts" (Rorty,

1989). There simply is no way to get in touch with reality that completely transcends the contingencies of language.

In this chapter, we construe different perspectives on interpersonal communication as alternative metaphors for dealing with the social world in different ways and for different purposes. We do not see the choice of a perspective or a paradigm as a decision made on the basis of correspondence to reality or fit with the nature of human beings. Following Rorty (1979, 1982, 1989), we think of perspectives as vocabularies that function as tools for dealing with the world for one purpose or another, rather than as vocabularies that fit reality or represent intrinsic nature. Accordingly, we think the choice of a perspective ought to be made not on the basis of its correspondence to reality but because it is suitable to or useful for certain purposes. This way of construing perspectives shifts the focus of conversation away from the epistemic question, What are the facts and how do we know them? and toward the pragmatic question, What are our goals and how can we deal with them?

The shift from an epistemic to a pragmatic orientation has important methodological implications. Interpersonal communication becomes a subject that can be described legitimately in several different vocabularies with several different purposes in mind. As a "human science," interpersonal communication has no uniquely correct scientific perspective because, as Bateson suggested, there are always a variety and plurality of descriptions for natural processes, depending on one's point of view (Bateson, 1979). The willingness to accept plurality has the effect of undermining the venerable idea that there is a universal method of science or that scientific inquiry is monolithic in purpose (prediction and control). Since predicting and controlling are only two of the things we may want to do with human beings, our studies of interpersonal life must self-consciously address the correspondence between research objectives and methodologies. For example, when the goals of inquiry shift from prediction and control (collecting facts) to interpretation and understanding (interpreting meanings) or to criticism and social change (altering values), it becomes necessary to expand our range of acceptable methodologies (Bochner, 1985). The question shifts from the absolute (Which methods are scientifically acceptable?) to the relative (Which methods are best suited to our objectives?). Consequently, the line separating "scientific" from "humanistic" modes of inquiry becomes less distinct. More than a decade ago, Geertz (1980) discussed this shift as a "blurring of genres" in which, "freed from having to become taxonomically upstanding, because nobody else is, individuals thinking of themselves as social (or behavioral or human or cultural) scientists have become free to shape their work in terms of its necessities rather than received ideas as to what they ought or ought not to be doing" (pp. 166–167).

Our purpose in this chapter is to draw some distinctions among a few of the most widely discussed and familiar perspectives on interpersonal communication. Each perspective is a metaphoric description that offers a certain way of thinking about interpersonal communication and, consequently, orients research toward certain goals and necessitates certain methodological choices. Underlying each perspective are certain premises about interpersonal life. These premises are not always stated explicitly, but they become evident when research associated with the perspective is examined closely. Each of these different ways of talking about interpersonal communication tells a somewhat different story about the connections between self and other and the ordinary problems of interpersonal life toward which research should be directed.

Conceptualizing Interpersonal Communication

There is no single right or correct way to conceptualize and study interpersonal communication. Although writers will undoubtedly continue to justify their singular points of view by appeals to the nature or essence of interpersonal communication, these foundational appeals cannot be sustained because there are no criteria that can be used to decide which is the "real" nature. It is just as well to assume that interpersonal communication does not have a nature. Since we are stuck with the contingencies of description, it makes more sense to us to focus on the ways of thinking and modes of action that are opened up or closed down by different ways of talking about interpersonal communication than to assume that we can arrive at a single, universally valid description that represents the essential conditions of what it means to be human or to communicate.

Every inquiry begins with a description of an issue or the statement of a problem—the story on which the inquiry is based. The terms in which the problem is cast express *one* way of seeing the problem. Over time, however, *one* way of seeing the problem often becomes *the* way of seeing it (see discussion by Duck & Montgomery, Chapter 1). When this happens, one set of terms or one way of telling the story achieves the status of a privileged description. It becomes a habitual way of thinking about and enacting the problem. Rorty (1989) refers to this process as literalizing a metaphor. The result is that we come to see a particular description as closer to reality or more essential to the core or nature of our subject. We forget that every description is a tool for doing something and is better or worse only in relation to the purposes to which it is directed. A problem can always be redescribed, however, in a different vocabulary. The purpose of redescription is not to achieve a better fit with reality but to change what we can do and how we can think about the problem.

Consider the example of descriptions of interpersonal communication that are cast in the metaphors of "strategy" and "tactics" (Miller & Steinberg, 1975; Roloff, 1981). The terminology of strategic communication advances a corpus of military metaphors, such as control maneuvers, subtle tactics, and ruses (Kellerman, Reynolds, & Chen, 1989), in which interpersonal communication is seen as a largely unilateral activity involving the strategic triumph of one person over another. The vocabulary of strategic communication celebrates autonomous individuals who can do unto others as they would not want others to do unto them. Normally, when interpersonal communication is studied as strategic, subjects are asked to respond to questions about how they get their way, that is, what they say and do to produce favorable outcomes. As a result, much of this research has concentrated on taxonomies of strategies and tactics that tend, when applied to research about interpersonal influence, to yield a rational, unilateral, and uncomplicated description of interpersonal encounters (Bochner, 1989). The research designs used to formulate taxonomies of strategies and test hypotheses about the use of strategies have been premised on the assumption of unilateral control and have been mainly restricted to methodologies that take for granted the "rational nature" of the influence process.

For the purposes of predicting and controlling influence and, perhaps, for improving our ability to train communicators to be more competent communicators, this perspective may be useful. But it would be a mistake to conclude that human beings are essentially or "by nature" strategic or to privilege the strategic mode of description over other ways of describing interpersonal communication. The same events that are described as instances of "strategic communication," in which unilateral action and rational choice are assumed, can be redescribed as instances of "paradoxical communication," in which one person's choices are seen as interdependently and emotionally tied to another's and the patterns of their interaction as culturally regulated. There are no criteria by which it can be decided that one of these descriptions is closer to reality than another. The preference for one way of describing (or redescribing) an event over another is simply the preference for one way of coping with our subject (the world) over another. A preference for a rational description over an emotional one, or one which is premised on autonomy instead of interdependence, may say more about how we would *like* things to be than the way they are. As Jasper Griffen (1990) argues in relation to the subject of sexual relations:

> The relation of the sexes is a subject on which it is perhaps impossible to tell the truth, even if one tried, and on which almost nobody has ever wanted to tell the truth. Most generalizations about the way men behave, or what women do, are not so much reliable statements of sociological fact as the expression of hopes, or the venting of criticisms, or the attempt at propaganda. (p. 9)

Even a cursory consideration of the parameters of interpersonal episodes suggests many possible points of departure for theory and research. The most general meaning of the term interpersonal communication is simply "communicating between persons." Research on interpersonal communication, however, is usually guided by a narrower and more specific conceptualization (Bochner, 1989). The anchor points for such a conceptualization are (1) at least two communicators intentionally orienting toward each other, (2) as both subject and object, (3) whose actions embody each other's perspectives both toward self and toward other. In an interpersonal episode, then, each communicator is both a knower and an object of knowledge, a tactician and a target of another's tactics, an attributor and an object of attribution, a codifier and a code to be deciphered. It should come as no suprise, then, that the literature on interpersonal communication is replete with studies of information seeking (knowledge), strategic communication (tactics), cognitive processes (attribution), and dimensions of symbolic interaction (codes). Any of these terms could serve our purpose of comparing optional descriptions of interpersonal communication. We have chosen, however, to focus more macroscopically on the relation between self and other presupposed by several generic perspectives on interpersonal communication. The metaphors we have rather arbitrarily chosen to use are *control, coordination,* and *contextualized interaction.*

Control

Interpersonal communication has been viewed as a *problem of control* in which self seeks to control the outcomes of other. Interpersonal situations are seen as "uncertain" (Berger & Calabrese, 1975) or precarious encounters. It is assumed that uncertainty can be reduced or overcome by choosing rational message strategies based on "social knowledge" (Roloff & Berger, 1982). Thus, interpersonal communication is described as a rational, goal-oriented activity in which the probability of success or effectiveness is determined largely by whether self has enough social knowledge and/or social skill to *predict* and *control* other's responses. Accordingly, psychological processes function as analogues to interpersonal processes. The explanation for what is going on between self and other is presumed to be dependent on what is going on inside or under the skin of the individual communicators.

The control perspective has given rise to several lines of research emphasizing strategic communication. The terms used most frequently to describe these research traditions are (1) compliance gaining, (2) social cognition, and (3) constructivist.

COMPLIANCE GAINING

This line of research defines the goal of interpersonal communication as compliance. Consequently, the focus of research is on self's ability to elicit compliance from other. It is assumed that compliance is gained by selecting and enacting appropriate message strategies. Research on compliance gaining has been guided by a "strategic choice model" that is concerned with the selection, construction, and/or enactment of instrumentally optimal strategies of communication (Seibold, Cantrill, & Meyers, 1985). The strategic choice model portrays self as an agent of influence seeking control over other's responses. Self is assumed to be conscious of available options, rational, and in possession of a well-organized cognitive map on the basis of which choices of message strategies are made.

In order to test hypotheses about compliance gaining, it is necessary to formulate a relatively comprehensive repertoire of message strategies and tactics and then create or have subjects recall situations in which they enacted particular strategies "to get their way." As a result, research on compliance gaining has focused largely on developing taxonomies of tactics or categories of message strategies and on determining the conditions under which communicators select different strategies. Unfortunately, this corpus of research has not progressed beyond the point of asking individuals to report which strategies they would select in a hypothetical situation or to recall what they did to get their way in the past. Researchers have not examined compliance gaining as an immediate experience or as a process involving actions and reactions between self and other. The responses of other to self have not been observed. Indeed, compliance gaining typically has been studied as an event that occurs at a single point in time rather than as an interdependent sequence of maneuvers and countermaneuvers between self and other.

The conversation between Michael and Cathy Stone, the sample interaction of this text, can be viewed as a compliance-gaining encounter in which Cathy attempts to get Michael to share more of the responsibility for household chores. Cathy chooses a sequence of assertive message tactics to get her way. She seizes an opening, innocently provided by the Millers, to imply that she does all the housework ("I do it all"). She subsequently provides a litany of examples of Michael's unwillingness to contribute or his lack of awareness about his share of the responsibilities and, finally, she asserts that he just doesn't think (about his responsibilities for chores). While these assertive messages can be exemplified by utterances in the conversation, compliance-gaining research has typically operated at a level that is at least one step removed from actual conversation. In an actual compliance-gaining study, Cathy probably would be asked to report which strategies she used from a list of strategies provided by the investigator.

SOCIAL COGNITION

Research on social cognition emphasizes the structures of knowledge that bring self to an encounter with other and examines how self gathers, retrieves, processes, and applies social information during the course of an interaction. Greene (1984) outlined three assumptions associated with social cognition: (1) as a social actor, self acts purposefully and is "capable of formulating behavioral alternatives and choosing among those alternatives on the basis of expected outcomes" (p. 242); (2) self's actions toward other are based on the meanings that self assigns to social and environmental stimuli; and (3) self's cognitive system is the most significant predictor of self's social behavior. Greene concludes that from the perspective of social cognition, "social behavior is directly the result of processes of meaning analysis, planning, and generation of efferent commands which take place in the information-processing system" (p. 342). All events in the social world, then, are assumed to be mediated by cognitive systems.

Returning to the dialogue between Cathy and Michael, we can ask, from the perspective of social cognition, what social knowledge Cathy has applied in order to perceive the situation as one in which it is appropriate to confront Michael about his lack of responsibility in carrying out his household obligations. Obviously, some individuals would not want to "make a scene" in front of friends. Why does Cathy construe this situation as she does and why does she act differently than others would in the same situation? Research on the cognitive structures of individuals would attempt to predict the ways in which individuals with different cognitive systems would perceive and act in social situations similar to the one facing Cathy.

CONSTRUCTIVIST

The constructivist perspective is a program of research that corresponds closely with the assumptions of social cognition. Constructivists hypothesize a causal relationship between an individual's system of constructs and the messages the individual will produce in an interpersonal encounter. A system of constructs is the organized cognitive structure by which self anticipates, interprets, and evaluates other's responses. Constructs thus constitute a system of interpretation by which, "through the application of cognitive schemes, experience is segmented into meaningful units and interpreted, beliefs about the world are created and integrated, and behavior is structured and controlled" (Delia, O'Keefe, & O'Keefe, 1982, p. 151).

Constructivists maintain that the more differentiated and abstract the self's system of constructs, the more likely it is that self will form multiple goals and identify multiple obstacles to achieving these goals. An individual with a complex construct system is thought to possess a more highly developed repertoire of strategies. This type of individual has learned to approach interpersonal communication as a situation involving complex communication tasks and has developed a wide variety of interpersonal tactics to cope with this complexity. The hypothetical conflict between Cathy and Michael could be used as a stimulus in constructivist research to test hypotheses about the effects of different levels of construct differentiation and complexity. By asking subjects to play Cathy's (and/or Michael's) role, we could learn whether there are consistent differences in the variety and complexity of tactics chosen by subjects with more or less differentiated construct systems.

The constructivist perspective extends the scope of research on interpersonal strategies beyond compliance by acknowledging the multiple intentions that self may have when encountering other. Message selection and production, however, still are examined from the individualistic perspective of the message producer.

Coordination

Interpersonal communication has been described as "a problem of coordination" in which self and other coordinate their lines of action in order to achieve their personal and collective goals. In contrast to the monadic and individualistic premises of the control perspective, coordination promotes a dyadic conception of interpersonal communication that views the relation of self to other as a coorienting process that involves something more than merely aggregating what each person brings to the encounter. The dyadic model can be traced back to John Dewey (Dewey & Bentley, 1949) and George Herbert Mead (1934) in interactionist social science, to Theodore M. Newcomb (1961) in social psychology and to Alfred Schutz (1970) in phenomenological sociology. Terms such as *role taking, intersubjectivity,* and *joint-consciousness* have been coined to show how each person projects part of the other's consciousness onto his or her own, thus merging, at least temporarily, into a single interaction system. The coordination perspective is typified by two lines of inquiry on interpersonal communication: (1) coorientation research (often referred to as interpersonal perception method), in which self's behavior is in part a function of different levels of perception between self and other (McLeod & Chaffee, 1973) and (2) research on the "coordinated management of meaning" (often referred to as rules theory), the procedures by which individuals coordinate their lines of action (Pearce & Cronen, 1980).

COORIENTATION

The empirical work on coorientation in interpersonal communication was inspired largely by the observations and research methods developed by R. D. Laing and his associates (Laing, Phillipson, & Lee, 1966). Their focus was on the mediation between behavior and experience. They observed that the behavior of self toward other, and other toward self, is mediated by the experience of each by the other, and each one's experience is mediated by each one's behavior. From this deceptively simple proposition, Laing, Phillipson, and Lee elaborated a set of concepts representing levels of interexperience and a methodology for investigating conjunctions and disjunctions in dyadic experience. Their conception of coorientation distinguished between three levels of perception—the *direct perspective* (what each person thinks about an issue in their relationship), the *metaperspective* (what each person thinks the other thinks about the issue), and the *metametaperspective* (what each person thinks the other person thinks he or she thinks about the issue)—and three empirical concepts for representing levels of collective experience—*agreement* (a comparison of self's direct perspective with other's direct perspective), *understanding* (a comparison of self's metaperspective with other's direct perspective, and vice versa), and *realization* (a comparison of self's metametaperspective with other's metaperspective, and vice versa). The relationship issues on which the interpersonal perception method focuses included numerous crucial concerns, such as interdependence and autonomy, concern and support, disparagement and disappointment, contradiction and confusion, and extreme denial of autonomy.

The dialogue between Michael and Cathy Stone can be used to speculate about dimensions of coorientation in their relationship. Of course, we only have their words to go on, not their perceptions of each other. The dialogue suggests that Cathy and Michael disagree about their relative contributions to domestic chores. Michael seems to misunderstand Cathy's view. She seems to feel much more "put upon" or burdened by excessive household responsibility than Michael realizes. Cathy expresses a feeling of being misunderstood and of having her ideals about spousal equality unrealized.

Of course, these hypothetical speculations may be of less value than some of the empirical studies of coorientation in marriage. Surprisingly, levels of agreement and disagreement have been found to be less important to the perception of a good or satisfying relationship than is commonly thought (Bochner, Krueger, & Chmielewski, 1982), and the ideal of good communication as a panacea for developing greater understanding and satisfaction in marriage has not been supported empirically (Sillars, Pike, Jones, & Murphy, 1984; Sillars, Weisberg, Burggraf, & Zietlow, 1989).

COORDINATED MANAGEMENT OF MEANING

The metaphor of coordination is a tool for dealing with "interpersonal realities" that are presumed to be socially constructed and socially sustained. The premise of a socially constructed reality embodies three important propositions: (1) meanings are learned through speech, (2) speech is a social process governed by rules, and (3) without rules there can be no meanings. Thus, there is an inextricable connection between speech acts, rules, and meanings. This corpus of concepts is central to an approach to the study of interpersonal communication referred to as "rules perspectives."

One of the most widely discussed rules perspectives is the coordinated management of meaning (Pearce, 1988; Pearce & Cronen, 1980), a theory that construes interpersonal communication as a process of coordination in which "each person interprets and responds to the acts of another, monitors the sequence, and compares it to his or her desires and expectations" (Cronen, Pearce, & Harris, 1982, p. 68). Research is guided not by the empiricist goal of prediction and control but by the interpretivist purpose of understanding and intelligibility. Instead of asking what antecedents lead to what consequences, the coordinated management of meaning stresses *how* and *in what form* coordination is achieved (Pearce, 1988). The theory defines rules as cognitions existing in the heads of individual actors. Rules organize the meanings of actors (constitutive rules) and also regulate or shape sequences of actions (regulative rules). Since self and other are frequently guided by different rules, however, this theory draws attention to cases in which coordination ironically requires self and other to assign different meanings to the same messages. The emphasis is on "managing" meanings, not on "sharing" them.

Indeed, the conventional assumption that interpersonal communication is commensurate with the achievement of shared meaning cannot be sustained. Meanings are not fixed by messages. In fact, only the most trivial messages are transparent. We may wish for a world in which whatever can be meant can also be said and understood, but this ideal of expressibility probably has no meaningful application outside the realm of unequivocal literal expressions. In the world of ordinary discourse between human beings, the main qualities of expression are nonliteralness, ambiguity, vagueness, deniability, and incompleteness. Speakers are rarely able to say what they mean (Rommetveit, 1980).

The coordinated management of meaning emphasizes that both self and other must assume responsibility for the co-creative parts each plays in managing the meanings of their relationship. The process of coordination is complicated by the high probability that self and other will have their own ways of acting and perceiving and their own ways of understanding each other's ways of acting and perceiving. Typically, self and other have different knowledge and beliefs about the world, and encounters between such different private worlds cannot be expected to produce "shared meaning" in the ordinary sense of that term. Rather than the ideal of a pure intersubjectivity based on the possibility of a free and complete interchange of dialogue roles, the 'real' world of interpersonal relations is only a partially shared one in which a sense of sharing is the product of mechanisms of control over meanings as well as mutual faith in a shared social world (Rommetveit, 1980).

The disagreement between Cathy and Michael may be looked at as an episode that calls into question each one's definition of what it means to be a close, loving couple and of the rules for engaging in conflict that regulate their interaction. Cathy may see this episode as a demonstration of their closeness and the security of the relationship because "a serious argument in front of close friends shows how close and trusting we are" whereas Michael may feel emotionally violated by the embarrassment of enacting a private conflict in a relatively public setting, a behavior he feels is inappropriate and unloving. In the episode, Michael seems to operate according to the rule that when he is criticized by Cathy he should defend himself or at least give an account, whereas Cathy seems to behave according to the premise that she should rack up points rapidly and argue relentlessly until Michael admits that she is right (or is willing to assume more responsibility). The rules—such as they evolve in this or any other relationship—are the procedures by which self and other coordinate their respective systems of meaning into a coherent and organized relationship. These rules can be made intelligible by looking for repeated sequences of interaction and by close examination of the reports of the interactants, for example, through qualitative interviews (Denzin, 1989).

Contextualized Interaction

Interpersonal communication has been conceptualized as a problem of contextualized interaction in which self and other form a system that controls itself by following largely implicit rules established through a process of trial and error over time. In contrast to the monadic and dyadic perspectives embodied by the metaphors of control and coordination respectively, contextualized interaction incorporates an "N-adic" perspective that assumes "it is always the most complex that explains the most simple" (Ricci & Selvini-Palazzoli, 1984). This contextual orientation strongly implies that interactions between self and other normally implicate additional persons related or connected to the primary interactants. Thus, the boundaries of an interaction system must be extended to include other interactants implicated in transactions between self and other. Moreover, the observer of an interaction system (the researcher) cannot be completely detached from the system being observed. Methodologically, this means that the observer must be recognized as part of the system being observed. The researcher's background, cultural premises, and emotions are part of the research process (Ellis, in press; Steier, in press), not outside it. When interpersonal communication is viewed as contextualized interaction, the observer is placed within, not outside, the observed system.

The contextualized interaction perspective evolved mainly from the cybernetically informed theorizing of Gregory Bateson (1972). Families and other naturally evolving groups were described by Bateson and his colleagues in the terminology of a loosely applied cybernetics. Principles of self-regulation explained how bonds evolve over time through a sequence of transactions and feedbacks until the members become a unit governed by stable rules unique to them alone. Cybernetically, the members of an interaction system are seen as elements in a circuit of interaction. While it is acceptable to assume that each member has influence, it is unacceptable to conclude that any one member's behavior *causes* the behavior of others. As elements in a circuit, none of the members has unidirectional power over the whole. The part cannot control the whole or, as system theorists express the point, "the power is only in the rules of the game," which cannot be changed by the players (Selvini-Palazzoli, Boscolo, Cecchin, & Prata, 1978).

THE INTERACTIONAL VIEW

The principles of contextualized interaction are sometimes classified as part of a pragmatic perspective on communication referred to as the "interactional view" (Watzlawick, Beavin & Jackson, 1967; Wilder-Mott & Weakland, 1981). This view emphasizes directly observable messages, that is, statements or actions of the interactants. This focus on messages draws attention to several significant features of interaction.

First, it is assumed that "there is no such thing as a simple message" (Weakland, 1976, p. 117) because communicators are sending and receiving messages simultaneously. Some messages necessarily qualify or modify the meaning of other messages. Thus, no single message can be adequately understood without considering the messages that qualify or frame its meanings. Second, the analytical distinction between the report and command level of messages (Ruesch & Bateson, 1951) indicates that every message is a double message insofar as it is both a stimulus and a response; that is, it serves both informative and directive functions. The directive functions of a message are particularly important since, as Weakland (1976) observes, "small signals may easily have large effects [and thus] the potential importance of communicative influence on behavior is great, and should never be neglected" (p. 117). Third, ongoing sequences of interaction have no beginning or end. What is counted as a stimulus or as a response is an arbitrary decision, as is the distinction between the source and the receiver. Nevertheless, interactants tend to punctuate their sequences in a linear fashion, as if these arbitrary distinctions were real. For example, in a conflict, one is viewed as "to blame" or "at fault," and the other becomes the "innocent victim." These sorts of causal punctuations are viewed as a major source of relational difficulty. Fourth, interactional sequences are self-perpetuating and repetitive. Normally, members of an interaction system behave in whatever way is necessary to keep the sequence going (Haley, 1976). Fifth, no matter how unusual a particular person's behavior may seem, it is sensible within its own particular interactional context. The questions to ask are the following: (1) What function does the behavior serve in the context of this relationship (marriage, family, etc.)? and (2) How does the behavior fit within the repetitive interactional sequences of the system?

These questions are applicable to the episode involving Cathy and Michael Stone. It would be useful to know how the Stones could reframe their sequence as a joining or negotiating sequence instead of a blaming or attacking one, as it seems to be. Other sequences would need to be observed to draw conclusions about the functions of Cathy's or Michael's behavior or their fit in the repetitive patterns of their relationship.

RADICAL CONSTRUCTIVIST

Another form of the contextualized interaction metaphor is the metatheoretical perspective referred to as "radical constructivist." This view assumes that knowledge is something that individuals formulate by establishing repeatable experiences that help them cope with the "amorphous flow of experience" (von Glasersfeld, 1984). Radical constructivists emphasize the worldviews or belief structures that individuals use to organize and/or operate on their experience. Interpersonal relationships (such as close friendships, marriages, and, particularly, families) are seen as the places where each individual builds a blueprint of the world and a sense of "the way things are" (Sluzki, 1983). This blueprint becomes a relationship ideology that is reflexively tied to the interaction patterns of primary relationships, which means that it turns or bends back on itself in a circular fashion. Another way to say this in the case of families, for example, is that interaction patterns evolve from the family's ideology and reinforce it.

Steier (in press) argues that in a radical constructivist framework of research, the observer must become part of the data to be analyzed because the researcher is always a coparticipant or cocreator in what will count as "facts." After all, it is normally the researcher's categories, the researcher's distinctions, or the researcher's language, that establishes the context of inquiry. Thus, the reflexivity of ideology is not confined to the system being observed but is extended to links between the observer and the observed system.

From the point of view of radical constructivist methodology, every observation made in this book about the episode involving Cathy and Michael Stone can be viewed as both an invention of and an intervention into their relationship (Steier, in press). Many critical questions associated with studying interaction are raised once this position is taken seriously, including the following: How are our ideals or values as observers reflected in what we think we see "in" this discourse? Why might a male and a female observer see what is going on here differently? What difference does it make whether we see this as a "battle for equality or dominance," "an effort to cope with embarrassment," "a negotiation on rules for the relationship," an "expression of frustration and exasperation," or any other interpretation offered in this book? Does the fact that there are so many plausible ways of construing this episode mean that how it is seen or what questions researchers may ask about it reflect the sense that all research may be viewed as autobiographical? Why do researchers decide to ask certain questions and not others anyway? What if Cathy and Michael see their sequence differently or use different terms than the researchers do to explain what they think they were doing? Although questions like these have been largely ignored in the past, it now seems clear that what counts as knowledge about interaction is highly contingent on answers to such questions.

Conclusion

This book focuses on procedures and methods of gathering and analyzing data on interaction. Methodology books sometimes have the unintended effect of creating false dualisms or implying that the choice of a method precedes the choice of a problem for which the method is suitable. Certainly, it is not uncommon to find scholars who identify themselves as "quantitative" or "qualitative," "experimental" or "field," or "mainstream" or "interpretive," as if these choices needed to be made before one decided what phenomena to study and with what purpose in mind. Students are given the impression that truth is dependent on method.

This book, on the other hand, views decisions about methodology as contingent on the purposes of inquiry. Judgments about which methods are better or worse are dependent upon the purposes for which the methods are applied. Correspondingly, this chapter assumes that truth is a function of the describing operations of investigators: "where there are no sentences there is no truth" (Rorty, 1989, p. 5). Respect for facts is not enough; we need to have respect for the power of language to create new and different visions about who we are and what we can do. The way we see it, the question that needs to be asked is whether there is sufficient correspondence between the objectives of a study and the methods used to fulfill the objectives. All too often, studies of interaction transform stories into graphs. We think there are times when it is valuable to preserve the narrative truth of the story and other times when the story ought to be about the graph.

We think that one way to draw more attention to the methodological necessities of perspectives on interpersonal communication is, as Rorty (1989) suggests, to change the question that seems crucial from How do you know? to Why do you talk that way? The way we talk about interpersonal communication tells us a great deal about how we think about people relating to other people (Duck, 1984, 1987, 1990). Our metaphors also tell us a great deal about what we assume we can do. The metaphors of interpersonal communication that we have emphasized cannot be judged against a set of objective facts that will help us decide whether the "real" problem of communication is control, coordination, or contextualization. They can only be compared with each other in terms of how they help us cope with conditions of social experience. Obviously, a language of strategy, a language of rules, and a language of patterns or connections offer quite different visions of such common concerns as power, equality, freedom, and justice. Such a comparison is beyond the scope of this chapter, but it is worth noting that the options for conceptualizing and describing interpersonal communication are not and should not be limited to these metaphors. While these metaphors have dominated our ways of thinking about interpersonal communication, they do not exhaust the possibilities for telling new stories about interaction. A question that remains is, What other stories do we want to tell about interaction and how shall we tell them?

Shweder and Fiske (1986) have argued that the distinctive subject matter of the social sciences is subjectivity. The study of interaction is to a large extent the relation of one domain of subjectivity to another— intersubjectivity. We believe it is time to address more self-consciously the content of subjectivity and intersubjectivity, namely, emotions, values, moral choices, ideas, and ideals. Relationships between persons ordinarily involve emotional reactions, hidden and explicit values, and moral premises. How can we as researchers cope with these highly significant dimensions of interaction between people? The metaphors that have dominated how researchers think and what researchers do provide few options and little insight into the emotional and moral sides of interactional experience.

Our commitment to plurality over universality and to many ways of talking over one way of knowing mandates that we embrace the goal of radical redescription. We need new terms that will make it possible, important, and likely that crucial aspects of subjective and intersubjective experience that have been transformed, overlooked, or marginalized will be placed side by side with the already privileged modes of description that have dominated our ways of thinking, acting, and inquiring. As Koch (1985) concluded about the history of psychology as a science, it may be necessary for the conception of the entire enterprise to be profoundly changed.

References

Bateson, G. (1972). *Steps to an ecology of mind*. New York: Ballantine.

Bateson, G. (1979). *Mind and nature: A necessary unity*. New York: Dutton.

Berger, C. R., & Calabrese, R. J. (1975). Some explorations in initial interaction and beyond: Toward a developmental theory of interpersonal communication. *Human Communication Research, 1,* 99–112.

Bochner, A. P. (1985). Perspectives on inquiry: Representation, conversation, and reflection. In M. L. Knapp & G. R. Miller (Eds.), *Handbook of interpersonal communication* (pp. 27–58). Beverly Hills, CA: Sage.

Bochner, A. P. (1989). Interpersonal communication. In E. Barnouw (Ed.), *International Encyclopedia of Communications* (Vol. 2, pp. 336–340). New York: Annenberg School of Communications, University of Pennsylvania, and Oxford University Press.

Bochner, A. P., Krueger, D. L., & Chmielewski, T. L. (1982). Interpersonal perceptions and marital adjustment. *Journal of Communication, 32*(3), 135–147.

Cronen, V. E., Pearce, W. B., & Harris, L. M. (1982). In F. E. X. Dance (Ed.), *Human communication theory: Comparative essays* (pp. 61–89). New York: Harper & Row.

Delia, J. (1977). Constructivism and the study of human communication. *Quarterly Journal of Speech, 63,* 66–83.

Delia, J., O'Keefe, B., & O'Keefe, D. (1982). The constructivist approach to communication. In F. E. X. Dance (Ed.), *Human communication theory: Comparative essays* (pp. 147–191). New York: Harper & Row.

Denzin, N. K. (1989). *Interpretive interactionism*. Newbury Park, CA: Sage.

Dewey, J., & Bentley, A. F. (1949). *Knowing and the known*. Boston: Beacon Press.

Duck, S. W. (1984). A rose is a rose (is a tadpole is a freeway is a film) is a rose. *Journal of Social and Personal Relationships, 1,* 509–510.

Duck, S. W. (1987). Adding apples and oranges: Investigators' implicit theories about relationships. In R. Burnett, P. McGee, & D. Clarke (Eds.), *Accounting for relationships* (pp. 215–224). London: Methuen.

Duck, S. W. (1990). Relationships as unfinished business: Out of the frying pan and into the 1990s. *Journal of Social and Personal Relationships, 7,* 5–28.

Ellis, C. (in press). Emotional sociology. In N. Denzin (Ed.), *Studies in symbolic interaction* (Vol. 12). Greenwich, CT: JAI Press.

Geertz, C. (1980). Blurred genres: The refiguration of social thought. *The American Scholar, 49,* 165–182.

Greene, J. O. (1984). Evaluating cognitive explanations of communication phenomena. *Quarterly Journal of Speech, 70,* 241–254.

Griffin, J. (1990, March 29). Love and sex in Greece. *New York Review of Books, 37*(5), p. 6, 8–12.

Haley, J. (1976). *Problem-solving psychotherapy.* San Francisco: Jossey-Bass.

Kellerman, K., Reynolds, R., & Chen, J. (1989, November). *Strategies of conversational retreat: When parting is not sweet sorrow.* Paper presented at the Speech Communication Association Convention, San Francisco.

Koch, S. (1985). Afterword. In S. Koch & D. E. Leary (Eds.), *A century of psychology as science* (pp. 928–950). New York: McGraw-Hill.

Laing, R. D., Phillipson, H., & Lee, A. R. (1966). *Interpersonal perception: A theory and a method of research.* New York: Perennial Library.

McLeod, J. M., & Chaffee, S. H. (1973). Interpersonal approaches to communication research. *American Behavioral Scientist, 16,* 469–499.

Mead, G. H. (1934). *Mind, self, and society.* Chicago: University of Chicago Press.

Miller, G. R., & Steinberg, M. (1975). *Between people: A new analysis of interpersonal communication.* Chicago: Science Research Associates.

Newcomb, T. (1961). *The acquaintance process.* New York: Holt, Rinehart, & Winston.

Pearce, W. B. (1988). *Communication and the human condition.* Carbondale, IL: Southern Illinois University Press.

Pearce, W. B., & Cronen, V. E. (1980). *Communication, action, and meaning: The creation of social realities.* New York: Praeger.

Ricci, C., & Selvini-Palazzoli, M. (1984). Interactional complexity and communication. *Family Process, 23,* 169–176.

Roloff, M. E. (1981). *Interpersonal communication: The social exchange approach.* Beverly Hills, CA: Sage.

Roloff, M. E., & Berger, C. R. (1982). *Social cognition and communication.* Beverly Hills, CA: Sage.

Rommetveit, R. (1980). On "meanings" of acts and what is meant and made known by what is said in a pluralistic social world. In M. Brenner (Ed.), *The structure of action* (pp. 108–149). New York: St. Martin's Press.

Rorty, R. (1979). *Philosophy and the mirror of nature.* Princeton, NJ: Princeton University Press.

Rorty, R. (1982). *Consequences of pragmatism (Essays: 1972–1980).* Minneapolis: University of Minnesota Press.

Rorty, R. (1989). *Contingency, irony, and solidarity.* Cambridge: Cambridge University Press.

Ruesch, J., & Bateson, G. (1951). *Communication: The social matrix of psychiatry.* New York: Norton.

Schutz, A. (1970). *On phenomenology and social relations.* Chicago: University of Chicago Press.

Seibold, D. R., Cantrill, J. G., & Meyers, R. A. (1985). Communication and interpersonal influence. In M. L. Knapp & G. R. Miller (Eds.), *Handbook of interpersonal communication* (pp. 551–611). Beverly Hills, CA: Sage.

Selvini-Palazzoli, M., Boscolo, L., Cecchin, G., & Prata, G. (1978). *Paradox and counterparadox: A new model in the therapy of the family in schizophrenic transaction* (E. V. Burt, Trans.). New York: Jason Aronson.

Shweder, R. A., & Fiske, D. W. (1986). Introduction: Uneasy social science. In D. W. Fiske & R. A. Shweder (Eds.), *Metatheory in social science* (pp. 1–18). Chicago: University of Chicago Press.

Sillars, A. L., Pike, G. R., Jones, T. S., & Murphy, M. A. (1984). Communication and understanding in marriage. *Human Communication Research, 10,* 317–350.

Sillars, A. L., Weisberg, J., Burggraf, C. S., & Zietlow, P. H. (1989, November). *Communication and understanding revisited: Married couples' understanding and recall of conversations.* Paper presented at the Speech Communication Association Convention, San Francisco.

Sluzki, C. (1983). Process, structure and world views: Toward an integrated view of systemic models in family therapy. *Family Process, 22,* 469–476.

Steier, F. (in press). Toward a radical and ecological constructivist approach to family communication. *Journal of Applied Communication Research.*

Von Glasersfeld, E. (1984). An introduction to radical constructivism. In P. Watzlawick (Ed.), *The invented reality* (pp. 17–40). New York: Norton.

Watzlawick, P., Beavin, J. H., & Jackson, D. D. (1967). *Pragmatics of human communication.* New York: Norton.

Weakland, J. H. (1976). Communication theory and clinical change. In P. Guerin (Ed.), *Family therapy: Theory and practice* (pp. 111–128). New York: Gardner.

Wilder-Mott, C., & Weakland, J. H. (Eds.). (1981). *Rigor and imagination: Essays from the legacy of Gregory Bateson.* New York: Praeger.

Chapter 3

Multiple Perspectives on Interaction: Participants, Peers, and Observers

CATHERINE A. SURRA
CARL A. RIDLEY

Researchers usually make one of two assumptions about the meaning of interaction. On the one hand are investigators who believe that behavior has one objective interpretation and that outside observers, peers, and participants in relationships ideally should agree on what that interpretation is. For these researchers the correct meaning is that attributed by observers. The fact that participants and observers differ in the meaning they ascribe to behavior is disconcerting to them. Any discrepancy is thought to indicate errors of measurement that arise from participants' inability to accurately describe their behavior (e.g., Floyd & Markman, 1983; Jacobson & Moore, 1981).

On the other hand are researchers who fully expect the meaning of interaction to differ depending on who is asked. In this case researchers assume that the differences represent reliable variations in how participants, peers, and observers experience the same behavior. The goals are to describe the various perspectives and to understand why the discrepancies occur (e.g., Duck & Pond, 1989; Duck & Sants, 1983; Noller & Guthrie, in press; Olson, 1977).

The fact that we have written this chapter and titled it "Multiple Perspectives" tells the reader where we stand. In the sample interaction of this text, the editors have given us a blow-by-blow account of an argument between Michael and Cathy Stone, which took place in front of their long-term friends, James and Holly Miller. What does the account tell us? We know exactly what Cathy and Michael said. From this, we may even conclude something about the meaning for the participants of what was said. Yet we know nothing about what Cathy and Michael actually thought and felt. We know even less about their friends. Did James and Holly say anything during the argument? How did they feel? Astonished? Embarrassed? Amused? Pleased it was not their problem? What did James, Holly, Cathy, and Michael learn about their relationships from watching the argument? As these questions illustrate, we are interested not only in the behavioral events that transpire during interaction but also in their subjective interpretation and implications. We want to understand the bases of similarities and differences between insiders' and outsiders' viewpoints on interaction. Instead of viewing insiderness–outsiderness as a dichotomy, however, we will follow Levinger's (1977) lead: we will treat insiderness as a continuum of degree of relationship between observers and the target pair.

We will analyze different perspectives on the interaction scenario according to how close the observer is to the observed. Drawing on current models of relationships, we will first define degree of relationship in terms of variations in behavioral and subjective interdependence. Then we will arrange people privy to the interaction on a continuum of "degree of relationship." Next, we will review the literature on perspectives on interaction for each pair on the continuum, with an emphasis on the theoretical reasons for variation in perspectives. We conclude with a commentary on the connections between research methods and degree of relationship between observer and observed.

Relationships as Behavioral and Cognitive Interdependence

Our position in this chapter is that the best way to analyze various perspectives on interaction is to consider the degree of closeness or relationship between the source of the perspective and the targets. The degree of relationship between any target and any observer, an insider or an outsider, can be defined in terms of behavioral and cognitive interdependence. Behavioral interdependence refers to the interconnections between the behaviors partners perform during interaction, where interconnections consist of mutual influence between partners (Kelley et al., 1983). One partner influences another when he or she elicits a behavioral, cognitive, and/or affective response from the other. The degree of closeness of a relationship is determined by such qualities as the frequency and strength of influence, the diversity of influence across different behaviors, and the length of time the relationship has endured. In a close relationship, influence is frequent, diverse, strong, and enduring (Kelley et al., 1983).

Research on relationships confirms the idea that partners' behavioral, cognitive, and affective responses are interconnected. Gottman and others have found, for example, that spouses' verbal and nonverbal behaviors follow one another in predictable sequences, particularly for dissatisfied partners (Gottman, 1979; Gottman & Levenson, 1984). Other research demonstrates that interacting partners influence one another affectively. In a study of physiological responsiveness during marital interaction, Levenson and Gottman (1983) observed that the physiological responses of dissatisfied couples were more strongly linked to one another than those of satisfied couples. Using a method that allowed them to study the cognitions and feelings that partners experience during interaction (Ickes & Tooke, 1988), Ickes and colleagues (Ickes, Robertson, Tooke, & Teng, 1986) found that behavioral measures of dyadic involvement coded by outsiders, such as directed gazes, were positively correlated with the amount of partners' self-reported thoughts and feelings and the amount of positive thoughts and feelings. The results suggest that one partner's behavioral responses may stimulate increased subjective activity on the part of the other, and increased subjective activity may generate involving behavioral responses. In another study Ickes and colleagues (Ickes, Tooke, Stinson, Baker, & Bissonnette, 1988) found evidence of intersubjectivity, or similarity in the content of partners' thoughts and feelings that develops from interaction.

The definition of relationship discussed so far has focused on immediate, moment-to-moment interaction events. In this analysis the locus of the definition is primarily behavioral because it is the observable behaviors of one partner that elicit responses in the other. This is only part of the way partners are interconnected, however. Degree of relationship also can be defined according to the amount of cognitive interdependence between partners.

Cognitive interdependence refers to the interconnections between partners' thoughts and knowledge about the relationship (Surra & Bohman, in press; Wegner, Giuliano, & Hertel, 1985). Over time partners develop relational knowledge structures, or sets of organized beliefs about the other and their relationship (Surra & Bohman, in press). With respect to cognitive interdependence, degree of closeness is determined by these properties: how distinctive and detailed the knowledge is; how well integrated it is with other knowledge structures; how much overlap there is between the partners' knowledge; and the extent to which one partner's actions are able to elicit cognitive and affective responses on the part of the other. In a close relationship knowledge about the partnership is specific, complex, and unique compared with our knowledge of others; it is shared to some extent with the other; and it is highly integrated with other knowledge structures.

In close relationships partners' actions have the capacity to profoundly affect one another's relational knowledge. (Surra & Bohman, in press).

Although research on cognitive interdependence is in its infancy, what we know about it is consistent with the definition of closeness just described. Work on impression formation in newly forming relationships suggests that partners do develop abstract representations of the other's traits and behaviors fairly quickly, as the result of partners' closely attending to what transpires between them (Park, 1986; Wilkinson, 1987). Although initial representations are fairly stable, they are modified by partners' actions and by recent events occurring in the relationship (Miell, 1987; Park, 1986; Wilkinson, 1987). Research on more well-established relationships further indicates that relational knowledge structures are closely linked to at least three other types of knowledge: general knowledge about classes of close relationships (e.g., what marriages typically are like); knowledge about specific other close relationships; and knowledge about the self (Planalp & Rivers, 1988; Surra, Arizzi, & Asmussen, 1988; Surra & Milardo, in press; Wilkinson, 1987). There is also evidence that the degree of overlap in partners' relational knowledge may increase as they become more involved (Stephen, 1985).

Once in place, knowledge structures represent the subjective reality of a close relationship. Such knowledge enables each partner to know how to behave toward the other and to understand, predict, and interpret the other's behavior towards the self (Hewes & Planalp, 1987; Planalp, 1987).

Along both dimensions of interdependence—behavioral and cognitive—insiders and outsiders have different degrees of relationship with the target partners. We turn now to an examination of how degree of relationship affects perspectives on interaction.

Multiple Perspectives on Interaction as Degrees of Relationship

In the interaction scenario transcribed in the beginning of this volume, Cathy and Michael have a close association, representing one extreme of closeness. For our purposes, we need to fill in some of the details of the spouses' association with their friends. Let us assume that Holly is closer to Cathy than Michael is to James. The women have known each other since high school and have been best friends for years. James and Michael got to know each other through their wives and have known one another four years. Though they like each other, they rarely do things together outside of their interaction with their wives. Let us also introduce Fred, the contractor, who overhears the argument as he cleans up after his day's work remodeling the next room. He has gotten to know Cathy and Michael to some extent, since he has witnessed most of their day-to-day life for the past two weeks.

For the purposes of analysis, Cathy, Michael, Holly, James, and Fred constitute a small social network in which each dyad has a different degree of relationship. Cathy (one partner, P) and Michael (the other, O) are the insiders and have the target relationship we wish to study. Holly and James are close third parties (Xs), but they have varying degrees of association with P and O. Fred is another "X," a mere acquaintance with a weak association to the others present. In addition, we are outside observers, other Xs, who have no relationship to any of the other parties, although we do have a written transcript of the interaction and general knowledge about marriage. Thus, outsiders may be objective outsiders (us) or subjective outsiders like Fred, James, and Holly (see Olson, 1977). In this way, third parties vary in terms of their degree of relationship to P and O. When viewed in this manner, it is confusing to talk about outsiders and insiders as a dichotomy and more accurate to represent degree of relationship to targets on a continuum (Levinger, 1977):

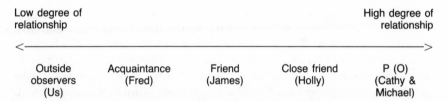

Low degree of relationship				High degree of relationship
<——>
Outside observers (Us)	Acquaintance (Fred)	Friend (James)	Close friend (Holly)	P (O) (Cathy & Michael)

What distinguishes those at the left end of the continuum from those at the right? Outside observers may have a transcript or audiotape of an interaction, but they have no behavioral, affective, or cognitive interconnection with the targets and no idiosyncratic relational knowledge. In this sense, they are objective observers. Acquaintances like Fred, the contractor, have weak behavioral, affective, and cognitive connections to the targets. Although acquaintances have some relational knowledge about the target, it is relatively sketchy, loosely linked to other knowledge structures, and unstable. Friends, close friends, and members of the target relationship influence one another behaviorally, affectively, and cognitively during interaction and have well-developed knowledge about the target relationship. This knowledge affects their interpretation of the interaction. For example, based on her knowledge that Michael frequently alludes to ending their marriage when they fight, Cathy interprets Michael's statement "Sometimes I think about how I'd do [housework] more often probably if you weren't around" as a threat to leave the relationship (see segment no. 11). Because outsiders do not share this knowledge, however, they might draw on their stereotypic beliefs about men and housework and interpret Michael's statement to mean that he would be more responsible if he were on his own. Holly, another insider, might interpret Michael's message in the same way that Cathy did because she shares some of Cathy's knowledge about her marriage. In the next section, using our continuum as a guide, we review research relevant to perspectives on interaction for each pair and discuss further where variation in perspectives comes from.

The Perspective of Outside Observers

Two characteristics mark the relationship between an outside observer and the interactants: (1) there is no mutual influence between the behavioral, affective, and cognitive responses of the observer and the participants and (2) they are not cognitively interdependent because they do not have unique subjective knowledge about one another. The only knowledge outside observers of the relationship have is a generalized concept of marriage. In short, observers at the far end of the continuum have no unique interpersonal relationship with participants.

The condition of "no-relationship" is the hallmark of observational research on interaction. It is necessary in order to achieve an objective record of interaction. The goals of observational research are to eliminate and control the impact of subjectivity, both investigators' and participants', on the record of interaction that is obtained. One way to minimize subjectivity is to prohibit actual interaction between observer and observed. Thus, observers are usually physically separated from participants, and interaction often is recorded using videotapes or audiotapes. Observers have limited opportunities to form any impression of participants that might affect their interpretation of what they see.

Physical separation also limits participants' knowledge of the observer, which helps to control the impact of demand characteristics and ensure a more objective sampling of interaction. By having participants come to their lab so that interaction can be recorded, investigators separate participants from the influence of their everyday social surroundings. In this way researchers are able to record the objective reality of interaction and minimize the influence of context. They assume that interaction is minimally affected by context anyway because participants are "leaky"—that is, unable to mask their true or typical interaction (Weiss, 1989).

The fact that observers have no unique subjective knowledge about the relationship they are observing does not mean that they have no knowledge about it at all. Observers do have a cognitive representation of relationships that comes from at least two sources: (1) normative or conventionalized beliefs about the meaning of behaviors (Bakeman & Gottman, 1986; Hewes & Planalp, 1987; Noller & Guthrie, in press), and (2) the common theoretical meaning attributed to various behaviors by scientists.

With respect to the first source of meaning, observers of social interaction are "cultural informants" who presumably understand the meaning of behaviors because they use the same cultural and social filters to interpret them as participants use (e.g., Bakeman & Gottman, 1986; Weiss, 1989). Cultural informants are not merely objective detectors of what is there (Bakeman & Gottman, 1986) but are "pretrained as it were in the interpersonal significances of cultural symbols and gestures" (Weiss, 1989, p. 137). According to communication theorists, viewing coders as cultural informants assumes that coders are tapping into the conventionalized meaning of acts or the shared cultural meaning attributed to the same behaviors (Hewes & Planalp, 1987). The objective reality imparted by coding schemes is, in part, a normative reality.

In addition, observers' knowledge is shaped by the instructions and coding definitions taught to them (Weiss, 1989). Coders' knowledge about behaviors not only is based on conventionalized meanings but also derives from theoretical notions about which behaviors are important to study, which are not, and what they mean. In constructing the Couple Interaction Scoring System (CISS), for instance, Gottman (1979) devised content codes partly from the work of the Oregon group (Hops, Wills, Patterson, & Weiss, 1972) on the Marital Interaction Coding System (MICS) and partly from personal experience. Drawing on an accumulated body of theoretical knowledge is another means of getting an objective representation of reality (Thompson, 1987), and using coding schemes that are theoretically based ensures that different investigators contribute to a common core of theory.

The assumption underlying both sources of observer knowledge is that the objective picture painted by observers bears a close resemblance to what participants themselves are experiencing. To the extent that the conventionalized meaning applied by coders is indeed normative and culturally shared, participants should interpret their behaviors in the same way as coders. To the extent that our theories and scientific knowledge about relationships are valid, participants' interpretations should map onto interpretations assumed by theories and represented in coding schemes.

That this assumption is accurate is extremely important. As Folger and Poole (1982) have pointed out, the interpretation of results from observational studies usually relies on the presupposition that codes are consistent with participants' understandings of behavior. The significance, for example, of the reciprocity of negative affect observed in distressed spouses (Gottman, 1979) lies in the fact that such spouses feel badly and are causally linked in a cycle of feeling badly. In addition, our ability to explain interaction processes and to derive meaningful theory about them is based on the assumption that codes are consistent with participants' interpretations (Folger & Poole, 1982). To continue with the example, the theoretical significance of negative affect reciprocity, and of feeling badly, is that the more general subjective condition of marital distress produces and/or results from it. In this way, knowing how participants feel about their interaction is crucial to building strong theory about the causes and consequences of marital distress.

The evidence suggests, however, that the knowledge of relationships used by observers does not correspond well with participants' own. Research comparing observers' perspectives on interaction with participants' clearly indicates that observational research taps a reality different from the participants' reality. After reviewing studies comparing self-reports with observers' reports, Sullaway and Christensen (1983) concluded that agreement between the perspectives is moderate at best. Robinson and Price (1980) had observers do in-home observations of the frequency of pleasurable behaviors spouses emitted and received and had spouses record the frequency of pleasurable behaviors during the time observers were present. Self-reported rates of pleasurable behaviors were moderately correlated with those of observers for both emitted and received behaviors ($r = .57$, $p < .001$, and $r = .41$, $p < .01$, respectively). Low marital adjustment spouses underestimated rates of pleasurable events by about 50% relative to high adjustment spouses. Using the observer as a standard, high adjustment couples were more "accurate" in their reports than low adjustment couples.

Floyd and Markman (1983) compared spouses' own ratings of messages with those of untrained observers by means of the talk table, a procedure in which partners seated opposite one another rate the positivity of messages sent and received. Compared with observers, spousal ratings of the impact of messages sent were significantly more positive. In a study of global ratings of interaction in families with adolescents, Noller and Callan (1988) found that family members' ratings of one another were often uncorrelated or negatively correlated with observers' ratings, although self-ratings were positively correlated with observer ratings. These results are consistent with the conclusions reached by Sullaway and Christensen in their 1983 review, namely, agreement between perspectives is better when participants report on their own behavior rather than another family member's. Agreement is also better when participants and observers report on specific, recent behaviors.

The difference between the perspectives of participants and observers is systematic. Observers rate interaction events more negatively than participants. A study that employed the talk table with depressed, nondepressed, and nonclinical–nondepressed spouses showed that untrained observers rated a higher percentage of spousal messages as negative and a lower percentage as positive than did the spouses themselves (Kowalik & Gotlib, 1987). Margolin, Hattem, John, and Yost (1985) also found that agreement between observers and spouses was especially low for negative messages and that the effect held only when couples were rating their own interaction, not that of another couple. Floyd and Markman (1983) reported similar findings and also found gender and marital adjustment differences in the effect. Observers rated husbands' messages more positively than wives' messages, but spouses rated wives' more positively than husbands (also see Gottman, 1979). The latter effect was mostly due to husbands in distressed marriages rating their wives more positively than did observers. Similar results were obtained by Notarius, Benson, Sloane, Vanzetti, and Hornyak (1989). Trained observers were 7.9 times as likely to code nondistressed wives' behavior as positive than they were to code distressed wives' behavior as positive. Yet there were no differences in the way husbands of distressed and nondistressed wives subjectively evaluated their wives' (objectively coded) negative behaviors. Weiss (1984) had spouses rate the helpfulness of their partners' behavior during problem-solving interactions and found that the ratings were correlated with behaviors coded as positive by outsiders but not with those coded as negative.

Why is it that observers, both trained and untrained, and participants have different perspectives on interaction? The most important reason is that communication has subjective, idiosyncratic meaning for participants, as well as conventionalized or normative meaning (Folger & Poole, 1982; Hewes & Planalp, 1987; Montgomery, 1988). While direct observation by outsiders taps conventionalized meaning, it ignores the impact of partners' relational knowledge acquired through a history of interaction. The evidence that observers code interaction more negatively than participants, even when the participants are depressed or in unhappy marriages, suggests that participants may see their own and their partners' behavior in a more positive light or that participants are more tolerant of one another than are observers. Observers may rate interaction more negatively due to their reliance on conventional views of close relationships as something that should be "warm and fuzzy." Moreover, observers who have had extensive experience coding interaction in distressed marriages may develop generalized beliefs about the negativity of interaction in these relationships. Such observers may code behaviors in ways that verify their beliefs. Thus, for the sample interaction transcribed in the beginning of this text, an observer might code Cathy's statement (segment #03) "You don't cook, you don't clean . . ." negatively as an "evaluative" message, whereas Michael's response "Come on—that's not fair" might be coded as "defensive," further supporting the negative coding of Cathy's previous statement. From his perspective, Michael might simply be questioning the accuracy of Cathy's statement.

Other evidence suggests that observers may be influenced by stereotypes of gender roles in marriage. The fact that observers saw husbands' messages as more positive than wives' messages but spouses saw the reverse (Floyd & Markman, 1983) indicates that observers may be affected by stereotypic views of wives as whiners and naggers. Furthermore, the fact that observers saw wives in unhappy marriages as more negative than did their husbands indicates that observers may be interpreting interaction in light of the traditional view that the quality of the relationship is the wife's responsibility.

An alternative interpretation of the data that show observers to be more negative than participants is that participants are affected by social desirability (see Sullaway & Christensen, 1983). Such an effect would induce participants to present themselves and others as feeling more positive than they actually do feel. This interpretation is inconsistent, though, with the pattern of gender differences in findings and with the fact that the findings hold for unhappy and depressed spouses as well as for happy and nondepressed ones.

Another reason why observer–participant perspectives do not match is that coding schemes may not adequately tap conventionalized meanings; that is, the schemes may lack representational validity (Poole & Folger, 1981). Using multidimensional scaling, Poole and Folger (1981) compared the meaning of interaction attributed by cultural informants to that attributed by coders, who used three systems to code small group decision making (Bales's Interaction Process Analysis System [IPA], Fisher's Decision Proposal Coding System, and Mabry's Pattern Variable Coding System). The results showed that the IPA and Fisher's systems matched subjects' own interpretation of behaviors better than the Mabry system, although the match between subjects and coders was imperfect for all three systems. The degree of representational validity of other commonly used coding schemes is yet to be determined.

Finally, observers and participants may disagree about how to interpret interaction because coding schemes may be based on faulty theoretical assumptions about which behaviors are important to participants and why. Floyd, O'Farrell, and Goldberg (1987) compared results obtained when two popular schemes—the MICS and the Communication Skills Test, an economical alternative to Gottman's CISS—were used to code marital interaction. The summary scores for the same behavior categories in the two systems were uncorrelated. The schemes produced different results for base rate reciprocity and for the behavioral correlates of marital satisfaction. The researchers concluded that the differences were due to the different coding units used in the schemes and suggested that coding units should better match those used by spouses to evaluate behaviors. The results also question the extent to which the schemes share a similar theoretical basis.

Participants' Perspectives on Their Own Interaction

At the far right end of the continuum are the members of the relationship we wish to study. These people have a high degree of relationship. Their behavioral, affective, and cognitive responses during interaction are highly interconnected, and each person has well-developed relational knowledge. The implications of such interconnections are that "each person may be, at the same time, the other's most knowledgeable *and* least objective observer" (Sillars & Scott, 1983, p. 154). In one respect, participants in relationships are in a position to be consummate objective investigators, since they have access to a large and diverse sampling of behavior. Yet what partners in a relationship make of these data is inherently subjective and idiosyncratic, not only with respect to outside observers, but also one another.

Information about the idiosyncratic nature of participants' knowledge, relative to outsiders, is available from studies comparing insiders' with outsiders' interpretations of interaction. This research is especially telling about the private message system couples use to send and receive information. The existence of the private message system is confirmed by evidence showing that spouses agree more when coding their own interaction than when coding that of another couple and by the higher correlation between spouses' ratings of their interaction compared with observer–spouse ratings (Margolin et al., 1985). Idiosyncratic interpretations of messages are most likely when wives are the message senders and husbands the receivers (Noller, 1984). Although some studies indicate that the private message system is better developed for satisfied than dissatisfied couples (Gottman, 1979; Gottman & Porterfield, 1981), other studies find no marital satisfaction effect (Margolin et al., 1985; Noller, 1984).

The nature of private message systems apparently involves the way negative messages are interpreted. As we saw earlier, objective observers are more likely than spouses to code behavior as negative, especially the behavior of wives in distressed marriages. Yet husbands of distressed wives tend to interpret these behaviors more positively, or at least do not differ from nondistressed husbands in their interpretation. Thus, the interpretation of negative messages by spouses is particularly idiosyncratic (Weiss, 1984).

A recent study by Notarius et al. (1989) sheds some light on the nature of the idiosyncracy of negative messages. Although nondistressed and distressed husbands did not differ with regard to their subjective evaluations of their wives' objectively negative behaviors, distressed and nondistressed wives did differ: that is, wives in distressed marriages were much more likely to rate their husbands' objectively negative behaviors as negative than were nondistressed wives (64% of the time vs. 36%). Nondistressed wives appear to be influenced by positive sentiment override; that is, they often experience their husbands' negative messages as positive or neutral. Distressed wives, in contrast, more often experience their husbands' negative messages negatively; in a sense, they are more accurate decoders of their husbands' messages. In addition, distressed wives more often interpreted husbands' neutral behaviors as negative, demonstrating negative sentiment override. These data suggest one mechanism by which the private knowledge structures of spouses alter, relative to observers, the affective and cognitive impact of behavior.

Relational knowledge also seems to affect the behavioral responses elicited by the spouse in ways an objective observer would not expect. Exchange theory dictates, for example, that one spouse's positive or negative behavior will be responded to in kind by the other (Gottman, 1979). Yet in the study by Notarius et al. (1989) both distressed and nondistressed spouses evidenced cognitive editing, whereby partners do not match the affect of the antecedent message of the spouse (see Gottman, 1979). Nondistressed wives, for example, were more likely to edit by following their husbands' negative behaviors (experienced negatively) with a positive one, thereby breaking cycles of negative affect. Distressed wives, in contrast, were more likely to follow their husbands' neutral messages, which were experienced neutrally, with negative messages, perhaps instigating cycles of negative affect.

One feature of relational knowledge seems especially influential in shaping how insiders' interpret and are affected by interaction: their expectations for and prior knowledge about what their discussions usually are like. Levenson and Gottman (1985) first noticed the impact of expectations in their 3-year longitudinal study of the links between marital satisfaction and affective responses, measured physiologically. Though they expected the link to differ depending on such variables as whether the spouses were discussing a conflict or simply having a conversation, they found that higher levels of arousal predicted declines in marital satisfaction regardless of what was being discussed. The association held even for the physiological baseline measurement, during which time couples simply sat near each other without talking. The fact that the association between arousal and satisfaction was so pervasive led the investigators to conclude that simply the expectation of interaction is stressful for unhappy couples, presumably because they know what is to come.

In a more detailed study of expectations, Weiss (1984) found that spouses' preconceived ideas about their interaction predicted their subjective experience during a conflict interaction, as well as objective ratings of their behavior during conflict. Expectations predicted somewhat better than more generalized sentiments about the relationship (e.g., love and satisfaction). These results suggest that a history of interaction shapes couples' scripts of how interactions typically are played out and that the scripts, in turn, affect what actually happens during interaction. The interaction between Cathy and Michael in the example may be another episode of Cathy's "how to get Michael's attention" script and Michael's "how to get Cathy off my back" script.

Even within the same close relationship, participants have divergent perspectives on their interaction. Studies of the amount of agreement between spouses on the occurrence of behavioral events generally find moderate levels of agreement (Sullaway & Christensen, 1983), indicating that partners' perspectives on behavior substantially depart from one another. Agreement is better, however, and reaches levels indicative of good reliability when the behaviors sampled are more objective, recent, clearly observable, and more molecular (Christensen, Sullaway, & King, 1983). Within-couple agreement tends to be better for more subjective features of relationships, such as satisfaction or estimates of the probability of marriage, than for behavior (Sullaway & Christensen, 1983). Agreement on subjective features also does not deteriorate over time the way agreement on behavior does.

In discussing the nature of cognitive independence, we noted that partners in close relationships vary in the extent to which their relational knowledge overlaps. The moderate to high levels of agreement between partners reflect this variance in overlap and suggest why overlap might be higher under some conditions than others. One factor affecting the degree of common knowledge is the quality of the relationship between partners. There is considerable evidence that spousal agreement on behavioral events increases with happiness with the relationship (see Sullaway & Christensen, 1983, and Sillars & Scott, 1983, for reviews). For dating couples, agreement on subjective measures of intimacy was higher in stable relationships than in unstable ones (Hill, Peplau, & Rubin, 1981). Even for newly formed acquaintanceships, different impressions of the nature of the relationship were associated with imminent relationship breakdown (Wilkinson, 1987).

The fact that relationship quality is better when coupled partners share similar perspectives probably results from several interacting processes. First, poor communication processes may lead to a lack of consensus about the nature of the relationship. According to Montgomery (1988), private message systems, or relational standards, arise primarily from implicit communication processes that operate at the relational level of messages. Thus, problems with the encoding and decoding of nonverbal messages may especially contribute to within-couple discrepancies in knowledge (see Noller, 1984). The verbal content of messages also is important to the formation of joint knowledge. Simply not sharing new or important information may limit joint knowledge. Lower levels of self-disclosure among daters, for example, are associated with less agreement about just how intimate the relationship is (Hill et al., 1981). In addition, some individuals have better speaking skills and are more adept at sending verbal messages that bring their listener's knowledge closer to their own (Hewes & Planalp, 1987).

Second, the cognitive processing of information during interaction may affect the extent to which partners share common knowledge. Intersubjectivity will be greater to the extent that partners attend to the same stimuli and process, store, and retrieve information in the same way (Hewes & Planalp, 1987). Research on the phenomenon of egocentric bias demonstrates how one of these processes, selective retrieval, can limit agreement. Studies consistently show that married and dating partners overestimate their own contributions to behavioral events relative to their partners' (Christensen et al., 1983; Ross & Sicoly, 1979; Thompson & Kelley, 1981) and further suggest that overestimation results from the ease with which self-relevant behaviors are recalled (Ross & Sicoly, 1979; Thompson & Kelley, 1981).

Third, the extent to which partners' relational knowledge is based on culturally shared norms and in similar views of close relationships will affect the amount of overlap in knowledge. As we described previously, knowledge about a particular relationship derives, in part, from knowledge about that class of relationships generally. Montgomery (1988) noted that unique relational knowledge incorporates, adds to, or supplants societal ideologies. For some partners the normative basis of their knowledge is extensive and extensively shared. For others it is not, making it difficult to develop unique, shared views. To return to our sample interaction, Michael may believe that women should be primarily responsible for household chores and that men at most are clumsy and inconsistent helpers whereas Cathy may think that men help when wives work. This discrepancy may make it difficult for Cathy and Michael to develop a shared relational belief about division of household labor.

Studies of the correlates of within-couple agreement attest to the influence of norms on shared relational knowledge. This is particularly obvious in studies of family power, in which estimates of who has more power tend to align with prevailing norms (Sullaway & Christensen, 1983). The association between spousal agreement and social desirability can be viewed as another manifestation of the impact of norms on private knowledge. Although spouses agreed more on behaviors when they were more socially desirable, this was not true for daters (Christensen et al., 1983), perhaps because norms for marital behavior are more explicit than those for dating. To the extent that social desirability reflects ideas about what relationships should be like, this response bias reflects partners' shared, cultural views.

The Perspectives of Subjective Outsiders

Returning to the middle of our continuum, we see represented three people, each of whom has a different relationship with our participants, Cathy and Michael. To borrow Olson's (1977, p. 118) language, each of these individuals is a "subjective outsider" with respect to Cathy and Michael. The three vary a great deal with regard to the degree of behavioral and cognitive interdependence each has with the spouses. Fred has known the couple only

2 weeks and has weak behavioral and cognitive interconnections with them. James is somewhat more interdependent with both insiders, since he interacts with them regularly and knows each fairly well. His interaction with them is mostly in couple and group situations, however. As a result, he has little knowledge of either as an individual and his knowledge about his unique relationship with each insider is not well developed. Holly is a highly subjective outsider, by virtue of her long-lasting best friendship with Cathy and her frequent interaction with her. Holly and Cathy's relationship shares many of the same features as Cathy and Michael's relationship, described in the previous section, such as its own private message system, clear expectations for how their encounters typically proceed, and a high degree of overlap between the partners' knowledge.

Beginning with the least subjective "subjective outsider," we can say that Fred's perspective on the couple's argument probably would be more similar to an outside observer's than to either the friends' or to an insider's perspective. Although research comparing views of subjective outsiders and with objective outsiders is scarce, the studies that have been done show consistent findings. Margolin et al. (1985) had spouses and outside observers rate videotapes of the spouses themselves interacting and of actors playing a married couple. Agreement was better between spouses' and outside observers' coding of the actors' interaction than it was between the spouses' and outside observers' coding of the spouses' interaction. Similarly, Noller and Callan (1988) gathered three sets of family interaction ratings: from family members themselves, from an outsider family with a similar structure, and from outside observers. Ratings of involvement and dominance were more highly correlated between outsider families and outside observers than between insider families and outside observers, regardless of which family member was being rated. Montgomery (1984) obtained ratings of interactants' openness during small-group discussions and found higher agreement between peer and observer ratings than between self and observer ratings. Similarity in the views of subjective and objective outsiders, combined with other results, led Montgomery (1986) to conclude that valid and reliable assessments of (objective) interaction can be obtained from previously unacquainted or newly acquainted peers.

One can expect the similarity between the perspectives of objective and subjective outsiders to deteriorate rapidly as one moves further to the right on the continuum. This is because of the changes in degree of relationship represented in each pair. One way to analyze these changes is to view them developmentally, as a cross-sectional look at developmental growth in degree of relationship. Initially, partners in interaction rely heavily on cultural norms and stereotypes to interpret information (Levinger & Snoek, 1972; Sillars & Scott, 1983; Surra & Bohman, in press). The fact that outside observers use much the same sources of information in their coding probably contributes to the high degree of agreement between subjective outsiders at the left end of the continuum and objective outsiders. As the relationship evolves, knowledge becomes more individualized and unique to the relationship (Sillars & Scott, 1983; Surra & Bohman, in press). This knowledge colors the partners' interpretations of interaction such that they will no longer match very well the interpretations of outside observers. Instead, the partners' (insiders') perspectives will become more similar to each other than to outside observers'. Thus, we can expect James's, and especially Holly's, interpretation of the argument to align more closely with the spouses' own than with either Fred's or ours as outside observers.

Another developmental change concerns the detection, perception, and representation of interaction events. We described previously how the formation of initial impressions proceeds rapidly and is highly changeable (Park, 1986; Wilkinson, 1987). Individuals who are forming initial impressions of one another may closely monitor interaction events for information, and their knowledge may change readily in response to them. In a study of initial interaction between previously unacquainted pairs, Ickes, Stinson, Bissonnette, and Garcia (1989) found that the accuracy with which one partner reads the content of another's thoughts and feelings was related to verbal and nonverbal behaviors (e.g., asking questions, smiling) during interaction, to the processing of information during interaction (e.g., making attributions about the character of the other), as well as to other attentional and motivational factors. The intensive focus on interaction events and the resulting changes in knowledge characteristic of early encounters is much like the "coding" and processing of information by outside observers—another factor that may account for the similarity between perspectives of outside observers and newly acquainted peers.

As time goes on, an individual's knowledge about the other is likely to become more entrenched and resistant to change in response to routine interaction events (Sillars & Scott, 1983; Surra & Bohman, in press). As our review of research has suggested, insiders are more likely to interpret interaction based on preexisting expectations and idiosyncratic knowledge than on ongoing interaction events; therefore, the interpretation of subjective outsiders begins to depart from objective outsiders.

Because James's and Holly's interpretations are based more on what they know about Cathy and Michael than in what they see or in their shared cultural norms, their interpretations of the interaction will diverge from Fred's and from an outside observer's. Their interpretations are likely to be more similar to Cathy and Michael's interpretations than to either Fred's or ours. In addition, James's and Holly's unique relationship with each spouse means that their perspectives will differ from one another and from the insiders'. The similarity between any subjective outsider and an insider is a function of the degree of overlap in their relational knowledge about each other and the target relationship. Because overlap is likely to increase with behavioral and cognitive interdependence, we can expect more similarity between Cathy's and Holly's perspectives than between James's and either Cathy's or Michael's.

Conclusions: Some Observations on Research Methods and Multiple Perspectives

In the same way that the degree of relationship between observer and observed varies, different research methods make different assumptions about the nature of reality and the importance of subjectivity in defining reality (see Morgan & Smircich, 1980). As we described previously, the aim of observational research is to record the objective, accurate reality of interaction as a concrete structure. The best way of doing this is to minimize the influence of observers' and participants' subjectivity. This is done not only by physically separating them but also by dissecting participants into variables, by relying on accumulated scientific theory as a knowledge base, by gathering data using experimental control or large surveys, and by using sophisticated statistical analyses (Thompson, 1987). Indeed, the chief investigator who conceptualizes and designs the study is usually not the one doing the data gathering and coding. Such techniques separate the scientist from the social world of the objects of study (Thompson, 1987). All of these techniques are used in interaction research to separate investigators physically *and psychologically* from those they study in order to ensure that the external social world is accurately represented.

At the other extreme are research methods designed to assess a reality that is assumed to be socially constructed (see Morgan & Smircich, 1980). Unlike objectivist approaches, in which investigators want to eliminate the influence of subjectivity, those who study insiders' reality wish to capitalize on it. Their goal is to understand the subjectivity of their subjects in order to understand interaction. This goal is accomplished by means of methods that maintain a close association between the researched and the researcher (Thompson, 1987) and by allowing participants to speak for themselves rather than relying on outsider reports. In addition, investigators achieve a relationship with the researched by having personal contact with them and by using empathy with them as a means of identifying and correcting for the influence of their own subjectivity (Thompson, 1987). A good example of this sort of approach is Wilkinson's (1987) study of impression formation, in which she reconciled her point of view with that of her participants by becoming a participant herself, by allowing her participants to comment on the research and to critique her analyses of their data, and by permitting them to determine whether, how, when, and where they were to meet and what they would record about their meetings (see also Chapter 7).

In the middle are research methods that combine features of each approach. These methods are based on the worldview that there are two realities, subjective and objective (see Morgan & Smircich, 1980) and emphasize the connections between the two realities. Such methods have been used in many of the studies reviewed in this chapter, in which outsiders' coding is combined with insiders' coding in the same design. With these approaches, objective reality often is treated as the standard against which participants' subjectivity is judged for its accuracy or bias, rather than assuming each reality is correct but different. In addition, these approaches often make assumptions about what insiders' feel and think by predetermining what dimensions participants should use to interpret interaction and when the stream of conversation should be interrupted for subjective evaluation. They also presuppose that the social setting in which the interaction occurs does not interfere with either the subjective or objective representation of interaction (for an interesting exception see Notarius et al., 1989, who discuss how an interaction lab might influence the subjective and objective data obtained). Current theories about interaction are most comfortable with this middle ground, stressing the interface between subjective and objective reality (e.g., Noller & Guthrie, in press; Notarius et al., 1989).

Our belief is that we will understand interaction only when results from all these methods are accepted by the research community and when we stop treating subjectivity as error and participants' views as bias. As we demonstrated in this chapter, this belief is rooted in theories of relationships that are multidimensional and require multimethods for testing them.

References

Bakeman, R., & Gottman, J. M. (1986). *Observing interaction: An introduction to sequential analysis.* Cambridge: Cambridge University Press.

Christensen, A., Sullaway, M., & King, C. E. (1983). Systematic error in behavioral reports of dyadic interaction. *Behavioral Assessment, 5,* 129–140.

Duck, S., & Pond, K. (1989). Friends, Romans, countrymen, lend me your retrospections: Rhetoric and reality in personal relationships. In C. Hendrick (Ed.), *Close relationships: Review of personality and social psychology* (Vol. 10, pp. 17–38). Newbury Park, CA: Sage.

Duck, S., & Sants, H. (1983). On the origins of the specious: Are personal relationships really interpersonal states? *Journal of Social and Clinical Psychology, 1,* 27–41.

Floyd, F. J., & Markman, H. J. (1983). Observational biases in spouse observation: Toward a cognitive/behavioral model of marriage. *Journal of Consulting and Clinical Psychology, 51,* 450–457.

Floyd, F. J., O'Farrell, T. J., & Goldberg, M. (1987). Comparison of marital observation measures: The Marital Interaction Coding System and the Communication Skills Test. *Journal of Consulting and Clinical Psychology, 55,* 423–429.

Folger, J. P., & Poole, M. S. (1982). Relational coding schemes: The question of validity. In M. Burgoon (Ed.), *Communication yearbook 5* (pp. 235–247). New Brunswick, NJ: Transaction Books.

Gottman, J. M. (1979). *Marital interaction: Experimental investigations.* New York: Academic Press.

Gottman, J. M., & Levenson, R. W. (1984). Why marriages fail: Affective and physiological patterns in marital interaction. In J. C. Masters & K. Yarkin-Levin (Eds.), *Boundary areas in social and developmental psychology* (pp. 67–106). Orlando, FL: Academic Press.

Gottman, J. M., & Porterfield, A. L. (1981). Communicative competence in the nonverbal behavior of couples. *Journal of Marriage and the Family, 4,* 817–824.

Hewes, D. E., & Planalp, S. (1987). The individual's place in communication science. In C. R. Berger & S. H. Chaffee (Eds.), *Handbook of Communication Science* (pp. 146–183). Newbury Park, CA: Sage.

Hill, C. T., Peplau, L. A., & Rubin, Z. (1981). Differing perceptions in dating couples: Sex roles vs. alternative explanations. *Psychology of Women Quarterly, 5,* 418–434.

Hops, H., Wills, T. A., Patterson, G. R., & Weiss, R. L. (1972). *The marital interaction coding system (MICS).* Unpublished manuscript, University of Oregon, Eugene, OR.

Ickes, W., Robertson, E., Tooke, W., & Teng, G. (1986). Naturalistic social cognition: Methodology, assessment, and validation. *Journal of Personality and Social Psychology, 51,* 66–82.

Ickes, W., Stinson, L., Bissonnette, V., & Garcia, S. (1989). *Naturalistic social cognition: Empathic accuracy in mixed-sex dyads.* Unpublished manuscript, The University of Texas at Arlington, Arlington, TX.

Ickes, W., & Tooke, W. (1988). The observational method: Studying the interaction of minds and bodies. In S. W. Duck, D. F. Hay, S. E. Hobfoll, W. Ickes, & B. Montgomery (Eds.), *Handbook of personal relationships: Theory, research, and interventions* (pp. 79–97). Chichester, UK: Wiley.

Ickes, W., Tooke, W., Stinson, L., Baker, V. L., & Bissonnette, V. (1988). Naturalistic social cognition: Intersubjectivity in same-sex dyads. *Journal of Nonverbal Behavior, 12,* 58–84.

Jacobson, N. S., & Moore, D. (1981). Spouses as observers of the events in their relationship. *Journal of Consulting and Clinical Psychology, 49,* 269–277.

Kelley, H. H., Berscheid, E., Christensen, A., Harvey, J. H., Huston, T. L., Levinger, G., McClintock, E., Peplau, L. A., & Peterson, D. R. (Eds.). (1983). *Close relationships.* New York: Freeman.

Kowalik, D. L., & Gotlib, I. H. (1987). Depression and marital interaction: Concordance between intent and perception of communication. *Journal of Abnormal Psychology, 96,* 127–134.

Levenson, R. W., & Gottman, J. M. (1983). Marital interaction: Physiological linkage and affective exchange. *Journal of Personality and Social Psychology, 45,* 587–597.

Levenson, R. W., & Gottman, J. M. (1985). Physiological and affective predictors of change in relationship satisfaction. *Journal of Personality and Social Psychology, 49,* 85–94.

Levinger, G. (1977). Re-viewing the close relationship. In G. Levinger & H. L.

Raush (Eds.), *Close relationships: Perspectives on the meaning of intimacy* (pp. 137–161). Amherst, MA: University of Massachusetts Press.

Levinger, G., & Snoek, J. D. (1972). *Attraction in relationships: A new look at interpersonal attraction.* Morristown, NJ: General Learning Press.

Margolin, G., Hattem, D., John, R. S., & Yost, K. (1985). Perceptual agreement between spouses and outside observers when coding themselves and a stranger dyad. *Behavioral Assessment, 7,* 235–247.

Miell, D. (1987). Remembering relationship development: Constructing a context for interactions. In R. Burnett, P. McGhee, & D. D. Clarke (Eds.), *Accounting for relationships: Explanation, representation, and knowledge* (pp. 60–73). London: Methuen.

Montgomery, B. M. (1984). Behavioral characteristics predicting self and peer perceptions of open communication. *Communication Quarterly, 32,* 233–242.

Montgomery, B. M. (1986). An interactionist analysis of small group peer assessment. *Small Group Behavior, 17,* 19–37.

Montgomery, B. M. (1988). Quality communication in personal relationships. In S. W. Duck, D. F. Hay, S. E. Hobfoll, W. Ickes, & B. Montgomery (Eds.), *Handbook of personal relationships: Theory, research, and interventions* (pp. 343–359). Chichester: Wiley.

Morgan, G., & Smircich, L. (1980). The case for qualitative research. *Academy of Management Review, 5,* 491–500.

Noller, P. (1984). *Nonverbal communication and marital interaction.* New York: Pergamon Press.

Noller, P., & Callan, V. J. (1988). Understanding parent–adolescent interactions: Perceptions of family members and outsiders. *Developmental Psychology, 24,* 707–714.

Noller, P., & Guthrie. (in press). Studying communication in marriage: An integration and critical evaluation. In W. H. Jones & D. Perlman (Eds.), *Advances in personal relationships* (Vol. 3). London: Jessica Kingsley.

Notarius, C. I., Benson, P. R., Sloane, D., Vanzetti, N. A., & Hornyak, L. M. (1989). Exploring the interface between perception and behavior: An analysis of marital interaction in distressed and nondistressed couples. *Behavioral Assessment, 11,* 39–64.

Olson, D. H. (1977). Insiders' and outsiders' views of relationships: Research strategies. In G. Levinger & H. L. Raush (Eds.), *Close relationships: Perspectives on the meaning of intimacy* (pp. 115–135). Amherst, MA: University of Massachusetts Press.

Park, B. (1986). A method for studying the development of impressions of real people. *Journal of Personality and Social Psychology, 51,* 907–917.

Planalp, S. (1987). Interplay between relational knowledge and events. In R. Burnett, P. McGhee, & D. D. Clarke (Eds.), *Accounting for relationships: Explanation, representation, and knowledge* (pp. 175–191). London: Methuen.

Planalp, S., & Rivers, M. (1988). *Changes in knowledge of relationships.* Paper presented at meeting of the Interpersonal and Small Group Division, International Communication Association, New Orleans.

Poole, M. S., & Folger, J. P. (1981). A method for establishing the representational validity of interaction coding systems: Do we see what they see? *Human Communication Research, 8,* 26–42.

Robinson, E. A., & Price, M. G. (1980). Pleasurable behavior in marital interaction: An observational study. *Journal of Consulting and Clinical Psychology, 48,* 117–118.

Ross, M., & Sicoly, F. (1979). Egocentric bias in availability and attribution. *Journal of Personality and Social Psychology, 37,* 322–336.

Sillars, A. L., & Scott, M. D. (1983). Interpersonal perception between intimates: An integrative review. *Human Communication Research, 10,* 153–176.

Stephen, T. D. (1985). Fixed-sequence and circular-causal models of relationship development: Divergent views on the role of communication in intimacy. *Journal of Marriage and the Family, 47,* 955–963.

Sullaway, M., & Christensen, A. (1983). Couples and families as participant observers of their interaction. In J. P. Vincent (Ed.), *Advances in family intervention, assessment, and theory* (Vol. 3, pp. 119–160). Greenwich, CT: JAI Press.

Surra, C. A., Arizzi, P., & Asmussen, L. (1988). The association between reasons for commitment and the development and outcome of marital relationships. *Journal of Social and Personal Relationships, 5,* 47–63.

Surra, C. A., & Bohman, T. (in press). The development of close relationships: A cognitive perspective. In G. Fletcher & F. Fincham (Eds.), *Cognition in close relationships.* Hillsdale, NJ: Erlbaum.

Surra, C. A., & Milardo, R. M. (in press). The social psychological context of developing relationships: Interactive and psychological networks. In W. H. Jones & D. Perlman (Eds.), *Advances in personal relationships* (Vol. 3). London: Jessica Kingsley.

Thompson, L. (1987). *Objectivity and subjectivity in feminist and family science.* Paper presented at the Pre-Conference Workshop on Theory Construction and Research Methodology, National Council on Family Relations, Atlanta.

Thompson, S., & Kelley, H. H. (1981). Judgments of responsibility for activities in close relationships. *Journal of Personality and Social Psychology, 41,* 469–477.

Wegner, D., Giuliano, T., & Hertel, P. (1985). Cognitive interdependence in close relationships. In W. Ickes (Ed.), *Compatible and incompatible relationships* (pp. 253–276). New York: Springer.

Weiss, R. L. (1984). Cognitive and behavioral measures of marital interaction. In K. Hahlweg & N. S. Jacobson (Eds.), *Marital interaction: Analysis and modification* (pp. 232–252). New York: Guilford Press.

Weiss, R. L. (1989). The circle of voyeurs: Observing the observers of marital and family interactions. *Behavioral Assessment, 11,* 135–147.

Wilkinson, S. (1987). Explorations of self and other in a developing relationship. In R. Burnett, P. McGhee, & D. D. Clarke (Eds.), *Accounting for relationships: Explanation, representation, and knowledge* (pp. 40–59). London, Methuen.

Chapter 4

Levels of Analysis:
The Individual, the Dyad,
and the Larger Social Group

GEORGE J. MCCALL
J. L. SIMMONS

Human begings engaged in interaction interpret meanings on many levels simultaneously, occupy many roles at once, are concurrently members of several groups, and often convey messages ambiguously. For these reasons, a kiss is never *just* a kiss and no human act is simply straightforward body movement; rather, each exists at the converge of multiple contexts of meanings. To understand any episode of human interactions is thus to comprehend the multilayered meaning of an interchange of messages, a "conversation of gestures" (Mead, 1934). Not only does the ambiguity of messages permit alternative readings, it requires the audience to judge whether that ambiguity was intended. The inferred attitude of the sender toward his or her own gesture influences whether the audience takes that gesture at face value or as requiring some deeper interpretation. Messages and gestures can thus reveal much about the persons who make and receive them and about the dynamic web of relationships and social groupings that includes and connects those individuals. Certainly this is true of the sample research problem, the dinner conversation between Cathy and Michael Stone.

This consequential layering of meaning poses major methodological difficulties for the interaction researcher: How many—and which—layers can be adequately handled in a particular study? The choice of a level of analysis (that is, deciding whether to employ molecular or molar units of observation) has been a long-standing issue in the empirical study of interaction (Hollenbeck, 1978; McCall, 1984). Analysis at multiple levels has also been increasingly urged (Lamb, Suomi, & Stephenson, 1979); criteria and techniques for aggregating molecular units into molar units have been discussed extensively (van Hooff, 1982), though without adequate attention to the logical problems of aggregation and disaggregation long familiar to sociologists (Hannan, 1971).

This chapter aims to (1) develop a new understanding of "levels" and "units" of analysis, (2) explicate the inherent dilemmas of multiple-level analysis, and (3) illuminate the fundamental undesirability of single-level analysis of interaction. Although existing schemes for multiple-level study are inherently flawed, single-level study yields a flat picture lacking the natural depth of human interaction. In the concluding section we propose instead a novel, "stereoscopic" alternative for retrieving some depth of comprehension.

Layers of Meaning, Levels, and Units of Analysis

"Individual" behaviors—such as Cathy Stone's remark that she does all the work in preparing dinner parties—not only occur in a social context but are fundamentally influenced by it and serve to illuminate some of the ways in which social forces operate upon individuals. That is to say, behaviors signify; they point to deeper meanings.

> Behavior is said to make sense when a series of actions is interpretable as indicating that the actor has in mind some role which guides his behavior. . . . The individual acts as if he were expressing some role through his behavior and may assign a higher degree of reality to the assumed role than to his specific actions. The role becomes the point of reference for placing interpretations on specific actions, for anticipating that one line of action will follow upon another, and for making evaluations of individual actions. (Turner, 1962, p. 24)

Fully human beings never meet as individuals simpliciter, but always in multiple, social roles. Filtering and shaping the contact between Cathy and Michael Stone are their respective age roles, sex roles, economic roles, political roles, religious roles, ethnic roles, and the like—as well as their more specific marital and family role relationships. It is the multiplicity and the hierarchy of roles that engender the multiple layering of meaning when human beings interact.

In the study of interaction, the "units of observation" are individual behaviors (e.g., gestures) whereas the "units of classification" (serving to categorize and interpret such behavioral gestures) are social roles. The "units of analysis" are the social units that these roles constitute (e.g., dyads, groups, associations, communities, and the like). It is just this hierarchy of organizational scope/complexity of social units (Bash, 1989, Bates & Peacock, 1989; Brent, 1984; McCall & Simmons, 1982) that creates levels of analysis in the study of human interaction.

THE LEVEL-OF-ANALYSIS PROBLEM

Although higher-level social units manifest themselves by influencing (even generating) all sorts of lower-level social units, they are not *constituted* by those effects but stand as emergent realities. Therefore, statistical aggregation of observations on lower-level units cannot be relied on to reveal much about higher ones:

> In the life of many little groups, occasions regularly arise when all the members and only the members come together and jointly sustain a situated activity system or encounter: they hold a meeting, play a game, or take a cigarette break together. To call these gatherings "meetings of the group" can easily entrap one into thinking that one is studying the group directly. Actually, these are meetings of persons who are members of a group, and even though the meeting may have been called because of issues faced by the group, the initial data concern participants in a meeting, *not* members of a group.
>
> It is true that on such occasions there is likely to be a correspondence between the realm of group life and the realm of face-to-face interaction process. For example, leadership of a little group may be expressed during gatherings of members by the question of who is chairman or who talks the most, or who is most frequently addressed. It is also likely that the leadership demonstrated in the gathering will both influence, and be influenced by, the leadership in the group. But group leadership is not made up exclusively of an "averaging" of positions assumed during various gatherings. In fact, the group may face circumstances in which its leader is careful to let others take leadership during a meeting, his capacity to lead the group resting upon the tactful way in which he plays a minor role during gatherings of group members. The group leader can do this because "taking the chair" is intrinsically a possibility of gatherings, not groups. (Goffman, 1961, pp. 11–12; italics added.)

That certain actions are specific to the distinctive role systems of differing social units clearly illuminates the concept of an emergent property. Even such a basic interaction research variable as leadership thus proves to be analogous, not homologous, between social units. Researcher confusion about the social roles operating in an empirical situation may lead to misclassification of behaviors and thus to confounding of levels of analysis.

LIMITATIONS OF MULITIPLE-LEVEL ANALYSIS

All this is not to deny that a single episode of human interaction, such as the dinner conversation at the Stone home, might afford a glimpse of organizational life at more than one level. Indeed, much of this chapter seeks to show in detail just how it might do so.

However, multiple-level analysis of a single episode offers no warrant for multiple-level analysis of any given *set* of episodes (as proposed by Bales & Cohen, 1979; Lamb et al., 1979; van den Eeden & Huttner, 1982). To study the group composed of the Stones and the Millers, we would want data from one set of episodes, whereas to study the Stones as a dyad we would want data from a largely different set of episodes. To study Cathy Stone as an individual would require yet a third set. For example, in studying Cathy we would desire a representative sample of her entire population of encounters, few of which would have bearing on the dyad and even fewer of which would pertain to the dinner group (See Chapter 15).

Analogously, a linguist observing the dinner conversation at the Stones could analyze that one stretch of talk at multiple levels: phonological, morphological, syntactic, and so on. None of these analyses precludes a reading at another level. Again, however, the set of samples of English conversations that would satisfy the research needs of phonologist would almost certainly prove inadequate to the needs of a grammarian and quite deficient for the purposes of a cultural anthropologist. The moral of the story is this: Rare is the data base that permits rigorous, nomothetic analyses at different levels.

LIMITATIONS OF SINGLE-LEVEL ANALYSIS

Each level is scientifically legitimate and raises legitimate research questions. However, it is also true that each level alone and in isolation is subject to "scientific tunnel vision" because of the questions never asked (Simmons & McCall, 1985).

In analyzing episodes at any of the lower organizational levels, we must not lose sight of the crucial fact that these smaller organizations operate within the web of all the higher-level organizations. This overarching organizational web forms the stage or ground within which individual lines of action are expressed, channeled, and constrained. But it is this web that provides the opportunities. Thus, social organization is a necessary condition for individual lines of action: without the Stones' marriage, the argument would never have occurred the way it did.

The larger organizations act as "contextual variables," that is to say, they provide a vast panoply of potential raw materials from which actions at the lower levels grow. The individual, pair, or group can choose to fashion from these raw materials a multitude of alternative scripts. However, the contextual variables do render the occurrence of any script either very likely, likely, unlikely, very unlikely, or impossible (McCall & Simmons, 1978). Think for a moment how the dinner would have been different, given the same players, had it occurred in, say, Iran or precontact Borneo, instead of late 20th-century America. Even though human understanding relies heavily upon context, any single-level analysis of interaction necessarily strips away the contextual influences of higher-level social units.

Making Sense of Interaction

These several methodological implications all flow from our thesis that in the study of human interaction "units of analysis" are social organizational units and that "levels of analysis" pertain to levels of organizational scope of those social units. In this section of the chapter we develop further the rationale for such an unabashedly social organizational approach to the study of human interaction. Subsequent sections examine more closely the organizational nature of three most relevant "units of analysis" (group, dyad, social self) and how interaction episodes might be studied at the corresponding levels of analysis.

WHAT DO WE SEE IN INTERACTION ANYWAY?

Through episodes of human interaction we catch glimpses of organizational life. At all but the very lowest levels, the scope of social organization of human interaction is too great to be contained, or made available, in any single episode or communication event. Yet it is only through such episodes and events that the larger-scale organization of human interaction can ever be glimpsed. Peeking through the keyhole of a live interaction, we may catch glimpses of the vast organizational framework on which that episode depends. The group, for example, provides a framework for the gathering, just as a house could be said to provide a framework for home-living.

The research significance of interaction episodes resides in their constituting "keyholes" on the larger social life. As Bogey put it in the film *Casablanca*, "the troubles of two little people in this world don't amount to a hill of beans." Of greater moment are community, human institutions, and the sweep of history, as these are played out within the mundane and puny interactions between individuals. Even at this immense remove in time, through the conversations among the pilgrims in Chaucer's *Canterbury Tales* we catch glimpses not only of their party but of the entire structure and dynamics of medieval English life, the English language, and the human condition. So it is with the more prosaic dinner conversation at the Stone home: their particular dyadic interaction illustrates, signifies, and stands for more general principles of social organization.

APPLYING ORGANIZATIONAL KNOWLEDGE

What enables us to glimpse, through an interaction episode, the operation of some larger, framing organization is the fundamental human talent for role-taking—to discern through another's behaviors the role that person is performing, the line of action that gives those behaviors direction, coherence, and meaning. Roles constitute and express social organization. Seeing that an individual is performing a role (or roles) allows us to make some sense of his or her actions and to detect the framing effects of a social organization.

But organizational life transcends the performance of roles. To apprehend life in and of organizations requires more than role-taking ability; it demands the application of organizational knowledge. In fact, three kinds of organizational knowledge are necessary. Of these, the most abstract and the most strategic is "generic" organizational knowledge, i.e., concepts and principles that apply to organizations of whatever sort. "Typical" organizational knowledge is that which applies only to organizations of a particular type (i.e., level or form). "Unique" organizational knowledge applies to only one specific, concrete organization.

The founts of knowledge about organizations are, of course, legion. Although we here draw primarily from our own analysis of social organization (McCall & Simmons, 1982), the points we shall make about applying organizational knowledge in no way depend on the specifics of that work.

Knowledge of the basics of organizational life provides fundamental frames of reference for conceptualizing what is going on when we encounter organizational life through an episode of human interaction. Illustratively, our own, process-oriented work suggests at least three such fundamental "logics of looking," or "schemata for seeing" organizational life. These three frames of reference constitute complementary, not mutually exclusive, ways of seeing.

Seeing Collective Action

First of all, through any episode of interaction the observer should look for—but cannot count on seeing—the collective action of some larger, framing organization. At the core of organizational life is collective action (Olson, 1971). In fact, we define a social organization as a "structured collectivity undertaking collective action to produce a collective good" (i.e., any good that is necessarily shared with at least some other members). A football championship, for instance, is a collective rather than an individual good, producible only through collective, rather than individual, action.

Collective action brings into focus the organization's aspect of unity, of *collectivity* (the sense of constituting one social unit to which the participating individuals "belong" or of which they are "members"). The organizational features underlying such collectivity include not only collective interests and collective resources (the wellsprings of collective action) but also *shared culture* (a fabric of shared meanings that generates a common reality for the participants).

While a social organization is, in this sense, a unitary collectivity, it also displays a diversity that is crucial to any understanding of it. Even in the most rudimentary organizations the membership is internally differentiated in terms of function, activity, and position—that is, members are organized to facilitate coordinated action. Without such internal differentiation of members, the 11 football players would be only a mob, not a team. This aspect of diversity we call *social structure,* a differentiated pattern in which members not only play distinctive parts in a division of labor but also occupy distinct, though interdependent, social positions. Out of this primary, functional differentiation of social position there always arise secondary social structures: various suborganizations and stratification systems that rest upon and foster divisive special interests.

The forms of collective action and of the collectivity it structures rest crucially on the nature of the collective good to be produced. Day-care center, dance company, and drug ring differ not contingently but necessarily, given the differing goods they seek to produce.

Through an episode of human interaction, the observer may be lucky enough to glimpse collective action. Lucky, first of all, because the means–ends logic linking collective action to production of a collective good affords a powerful and familiar basis for understanding what is going on, why, and with what probable consequences, and what is likely to happen next. Daily life examples abound, such as the cooperative efforts necessary for moving heavy furniture. Lucky, in the second place, because most organizations spend surprisingly little time actually engaged in their central and distinctive modes of collective action. Although organized to play football, even a professional team actually plays football no more than 3 hours a week for perhaps 20 weeks a year. A classroom teacher manages to engage in actual teaching only a small part of the school day, and pupils spend relatively little time on task.

Seeing Role Construction

Through any episode of interaction the observer also should look for, and expect to see, the role-construction process of some larger framing organization. The fundamental fact of organizational life is the ever-present tension between the aspect of unity and the aspect of diversity. Both individuals and organizations must somehow come to grips with this tension, because there is never a perfect fit between these two aspects. The flesh-and-blood social reality of a live social organization does not show up well in those "X-ray pcitures" we call tables of organization. That is to say, an organization is not only a structured collectivity but also very much a dynamic social *process* of organizing threads of human lives. Multiple actors—suborganizations as well as individuals—differing in positions, interests, and resources, are engaged in the pursuit of not only a web of collective interests but also a wide range of competing and conflicting special interests. This fact has vast implications and always colors social life. The differentiation and the coordination of lines of action proceed apace.

Through an episode of interaction, then, the observer ought always to be able to glimpse some process of organizing, that is, the construction or reconstruction of the roles of individuals. Roles are constructed jointly, through ongoing interchange between individuals and the organization to reshape their contours of participation. Individuals' organizational participation is determined through *recruitment*, defined through *socialization*, implemented through *interaction*, altered through *innovation*, and constrained through *social control*. Each of these is a two-sided process involving strategic and tactical moves by the individuals as well as the organization. Figure 4.1 shows how these five basic processes are dynamically interrelated and together suffice to determine the character of an individual's organizational role. Recruitment and socialization jointly determine his or her *prescribed role*. In turn, this prescribed role influences the interaction process, which determines his or her *performed role*, as he or she improvises to meet circumstances and pursue individual interests. Role performance always involves the individual in the innovation process, as a creative or deviant performer, which in turn involves him or her in the social control process through which creativity is rewarded and deviance is punished. Enriched and complicated by the operation of various feedback loops among these processes (McCall & Simmons, 1982, pp. 155–166), the linkages form an endlessly cycling system of social process that shapes and reshapes the individual's organizational role. Viewed over a short span of time, it is a system of role construction; over a longer time span, it is a system of organizational career development. The logical patterning of this system

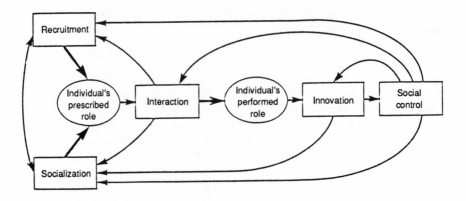

FIGURE 4.1 Interconnections among basic processes in the development of an individual's organization role.

distinctively illuminates much of what might be going on, why, what is likely to happen next, and what the likely consequences might be for the organization, for this system of processes, and for the individuals.

Seeing Logistics

Through any episode of interaction the observer should look for, and expect to see, indications of the operation of individual and organizational tactics in the struggle to accommodate the multiple memberships and multiple roles of individuals. Organizational life takes place in the shadow of other organizations, larger and smaller. That is, smaller organizations are embedded within the boundaries of larger ones. Embedding organizations usually claim some rights of surveillance over their embedded organizations and also some rights to shape and influence what goes on with them. Embedded organizations seek the collective goods of the embedding organizations but struggle to maintain their own freedom of action. Thus there is a perennial struggle over "degrees of freedom."

Every individual plays some role in the life of numerous organizations of different levels. By belonging to many organizations, the individual belongs fully to none. This fact virtually guarantees some organizational cross-pressure on any person (in the forms of role strain and role conflict) but also puts him or her in a position to play each organization against the others. That is, such multiple memberships engender the advantage of providing alternative opportunities for desired role-enactments. For instance, Cathy Stone might enjoy the alternatives of her own family, the women's movement, a valued work role, and so forth.

The joint process though which individuals and organizations strategically and tactically accommodate the multiple memberships of living individuals is one of *logistics,* the balancing and creative managing of the interests and capacities of both individuals and organizations. Through an episode of interaction, the observer ought always to be able to glimpse the process of logistics, especially individual-level tactics.

Organizations provide arenas for individual lines of action, which may or may not be complementary with the collective interests. No single organizational arena can encompass all of the individual's pursuits of valued identities and activities; he or she will perform in numerous such arenas, and in moving from one to another will bring along some of his or her other social roles. Indeed, this intrusion of external roles is one significant factor leading to the inevitable divergence between the role prescribed for the person within one arena and the actual pattern of performance there.

From the viewpoint of the individual, then, logistics is a matter of using the whole set of organizational arenas in whatever manner seems best suited to "satisficing" his or her obligations and wants. To the organization, on the other hand, logistics is a matter of juggling and adjudicating the demands that it places on its individual members in light of their differing external roles. These multiple memberships guarantee a looseness to social life that is the despair of every autocratic executive or family head and that refutes any "oversocialized conception of man" (Wrong, 1961).

Again, there never is likely to be a perfect fit between individual and organizational logistics. The five basic processes of role construction (i.e., recruitment, socialization, interaction, innovation and social control) adjust and lubricate this gap, but it remains for successful logistics strategies and tactics to make it all work out.

TAKING ACCOUNT OF EMERGENT REALITIES

These three generic schemas for seeing organizational life achieve sharper focus through the additional lens of "typical" organizational knowledge, that is, categorical knowledge that applies only to organizations of a particular level or form. The necessity for such an additional lens arises from the emergent properties distinctive to the various social units of analysis—properties that impart special twists to the processes of collective action, role construction, and logistics at different levels of analysis.

Group-, dyadic-, and individual-level analyses are examined in the following three sections of this chapter. In each we identify some key emergent properties of that social unit of analysis, explore the resultant special twists imparted to our "schemas for seeing," and ponder how the dinner conversation at the Stone home might be studied at that level of analysis.

Group-Level Analysis

Groups contrast with larger-scale social units such as associations (MacIver, 1937; Ridgeway, 1983) in that (1) purposes are general rather than limited; (2) collectivity is more developed than social structure; (3) relations tend to be informal and personal; and (4) cooperative interaction is direct, with personal characteristics more important than roles.

SEEING COLLECTIVE ACTION

At least in what sociologists call "primary groups," collective action assumes the rather distinctive form of "group process":

> The face-to-face group, though it admits of subsidiary and preparatory division of labor, is essentially a mode of sharing a common experience. . . . The members of a study group may undertake separate tasks in preparation for the activity of the group, but they must bring their results into a common process at the point where the group activity begins. . . . The members of a group discussing the same problem make different contributions, but they do not have separate functions; all participate in the same process. (MacIver, 1937, p. 240)

A primary group does not ordinarily cohere around some single like interest of its members but answers some overlapping ranges of like and complementary interests. For members of a primary group, the nature of *any* interest becomes both focused and enriched—objectified, in Mead's (1934) sense—through the group process.

> We see it through the eyes of others and thus it is in some measure freed from irrelevant personal implications. It is defined more closely for each of us, for being now both mine and yours it must have a common meaning. Before we can effectively pursue it together we must learn to perceive it together. Each seeing it from his own viewpoint seeks to convey that aspect to his associates. Thus the character of the interest is enlarged and enriched, as each contributes something different to the understanding of it . . . as the play of different minds is directed upon it. . . . The interest, by being shared, acquires a new significance, a new emphasis, a new valuation. (MacIver, 1937, pp. 237–239)

SEEING ROLE CONSTRUCTION

Unfortunately, in conventional analyses of most types of organization the role-construction process receives little or no systematic attention. In the case of the group, however, the informal constructing of roles has long been the very center of analysis (Turner & Colomy, 1988).

Students of group dynamics and of family dynamics tell us that, in most primary groups, role differentiation tends to rest on an implicit, often almost accidental, division of labor that comes to have the force of a group tradition. Norms applying to the membership as a whole are elaborated much more thoroughly than those position-specific norms we think of as role-expectations. More clearly marked (and often more influential) than role is one's place in the group's various stratification systems, the well-studied structures of power, status, leadership, communication, and liking.

Because every primary group is "a unity of interacting personalities" (Burgess, 1926), each of these participating personalities undergoes certain adaptations—of perception, judgment, belief, attitude, opinion, motivation, behavior, habit, and self-concept—through the give-and-take of the distinctive group process. Some of these changes can be attibuted to the informational influence of the defining and objectifying character of the group process itself (Klapper, 1961). Group process not only shows the individual how to think intelligently and how to see creative solutions the individual would never have found alone (Taylor & McNemar, 1955) but also provides him or her with seemingly credible group interpretations of ambiguous or contradictory situations and with social support or consensual validation for its social realities. Other personal changes can be attributed to the powerful normative influence of the group—that is, to members' desires to adhere to and live up to the norms of the group (Deutsch & Gerard, 1955)—and also to the facilitating and sustaining influence of group support in members' efforts to alter deeply entrenched attitudes and behaviors.

Of course, the individual remains an active agent within the group. As Mead has emphasized, the individual will actively seek to influence the normative structure, the definitions of situations, and all the secondary structures. For instance, he or she will recruit himself or herself into or out of particular gatherings and will actively socialize himself or herself in order to attain certain positions within the secondary structures.

SEEING LOGISTICS

Primary groups are a place to which an individual can take a wide range of personal problems in search of insight, assistance, and support. He or she can rely on a primary group to support, sharpen, and focus many of his or her personal interests. As a consequence, groups tend to be fun, and feeling at home in the group, one can display and receive some affirmation for most, if not all, of one's personal identities. The family, in particular, fulfills an "archival function" of retaining and affirming member's various external roles and identities—even "lost" identities such as the student council presidency of a now middle-aged son (Weigert & Hastings, 1977).

Also, a person can often count on primary groups to collude and conspire with him or her in managing the strains of external roles, by "covering" or speaking up for the person. Families collude with their members against unforgiving work organizations, and friendship groups collude with members against the demands of their marital relationships. Furthermore, for most individuals the family uniquely serves as "role budget center":

> For adult or child, the family is the main center of role allocation, and thus assumes a key position in solutions of role strain. Most individuals must account to their families for what they spend in time, energy, and money outside the family. . . . family members are often the only persons who are likely to know how an individual is allocating his total role energies, managing his whole role system; or that he is spending "too much" time in one role obligation and retiring from others. . . . Consequently, other family members can and do give advice as to how to allocate energies from a "secure center." Thus it is from this center that one learns the basic procedures for balancing role strains. (Goode, 1960, pp. 489–490, 493)

GROUP LIFE AMONG THE MILLERS AND THE STONES

Such typical knowledge of groups can be most useful in helping us to glimpse group life through the "keyhole" of that dinner conversation recounted in the Preface. In looking for collective action, we know to expect here only a subsidiary and preparatory division of labor, to watch here for different contributions rather than separate functions. In looking for role construction, we know that the ongoing processes of secondary social differentiation (e.g., status, power, communication, and liking) may be more visible than those of primary (role) differentiation. In looking for logistics, we know to expect that primary group members will feel obliged to make *some* accounting to the group of how they have been spending their time and energies.

To actually attain that degree of focus, however, will additionally require the use of certain "unique" organizational knowledge. In order to glimpse the life of some specific group, it is enormously helpful to know something of its particular social structure. What positions has this group evolved? How are they interconnected? Who occupies which position?

Similarly, we will need to know something of its culture. Every gang, family, and work group develops rather quickly its own, somewhat unique, little culture of norms, shared meanings, and distinctive traditions (McFeat,

1974; Fine, 1979; Ridgeway, 1983). To comprehend life in some specific group, or even the language, thoughts, feelings, and actions of its members, demands some grasp of that group's prevailing shared rhetoric of ritual and meaning.

Another key element of organizational culture is a group's sense of history. What are the present circumstances of the group? By what developmental path did it come to this? Where is the group headed? The natural history of a group, like the biography of an individual, affords a vital interpretive context. Without such historical knowledge we can be too easily led astray and make the mistake, so common in daily life, of evaluating only in terms of generic stereotypes (e.g., a couple fighting is automatically construed as marriage in trouble).

If the Millers and the Stones comprise a group, what unique knowledge of this group do we need? Beyond the scant account given of this group, what would we want or need to know in order to glimpse, through the episode of a dinner conversation, the life of that group?

About the gathering: we would want to know what occasioned this social dinner. Someone's birthday or anniversary? A holiday celebration? Reciprocation of an earlier dinner at the Miller home? Some domestic tragedy that has driven the Millers from their own home to that of their long-term friends? The monthly gathering of a small and informal "gourmet club"? An "occasioned gathering" (in Goffman's terminology) not only provides a setting, complete with props, but also constitutes a platform for and constraints upon the interaction that takes place therein.

About the interaction within that gathering: we would want to know at least two things. First, what led up to the argument? Knowledge of the verbal context in which Holly Miller came to ask the (innocent? provocative?) question would certainly be helpful. But actions as well as words preceded her query. Perhaps the preparation and serving of this meal had been plagued by a series of misfortunes, or perhaps this query arose after an hour of heavy drinking. Second, and perhaps more important, what were the Millers doing while this argument was going on? If their apparent silence indicates that they sank through the floor in embarrassment, group life seems absent. If the transcript merely omits their numerous paralinguistic and kinesic gestures toward rescuing the situation, group life might yet be glimpsed.

About the putative little group: we would want to know its "facts of life" as a structured collectivity, its collective goods, its shared role constructions, and logistics from the group's viewpoint. For instance, if the group is a letting-off-steam valve for the two couples, the argument would have one meaning; if it is a well-mannered, dress-up configuration, quite another. And if the group's purpose were spouse-swapping, the encounter would be evaluated still differently indeed.

The more we know (about gathering, conversation, and/or group), the more we can recognize, appreciate, and comprehend the organizational life that frames and animates an interaction episode.

Dyadic-Level Analysis

In most respects, a dyadic relationship is essentially a two-person group. As Simmel (1950) convincingly demonstrated, however, such an absolutely minimal "group" exhibits sharply distinctive features both as a collectivity and as a social structure.

Unlike most social organizations, dyadic relationships do not vary in membership size. Having only two members, the dyad is a peculiarly vulnerable organization, for the loss of a single member ends the organization as a whole. The dyad is, in fact, the only organization that can never expect to outlive any of its members. Consequently, the dyad is obsessed with its own mortality, an obsession that heightens the intrinsic sentimentalism distinguishing dyadic life and encourages the establishment of all sorts of interpersonal bonds as glue to hold the relationship together. For instance, the bonds of commitment, attachment, and investment loom especially large in dyads.

Internal social differentiation of any kind is absolutely minimal, for there are only two structural positions definable. For the same reason, as in no other type of organization, factional suborganization is necessarily and completely absent. Thus, no internal coalitions are available within the process of ratifying or stigmatizing innovations. While this entails that a member can never be outvoted, it also means that he or she can never obtain any internal backing in any dispute with another member. And, never forget, each member does have an ultimate veto power. Drawing on such "typical" organizational knowledge (Cappella, 1988; Ginsburg, 1988; McCall, 1982) can help us to focus our schemata for seeing dyadic life.

SEEING COLLECTIVE ACTION

In any relationship, a sense of shared fate tends to arise as members discover that the surrounding world treats them not so much as separate individuals but, rather, as a couple or unit. Married people, for example, are invited to social events not as persons but as couples. Awareness of this sort of "dual participation" (Waller, 1938) often leads members to appreciate more deeply the extent to which theirs is a shared fate and a common interest. This engenders a haunting quality to dyadic relationships, where one plus one never precisely equals two. This appreciation in turn reinforces their tendency to collective action, in the form of "pair-centered interaction"

(Waller, 1938). That is to say, married couples, friends, and colleagues typically act toward outsiders as teams, cooperating to maintain proper fronts of solidarity and to further their joint ventures.

SEEING ROLE CONSTRUCTION

Even in an institutionalized primary relationship such as marriage, where the official positions of husband and wife are allocated to members, knowing these positions tells us little about the actual division of labor. As the man and the woman informally differentiate their respective roles, each is guided by his or her own role-identities and by the presented persona of the other. The fit between their personas effectively requires them to avoid certain actions that are prescribed by their institutional role relationships but that happen to be inconsistent with a member's presented role identity, and allows them, conversely, to perform actions that deviate from institutional role prescriptions but that happen to be consistent with the presented role identities of the members. For such reasons, it may turn out that neither member of a marital couple will do any cooking or that in the privacy of their own apartment they speak to each other largely in baby talk. The negotiation processes through which such normative expectations are developed, applied, and refined are of great organizational significance (Ginsburg, 1988; Roloff, 1987). It appears, for example, that dyads tacitly negotiate their unique rules of relationship primarily through remedial episodes (Morris, 1985; Morris & Hopper, 1980; Stokes & Hewitt, 1976), that is, restorative sequences of reproach, account, and remedy.

SEEING LOGISTICS

Simmel (1950) identified within primary relationships a "strain toward totality" that operates to include ever-larger segments of members' self structures and ever-greater proportions of their time and other resources. Because every individual maintains and depends on an entire network of such "greedy" relationships, he or she must limit, adjudicate, and balance all these competing claims. With only 24 hours in a day and limited energies, how can he or she optimize his or her interactions with all these people? How can he or she simultaneously cultivate all these relationships? One's network represents a "personal economy" of relationships to be managed more effectively (Marks, 1977) through such tactics as scheduling, role segregation, audience segregation, stalling, working-in, compromising, and playing-off relationships. (As McCall and Simmons [1978] assert, these logistic dynamics deserve a book in themselves).

Personal economy dictates that we try to get as much as possible out of each relationship, to include as much of ourselves as is profitable. That is, one must try to include in a relationship all those aspects of self that would be reasonably well received by one's partner but exclude all those aspects that would threaten the continued existence of the relationship. The existence one has outside of and in addition to the relationship must not be allowed to have a deleterious influence upon it. This often takes some fancy footwork. Through tactics of information control—dramaturgical circumspection, revisionary autobiography, selective reporting, and audience segregation—we manage events to prevent disruption of a well-received persona.

DYADIC LIFE AMONG THE MILLERS AND THE STONES

In looking for collective action, we as researchers know enough to look for pair-centered interaction. In looking for role construction, we know to watch for remedial episodes. In looking for logistics, we know that we should be alert to how individuals manage their personal economies of relationships.

But again, "unique" organizational knowledge about the specific dyad—the Stones, for instance—is especially helpful. We would like to know about its social structure (e.g., the respective ranks of Cathy and Michael in the dyadic structures of power, status, liking, and leadership). Knowledge of this particular dyadic culture (Baxter, 1987; Oring, 1984)—for example, knowing whether theirs is a "conflict-habituated" marriage—certainly would be useful in grasping the local rhetoric (Hopper, Knapp, & Scott, 1981; Maynard & Zimmerman, 1984). Knowing something of the natural history of this dyad (Kellerman, 1987) would also help us to interpret their interaction (e.g., whether this argument is a routinized or an anomalous occurrence and what the reference to the cat box might stem from).

But perhaps most of all we would want to know about this dyad's interorganizational relations (to other dyads, groups, etc.). Among the Millers and the Stones, for example, there are to be found six different dyads and perhaps a group or two. In order to comprehend the episode of dinner conversation, we would do well to understand how all these little organizations relate to one another. Very likely, the two marital relationships dominate this organization set, in which case the gathering in question is a classic occasion for dual participation. Perhaps, however, it is the workplace-engendered relationship between the two women that dominates, or the over-the-back fence relationship of the two men. In either event, the gathering will tend to be structured by the two same-sex relationships. There remains, too, the possibility that three or four of these individuals do constitute a true group, which these various dyadic relations functionally complicate. Under any of these scenarios, it is the two cross-sex/nonmarital relationships that are least likely to feature prominently (but without unique knowledge, this is only a guess).

In this episode we certainly do not see any pair-centered interaction but, rather, the operation of a dyadic role-construction process. Does the Stones' argument represent a serious and direct attempt by Cathy to reshape the dyadic division of labor, or might it instead represent her attempt to test the strength of the marital relationship (Baxter & Wilmot, 1984; Kurth, 1970)?

What would we want or need to know in order to decide what is really going on? Certainly we will again want to know what occasioned the gathering, what led up to the argument, and what the Millers were doing during the argument. About this dyad we would want to know its natural history and culture, the collective goods it encompasses, and its pair logistics (e.g., what plans have the Stones toward the Millers?).

Individual-Level Analysis

What makes the human individual a social unit is the achievement of selfhood, or reflexivity. According to George Herbert Mead (1934), this achievement occurs when the individual first begins to act toward himself or herself in more or less the same fashion in which he or she acts toward other people—that is, when a "me" emerges alongside the "I." For Mead, the "I" is the essentially unknowable active agent, that which does the thinking, the knowing, the planning, the acting. The "me" is all those perspectives on oneself that the individual learned from others—the attitudes that the "I" assumes toward his or her own person when he or she is taking the role of the other toward himself or herself.

> If the "I" and the "me" constitute the totality of the self, this self is best seen in what Mead called the "inner forum," the silent internal conversation that is continually going on inside the human organism. But the reader should avoid the fallacy of thinking of this conversation as a simple dialogue between something called the "I" and something called the "me." . . . The human mind is not so simple and monolithic. Ordinarily, one's mind is reacting to what one is saying or thinking *as one is saying or thinking it.* One does not wait until he has said something to see just what it is that he was going to say. One monitors oneself *throughout* the process and from a multiplicity of perspectives and contexts. And it is this organization of multiple perspectives and contexts for reaction that is the "me," in Mead's terms. The "me" is best thought of, not as the antagonist in a dialogue

with the "I," but as an *audience*, all the people in a *multiperson discussion* who are temporarily silent while the "I" holds the floor. But though they are politely silent, they are evaluating and criticizing all the while that the "I" is talking. Each has a somewhat different reaction, corresponding to his unique perspective, and when the "I" has finished and relinquished the floor, so to speak, every member of this metaphorical audience strives to inform him of his own personal reaction to what was said. It is not accidental that Mead chose the metaphor of "inner *forum*." And, of course, if any of the "audience" objects really strongly to what the "I" is saying or doing, he may not restrain himself until the "I" has completed his act but may instead rudely interject his reactions and disrupt or suspend the ongoing action.

But of course metaphors are merely crutches, and we must not allow ourselves to hypostatize this picture of the self as inner forum. . . . *The "me" is merely the organized cognitive frames of reference in terms of which the mind appraises and evaluates and monitors the ongoing thought and action of its own person, the "I."* (McCall & Simmons, 1978, pp. 53–54)

Such self-monitoring, we can therefore presume, was occurring "within" both Michael and Cathy during the course of their argument.

SEEING COLLECTIVE ACTION

For the social self, collective action is precisely the operation of the "inner forum"—the continual self-appraisal carried on in terms of standards internalized from significant others, creatively adapted, and individually elaborated. As Mead and others have suggested, this process is the basis for that intelligent, controlled, socialized behavior that is the singular accomplishment of the human animal.

One thing that distinguishes man from the lower animals is the fact that he has a conception of himself, and once he has defined his role he strives to live up to it. . . . Instead of acting simply and naturally, as a child, responding to each natural impulse as it arises, we seek to conform to accepted models, and conceive ourselves in some one of the conventional and socially accepted patterns. In our efforts to conform, we restrain our immediate and spontaneous impulses, and act, not as we are impelled to act, but rather as seems appropriate and proper to the occasion. (Park, 1927, pp. 738–739)

The visible product of self-apprasial through the inner forum is, then, *conduct,* that sophisticated "form of behavior we expect in man when he is conscious of the comment that other men are making, or are likely to make, upon his actions." (Park, 1931, p. 36) However, until we know something of the individual actors' unique history and reference groups we cannot say who and what they may be conforming to in their lines of conduct.

SEEING ROLE CONSTRUCTION

These conceptions of self-in-a-role, or *role-identities*, motivate and guide the development of lines of action. Each of the person's many role-identities suggests (or contains within itself) many concrete actions or performances that the person would like to stage, being the sort of person he or she likes to think of himself or herself as being. Performances suggested by one role-identity are, however, often incompatible with certain performances suggested by other role-identities of the same individual. Among the factors causing certain identities to figure more saliently as sources of suggested performances in the situation are (1) prominence, or relative importance to the person; (2) the relative needs of these identities for role-support, the person's need or desire for the kinds and amounts of (a) intrinsic and (b) extrinsic gratification ordinarily gained through their performance; and (3) the perceived degree of opportunity for the profitable enactment of such an identity in the present circumstances.

It is of great importance to recognize that the actual performance of any person is multiply relevant; that is, it is relevant to, or involves, a number of the person's role-identities. That subset that one strives to incorporate in one's performance in a given situation constitutes the character one seeks to assume in that situation. The individual's performance before the other persons present is devised with the aim of acting in a manner consistent with and expressive of that character, in order to legitimate those identities. One thus improvises an interactive role for oneself in the form of a line of conduct characteristic and expressive of a person with a particular self-structure (character). If the actual performance is indeed consistent with and expressive of this self-structure, the audience confers that character upon the performer. This performance not only expresses an image of who one is, but it also simultaneously expresses an image of who one takes the others to be (Turner, 1968; McCall, 1987).

But when one person's expressive processes of presentation of self (Goffman, 1959; Schlenker, 1980; Tedeschi, 1981) and altercasting (Weinstein & Deutschberger, 1963, 1964) do not manage to structure the encounter for everyone, they at least suggest to others the direction in which that person would like to modify the roles of each party, through the negotiation of social identities (McCall & Simmons, 1978). Thus the encounter is negotiated—smoothly or roughly (or even savagely)—by the individuals involved. This is done essentially through our five basic processes of role construction (i.e., recruitment, socialization, interaction, innovation, and social control), which are ever-present, in however rudimentary a form.

SEEING LOGISTICS

For such reasons, the individual cannot safely stake his or her self on a single encounter but must evolve means of staking it on an indeterminate series of encounters. One learns to select and arrange those encounters in which one may safely enact the character one would like to be and to avoid those situations, acts, and persons that would threaten one's role-identities. Thus again, the individual is an active agent in his or her own social life.

Because no single performance can satisfy all a person's needs and desires, a series of qualitatively different performances must be staged in order to cover all these needs. Since they are different in content, some of these performances may be less than compatible and will at least differ in the types of audience, resources, and other elements that they require for successful staging. To cope with these incompatibilities and differential requirements, the person must set up agendas, or schedules of performances. These agendas (or life plans) come in all different sizes, some roughly covering the remainder of the life span, some covering only the rest of the week, and some covering the remainder of the day or even the rest of the hour. Once the agenda is tentatively set, one moves from stage to stage according to schedule, staging this performance in the setting most favorable to its success and staging that one over there.

But agendas, like performances, are interactively negotiated and not necessarily with equal voice by each participant. Settings, audiences, supporting casts, and dramaturgical discipline are the sorts of things characteristically controlled by social organizations, of all sizes and forms. At this level one must bargain with one's entire organizational set to negotiate one's life round (McCall & Simmons, 1982, pp. 425–442).

But what bargains does the individual seek to strike? Without some understanding of the subjective cost/reward calculus, it is not possible to fully understand what an individual is doing.

INDIVIDUAL LIFE AMONG THE MILLERS AND THE STONES

In seeking to glimpse the operation of social selves, we know not to bother looking for collective action, which at this level amounts to unobservable intrapersonal communication; only its product (conduct) may be seen. In looking for role construction, we know that through observing an individual's presentation of self and altercasting, we may detect inferentially the role he or she has improvised for himself or herself in that social situation. In looking for logistics, we know to watch for agendas (hidden or official) and the process of their negotiation.

"Unique" organizational knowledge about some specific social self—say, Cathy Stone's—can greatly help us to fine-tune our looking. For example, we might be tempted to view her remarks to Michael as both presentation of self and altercasting. We could better evaluate that possibility if we knew something about this specific self's structure (e.g., that her identity as a woman is at the top of her prominence hierarchy of role-identities), "culture" (e.g., gender-role definitions), and history (e.g., that her role-identity as a woman has been significantly changing in content and/or prominence).

Or perhaps we instead might construe her remarks as logistical negotiation, seeking to reallocate her scarce store of time and energies across endeavors. Here, specific knowledge about this self's "interorganizational relations" (the web of Cathy's interdependencies with other individuals, dyads, groups, etc.) would be particularly helpful in evaluating this interpretation.

What more would we want or need to know about the episode itself? Again, we would like to know what occasioned the gathering. Private gatherings for pure sociability, for example, are framed for identity support (Pin & Turndorf, 1985). If the gathering at the Stone home were of that sort, that certainly would influence our interpretation of the interaction. About the interaction itself, we would again like to know what led up to the argument (e.g., had there been earlier mentions of gender issues?) and what the Millers were doing during the argument (gaping? nodding affirmatively? averting their eyes?).

Some Alternative Strategies of Analysis

Through knowledge of collective action, role construction, and logistics—as these processes play out distinctively at the levels of the group, dyad, and individual—we are certainly more likely to make sense out of our dinner-table conversational fragment. But again, the multiple-level analysis of a single episode offers no warrant for multiple-level analysis of any given set of episodes.

A far too common response to this difficulty has been to adopt a strategic (if not ideological) preference for restricting analysis to either the highest or the lowest available level. Yet an unbending holistic approach that fixates only on the highest macrolevel is just as misleading as a rigid reductionistic approach that blindly fixates only on the most micro of levels (Bohm 1980). Polemics and imperialisms are useless, sectarian, and trivializing, off the track of true science.

Preferable to any such fixed mode would be either a "top-down" or a "bottom-up" strategy, offering a starting point, a focus, and a direction of analysis. Through such "directional" strategies of analysis and interpretation, the limitations of a given data base can still be respected while affording some chance for major emergent realities of other levels to be uncovered.

Better yet would seem to be a "contextualist" strategy in which analysis centers on some focal level in the context of the influencing levels above and below. In this sandwich approach, the chosen level of analysis is the "meat" and the levels above and below serve as the enveloping slices. These surrounding contextual "slices" cannot safely be ignored. A dyadic-level analysis, for instance, must take some (albeit incomplete and imperfect) account of the social selves of the dyad's members and of the embedding organizations within which that dyad is nested (Kenny & Kashy, in Chapter 15, describe a particular methodology that accommodates such a contextualist strategy).

Such a "stereoscopic," contextualist strategy, respecting the multi-layered meaning of human interaction, allows the analyst to preserve some of the real-life depth of significance that is lost by reduction to any single plane of analysis.

References

Bales, R. F., & Cohen, S. P. (1979). *SYMLOG: A system for the multiple-level observation of groups.* New York: Free Press.

Bash, H. H., (1989). An exchange on vertical drift and the quest for theoretical integration in sociology. *Social Epistemology, 3,* 229–246.

Bates, F. L., & Peacock, W. G. (1989) Conceptualizing social structure: The misuse of classification in structural modeling. *American Sociological Review, 54,* 565–577.

Baxter, L. A. (1987). Symbols of relationship identity in relationship cultures. *Journal of Personal and Social Relationships, 4,* 261–280.

Baxter, L. A., & Wilmot, W. (1984). Secret tests: Social strategies for acquiring information about the state of the relationship. *Human Communication Research, 11,* 171–201.

Bohm, D. (1980). *Wholeness and the implicate order.* Boston: Routledge.

Brent, S. B. (1984). *Psychological and social structures.* Hillsdale, NJ: Erlbaum.

Burgess, E. W. (1926). The family as a unity of interacting personalities. *The Family, 7,* 3–9.

Cappella, J. N. (1988). Personal relationships, social relationships and patterns of interaction. In S. Duck, D. F. Hay, S. E. Hobfoll, W. Ickes, & B. Montgomery (Eds.), *Handbook of personal relationships: Theory, research and interventions* (pp. 325–342). Chichester, UK: Wiley.

Deutsch, M., & Gerard, H. B. (1955). A study of normative and informational social influences upon individual judgment. *Journal of Abnormal and Social Psychology, 51,* 629–636.

Fine, G. A. (1979). Small groups and culture creation: The idioculture of Little League baseball teams. *American Sociological Review, 44,* 733–745.

Ginsburg, G. P. (1988). Rules, scripts and prototypes in personal relationships. In S. Duck, D. F. Hay, S. E. Hobfoll, W. Ickes, & B. Montgomery (Eds.), *Handbook of personal relationships: Theory, research and interventions* (pp. 23–40). Chichester, UK: Wiley.

Goffman, E. (1959). *The presentation of self in everyday life.* Garden City, NJ: Doubleday.

Goffman, E. (1961). *Encounters: Two studies in the sociology of interaction.* Indianapolis: Bobbs-Merrill.

Goode, W. J. (1960). A theory of role strain. *American Sociological Review, 25,* 483–496.

Hannan, M. T. (1971). *Aggregation and disaggregation in sociology.* Lexington, MA: Lexington.

Hollenbeck, A. R. (1978). Problems of reliability in observational research. In G. P. Sackett (Ed.), *Observing behavior II: Data collection and analysis methods* (pp. 79–98). Baltimore: University Park.

Hopper, R., Knapp, M. L., & Scott, L. (1981). Couples' personal idioms: Exploring intimate talk. *Journal of Communication, 31,* 23–33.

Kellerman, K. (1987). Information exchange in social interaction. In M. E. Roloff & G. R. Miller (Eds.), *Interpersonal processes: New directions in communication research* (pp. 188–219). Newbury Park, CA: Sage.

Klapper, J. T. (1961). *The effects of mass media.* New York: Holt, Rinehart & Winston.

Kurth, S. B. (1970). Friendship and friendly relations. In G. J. McCall (Ed.), *Social relationships* (pp. 136–170). Chicago: Aldine.

Lamb, M. E., Suomi, S. J., & Stephenson, G. R. (Eds.). (1979). *Social interaction analysis: Methodological issues.* Madison: University of Wisconsin Press.

MacIver, R. M. (1937). *Society.* New York: Farrar & Rinehart.

Marks, S. R. (1977). Multiple roles and role strain: Some notes on human energy, time and commitment. *American Sociological Review, 42,* 921–936.

Maynard, D. W., & Zimmerman, D. H. (1984). Topical talk, ritual and the social organization of relationships. *Social Psychology quarterly, 47,* 301–316.

McCall, G. J. (1982). Becoming unrelated: The managment of bond dissolution. In S. Duck (Ed.), *Personal relationships: 4. Dissolving personal relationships* (pp. 211–232). New York: Academic Press.

McCall, G. J. (1984). Systematic field observation. *Annual Review of Sociology, 10,* 263–282.

McCall, G. J. (1987). The self-concept and interpersonal communication. In M. E. Roloff & G. R. Miller (Eds.), *Interpersonal processes: New directions in communication research* (pp. 63–76). Newbury Park, CA: Sage.

McCall, G. J. (1988). The organizational life cycle of relationships. In S. Duck, D. F. Hay, S. E. Hobfoll, W. Ickes, & B. Montgomery (Eds.), *Handbook of personal relationships: Theory, research and interventions* (pp. 467–484). Chichester, UK: Wiley.

McCall, G. J., & Simmons, J. L. (1978). *Identities and interactions* (rev. ed.). New York: Free Press.

McCall, G. J., & Simmons, J. L. (1982). *Social psychology: A sociological approach.* New York: Free Press.

McFeat, T. (1974). *Small-Group cultures.* New York: Pergamon Press.

Mead, G. H. (1934). *Mind, self, and society.* Chicago: University of Chicago Press.

Morris, G. H. (1985). The remedial episode as a negotiation of rules. In R. L. Street & J. N. Capella (Eds.), *Sequence and pattern in communicative behaviour* (pp. 70–84). London: Edward Arnold.

Morris, G. H., & Hopper, R. (1980). Remediation and legislation in everyday talk: How communicators achieve consensus on rules. *Quarterly Journal of Speech, 67,* 266–274.

Olson, M., Jr. (1971). *The logic of collective action* (rev. ed.). New York: Schocken.

Oring, R. (1984). Dyadic traditions. *Journal of Folklore Research, 21,* 19–28.

Park, R. E. (1927). Human nature and collective behavior. *American Journal of Sociology, 32,* 733–741.

Park, R. E. (1931). Human nature, attitudes, and mores. In K. Young (Ed.), *Social attitudes* (pp. 17–45). New York: Holt.

Pin, E. J., & Turndorf, J. (1985). *The pleasure of your company: A socio-psychological analysis of modern sociability.* New York: Holt.

Ridgeway, C. L. (1983). *The dynamics of small groups.* New York: St. Martins.

Roloff, M. E. (1987). Communication and reciprocity within intimate relationships. In M. E. Roloff & G. R. Miller (Eds.), *Interpersonal processes: New directions in communication research* (pp. 11–38). Newbury Park, CA: Sage.

Schlenker, B. R. (1980). *Impression management.* Monterey, CA: Brooks/Cole.

Simmel, G. (1950). *The sociology of Georg Simmel.* New York: Free Press.

Simmons, J. L., & McCall, G. J. (1985). *Social research: The craft of finding out.* New York: Macmillan.

Stokes, R., & Hewitt, J. P. (1976). Aligning actions. *American Sociological Review, 41,* 838–849.

Taylor, D. W., & McNemar, O. W. (1955). Problem solving and thinking. *Annual Review of Psychology, 6,* 455–482.

Tedeschi, J. T. (1981). *Impression management theory and social psychological research.* New York: Academic Press.

Turner, R. H. (1962). Role-taking: Process versus conformity. In A. M. Rose (Ed.), *Human behavior and social processes* (pp. 20–40). Boston: Houghton Mifflin.

Turner, R. H. (1968). The self-conception in social interaction. In C. Gordon & K. J. Gergen (Eds.), *The self in social interaction* (Vol. 1, pp. 93–106). New York: Wiley.

Turner, R. H., & Colomy, P. (1988). Role differentiation. In E. J. Lawler & B. Markovsky (Eds.), *Advances in Group Processes,* Volume 5. Greenwich, CT: JAI Press.

van den Eeden, P., & Huttner, H. J. M. (1982). Multi-level research. *Current Sociology, 30,* 1–182.

van Hooff, J. A. R. A. M. (1982). Categories and sequences of behavior: Methods of description and analysis. In K. R. Scherer & P. Ekman (Eds.), *Handbook of methods in nonverbal behavior research* (pp. 362–439). Cambridge: Cambridge University Pres..

Waller, W. (1938). *The family: A dynamic interpretation.* New York: Dryden Press.

Weigert, A. J., & Hastings, R. (1977). Identity loss, family, and social change. *American Journal of Sociology, 82,* 1171–1185.

Weinstein, E. A., & Deutschberger, P. (1963). some dimensions of altercasting. *Sociometry, 26,* 454–466.

Weinstein, E. A., & Deutschberger, P. (1964). Tasks, bargains, and identities in social interaction. *Social Forces, 42,* 451–456.

Wood, J. T. (1982). Communication and relational culture: Bases for the study of human relationships. *Communication Quarterly, 30,* 75–83.

Wrong, D. (1961). The oversocialized conception of man. *American Sociological Review, 26,* 183–193.

Chapter 5

Incorporating Time

REBECCA WARNER

Why consider time in research on interaction and relationships? One reason is to correct past neglect. The time dimension has been fundamental in natural science research, but it has been curiously absent from many theories in social and behavioral science (McGrath, 1988). This neglect was due in part to the cost and difficulty of doing detailed time series observational studies. However, the advent of automated systems for coding expressive behaviors has made such studies more feasible.

Another, more compelling reason to be concerned with time is that research about relationships and social interaction naturally includes developmental issues (e.g., Which behaviors are stable over time, and which behaviors change? What is the profile of behaviors over time?) It also includes questions about reciprocity or mutual influence (how do relationship partners influence each other's behavior over time?) Researchers are now beginning to raise questions about the connection between temporal factors and relationship quality. Two examples of such questions are the following: If a mother's behavior is strongly influenced by her infant's behavior, is that evidence of greater responsiveness or stronger attachment? (cf. Bakeman & Brown, 1977). If a husband allocates more time to leisure activities and less time to job, how does that affect marital satisfaction? (Blaney, Brown & Blaney, 1986).

Time as Resource

Implicit in such questions about relationship quality and temporal aspects of behavior is the assumption that time allocation and sequencing of behavior are evaluated by people. That is, some temporal behavior patterns may be perceived as pleasant or rewarding whereas others are evaluated as unpleasant. This evaluation may be conscious, or it may occur with little conscious attention. All the research reviewed in this chapter shares this common assumption, although researchers differ—sometimes drastically— in their views about the reward value of particular temporal patterns in behavior. Specifically, researchers who follow Chapple (1970) argue that rhythmic or predictable behavior is rewarding and that people prefer well-coordinated interactions. This view comes from research on biological rhythms, where it is assumed that rhythm is essential to the optimal functioning of all living systems, including social systems (Iberall & McCulloch, 1969). Other researchers, following Gottman (1979a), have argued that the more predictable or structured a behavior sequence is, the more negative the affect. This view is based on clinical experience with distressed married couples; predictable behavior or behavior that is strongly contingent on partner behavior is viewed as an indication of loss of flexibility or spontaneity. While these two points of view seem contradictory, it is possible that each is correct in certain situations; this issue will be discussed further in a later section of this chapter.

The idea that timing of behavior has positive or negative value to people and can therefore be a source of reward or conflict is not new. Parsons (1951) pointed out that time is an intrinsically limited resource (given the finite human life span). Time allocation is thus a potential focus of conflict and negotiation in social relationships. A similar point was made by Strauss, in an introduction to Mead (1964):

> One way of translating Mead's conception [of the temporal order of social organization] is to take seriously the idea that people bring to any organization their own temporal concerns and that their actions on the organizational site are profoundly affected by those concerns. . . . Something like a concept of 'negotiated order' seems implied by Mead's views.
>
> (Mead, 1964, p. xiv).

Exchange theory predicts that relationships will be happier when the partners perceive the exchange of resources between them to be equitable and satisfactory. Theories about interpersonal resources have not usually included time explicitly; for example, Foa and Foa (1980) included love, services, goods, money, information, and status in their list of interpersonal resources. However, time can be included in resource exchange assessment by recording frequency and duration of relevant behaviors (e.g., how often does your spouse tell you that he/she loves you? How much time does your spouse spend in child care?)

Several types of data can be used to assess time allocation and its effects on relationship satisfaction and commitment. First, observational data on frequency and duration of behaviors can be obtained using human observers or automated activity detection systems on live interaction or videotaped records. These methods provide detailed data, but are too costly and intrusive to be practical in some situations. Second, one can employ self-report, by having people keep time diaries summarizing their time allocation (see Chapter 8) or by using surveys to assess perceptions of time spent in various activities and satisfaction with time spent. Rettig and Bubolz (1983) found that interpersonal resource exchanges (assessed by self-report questionnaire that included questions about frequency of behaviors) were good predictors of marital satisfaction. The advantage of self-report is that data are relatively easy to obtain. The disadvantage is that these subjective judgments of frequency and duration may not be an accurate description of actual time allocation. However, it is only through self-report that evaluations of satisfaction with time allocation can be otrained. Differences in expectations about how time will be spent can be sources of conflict; for instance, spouses may differ in their expectations about how much time each spouse should spend doing housework or child care. The amount of time spent in housework changes over the life cycle of a marriage, and expectations must also be changing (Rexroat & Shehan, 1987). We see, quite vividly, the possibilities for differing time perspectives in a scene from Woody Allen's film *Annie Hall* in which partners Alvie and Annie are each discussing their sex life with their therapists. In response to a question about how often they make love, Alvie says "Almost never—three or four times a week" whereas Annie says "Constantly—three or four times a week." Clearly they agree about objective frequency but evaluate that frequency quite differently.

Time Urgency and Relationships

Time perception and temporal regulation of behavior are important in communication, as illustrated by Rifkin's (1987) description of "computer compulsives"; people who interact extensively with computers become accustomed to the computer's immediate response and predictable behavior, and Rifkin speculates that they may lose the temporal skills that enable them to interact and coordinate their behaviors with other (relatively slow and unpredictable) human beings. It is possible that the rapid pace of life in contemporary American society is generally detrimental to personal relationships.

An example of how time urgency can affect the quality of relationships is the Type A behavior pattern. The Type A person typically exhibits a time urgent, competitive, hostile behavioral style and tends to be a workaholic. The Type A person prefers a rapid pace and hates to "waste time" by waiting. Becker and Byrne (1984) reported that Type A husbands communicated less with their wives, worked more around the house, and reported less pleasure from socializing. Other studies (e.g., Blaney et al., 1986; Burke, Weir, & DuWors, 1979) suggest that Type A behavior results in lower marital satisfaction. Furthermore, Type As have a characteristic speech style, characterized by a rapid and accelerated speech rate, loudness, explosive consonants, and frequent interruptions (Dembroski & Mac-Dougall, 1985; Siegman, Feldstein, Tomasso, Ringel, & Lating, 1987). This style reflects the general time urgency of Type As and seems more conducive to confrontation than to intimacy. Thus, time urgency may contribute to poor relationship quality in a variety of ways, ranging from the amount of time spent in social activity to the way in which people talk to each other.

To summarize, time allocation and the timing and coordination of behaviors may affect the quality of our relationships. Time urgency has become a major American cultural preoccupation, and it is important to understand how time urgency affects the quality of relationships. These are important justifications for incorporating time into our research on personal relationships.

Methodological Issues Involving Time

Three methodological issues involving time are (1) time sampling; (2) the role of time as an independent versus dependent variable in social interaction research; and (3) issues in the analysis of time series data. Each of these issues will be briefly discussed in a nontechnical way; subsequent sections of this chapter will then turn to more formal analyses of cyclical versus noncyclical patterns in social interaction.

TIME SAMPLING AND GENERALIZABILITY

Behavioral scientists assume the need for adequate sampling of subjects in order to establish generalizability of results but often ignore the need for adequate sampling of other factors in their research design, such as situations, tasks, settings, experimenters, and time periods (Dukes, 1965). Gergen (1973) argued that social psychology resembles history more than it resembles natural sciences, because "it deals with facts that are largely nonrepeatable and which fluctuate markedly over time" (p. 310). These critiques suggest that a particular finding (e.g., a high correlation between physical attractiveness and liking) cannot be assumed to hold true across different historical epochs or across the life span of individuals and relationships unless time sampling has covered these domains. Physical attractiveness becomes less important as a predictor of liking as people become better acquainted, for instance (Murstein, 1973). These critiques suggest that we need to sample more extensively from the time domain, even when our primary interest is not in time; only through adequate time sampling can we assess the generalizability of research findings. Obviously, when time is a major focus of the research, adequate sampling of time periods becomes an even more important need.

Time sampling decisions effectively determine what types of structure in behavior we will be able to see, much like levels of magnification in a microscope (Warner, 1979). For instance, if a record of vocal activity is 5 seconds long and the sampling frequency is 20,000 times per second, we can look at the spectral characteristics that define phonemes; if the data record is 5 minutes long and vocal activity is sampled once a second, we can look at turn-taking behavior within a brief conversation; if the data record is several days long and amount of vocal activity is reported once every 5 minutes, we can look at daily or hourly variations in amount of social activity.

TIMING AS DEPENDENT VERSUS INDEPENDENT VARIABLE

In some studies timing of behavior is treated as a dependent variable. Factors that influence the overall amount of activity and the timing, sequencing, or coordination of behaviors include the tempo of cognitive processes, internal physiological states that influence the readiness for initiation or continuation of activity, and social norms that regulate interpersonal behavior (Warner, 1979). These cognitive and physiological factors (and therefore the timing of expressive behaviors) differ across individuals (e.g., Allport, 1961; Allport & Vernon, 1933). Normative factors that influence behavior timing differ across cultures (Hall, 1959; J. Jones, 1988; Levine, 1988). Also, different relationships (and relationships at different stages of development) may be governed by different norms for the timing and coordination of social behavior. The degree to which children show coordinated interpersonal timing may be a useful index of degree of socialization (Welkowitz, Cariffe, & Feldstein, 1976). Social status is a particularly important factor influencing the timing of activities; in an interaction between a high-and low-status person (such as physician and client), the low-status person has to wait until the high-status person is available for consultation. By implication, the high-status person's time is more valuable and should not be wasted. Finally, task demands or situational factors may also affect the timing, sequencing, and coordination of social behavior (e.g., Dabbs, 1983; McGrath et al., 1989).

Alternatively, researchers can treat timing and coordination of social behavior as independent variables and look for consequences of timing. For instance, person perception is influenced by overall amount of talk (Hayes & Meltzer, 1972) and speech rate (Brown, Strong, & Rencher, 1974). Evaluations of the quality of a relationship may be influenced by the strength of coordination between partner activity or the degree to which one partner's behavior is predictable from the other partners' behavior (Warner, 1988).

Most studies of timing of social behavior are correlational and thus do not provide information about direction of causality. Many of the studies cited in the following paragraphs simply report an association between temporal behavior patterns and observer ratings of traits of individuals and/or qualities of relationships. Obviously, in order to make causal inferences, it is necessary to either manipulate antecedent conditions and observe how timing of behavior is affected or artificially control the timing of behaviors to see how variations in timing influence perceptions and evaluations of the behavior. Experimental work along these lines has begun fairly recently.

TIME SERIES DATA: TIME AS DIMENSION

Time series data provide a description of social interaction processes over time. Depending on the time scale of interest, behavior can be sampled very frequently (e.g., once per second) or infrequently (e.g., once a year or at longer intervals). Depending on the nature of the research question, the time series record may span only a few minutes (if the researcher is interested in brief conversations) or a period of many years (if the researcher is interested in life span developmental issues). At each time period sampled the investigator may either code behaviors into categories (as in Gottman, 1979a, or Tronick, Als, & Brazelton, 1980) or measure the amount of activity that is occurring within each sampling interval (as in Warner, 1979, where the percentage of time spent talking by each speaker was recorded for each 5-second time interval during a conversation).

If the variable in a time series study is continuous (interval-ratio level of measurement), then time series regression analysis or spectral analysis may be used to describe temporal patterns. For these analyses, a minimum of at least 50 observations per time series is advisable (McCleary & Hay, 1980). If the variable is categorical, then the required number of observations depends on the number of categories and probability of occurrence of categories (see Bakeman & Gottman, 1987, pp. 137–138); ideally, each category should have a reasonably high frequency of occurrence. Whether the data are continuous or categorical, the time series data should be plotted and examined carefully before doing statistical analyses. If there is little variance in behavior over time (as in a hypothetical mother–infant interaction where the infant is continually crying for 5 minutes while the mother continually comforts the infant) then elaborate statistical analyses would be inappropriate.

Time series data may be obtained from coding by human observers (which usually yields category data but may take the form of ratings on a continuum) or from automated coding systems, which can code on–off occurrence of events or do measurements of amount or intensity of activity. Observations derived from a complex coding scheme requiring interpretive judgments by human observers are costly but may contain a wealth of detail. Data obtained from automated recording systems—such as the Automatic Vocal Transaction Analyzer (Feldstein & Welkowitz, 1987), which records on–off vocal activity for speakers in conversations—are inexpensive and reliable but do not contain detailed information about the intent or content of communications. Both approaches (detailed human coding and automated recording systems) are valuable and provide complementary information.

Time series designs have both methodological advantages and limitations (Campbell & Stanley, 1966). Cook and Campbell (1979) describe interrupted time series designs that compare time series observations before and after an intervention. Their list of "threats to internal validity" in pretest–posttest and time series designs is excellent cautionary advice for social interaction researchers, because it includes factors that researchers interested in relationships wish to study (e.g., maturation) along with other factors that may be confounded with maturation (e.g., history, changes in instrumentation). Changes in data over time can be due to history, that is, environmental events that are not of direct interest. For instance, an increase in fussiness in a mother–infant interaction being observed in the laboratory might be due to changes in room temperature or noise level. Changes in the data over time can also be due to changes in instrumentation; coding done by a human research assistant may become more reliable over time due to practice (or less reliable due to fatigue) or the use of coding categories may change over time as the assistant begins to conceptualize the categories differently. It is essential to control for these extraneous variables in social interaction research. In any event, nonexperimental time series data do not provide a basis for strong causal inference although they provide rich descriptive information.

Some questions about time series data can be answered by calculating simple summary statistics (e.g., the mean, variance, proportion of time spent in each behavioral state). However, many research questions have to do with patterns over time (sequencing, trends, cycles) or with interdependence between partners. Special statistical methods are required for these questions (e.g., Markov chain analysis, lagged conditional probabilities, time series analysis; see Chapters 14 and 16 for details). The nonindependence of observations must be taken into account by choosing statistics that are suitable for correlated observations. Nonindependence arises because partners influence each other's behavior and therefore their behaviors are correlated (see Chapter 15), and also because neighboring observations in time series are typically correlated with each other (see Chapter 14). Later sections of this chapter deal more extensively with formal statistical analysis of patterns over time in social interaction.

Research Trends in Incorporating Time

Research on the structure of social interaction can be divided into two areas. One group of researchers has assumed that social interaction is organized cyclically and, influenced by the work of Chapple (1970), has described partner influence in terms of synchronized activity cycles. (Note that if behavior tends to vary cyclically, the implication is that current behavior is predictable from past behavior; however, current behavior can be predictable from past behavior in the absence of cyclicity.) A second group of researchers has assumed that there is predictable sequencing in social interaction, but they have not been interested in cyclicity. (In fact, they typically remove any cyclical patterns from the time series data before analyzing behavior sequences).

Each of these two research areas has considered the same three basic questions. These questions are as follows: (1) How is behavior structured over time? In other words, what is the nature of predictable patterning in social interaction? For the first group of researchers, this question has been answered by looking for cycles in activity; for the second group, it has been answered by fitting time series regression models to describe how current behavior is predictable from the partner's recent past behavior and the actor's own recent past behavior. (2) How do partners influence each other's behavior, and how can we measure the strength of partner influence? The first group of researchers has answered this question in terms of synchronization or mutual entrainment of cycles. The second group of researchers has answered this question by partitioning variance in time series regression models, that is, to see what proportion of the variance in the time series is explained by actor's own past behavior and what proportion by the partner's past behavior. Both groups of researchers are now turning to the more interesting question: (3) How are these features of behavior (e.g., the degree to which behavior is predictable and structured; the degree to which partners influence each other's behavior) associated with the quality of the relationship? That is, do relationships or interactions that are going well (according to the evaluations of the participants or clinical assessments) differ from relationships or interactions that are not going well? Subsequent sections of this chapter review how each of these questions has been addressed by those researchers who look for cyclical patterns and by those who look for other (noncyclical) types of behavior sequencing.

CYCLES IN SOCIAL INTERACTION

Most investigators who are interested in cyclicity measure amount of activity for each observation period. That is, they have tended to use continuous rather than categorical data. For instance, Warner (1979) recorded percentage of time spent speaking in each 5-second time interval (however, cyclicity can be analyzed in dichotomous time series data; see Gottman, 1979b). Simple summary statistics such as the mean and variance can be calculated as one way of characterizing the subject's behavior. Other statistics provide information about patterns over time: for instance, linear and nonlinear trends can be fitted to the time series. Spectral analysis (Bloomfield, 1976; Gottman, 1981) can be used to analyse cyclic patterns such as alternations between high and low levels of talk. Within this theoretical framework, these cycles are seen not as a mere curiosity but as an important organizational feature of social interaction that facilitates coordination between partners.

Chapple (1970) has argued that rhythmic or cyclical social interactions in which the activity patterns of partners are closely coordinated are evaluated as more pleasant and rewarding than nonrhythmic interactions. Chapple's theory depicts a social system as a "population of oscillators". By this he meant that each actor has a distinctive constellation of physiological rhythms (cycles in respiratory, cardiovascular, and other physiological processes) and that the actor's behavioral rhythms are related to these physiological rhythms. According to Chapple, an individual has a preference for a particular interaction tempo, a distinctive pattern of alternation between mostly talking and mostly listening that is coupled with his or her internal physiological rhythms. This interaction tempo can be described as a cycle. During the first half of the cycle the person exhibits a high level of activity, such as talking; during the second part of the cycle the person exhibits a lower level of activity. The duration of a high/low activity cycle is theorized to be consistent within an individual speaker but different between speakers.

During social interaction, partners try to coordinate their behavioral rhythms (e.g., they adjust the durations of their utterances and pauses in order to achieve a coordinated conversation). According to Chapple's theory, this coordination may be easy or difficult: if the partners have complementary preferred interaction tempos (that is, the overall percentage of time spent talking by persons A and B sum to approximately 100% and persons A and B have the same cycle lengths), then they should find it easy to coordinate their behavioral rhythms and achieve a smooth conversation with few interruptions and few extended pauses. The process through which speakers achieve coordination involves modulations of each speaker's cycle length. If person A has a 4-minute cycle and person B has a 6-minute cycle, A's cycle may lengthen and B's cycle may shorten as they interact with each other until they converge on a new, shared cycle length of 5 minutes; this modulation of cycle length is called "mutual entrainment" by Chapple and has been called "synchronization" by others. Note, however, that the term "synchrony" has been used by various researchers to refer to many different types of coordination between partners; the term "mutual entrainment" is preferable since it has a more specific meaning.

Chapple (1970) hypothesized that people find it pleasant and rewarding to engage in social interactions that permit them to express their own preferred interaction tempo (and to maintain coupling between their behavioral rhythms and their internal physiological rhythyms). He predicted that ease of achieving coordination through mutual entrainment will lead to attraction, other things being equal. Obviously, there are many other factors, such as similarity of attitude and background, that influence attraction, and interaction tempo would just be one among many factors. Conversely, Chapple argued that if a person is forced to engage in social interaction at a tempo that is desynchronized from his or her internal physiological rhythms, or if smooth coordination of behavior between partners cannot be achieved, the interaction would be experienced as unpleasant. A poorly coordinated conversation would involve frequent interruptions (just as A starts talking, B starts talking) and extended mutual pauses when neither partner has anything to say. Chapple suggested that frequent interruptions may be interpreted as an attempt to dominate or may suggest that the interrupter is not really listening; long response latencies (one partner does not respond after the other finishes speaking) would probably be interpreted as evidence of lack of interest or involvement.

Theories similar to Chapple's have been independently advanced by others. Iberall and McCulloch (1969) have argued that rhythm is the fundamental organizing principle of all living systems, including individual organisms and social systems. Field (1985) described attachment in terms of mutual entrainment of behavioral and/or physiological rhythms of mothers and infants. Hofer (1984) suggested that social interactions may modulate physiological rhythms in ways that may be beneficial or detrimental to physical health. Others (Altman, 1975; Altman, Vinsel, & Brown, 1981) have suggested that people alternate between periods when they desire privacy and periods when they desire social interaction; this description applies to behavior over longer periods of time but seems similar in spirit to Chapple's model and might be amenable to a similar type of analysis. A more extensive review of rhythm in social interaction is given by Warner (1988).

To summarize, Chapple's two primary predictions are the following:

(1) Behaviors (such as amount of vocal activity) tend to vary cyclically during social interaction, and (2) rhythmic and well-coordinated social interactions are perceived as more pleasant than nonrhythmic and poorly coordinated interactions (other predictions derived from Chapple's model are reviewed in Warner, 1988).

Empirical evidence supports Chapple's predictions. Cyclic variations in vocal activity (cycles on the order of 3 to 6 minutes long) have been reported by several investigators (Kimberly, 1970; Warner, 1979; and Warner, Malloy, Schneider, Knoth, & Wilder, 1987). Shorter cycles in vocal activity were reported by Cobb (1973) and Dabbs (1983); longer cycles were found by Hayes and Cobb (1979). Wade, Ellis, and Bohrer (1973) reported 10- to 15-minute cycles in heart rate in children during free play; this was interpreted as an index of gross motor activity. Cycles on the order of 10 seconds long have been reported in mother–infant interaction (Cohn & Tronick, 1988, Lester, Hoffman & Brazelton, 1985).

Two other predictions from Chapple's model are that behavioral and physiological rhythms should be coupled or correlated and that individual differences in cycle length should be consistent across situations. The limited available evidence suggests that both these predictions may be correct. Warner, Waggener and Kronauer (1983) found that ventilation (respiration) tended to covary with amount of talking for some speakers, although not for all. Warner et al. (1987) reported moderate associations between cyclical variations in heart rate and amount of talking in conversations. Warner and Mooney (1988) found evidence that a speaker's cycles in amount of vocal activity tend to be consistent in length across nine conversations (three conversations with each of three partners).

A few studies have assessed Chapple's prediction that close coordination of activity cycles is associated with more positive affect. Watts (1982) reported that differences between roommates in circadian rhythms (24-hour cycles in waking/sleeping, body temperature, and overall activity level) were associated with negative evaluations of the relationship between roommates. Warner et al. (1987) examined observer ratings of conversations that varied in the degree to which they were rhythmic (rhythmicity was defined as the percentage of variance in the time series explained by a few cyclic components), and their results suggested a curvilinear relationship between rhythmicity of vocal activity and affect, with moderately rhythmic conversations rated most positively.

There is evidence from other sources supporting Chapple's argument that breakdown of coordination between behavioral and physiological rhythms is detrimental. Healy and Williams (1988) have argued that a breakdown in the organization among circadian rhythms is associated with depression (although the direction of influence is not known). Hofer (1984) has speculated that the detrimental effects of bereavement on immune function and physical health may be mediated, in part, by the loss of important social cues that modulate physiological rhythms.

BEHAVIOR SEQUENCES AND NONCYCLICAL PATTERNS
IN SOCIAL INTERACTION

Other research on social interaction process is based on an alternative perspective that is quite different from Chapple's model. Rather than looking at cyclicity, these researchers try to describe typical noncyclical behavior sequences and assess the relative importance of actor's and partner's past behavior as predictors of actor's current behavior (Gottman, 1979a; Bakeman & Gottman, 1987). Behavior can be highly predictable from earlier behavioral events without showing cyclicity. Typically, only short-term influences are considered; for example, researchers might ask, To what extent are mother and infant behaviors predictable from mother and infant behaviors within the preceding 1 or 2 seconds? However, some studies include larger numbers of prior behavioral events as predictors of current behavior.

Many studies of behavior sequencing use categorical time series data; for instance, Bakeman and Brown (1977) coded whether the mother and infant were active or inactive in each 5-second time interval; Gottman (1979a) coded affect in husband–wife interactions. In principle, any number of behavioral categories can be included, but in practice, if there are more than three or four categories, the number of observations required to obtain a reasonable number of occurrences of all possible sequences of behaviors becomes prohibitively high (Bakeman & Gottman, 1987). Simple descriptive statistics, such as the proportion of time spent in each behavioral state, provide a convenient summary of the data, but most investigators also use Markov or log-linear analysis (or conceptually similar techniques) to describe behavior sequencing (see Chapter 14). These analyses involve calculating lagged conditional probabilities (e.g., how likely is it that the infant will stop crying, given that the mother begins to rock the infant in the previous time interval?). These analyses represent partner influence as a sort of moment-to-moment adjustment that partners make in response to changes in each other's behavior, rather than a process of mutual entrainment between cycles.

Continuous time series data can be analyzed using time series regression to assess the relative importance of actor and partner past behaviors as predictors of actor's current behavior (Gottman, 1981). This contrast between actor and partner influence is similar to ideas proposed by Jones and Gerard (1967). An individual's behavior can be viewed as the joint outcome of two influences. First, behavior is predictable to some extent from the actor's own past behavior, but it is also influenced by the partner's recent past behavior. Predictability from one's own past behavior reflects persistence or stability whereas predictability from partner's behavior reflects social influence or attachment (not necessarily positive attachment). Gottman (1979a) has argued that, in general, the more predictable and structured a social interaction is, the greater the pathology and the more negative the affect. Highly predictable behavior sequences are viewed as indicative of rigidity or lack of spontaneity. This contrasts with Chapple's view that cyclicity (a particular type of predictable sturcture) is associated with positive affect.

Most investigators have been more interested in partner influence than in predictability of an actor's behavior from his or her own past behavior. There is abundant evidence for mutual influence between partners in adult–adult and infant–adult interaction (Cappella, 1981, Chapter 6, this volume). This influence can either be reciprocal (e.g., when A increases self-disclosure, B responds with an increase in self-disclosure) or compensatory (when A increases self-disclosure, B responds with a decrease in self-disclosure). According to Cappella, matching or reciprocity tends to dominate for some behaviors (such as durations of pauses and switching pauses) whereas compensatory responses tend to occur for other behaviors (e.g., if A reduces interpersonal distance, B tends to respond with increased interpersonal distance and/or decreased gaze; Argyle & Dean, 1965).

The degree to which partners influence each other's behavior may be asymmetrical between partners. Gottman and Ringland (1981) suggested that if A's behavior is more strongly dependent on B's past behavior than B's behavior is on A's, then B may be seen as the dominant partner; that is, B is the one who is setting the tempo for the interaction. It is not clear how dominance defined in terms of asymmetrical partner influence is related to more traditional definitions of dominance or to observer judgements of dominance, but this would be an interesting subject for further study.

One major difference between Gottman's and Chapple's approaches is in terms of data analysis. Chapple's approach involves looking for cycles, whereas Gottman's approach involves first removing trend and cyclical components from time series data and then examining the residuals to see how they are correlated between partners. This is in the spirit of econometric analyses, where trends and cycles are removed because they are seen as possible sources of spurious correlation between time series. Removing trends and cycles from time series data is viewed by Gottman and others as a necessary but not sufficient precaution against spuriousness when evaluating partner influence. To assess partner influence, Gottman recommends using a time series regression model to partial out the effects of an actor's own recent past behavior before assessing partner influence (Gottman 1981, Chapter 25). For instance, husband's behavior may be predicted from both husband's and wife's recent past behavior. The R squared for the predictive usefulness of wife's behavior in this regression (with husband's past behavior partialled out) is taken as the index of partner influence (Levenson & Gottman, 1983). Similar models to predict current behavior from past behaviors of both actor and partner can be set up with categorical time series data (Allison & Liker, 1982; Chapter 14, this volume).

The important question for research is, How are strength of partner influence and predictability of an actor's behavior from the actor's own past behavior related to the quality of the communication or the relationship? For instance, we can ask whether strength of partner influence is correlated with clinical judgments about the quality of communication, with self-report ratings of satisfaction with the interaction, with stage of development in the relationship, or with other variables, such as task type.

Gottman's work on partner influence and marital distress has been extremely influential. He developed a Couples Interactive Scoring System (Gottman, 1979a) to code content of communication and classify behaviors as positive or negative. Analysis of behavior sequences yielded differences in the social interactions of distressed and nondistressed married couples: distressed couples were prone to engage in "cross-complaining" sequences whereas satisfied couples engaged in "validation sequences." In a cross-complaining sequence, spouse A responds to spouse B's complaint with a countercomplaint. In a validation sequence, when B makes a complaint, A assents by saying things like "yeah" and "un huh" and allows B to express complaints and receive acknowledgment of them. Then A has an opportunity to express complaints and be acknowledged (Gottman, 1982a). Others have obtained similar results supporting Gottman's claim that these types of behavioral sequences are associated with marital distress (e.g., Margolin & Wampold, 1981; Ting-Toomey, 1983).

Gottman's work on partner influence has not been limited to behavioral measures but has also looked at the psychophysiology of social interaction. Levenson and Gottman (1983) measured four physiological parameters (including heart rate and galvanic skin response) for husbands and wives during discussions of problems. Time series regression was performed to predict each husband's physiological reactions from his wife's physiological reactions (controlling for husband's own recent past physiological reactions) and the R squared for wife influence on husband was obtained for each dyad (similarly, in another set of regressions the wife's physiological response was used as the dependent variable). Levenson and Gottman (1983) found that strong coupling between physiological responses of spouses (large R squared's for partner influence in these regressions) was associated with concurrent marital dissatisfaction. This was interpreted as further evidence for the principle that greater structure or predictability in social interaction is detrimental.

Other researchers have obtained apparently conflicting results, suggesting that under certain circumstances more predictable or structured interactions are preferable. Tracey (1987) looked at topic initiation and topic following in the early, middle, and late stages of psychotherapy to see how more and less successful relationships differ. Behaviors were coded categorically, and log-linear analyses were done to assess the strength of intra-time series and inter-time series dependence (that is, dependence on own vs. partner's past behavior). More and less successful dyads were compared.

High inter-chain (between partner) dependencies were generally found, but this varied with stage and outcome. Clients and counselors in successful dyads had greater intra-chain dependency (predictability from actor's own past behavior) in later stages of therapy, and no such change occurred in the unsuccessful dyads. Tracey speculated that this high intra-chain dependency meant that the client was showing increased behavioral consistency and that the therapist was bringing more of himself or herself to the interaction. Faraone & Hurtig (1985) tape-recorded socially skilled and socially unskilled males during conversations with a female subject and coded interpersonal content. High-skill males had higher verbal productivity, more predictable behavior sequences, and showed more dominant behaviors toward their partners. This seems counter to Gottman's prediction (in this study, higher skill was associated with a more predictable or structured interaction). However, the investigators noted that in interactions with strangers (involving high levels of uncertainty), a more predictable or structured behavior sequence might be rewarding because it reduces uncertainty. On the other hand, in interactions with a spouse (involving low levels of uncertainty), a less predicatable or structured behavior sequence might be preferred since it would provide welcome novelty.

Given the inconsistent results across studies, it may be more appropriate to ask under what conditions it is optimal for interactions to be highly predictable or highly unpredictable, rather than to assume that unpredictability is always preferable.

To summarize, analyses of both cyclical and noncyclical patterns in social interaction have yielded interesting results. Very few studies have included both types of analysis (apart from Cohn & Tronick, 1988). The two approaches are not necessarily mutually exclusive; it is quite conceivable that partner coordination is achieved through both types of mechanisms (mutual entrainment of behavioral cycles and moment-to-moment adjustments in response to partner behavior). Results are mixed as to whether structured, predictable behavior sequences are evaluated positively or negatively; and further research is needed to specify under what conditions predictability of behavior is preferred.

Applications to the Case of Michael and Cathy Stone

The conflict in the sample problem transcribed at the beginning of this volume focuses on time allocation. Thus, time could be incorporated into the analysis in one of two ways. First, we could focus on the longer time durations that are the topic of discussion and collect objective time series data on behavior over a period of weeks or months. Time budget or diary-keeping studies can be used to obtain objective data on the amount of time each spouse typically spends in various activities (Robinson, 1988; Chapter 8, this volume).

It could be equally important to look at each partner's subjective time perception and evaluate the amount of time spent in various activities, to assess whether the conflict is over an objective fact (how much time does Michael really spend doing housework?) or an evaluation of interpersonal resource exchange (was the time he spent sufficient to maintain equity and satisfaction for Cathy?).

An alternative way to incorporate time into the analysis is to take the brief interaction excerpt itself as the object of study. Interaction sequences can be analyzed using any of the approaches outlined in previous sections of this chapter; however, these analyses would require a longer behavior sequence than presented in this vignette, both in terms of number of communicative acts and elapsed time. An automated system such as the Automatic Vocal Transaction Analyzer (Feldstein & Welkowitz, 1987) could be used to code on–off patterns in vocal activity. At least 5 minutes of dialogue would be required for this analysis. The on–off vocal activity could be analysed using Markov chain or log-linear analysis (see Chapter 14). Parameters such as mean duration of turn, switching pause, and in-terruptive and noninterruptive simultaneous speech could be estimated (see Feldstein & Welkowitz, 1987, for definitions of these terms). One notable feature of this brief excerpt of dialogue is that several utterances by Michael end with interruptions by Cathy. While interruptions are not always per-ceived negatively, in this instance it seems that they communicate anger and impatience.

To evaluate whether a mismatch of conversational rhythms (of the sort described by Chapple's theory) could be part of Cathy and Michael's problems, a longer dialogue would be needed (at least 20–40 minutes). For each speaker, amount of talk could be recorded once every 10 seconds (each observation would be the proportion of time spent talking in a particular 10-second time interval). Spectral analysis could be done to look for evi-dence of cycles on the order of 3 to 6 minutes; conversations that have a higher percentage of variance explained by such cycles may be experienced as more pleasant because they involve coordinated rhythms. Other statistics associated with spectral analysis, such as coherence (analogous to an R squared) assess more directly whether the cyclic variations in activity are coordinated between partners. If time series data were available on their activities over much longer periods of time, similar analyses could be done to evaluate whether there is generally poor coordination between their circadian activity cycles (Watt, 1982). This could include waking/sleeping schedules, leisure time, work schedules, and so forth. As Duck (1986) pointed out, poor coordination of daily activities in general may be a problem in close relationships.

The interaction sequence contained in the sample research problem could also be examined using a categorical coding scheme, such as the one proposed by Gottman (1979a). An interaction sequence of at least 10 to 15 minutes would be needed. Base rates (simple proportions) of each type of communicative act could be calculated. Lagged transition probabilities and other analyses such as log-linear analysis could be used to evaluate behavior sequencing and partner influence. The Stones' behavior sequencing could then be compared to the behavior of distressed and nondistressed married couples in past research. The brief communicative exchange in the sample interaction suggests that the Stones may be prone to cross-complaining sequences and escalation of negative affect (as described by Gottman, 1982a). Also, Michael's initial response to Cathy's complaint is to try to deflect it by making excuses rather than to respond to her complaint by acknowledging it. However, the sample vignette is quite brief, and one would want a representative sample of longer behavior sequences before making diagnostic judgments about this case, no matter which of these analyses are employed.

Conclusion

Gottman (1982b) has suggested that we need a "language of temporal form" for describing relationships. The research reviewed here suggests elements that might be included in such a language, including both cyclical and noncyclical patterns in social interaction. Many of the studies reviewed in this chapter found that various aspects of timing and coordination in social interaction are associated with affect or evaluation of the interaction. However, these studies are only a beginning; future research might focus on other issues. We might try to develop a kind of social psychophysics, that is, a description of the relationship between temporal features of behavior and evaluations of the quality of the interaction by participants and/or clinicians. This type of research would be of interest to those who want a more detailed understanding of social perception (e.g., the behavioral cues we rely on in judging quality of a relationship). It may also be of potential use to clinicians who seek more refined diagnostic tools for detection of distressed relationships and who want to identify teachable social skills that would be useful in therapy. It is conceivable that if distressed couples can be taught the communication patterns displayed by satisfied couples, they might become more satisfied. However, we should not automatically assume that this is true, since the communication style may be only a symptom of distress rather than the cause.

We also need further research to see how different antecedent conditions affect timing and coordination of behaviors. This would include experimental manipulations of task, setting, and other situational factors, and comparison of different types of dyads (e.g., same vs. different status partners, intimate versus nonintimate partners, different stages in relationship development). It would also be extremely useful to assess how well timing and coordination of social interaction predict affect and attraction compared to other factors that are already known to be predictive of liking or attraction, such as similarity of background, attitudes, and values.

Finally, future research should also address the question of the nature of the organization of behavior: studies that include assessment of both cyclical and noncyclical aspects of behavior need to be done in order to assess whether these approaches yield redundant or distinctive information and in order to assess which type of descriptive statistics (cyclical versus noncyclical) are more useful in predicting relationship quality. It is possible that both types of descriptive statistics are necessary for a thorough description of the temporal organization of social interaction.

References

Allison, P. D., & Liker, J. K. (1982). Analyzing sequential categorical data on dyadic interaction: A comment on Gottman. *Psychological Bulletin, 91*, 393–403.

Allport, G. W. (1961). *Pattern and growth in personality*. New York: Holt, Rinehart & Winston.

Allport, G. W., & Vernon, P. E. (1933). *Studies in expressive movement*. New York: MacMillan.

Altman, I. (1975). *The environment and social behavior: Privacy, personal space, territory, crowding*. Monterey, CA: Brooks/Cole.

Altman, I., Vinsel, A., & Brown, B. B. (1981). Dialectic conceptions in social psychololgy: An application to social penetration and privacy regulation. In L. Berkowitz (Ed.), *Advances in experimental social psychology* (Vol. 14, pp. 107–160). New York: Academic Press.

Argyle, M., & Dean, J. (1965). Eye-contact, distance, and affiliation. *Sociometry, 28*, 289–304.

Bakeman, R., & Brown, J. V. (1977). Behavioral dialogues: An approach to the assessment of mother–infant interaction. *Child Development, 48*, 195–203.

Bakeman, R., & Gottman, J. M. (1987). *Observing interaction: An introduction to sequential analysis*. Cambridge: Cambridge University Press.

Becker, M. A., & Byrne, D. (1984). Type A behavior and daily activities of young married couples. *Journal of Applied Social Psychology, 14*, 82–88.

Blaney, N. T., Brown, P., & Blaney, P. H. (1986). Type A, marital adjustment, and life stress. *Journal of Behavioral Medicine, 9*, 491–502.

Bloomfield, P. (1976). *Fourier analysis of time series: An introduction*. New York: Wiley.

Brown, B. L., Strong, W. J., & Rencher, A. C. (1974). Fifty-four voices from two:

The effects of simultaneous manipulations of rate, mean fundamental frequency, and variance of fundamental frequency on ratings of personality from speech. *Journal of the Acoustical Society of America, 55,* 313–318.

Burke, R. J., Weir, T., & DuWors, R. E. (1979). Type A behavior of administrators and wives' reports of marital satisfaction and well-being. *Journal of Applied Psychology, 64,* 57–65.

Campbell, D. T., & Stanley, J. C. (1966). *Experimental and quasi-experimental designs for research.* Chicago: Rand McNally.

Cappella, J. N. (1981). Mutual influence in expressive behavior: Adult–adult and infant–adult dyadic interaction. *Psychological Bulletin, 89,* 101–132.

Chapple, E. D. (1970). *Culture and biological man.* New York: Holt, Rinehart & Winston.

Cobb, L. (1973). Time series analysis of the periodicities of casual conversation (Doctoral dissertation, Cornell University, 1973). *Dissertation Abstracts International, 34,* 2764A.

Cohn, J. F., & Tronick, E. Z. (1988). Mother–infant face-to-face interaction: Influence is bidirectional and unrelated to periodic cycles in either partner's behavior. *Developmental Psychology, 24,* 386–392.

Cook, T. D., & Campbell, D. T. (1979). *Quasi-experimentation: Design and analysis issues for field settings.* Chicago: Rand McNally.

Dabbs, J. M., Jr. (1983). *Fourier analysis and the rhythm of conversation.* (ERIC Document Reproduction Service No. 222 959) Paper presented at the Annual Meeting of the American Psychological Association, Washington, D.C., August 23–27, 1982.

Dembroski, T. M., & MacDougall, J. M. (1985). Beyond global Type A: Relationships of paralinguistic attributes, hostility, and anger-in to coronary heart disease. In T. M. Field, P. M. McCabe & N. Schneiderman (Eds.), *Stress and coping* (pp. 223–242). Hillsdale, NJ: Erlbaum.

Duck, S. W. (1986). *Human relationships: An introduction to social psychology.* Beverly Hills: Sage.

Dukes, W. F. (1965). N = 1. *Psychological Bulletin, 64,* 74–79.

Faraone, S. V., & Hurtig, R. R. (1985). An examination of social skill, verbal productivity, and Gottman's model of interaction using observational methods and sequential analysis. *Behavioral Assessment, 7,* 349–366.

Feldstein, S., & Welkowitz, J. (1987). A chronography of conversation: In defense of an objective approach. In A. W. Siegman & S. Feldstein (Eds.), *Nonverbal behavior and communication* (pp. 329–378). Hillsdale, NJ: Erlbaum.

Field, T. (1985). Attachment as psychobiological attunement: Being on the same wavelength. In M. Reite & T. Field, (Eds.), *The psychobiology of attachment and separation* (pp. 415–454). New York: Academic.

Foa, U. G., & Foa, E. B. (1980). Resource theory: Interpersonal behavior as exchange. In K. G. Gergen, M. S. Greenberg, & R. H. Willis (Eds.), *Social exchange: Advances in theory and research* (pp. 77–94). New York: Plenum Press.

Gergen, K. (1973). Social psychology as history. *Journal of Personality and Social Psychology, 26,* 309–320.

Gottman, J. M. (1979a). *Marital interaction: Experimental investigations.* New York: Academic Press.

Gottman, J. M. (1979b). Detecting cyclicity in social interaction. *Psychological Bulletin, 86,* 338–348.

Gottman, J. M. (1981). *Time series analysis: A comprehensive introduction for social scientists*. Cambridge: Cambridge University Press.

Gottman, J. M. (1982a). Emotional responsiveness in marital conversations. *Journal of Communication, 32,* 108–120.

Gottman, J. M. (1982b). Temporal form: Toward a new language for describing relationships. *Journal of Marriage and the Family, 44,* 943–962.

Gottman, J. M., & Ringland, J. T. (1981). The analysis of dominance and bidirectionality in social development. *Child Development, 52,* 393–412.

Hall, E. T. (1959). *The silent language*. Garden City, NY: Doubleday.

Hayes, D. P., & Cobb, L. (1979). Ultradian rhythms in social interaction. In A. W. Siegman & S. Feldstein (Eds.), *Of speech and time: Temporal speech rhythms in interpersonal contexts* (pp. 57–70). Hillsdale, NJ: Erlbaum.

Hayes, D. P., & Meltzer, L. (1972). Interpersonal judgments based on talkativeness: Fact or artifact? *Sociometry, 35,* 538–561.

Healy, D., & Williams, J. M. G. (1988). Dysrhythmia, dysphoria and depression: The interaction of learned helplessness and circadian dysrhythmia in the pathogenesis of depression. *Psychological Bulletin, 103,* 163–178.

Hofer, M. A. (1984). Relationships as regulators: A psychobiological perspective on bereavement. *Psychosomatic Medicine, 46,* 183–197.

Iberall, A. S., & McCulloch, W. S. (1969). The organizing principle of complex living systems. *Journal of Basic Engineering, 91,* 290–294.

Jones, E. E., & Gerard, H. B. (1967). *Foundations of social psychology*. New York: Wiley.

Jones, J. M. (1988). Cultural differences in temporal perspective: Instrumental and expressive behaviors in time. In J. E. McGrath (Ed.), *The social psychology of time: New perspectives* (pp. 21–38). Beverly Hills: Sage.

Kimberly, R. P. (1970). Rhythmic patterns in human interaction. *Nature, 228,* 88–90.

Lester, B. M., Hoffman, J., & Brazelton, T. B. (1985). The rhythmic structure of mother–infant interaction in term and preterm infants. *Child Development, 56,* 15–27.

Levenson, R. W., & Gottman, J. M. (1983). Marital interaction: Physiological linkage and affective exchange. *Journal of Personality and Social Psychology, 45,* 587–597.

Levine, R. V. (1988). The pace of life across cultures. In J. E. McGrath (Ed.), *The social psychology of time: New perspectives* (pp. 39–60). Beverly Hills: Sage.

Margolin, G., & Wampold, B. E. (1981). Sequential analysis of conflict and accord in distressed and nondistressed marital partners. *Journal of Consulting and Clinical Psychology, 49,* 554–567.

McCleary, R., & Hay, R. A., Jr. (1980). *Applied time series analysis for the social sciences*. Beverly Hills: Sage.

McGrath, J. E. (1988). *The social psychology of time: New perspectives*. Beverly Hills: Sage.

McGrath, J. E., Kelly, J. R., Futoran, G. C., Harrison, D. A., VanderStoep, S. W., & Gruenfeld, D. H. (1989). *Conceptual, methodological, and substantive issues in the social psychology of time*. (Tech. Rep. No. 89–1). Urbana, IL: University of Illinois, Psychology Department.

Mead, G. H. (1964). *On social psychology* (Rev. Ed.). Chicago: University of Chicago Press. (Original work published 1934)

Murstein, B. I. (1973). Stimulus-value-role: A theory of marital choice. In A. F. Kline & M. L. Medley (Eds.), *Dating and marriage: An interactionist perspective* (pp. 183–217). Boston: Holbrook Press.

Parsons, T. (1951). *The social system.* New York: The Free Press.

Rettig, K. D., & Bubolz, M. M. (1983). Interpersonal resource exchanges as indicators of quality in marriage. *Journal of Marriage and the Family, 45,* 497–509.

Rexroat, C., & Shehan, C. (1987). The family life cycle and spouses' time in housework. *Journal of Marriage and the Family, 49,* 747–750.

Rifkin, J. (1987). *Time wars: The primary conflict in human history.* New York: Holt.

Robinson, J. P. (1988). Time-diary evidence about the social psychology of everyday life. In J. E. McGrath (Ed.), *The social psychology of time: New perspectives* (pp. 134–148). Beverly Hills: Sage.

Siegman, A. W., Feldstein, S., Tomasso, C. T., Ringel, M. A., & Lating, J. (1987). Expressive vocal behavior and the severity of coronary artery disease. *Psychosomatic Medicine, 49,* 545–561.

Strauss, A. (1964). Introduction. In G. H. Mead, *On social psychology* (Rev. Ed.), Chicago: University of Chicago Press. (Original work published 1934)

Ting-Toomey, S. (1983). An analysis of verbal communication patterns in high and low marital adjustment groups. *Human Communication Research, 9,* 291–302.

Tracey, T. J. (1987). Stage differences in the dependencies of topic initiation and topic following behavior. *Journal of Counseling Psychology, 34,* 123–131.

Tronick, E. Z., Als, H., & Brazelton, T. B. (1980). Monadic phases: A structural descriptive analysis of infant–mother face-to-face interaction. *Merrill-Palmer Quarterly, 26,* 3–24.

Wade, M. G., Ellis, M. J., & Bohrer, R. E. (1973). Biorhythms in the activity of children during free play. *Journal of the Experimental Analysis of Behavior, 20,* 155–162.

Warner, R. M. (1979). Periodic rhythms in conversational speech. *Language and Speech, 22,* 382–389.

Warner, R. M. (1988). Rhythm in social interaction. In J. E. McGrath (Ed.), *The social psychology of time: New perspectives* (pp. 63–88). Beverly Hills: Sage.

Warner, R. M., Malloy, D., Schneider, K., Knoth, R., & Wilder, B. (1987). Rhythmic organization of social interaction and observer ratings of positive affect and involvement. *Journal of Nonverbal Behavior, 11,* 57–74.

Warner, R. M., & Mooney, K. (1988). Individual differences in vocal activity rhythm: Fourier analysis of cyclicity in amount of talk. *Journal of Psycholinguistic Research, 17,* 99–111.

Warner, R. M., Waggener, T. B., & Kronauer, R. E. (1983). Synchronized cycles in ventilation and vocal activity during spontaneous conversational speech. *Journal of Applied Physiology: Respiratory, Environmental and Exercise Physiology, 54,* 1324–1334.

Watts, B. L. (1982). Individual differences in circadian activity rhythms and their effects on roommate relationships. *Journal of Personality, 50,* 375–384.

Welkowitz, J., Cariffe, G., & Feldstein, S. (1976). Conversational congruence as a criterion of socialization in children. *Child Development, 47,* 269–272.

Chapter 6

Mutual Adaptation and Relativity of Measurement

JOSEPH N. CAPPELLA

An understanding of relationships and communication patterns, in my view, can proceed only by our asking questions about the association between *patterns* of message interchange between partners and the partners' experienced state of the relationship. Elsewhere I have called these kinds of questions third-order questions (Cappella, 1987, 1988), if only to distinguish them from simpler questions that could be asked about interpersonal communication. These simpler questions concern (1) the types and structures of behaviors enacted in interpersonal encounters, (2) the processes of encoding and decoding such behaviors, and (3) the magnitude and type of influence, if any, that one person's overt behavior has on the partner. This last group of questions focuses on processes that have been called adaptation, mutual influence, synchrony, congruence, coordination, and a variety of other names.

In this chapter I give primary attention to the ways in which the interaction patterns exhibited by couples like the Stones might be measured and the implications of measurement assumptions on the kinds of findings that might be generated. But, frankly, most research in personal and social relationships bypasses the actual interaction patterns in favor of more static features of the relationship. Why, indeed, should the Stone's interaction patterns be the focus of our research efforts, given the complexity and cost of obtaining such information in contrast to simpler and cheaper methods?

Why Study Patterns of Interaction

Mutual adaptation is arguably the essential characteristic of every interpersonal interaction. In this sense the Stones could not even be said to have an interpersonal communication unless they exhibit mutual adaptation. The basis for this argument is fourfold.

1. *Mutual adaptation is the defining characteristic of interpersonal communication.* If Cathy Stone's behaviors do not affect Michael's uniquely and mutually (see Cappella, 1987), then contingent responsiveness is not present and she cannot be said to be observably sensitive to alterations in his actions. Without such contingent responsiveness it would be impossible to distinguish interleaved action from interaction.

The implications of this definition are several. First, patterns of interpersonal communication can be categorized in terms of the degree and type of mutual adaptation present (Cappella, 1988). Second, mutual adaptation is not inherently good or bad for relationships. For example, reciprocity of hostile affect between husbands and wives like the Stones is a strong type of mutual adaptation that is also associated with greater marital distress (Gottman, 1979). Third, the interactional domain is analyzed separately from the domain of relational state and personal competency, thereby allowing the proper study of third-order questions. Fourth, without assessing mutual adaptation one cannot know the degree of sensitivity, if any, that persons show to the behavior of their partners. Not only can the absence of sensitivity be informative, but also excessive sensitivity to certain types of remarks and actions may be diagnostic of relational difficulties.

2. *Mutual adaptation in verbal & nonverbal behavior is pervasive in interpersonal encounters.* A substantial body of research indicates that social interactions exhibit mutual adaptation for behaviors as diverse as accents, speech rate, vocal intensity, postural and gestural behaviors, movement, gaze, facial affect, self-disclosure, and excuses (Cappella, 1981; 1985; in press). The variety of behaviors implicated in mutual adaptation is testimony to the centrality of this process and the mechanisms behind it in human interaction. Deciding whether the Stones exhibit mutual adaptation, however, would require a richer data base, including both kinesic and vocal information, and a much longer stream of dialogue.

3. *Mutual adaptation pervades relationships even from the first instances of infant–mother interaction.* Studies reviewed by Cappella (in press) and Field (1987) show that infants who are weeks and, in a few cases, even hours old adapt to their adult partners in vocal, gaze, facial, and

movement behaviors. Such evidence underscores the centrality of mutual adaptation in human social interaction.

4. *Mutual adaptation covaries with important relational and individual conditions.* Positive social evaluations have been associated with certain types of mutual adaptation in interaction. Welkowitz and Kuc (1973) found that partners who were rated higher on warmth also exhibited greater similarity on speech latency. Street (1982) constructed audiotapes in which an interviewee's speech rate, latency, and duration converged, partially converged, or diverged with respect to that of an interviewer. The divergent speech of interviewees was evaluated more negatively on social competence by observers. Similar findings on rate, content, and pronunciation were obtained by Giles and Smith (1979). These findings have been replicated in naturalistic contexts as well (Street, 1984).

It is not only vocal features of speech that are related to evaluative social judgments. Davis and Martin (1978) found that the percentage of responsive comments, independent of their frequency, was positively related to attraction. Davis and Perkowitz (1979) observed that pleasurable shocks given by subjects to recipients depended on how responsive the recipient was and the appropriateness of the response by the recipient. Recent work by Bernieri (1988) found that judges' ratings of movement synchrony between high school students in a teacher–student setting were positively associated with the students' self-reports of rapport, a conclusion espoused by Tickle-Degnen and Rosenthal (1987) on the basis of their literature review. The research summarized above suggests that the presence of mutual adaptation is associated with positive assessments of interactions both by observers of the interaction and by participants.

Accumulating evidence is beginning to suggest that deviation from normal mutual adaptation processes may be characteristic of certain at-risk populations. Fararone and Hurtig (1985) studied socially skilled and unskilled males in interaction and found that conversations judged to be skilled ones showed a greater degree of sequential patterning than did the less skillful conversations. Feldstein, Konstantareas, Oxman, and Webster (1982) observed reciprocity in certain speech behaviors for counselors and parents of autistic children but not between the autistic children and their parents. Similar findings have been obtained with adult schizophrenics (Glaister, Feldstein, & Pollock, 1980) and depressives (Jaffe & Anderson, in press) who were less reciprocal than normals.

At the relationship level Gottman's (1979) widely cited findings are also relevant to the relationship between interaction and outcome. Although all of his couples tended to show reciprocity in hostile affect in discussions about common problems in their marriages, the less well adjusted couples showed greater hostile affect than the better adjusted couples. These findings have been replicated by Gottman (1979) using the data of Raush, Barry, Hertel, and Swain (1974) and in other contexts by Margolin and Wampold (1981) and Schapp (1982). Pike and Sillars (1985) also found greater reciprocity in negative vocal affect for dissatisfied, as opposed to satisfied, married couples. In Noller's (1984) study, using face-directed gaze rather than negative affect as a dependent variable, satisfied couples exhibited greater correlation between partners than did the dissatisfied couples. Overall, partners in satisfying, established relationships appear to differ from those in less satisfying relationships in the type of mutual influence seen in their interaction. Obviously, the patterns of interaction exhibited by the Stones would have to be evaluated on several levels of verbal and nonverbal content to determine what, if any, patterns are followed. Patterns could be reciprocal on certain behaviors and compensatory on others. The association between patterns and relational outcomes is a relative one and would require comparable observations on other couples who differed from the Stones in their relational satisfaction.

Measuring Interaction

Once one has chosen to study the observable patterns of interaction in a relational setting, one is faced with important measurement decisions. These decisions have implications for the cost of the research (in time and money), for the level at which processes are studied (microscopic to macroscopic), for the kinds of adaptation patterns that are observed (from reciprocal to compensatory) and possibly for the kinds of associations between patterns and outcomes that could be obtained. Measurement tools are certainly not neutral devices through which information is acquired. Rather, they are researchers' theory-driven constructions of the social world.

Approaches to the measurement of behaviors expressed in interaction are limited only by the imaginations of researchers who carry out those measurements. It is not possible to offer a comprehensive characterization of measurement schemes for interaction both because of space limitations and the fact that such schemes can be made obsolete with the next inventive leap. I will, however, try to represent those approaches to measurement that are amenable to quantitative application and that are in wide use.*

All measurement approaches to interaction have certain features in common. The measurement of an interactional event is a representation of

---

*Actions expressed in interaction can obviously be assessed through qualitative means, as evidenced by the vast upsurge of research employing conversation-analytic, ethnographic, and interpretive approaches (Cheney & Tompkins, 1988; Jacobs, 1988; Zimmerman, 1988).

the event in a specified "frame of reference" through a set of rules of translation. The interactional events may be live or may already have been modified through representation in another media, for example, videotape, audio recording, or typescript. The representation in the new frame of reference will always be a homomorphic transformation; that is, the representation is less informationally complex than the original. The "rules of translation" that give rise to the representation can be implicit or explicit, can span the spectrum from machine algorithms to human perceptions, and can be incredibly simple (for example, speech and nonspeech according to the rules of Jaffe & Feldstein, 1970) or numbingly complex (facial affect according to Ekman & Friesen, 1978).

All rules of translation will be inferential to some degree. The degree of inference can vary from the low end, which focuses primarily on the brute features of the behavior (e.g., talk vs. silence, face-directed gaze vs. gaze aversion) to the high end, which concerns interpersonal functions (or meanings) that the behavior serves (e.g., hostile affect, dominance). Even rules of translation derived from machine-based measurements involve some level of inference. For example, the assessment of fundamental frequency of voice depends on the algorithms for analyzing speech signals (Scherer, 1982).

RULES OF TRANSLATION

Four major approaches to interactional measurement are considered in this chapter: coding, rating, participant judgment, and observer judgment. I have chosen these four because each of them has been used in programmatic quantitative studies of adaptation in interaction and represents a class of translation rules for measuring interactional events. Any quantitative measure of social interaction involves the assignment of a value on some scale to a segment of interaction. The segment may be a thought unit, a turn, a fixed unit of time and so forth (see Cappella, 1987; Folger, Hewes, & Poole, 1984).

In the coding approach, values are objectively assigned to segments of the interaction according to precise rules applied by analog devices (e.g., pitch detectors) or by trained coders (of, for example, facial muscle positions indicative of smiling). In the rating approach, values are assigned to segments of the interaction by trained raters according to rules indicating the approximate quantity of behavior within the segment (e.g., smiling on an 11-point scale from "none at all" to "constant"). The coding and rating approaches are based on rules of translation supplied by the researcher and are carried out by translation "devices," which can be machines or trained individuals. In general, coding and rating approaches have employed low-level inference rules of translation. They have focused primarily on the more objective aspects of the interaction, rather than on aspects requiring more interpretive assessments. Neither approach requires low-level inferences in principle, but questions of reliability and validity (Cappella, 1987; Folger, Hewes, & Poole, 1984) certainly limit the use of high-level inference rating and coding systems.

In the judgment approach untrained persons, either participants or observers, act as judges, assigning values according to their perceptions of the "meaning" of the segment; for example, depending on the task, the segment may be perceived to be hostile or affiliative, synchronous or asynchronous, controlling or equalitarian and so on. The rules of translation in these approaches are supplied by the individual judges, either through their unique perspective on the interaction (e.g., as the partner of a participant) or their perspective as a competent member of the culture of observers. In general, the judgment approach has focused primarily on the more interpretive or meaningful, rather than the objective, aspects of the interaction. It makes little sense to have participants indicate frequency of certain types of acts when disinterested and trained observers can do so equally well or better. Despite this common practice one could use observers or participants as judges on low-level measurements about interactional events.

The record of the sample interaction of this volume, the Stones' dinner conversation, is a written transcript stripped of its rich vocal and kinesic textures. Despite this lack, the written transcript can be coded or rated by trained observers according to the dictates of the translation scheme adopted by the researcher. A group of judges, as cultural informants, can also be imported to evaluate segments of the interactional stream according to meaningful categories of judgment. Of course, the Stones themselves can do the same with regard to their own and their partner's behaviors.

APPLICATIONS IN STUDIES OF MUTUAL ADAPTATION

The above four approaches to measurement in social interaction have been chosen because each has been the method of choice of a particular research program committed to the study of mutual adaptation, and other facets of interaction as well. The coding approach characterizes my own approach to measurement (Cappella, Palmer, & Donzella, 1989; Cappella & Planalp, 1981; Street & Cappella, 1989). Gottman (1979) has employed both coding★ and participant judgment procedures in his studies of distressed and nondistressed married couples. Recently, however, Levenson and Gottman (1985) have argued that the only appropriate measure of a couple's expressed affective state is that provided by the couple:

★Gottman's (1979) coding rules appear to be a mix of coding and rating procedures, depending upon the behavior being evaluated.

> Compared with having an observer code or a professional rate marital satisfaction on the basis of a couple's behavior, the advantage of . . . having the couple provide affect ratings derives from a simple and perhaps obvious fact. The only observers who we can be certain are applying the appropriate normative metric to a couple's marital interaction are the husband and wife themselves. (p. 93)

Gottman (1979) reports that affect measured by coding and that measured by means of participant judgments are similar in the aggregate, but information on segment-by-segment similarity is not yet available.

Rating approaches have been employed by Burgoon (Baesler & Burgoon, 1987; Burgoon & Hale, 1988; Burgoon, Olney, & Coker, 1988) in her studies of interactional adaptation and in her other studies of nonverbal behavior. Advocates of rating argue that if trained, attentive raters can form reliable impressions of the interaction, then the more precise information provided by coding techniques may be unnecessary. Moreover, it is argued, participants may not process the features of social interaction as fully as coding approaches imply. In this view coding approaches are unnecessary both because of their cost and because they are more precise than participants' actual perceptions.

Observer judgment approaches have been the method of choice employed by Rosenthal and his colleagues (Bernieri, 1988; Bernieri, Rednick, & Rosenthal, 1988; Rosenthal, 1987). In this method, groups of observers are asked to make various judgments, often at a high level of inference, about multiple examples of interactional segments. The observers can be viewed as a group of cultural informants whose judgments of the segments, if reliable, could be treated as culturally accepted meanings. Reliability becomes as an effective reliability across judges and stimuli which are treated as replications (Rosenthal, 1987) so that high levels of correlation among judges are not necessary to achieve acceptable levels of reliability for the group.

Each of these approaches to measurement has had some predictive success in various domains, especially in studies of adaptation. Thus, predictive adequacy is not at issue. What appears to be at issue is which frame of reference offers the best representation of the reality that is being measured.

Some Comparisons of Measurement Approaches

The coding approach clearly has the capacity to provide more precise and accurate representations of interactional behaviors than other approaches. However, it does so at considerable cost in time and money. When multiple behaviors are to be coded, as is more and more frequently the case, researchers adopting a coding approach spend most of their time with training and coding activities. Coding approaches also implicitly assume that every behavior at every temporal segment is equally important. This is a dubious assumption in terms of what participants in an interaction are capable of noticing and responding to. The information density of social stimulation and its temporal variability certainly imply that participants and observers will employ some sort of simplifying heuristics in processing the incoming flux of stimulation (Cappella & Street, 1989). Coding approaches are also typically, though not necessarily, brute representations of interactional behavior. The meanings or functions of the behaviors must be ascertained indirectly through their predictive adequacy.

Rating approaches are similar to coding approaches in that the brute features of interactional behaviors typically are the central focus, rather than the meanings of the behaviors. Rating approaches are also more easily adjusted to include higher-level inferences (for example, fluency ratings) but are likely to encounter reliability problems with very high level inferences such as dominance ratings. Ratings are certainly more cost-effective than coding procedures, since longer segments are evaluated. They also handle the problem of excessive detail by allowing raters to act as perceptual filters reducing the level of detail that coding approaches necessarily provide.

In buying these advantages, a certain cost is incurred. One does not know if the ratings are veridical measurements of what is actually occurring during interaction or if the ratings represent filtering through what might be cultural stereotypes. For example, in rating fluency first and eye gaze on another pass through the data, a rater with a stereotype that gaze and fluency are signs of social competence might offer consistently higher ratings on these behaviors to a person who appears to be a competent interactant. The person who must code such behaviors has a cognitively more difficult task and would have to operate at a surface level of perception. In any case, there is no evidence, to my knowledge, about the relationship between ratings and codings in terms of accuracy.

The predictive success of both Gottman's and Rosenthal's work suggests that the judgment approach to measuring social interaction is an effective one. Certainly, the judgment approach is more efficient than either the rating or coding approaches in that it bypasses the problem of excessively detailed information that both ratings and codings provide and moves directly to the meanings that the participants or cultural observers would offer. Instead of representations of brute behaviors, the meanings of those behaviors are typically provided. Also, judgment approaches replace researcher-defined norms with norms from two privileged groups: those responding to the behavior and those representing the cultural group's norms.

However, the judgment approach provides no insight into which objective features of the interaction, if any, produce the participants' and observers' perceptions. Without information about how actual interactional behavior is translated into perceptual judgments, the pragmatic value of interactional research is limited. Training programs aimed at improving communication cannot be based merely on the perceptions that interaction creates but must be based on the features of the interaction that give rise to the perceptions. In effect, the knowledge about effective social interaction that is being generated by the judgment approach is at least one step removed from the interaction process itself, and conclusions about how interaction functions are really conclusions about how perception functions.

An Analogy

The four approaches to measuring social interaction provide four quite different frames of reference. The approaches can be compared on criteria such as precision, completeness, susceptibility to distortion, efficiency, meaningfulness, psychological reality (processing limitations), and utility. Each satisfies certain desirable criteria while failing on others. Can we choose among these approaches? Shall our studies of social interaction be measurement dependent so that, for example, the nature of mutual adaptation processes will depend on the frame of reference within which studies are conducted?

I think that these are the wrong questions. Consider an analogy. In the physical sciences the trajectories that projectiles are observed to follow depend on the frame of reference from which one does the observation (Hawking, 1988). Such apparent complexity does not lead to the conclusion that the physics of projectile motion is unique to each frame of reference. Rather, the physicist is led to search for methods of transforming the findings within one frame of reference to other frames of reference. The physics of projectile motion remains the same in all frames of reference, but the superficial manifestations differ as a function of the frame of reference of the observer.

My proposal is simply that the search for the privileged frame of reference for measuring social interaction not even begin. Instead, our search should be directed at transforming the results from one frame of reference to another by developing mappings from the more objective measurement frames to those represented by participant and observer judgments.

Research Strategies

The research being suggested is not simply a set of studies in the decoding tradition of verbal and nonverbal research (Duncan, 1969; Rosenthal, 1987). Such research is voluminous (Burgoon, Buller, & Woodall, 1989; Cappella & Palmer, 1989) but tends to be univariate rather than multivariate, static rather than dynamic, and aggregated at the group level rather than at the individual level.

To study the process of transformation from one frame of reference to another, one must have process data on codings, ratings, and participant and observer judgments for a representative set of interactions. Two studies directly relevant to the transformation question have been conducted in our laboratory. On the basis of the static studies of interpersonal dominance, Palmer (1989a) reasoned that turn-by-turn judgments of dominance should be related to the degree of floor holding and topical switching at each interactional turn. To test this hypothesis, he divided a transcript of a nondirected conversation into turns. One group of observers judged the degree of dominance by one partner or the other at each turn; another group judged the degree of topical relatedness to the previous conversational turn. The length of the turn was based on the number of words in each turn. Thus, three series of data were produced at each turn: degree of topic relatedness, turn length, and judged dominance.

Using time series regression procedures, dominance judgments were predicted from current and prior values of turn length and topic relatedness. Turn length was positively associated with judged dominance, and relatedness was negatively associated with it. These findings mean that the person holding the floor longer was seen as the more dominant, and the person whose topic differed to a greater extent from that of the partner's prior topic was seen as more dominant. Importantly, these judgments changed as turns evolved temporally, and more of the variance in judged dominance was carried by the topic differences than the turn length.

Although this study was limited in scope, its findings are significant for claiming that length of speaking turn and topic unrelatedness are perceived, at least by observers, as signs of interpersonal control. The study did not have participants' judgments or ratings of turn duration and so is of limited usefulness to the study of transformations.

A later study by Palmer (1989b) used a larger number of coded nonverbal behaviors, observers who judged both affiliation and dominance, and a larger set of stimuli. The study was unsuccessful. In this case, the temporal cross-correlations between the nonverbal codes (and various combinations of codes) did not predict reliable observers' judgments of either dominance or affiliation even though there was variance in these judgments.

With the little data that we have thus far we must conclude that the possibility of discovering transformations from one frame of reference for interactional meaning to another is uncertain. I believe, however, that the continued search is worth the effort.

Conclusion

Research on communication and personal relationships in my work takes the form of studying certain basic processes. These are the processes of mutual adaptation and the relativity of meaning across systems of coding.

The rationale for focusing on adaptation processes is, first, that adaptation is a defining feature of interpersonal communication. Its absence implies an insensitivity to the partner's behavior that undermines the apparent interpersonal character of face-to-face encounters. Second, adaptation is a process central to the functioning of the human organism and is perhaps diagnostic of interpersonal and individual competence. Although all the chapters of this book are aimed at evaluating the Stones' interaction, such work is atypical of the published research in personal and social relationships.

Studies of adaptation are difficult to carry out, being labor-intensive and employing techniques not generally taught in standard methodology courses. As one moves from studying adaptation per se to the relationship between patterns of adaptation and relational outcomes, issues of statistical power become significant. At a different level, the nature of the adaptive pattern likely to discriminate between relational types will depend on the kind of behavior to which adaptation is being made (Cappella, 1988). Thus, in a sense, it is not adaptation per se that is related to interpersonal outcome or to individual state but the adaptation by content interaction that is predictive.

One of the ways to understand the nature of interactional content is through its measurement from different frames of reference. To claim that the same content may be evaluated differently from different frames of reference (or measurement systems, since measurement is nothing more than a means of translation) is to make an uncontroversial claim. What is controversial and, in my opinion, deserving of thorough empirical scrutiny is whether alternative frames of reference can be transformed from one to another.

A variety of practical and theoretical outcomes could be realized from research on the mappings among measurement frames. First, the motivating question for this research asks whether participant or observer judgments of the meaning of social interaction can be accounted for in terms of more objective features of the interactions revealed by codings and ratings. If a mapping from objective interactional features to judgments can be found, then (1) training in the affected populations can be aimed at behaviors that give rise to interpretations deleterious to the functioning of the relationship, (2) the judgment approach to interactional measurement can be said to be a viable procedure for measuring interaction, rather than simply a nebulous form of global judgment, and (3) findings about relational outcomes based on the judgment approach to interaction can be viewed as statements about what is actually happening interactionally. If a mapping from codings and ratings to judgments cannot be found, then the judgment approach to measuring social interaction must be called into question. Since participants' judgments do predict relational satisfaction, the judgments must be based on some aspect of the setting not captured by the interactional features themselves. Judgments would still predict relational outcomes but would be unrelated to interactional patterns.

Second, if a mapping from codings and ratings to judgments can be found, then the data base for research into on-line impression formation will be significantly enhanced (Hastie & Park, 1986; Basili, 1989). People in interaction clearly cannot be processing all the sensory features of the stimuli to which they are being exposed. They must be using some short-cuts or heuristics in moving from the dynamic and information-rich interaction to judgments about it and the other person (Cappella & Street, 1989; Cappella & Palmer, 1989). The mappings from codings and ratings to judgments, if they can be found, would have the capacity to illuminate just what these shortcuts might be.

Third, the assumption of attribution theorists that participants in an interaction make judgments different from the judgments of observers (Cappella & Street, 1989; Jones & Nisbett, 1971; Kelley & Michela, 1980) can be tested by comparing the judgments of observers and participants in their continuous on-line perceptions of the interaction.

Fourth, the effectiveness of coding and rating approaches can be compared. Coding interaction is costly and labor-intensive, but it is also precise and less susceptible to bias. Rating interaction is more efficient in time and cost but also less precise and more likely to introduce biased scores; with ratings one can never be certain of the relationship between the ratings and what has actually transpired in the interaction. If, however, it can be shown that ratings predict judgments better than codings do, then they should be preferred to codings.

Fifth, a mapping between codings or ratings and judgments will provide information about the social meanings of objective behaviors in a way that is especially pertinent to their function in interpersonal encounters. Objective codings of interaction without knowledge of their meanings to the participants and to the culture at large (observers) are as useless as perceptions of the interaction without firm knowledge of what the perceptions are based on.

References

Baesler, E., & Burgoon, J. K. (1987). Measurement and reliability of nonverbal behavior and percepts. *Journal of Nonverbal Behavior, 11,* 205–233.

Basili, J. N. (Ed.). (1989). *On line impression formation.* Hillsadle, NJ: Erlbaum.

Bernieri, F. J. (1988). Coordinated movement and rapport in teacher–student interactions. *Journal of Nonverbal Behavior, 12,* 120–138.

Bernieri, F. J., Resnick, J. S., & Rosenthal, R. (1988). Synchrony, pseudosynchrony, and dissynchrony: Measuring the entrainment process in mother–infant interactions. *Journal of Personality and Social Psychology, 54,* 243–253.

Burgoon, J. K., Buller, D. B., & Woodall, W. G. (1989). *Nonverbal communication: The unspoken dialogue*. New York: Harper & Row.

Burgoon, J. K., & Hale, J. L. (1988). Nonverbal expectancy violations: Model elaboration and application to immediacy behaviors. *Communication Monographs, 55,* 58–79.

Burgoon, J. K., Olney, C. A., & Coker, R. (1988). The effects of communicator characteristics on patterns of reciprocity and compensation. *Journal of Nonverbal Behavior, 11,* 146–165.

Cappella, J. N. (1981). Mutual influence in expressive behavior: Adult–adult and infant–adult dyadic interaction. *Psychological Bulletin, 89,* 101–132.

Cappella, J. N. (1985). The management of conversations. In M. L. Knapp & G. R. Miller (Eds.), *The handbook of interpersonal communication* (pp. 393–438). Beverly Hills, CA: Sage.

Cappella, J. N. (1987). Interpersonal communication: Fundamental questions and issues. In C. R. Berger & S. Chaffee (Eds.), *The handbook of communication science* (pp. 184–238). Beverly Hills, CA: Sage.

Cappella, J. N. (1988). Interaction patterns and social and personal relationships. In S. Duck (Ed.), *Handbook of social and personal relationships* (pp. 325–342). New York: Wiley.

Cappella, J. N., & Palmer, M. L. (1989). The structure and organization of verbal and nonverbal behavior: Data for models of reception. *Journal of Language and Social Psychology, 8,* 167–192.

Cappella, J. N. (in press). The biological origins of automated patterns of human interaction. *Communication Theory.*

Cappella, J. N., Palmer, M. T., & Donzella, B. (1989, June). *The temporal stability of adaptation in social interaction.* Paper presented at the Nags Head Conference on Social Interaction.

Cappella, J. N., & Planalp, S. (1981). Talk and silence sequences in informal conversations III. Interspeaker influence. *Human Communication Research, 7,* 117–132.

Cappella, J. N., & Street, R. L. (1989). Message effects: Theory and research on mental models of messages. In J. J. Bradac (Ed.), *Message effects in communication science* (pp. 24–51). Newbury Park, CA: Sage.

Cheney, G., & Tompkins, P. K. (1988). On the facts of the text as the basis of human communication research. In J. A. Anderson (Ed.), *Communication yearbook 11* (pp. 455–481). Newbury Park, CA: Sage.

Davis, D., & Martin, H. J. (1978). When pleasure begets pleasure: Recipient responsiveness as a determinant of physical pleasuring between heterosexual dating couples and strangers. *Journal of Personality and Social Psychology, 36,* 767–777.

Davis, D., & Perkowitz, W. T. (1979). Consequences of responsiveness in dyadic interaction: Effects of probability of response and proportion of content-related responses on interpersonal attraction. *Journal of Personality and Social Psychology, 37,* 534–550.

Duncan, S. (1969). Nonverbal communication. *Psychological Bulletin, 72,* 118–137.

Ekman, P., & Friesen, W. V. (1978). *Unmasking the face: A guide to recognizing emotions from facial cues.* Englwood Cliffs, NJ: Prentice-Hall.

Fararone, S. V., & Hurtig, R. R. (1985). An examination of social skill, verbal productivity, and Gottman's model of interaction using observational methods and sequential analysis. *Behavioral Assessment, 7,* 349–366.

Feldstein, S., Konstantareas, M., Oxman, J., & Webster, C. D. (1982). The chronography of interaction with autistic speakers: An initial report. *Journal of Communicative Disorders, 15,* 451–460.

Field, T. (1987). Affective and interactive disturbances in infants. In J. D. Osofsky (Ed.), *Handbook of infant development* (2nd ed., pp. 972-1007). New York: Wiley.

Folger, J. P., Hewes, D. E., & Poole, M. S. (1984). Coding social interaction. In B. Dervin & M. L. Voigt (Eds.), *Progress in communication sciences* (Vol. 4, pp. 115–161). Norwood, NJ: Ablex.

Giles, H., & Smith, P. M. (1979). Accommodation theory: Optimal levels of convergence. In H. Giles & R. N. St. Clair (Eds.), *Language and social psychology* (pp. 45–65). Oxford: Blackwell.

Glaister, J., Feldstein, S., & Pollock, H. (1980). Chronographic speech patterns of acutely psychotic patients. *The Journal of Nervous and Mental Disease, 168,* (#4).

Gottman, J. M. (1979). *Marital interaction.* New York: Academic Press.

Hastie, R., & Park, B. (1986). The relationship between memory and judgment depends on whether the judgment task is memory-based or on-line. *Psychological Review, 93,* 258–268.

Hawking, S. (1988). *A brief history of time.* Toronto: Bantam.

Jacobs, S. (1988). Evidence and inference in conversation analysis. In J. A. Anderson (Ed.), *Communication yearbook 11* (pp. 433–443). Newbury Park, CA: Sage.

Jaffe, J., & Anderson, S. (in press). Speech rate studies in major depressive disorders: Degree of response to medication. In S. Feldstein, C. Crown, & J. Welkowitz (Eds.), *Speech sounds and silences: A social psychological approach to clinical concerns.* Hillsdale, NJ: Erlbaum.

Jaffe, J., & Feldstein, S. (1970). *Rhythms of dialogue.* New York: Academic Press.

Jones, E. E., & Nisbett, R. E. (1971). The actor and the observer: Divergent perceptions of the cause of behavior. In E. E. Jones, D. E. Kanouse, H. H. Kelley, R. E. Nisbett, S. Valins, & B. Weiner (Eds.), *Attribution: Perceiving the causes of behavior* (pp. 79–94). Morristown, NJ: General Learning Press.

Kelley, H., & Michela, J. (1980). Attribution theory and research. In M. R. Rosenweig & Porter (Eds.), *Annual reviews of psychology* (pp. 457–501). Palo Alto, CA: Annual Review.

Levenson, R. W., & Gottman, J. M. (1985). Physiological and affective predictors of change in relationship satisfaction. *Journal of Personality and Social Psychology, 49,* 85–94.

Margolin, G., & Wampold, B. E. (1981). Sequential analysis of conflict and accord in distressed and nondistressed marital partners. *Journal of Consulting and Clinical Psychology, 49,* 554–567.

Noller, P. (1984). *Nonverbal communication and marital interaction.* Oxford: Pergamon Press.

Palmer, M. T. (1989a). Controlling conversations: Turns, topics, and interpersonal control. *Communication Monographs, 56,* 1–18.

Palmer, M. T. (1989b). *Mapping relational inferences onto conversational behaviors: Cross-sectional and time-series analyses.* Unpublished doctoral dissertation, University of Wisconsin, Madison.

Pike, G. R., & Sillars, A. L. (1985). Reciprocity and marital communication. *Journal of Personal and Social Relationships, 2,* 303–324.

Raush, H. L., Barry, W. A., Hertel, R. K., & Swain, M. A. (1974). *Communication, conflict, and marriage.* San Francisco: Jossey-Bass.

Rosenthal, R. (1987). *Judgment studies: Design, analysis and meta-analysis.* Cambridge: Cambridge University Press.

Schaap, C. (1982). *Communication and adjustment.* Lisse, Netherlands: Swets & Zeitlinger.

Scherer, K. R. (1982). Methods of research on vocal communication: Paradigms and parameters. In K. R. Scherer & P. Ekman (Eds.), *Handbook of methods in nonverbal behavior research* (pp. 136–198). Cambridge: Cambridge University Press.

Street, R. L., Jr. (1982). Evaluation of noncontent speech accommodation. *Language and Communication, 2,* 13–31.

Street, R. L., Jr. (1984). Speech convergence and speech evaluation in fact-finding interviews. *Human Communication Research, 11,* 139–169.

Street, R. L., Jr., & Cappella, J. N. (1989). Social and linguistic factors influencing adaptation in children's speech. *Journal of Psycholinguistic Research, 18,* 497–519.

Tickle-Degnen, L., & Rosenthal, R. (1987). Group rapport and nonverbal behavior. *Review of Personality and Social Psychology, 9,* 113–136.

Welkowitz, J., & Kuc, M. (1973). Interrelationships among warmth, genuineness, empathy, and temporal speech patterns in interpersonal interaction. *Journal of Consulting and Clinical Psychology, 41,* 472–473.

Zimmerman, D. H. (1988). On conversation: The conversation analytic perspective. In J. A. Anderson (Ed.), *Communication yearbook 11* (pp. 406–432). Newbury Park, CA: Sage.

PART II

WHAT COUNTS AS DATA

Chapter 7

Accounts and Narratives

ROSALIE BURNETT

> It is a foolish thing to make a long prologue,
> and to be short in the story itself.
> *Old Testament, Maccabees, 2:32*

> Said my mother, "what is all this story about?"
> "A Cock and a Bull," said Yorick.
> *Laurence Sterne*, Tristam Shandy, *Bk. ix, ch 33*

By turning persons into research subjects with non-speaking parts in the script of social science, much investigation of interpersonal interaction can seem like an elaborate prologue to a play in which the characters are denied their lines. Unless we let actors say what they mean, then the content of that play is reduced; however elaborate an outsider's commentary on the central action, it is no substitute for the story itself as told by insiders. By contrast, I advocate an approach to studying social interaction using methods that include a means of accessing people's own meanings. Yet, as augured by the second quotation, there are research hazards in letting people speak for themselves. It is not simply that their open-ended accounts do not easily lend themselves to quantification. To invite people to provide their own account is to give them opportunity to show off, to ramble irrelevantly, and to deceive—in other words, to tell a cock-and-bull story. Even if they are honest, will they know their story well enough and will they be able to articulate it? On the horns of this dilemma, this chapter will address

121

the pros, cons, and underlying assumptions of a methodology utilizing accounts.

What Counts as an "Account"?

Accounts range from reflective efforts to understand to recollection of events organized into narrative form. People can account for themselves in the sense of explaining or justifying their actions, and the results could be simple statements without elaboration. Alternatively, people can give an account or story about themselves or an event, and here some elaboration and narrative-like features would typically be required. An account might be as short as a single-phrase statement or as long as a life story.

"Accounting," in its broadest sense, refers to all attempts to understand and explain experience. We are therefore dealing here with how people make sense of their world in their private reflection and analysis as well as in shared communication. Thus, accounts may be public (directed at others) or private (inward, unspoken, and not necessarily conscious), performable ("an account that is articulatable and can be examined as if it were a conscious social device . . . [and which] the person could choose to broad-cast") or unperformable ("one which is inarticulately operative on the person's actions and feelings . . . a mental representation . . . cognitively unavailable for public consumption," Antaki, 1987, pp. 97–98). The pur-pose of any account may be simply to describe, or else to explain cause or reason in order to further understanding, or the intention may be a moral one such as to justify or excuse action (Antaki & Fielding, 1981; Semin & Manstead, 1983; Scott & Lyman, 1968).

Narratives (or stories) are a specific form of account (though the terms are often used interchangeably), and they are usually long. Gergen and Gergen (1987) have set out five critical components of the "well-formed narrative": (1) it should have a goal-state, that is, there is a point in telling it; (2) events must be selected that are relevant to that goal state; (3) events are generally arranged chronologically; (4) one event should lead logically (often causally) to another; and (5) it has demarcation signs, such as "in the beginning." There can be many deviations from this ideal type.

There are other varieties of accounts apart from narratives or stories (which, of course, may be told either in writing or orally). People can explain themselves non-verbally and so, theoretically, an account could be pictorial: mimes and silent movies tell their stories well enough. And for an account presented in the form of graphs, see Miell (1987). Most rationales for studying accounts exclude these forms of communication, which are less explicit and direct than verbalized language. Finally, I do not deal with "diaries" or "texts," which are dealt with elsewhere (see Chapters 8 & 10).

How Can Investigation Benefit from People's Accounts?

Much that is of interest in social interaction is not observable. The most obvious case to be made for the value of accounts as data, therefore, is that they provide a direct route to information about persons' experiences. This is in contrast to expert interpretation or to inferences based on observation of behavior or to other indirect measures of experience, such as choices along a rating scale. Reference to the personal viewpoint and experience of the subject capitalizes on the advantage enjoyed by social scientists that their "subject" of study shares a common meaning system, speaks the same language, and may be willing to tell.

Use of accounts thus opens up a huge reservoir of potentially rich and varied information about private events, subjective experiences, and thoughts. Alternatively, accounts may be used to obtain more detailed, differentiated data than other methods achieve in order to explore individual differences, alternative perspectives, or depth of understanding. Further, by reference to accounts, researchers can seek to support their observations and theories by checking them against the first-hand explanations of the people whom they study. They can also use accounts to obtain detail that fills out and enlarges other sources of data; or accounts can be presented as illustrative case studies. Another virtue of an account methodology is that it allows a way of treating research participants on equal terms, in keeping with the status that they share with the investigator as human beings. Let us now look more closely at some of the other advantages of an account methodology.

ACCESS

An account methodology enlarges the data bank to include a mass of ready-made naturalistic data, including letters, books, lectures, diaries, and other archival sources. These have the advantage, as has been pointed out by Harvey, Turnquist, and Agostinelli (1988), that they are nonreactive: that is, the material was not produced especially for an experiment with the consequent risk of participant restraint and content bias.

PRIVATE WORLDS

Significant social interactive phenomena occur "behind closed doors," as part of intimate experience or private family life, and are therefore normally not readily available to researchers. Certainly, such events and experiences do not lend themselves to laboratory work. While many insightful contributions have hailed from psychotherapy, which has benefited from clients' disclosures about behavior not typically revealed, academic psychology has, by contrast, sometimes been charged with failing to get beneath the surface of social interchange. Liam Hudson (1972), in a critique of positivistic experimental psychology, lamented the fact that the researcher is denied the novelist's privileged access to individuals' emotions, interpretations, and private moments. Obviously, account data need not suffer from this problem.

SUBJECTIVE EXPERIENCE

Even in studies of public situations, a private stream of consciousness (thoughts, feelings, intentions, memories, uncertainties, and so on) may be deemed of relevance to the research issue, especially if these seem to be of central influence on the behavior in question. (I will consider this further in the following section). Examples of in-depth explorations of subjective experience based on accounts are Robert R. Bell's (1981) *Worlds of Friendship,* Lillian Rubin's (1983) *Intimate Strangers,* and Gail Sheehy's (1982) *Pathfinders*—works by a sociologist, a psychotherapist, and an anthropologist, respectively.

INDIVIDUAL DIFFERENCES

Although research is typically a search for common patterns from which to generalize, it may also focus on the way in which we are all different, or else may seek typical instances of such differences. Such a concern requires focus on specific cases, and accounts may be useful here. Also, attention to individuality in accounting may be useful for richness of detail and illustration of specific cases that exemplify a typology or that describe experiences with which readers can readily identify (e.g., Weiss's, 1975, work on experiences of marital separation and Blumstein & Schwartz's, 1983, exploration of American couples' private attitudes to work, money, and sex).

ALTERNATIVE PERSPECTIVES

The very employment of accounts is founded on the beliefs that there are alternative interpretations of experience besides the researcher's and that the participant's perspective is relevent to exposition or explanation of a phenomenon (see also Chapter 3). If a difference of viewpoint should lead to different responses, then it becomes especially important to explore individual accounts. This may be important in couple relationships because while we treat it as one relationship, each partner may have a view that is sufficiently unique to suggest the existence of "two relationships," while outsiders' views suggest a third or even more (Duck & Sants, 1983).

DIFFERENTIATION

The discrete categories and forced choices offered by rating scales and questionnaires can reveal nothing of the equivocations and interpretations that accompany their completion. Roiser (1974) recalls being a research subject himself and adding an uninvited page of text to explain what he really thought in answer to a bipolar question. Countless respondents must have felt similarly frustrated and misrepresented by their questionnaire responses. From that extreme of forced-choice and no latitude, the accounts method is open to real-life uncertainties and contradictions, in addition to richness of detail. For instance, where a questionnaire requires subjects to describe a partner as either patient or impatient, talkative or quiet, an account could reveal that the partner is impatient only when under pressure at work and is generally taciturn, although garrulous at parties. Thus, even Blumstein and Schwartz's (1983) 9-point rating scale for satisfaction with "how we communicate" gave participants none of the scope for descriptive explanation obtained in complementary open-ended interviews within the same study.

HUMANISTIC RESEARCH

The study of accounts essentially treats participants as equals of researchers and esteems their views. Ideal conditions for eliciting unrestrained and undefended discourse are conditions that provide safety, empathy, and shared goals. Often, participant and researcher become investigators together, each fulfilling the same requirements and each involved in the analysis. Apart from the practical gains of such equality (see Hollway, 1989; Wilkinson, 1981), this upgrading of participant status (plus the new value given to participant experience and perspective, in contrast to excluding this subjective dimension as orthodox psychology has done), is a more "humanistic" mode of investigation (Armistead, 1974).

COMMUNICATION AND MEANING

Instances mentioned so far concern a perhaps secondary role for accounts, that of providing alternative or multiple sources of data. A primary role for account data is indicated when "accounting" is treated as a communicative activity and a means of making sense of the world, that is, where such active communicating and understanding themselves become the areas of study. Here accounting provides not just a type of data but a whole social process, to be looked at as something that people do, a social act with an explanatory or communicative function.

In this performable form (Antaki, 1987), accounts merit investigation as a social device used to persuade, impress, save face, and serve other pragmatic purposes (Gergen & Gergen, 1987). Where they refer to negative personal events, such as relationship endings, they have a therapeutic role: "they may help people make better sense of the loss . . . achieve a better sense of psychological control regarding the loss, and they serve as a pathway for emotional release" (Weber, Harvey, & Stanley, 1987). Harvey and colleagues have highlighted the motivations for such retrospective account making; these include reinforcing self-esteem, emotional purging, establishing a sense of control, search for closure, and search for understanding. Thus, accounts are important forms of social action that merit investigation in their own right, over and above any merits that they have as a rich and alternative source of data about other forms of social action (Burnett, McGhee, & Clarke, 1987).

Problematic Aspects of Accounts as Method

Advocacy of accounts as a serious method does not imply that they are unproblematic. As with other methods, there are difficulties associated with their use.

CREDIBILITY

A central question is whether accounts and narratives can be believed or whether they are just "stories" (in the far-fetched sense!). Reactions against positivism and behaviorism can lead us to swing too far in the direction of taking words at face value, with more credence than anything the researcher might suggest. Hollway (1989) argues, "Humanist psychology and Verstehen-based sociology assume that accounts given in answer to sympathetic questioning will be an expression of the real person" (p. 42); it may be right to base research in people's experience, but it is another matter to proceed as if "accounts must be taken to mean exactly what they say" (p. 43). Researchers typically deal with this dilemma by comparing accounts with other sorts of data or by rejecting the positivist position endorsed by other approaches and upon which such an objection to accounts is based.

COMPETENCE

The participant may not know his or her views and feelings about the issue in question (at least consciously) and therefore may have difficulty in responding fully or at all. Similarly, respondents may be unsure about what is important to them; there may be unconscious motivations that the participant is unable to include in his or her explanations.

SELF-SERVING BIASES AND PRIVACY

Obvious drawbacks are also that people are likely to exaggerate or to hold back on the truth when asked to give accounts. What is communicated may be limited by self-serving biases or by social desirability and also by inhibitions and reticence. We humans bias what we report in order to raise our standing in others' eyes and best serve our intentions. In addition, the "inside" knowledge sought by research is, by definition, of a private nature and therefore tends to be disclosed reservedly, if at all. Vaughan (1987), in a chapter about separating couples "going public," refers to efforts "to sustain a public impression of the relationship in keeping with the image of what we want to convey" (p. 210). Partners who are breaking up each "attempt to neutralize or discredit the other's attempt to define the situation" and "both tailor their definitions of self, other, and relationship to best convince the audiences they address" (P. 214).

PROBLEMS OF MEANING

Additional ways in which accounts are problematic are timing (Is the person referring to a past or present experience?); function (What is the purpose of the account and what motives does the speaker have?); and form of account (Does it explain, describe, ascribe; does it "tell" as opposed to "report"?; see Shotter, 1981). Further, as identified by Hollway (1989, p. 43), there is a bias in Western culture towards a unitary rationalism; "participants usually strive for coherence and consistency in the narratives they produce (for research as well as for other purposes)," which means that subjects essentially simplify things. And since "social psychology has suppressed the variability that it finds in accounts" (Hollway, 1989, p. 36), there are indications that researchers try to simplify things, too! Hollway also argues that defense mechanisms are used to keep ambivalence, multiple meanings, and contradiction at bay; characteristics such as indecisiveness, uncertainty, ambivalence, and self-contradiction are thus repressed.

LINGUISTIC SKILLS AND LANGUAGE LIMITATIONS

Even when people want to, it is rarely a simple matter to tell it like it is; it can be a problem to find the right words. Novelist Peter Carey, in *Oscar and Lucinda,* has most graphically expressed this problem: "the declared meaning of a spoken sentence is only its overcoat, and the real meaning lies underneath its scarves and buttons" (p. 190). Elicitation procedures, such as consciousness-raising discussion groups (see Hollway, 1989) and negotiation of meaning (e.g., as with the guided autobiography procedure introduced by De Waele and Harré, 1979), are likely to be helpful in efforts to draw out meaning and to understand.

INCIDENCE OF ACCOUNT MAKING

Once obtained, accounts and narratives can beguile researchers into believing that participants are hugely thoughtful and rich in ideas about issues they have rarely considered but become verbose about "now you come to ask." Special occasions, such as the beginning and ending of intimate relationships, do seem to motivate sustained thoughts (Burnett, 1986, 1987). It becomes a priority to sort out ideas and articulate them (Weber et al., 1987). The research setting becomes another circumstance that stimulates interpretation and the construction of a "performable account" (Antaki, 1987). But such special occasions are relatively rare. Of course, the implicit, unarticulated nature of much understanding is not an argument against using accounts in research; but we ought to be cautious about regarding these produced accounts as indicative of ideas people carry around in their heads when *not* motivated to collect thoughts nor called upon to construct an account.

ACCOUNTS ARE NOT STATIC

Weber et al. (1987) imply that stories can be resources somewhat like photograph albums brought out to display major life events. Those narratives that keep good memories alive or that put a glow on a dark part of the past may indeed be maintained in the same form, ready to be put on view (as, for instance, in the "grave-dressing" stage of relationship breakdown; see Duck, 1982). An account that is good for the ego or that has been well received in the past might be preserved intact. But such stories are likely to be the exception, the more usual case being continual revision. Not only is meaning dynamic, but also the very activity of telling a story can often change it. Vaughan (1987) suggests that, for example, the transition from a private account to "going public" will result in its reconstruction. It is therefore useful to think of accounts as having "careers" (Weber et al., 1987).

PARTICIPANT SAMPLE BIAS

Research volunteers are ultimately always self-selected; even systematic and random sampling for participants will result in some people withdrawing or being unable to finish the task. Those people who are not forthcoming, not garrulous, and not accustomed to disclosing personal information will be less likely to agree to requests to give an account. Equally, there will be differences arising from prior interest and knowledge about the topic. The demands of the task can be an additional subject-eliminator. Educational background is likely to result in some account-givers being less articulate; thus, the content might be unclear and lacking in detail. Conversely, some people are born story tellers: they are people who like to talk, have the "gift of the gab," and can turn a good phrase. Wilkinson (1987) and Hollway (1989) decided in advance on the appropriate skills and inclinations (introspective, self-analytical, interested in the research topic) their participants should have and duly advertised for them. Where detail and subtlety of meaning are important, these unevennesses in participant suitability are significant restrictions on the confidence with which generalizations can be made.

Appropriateness of Accounts as Data

There is nothing new about the use of participants' accounts in social science. Unstructured depth interviewing, in which respondents are asked for their accounts through open-ended questions, as distinct from either–or questions, has a respectable and long enough history. Three examples pertinent to this volume's theme are Bott's (1957) classic study of family and social networks, Rapoport and Rapoport's (1971) research into dual career families, and Weiss's (1975) work on marital separation. Further, the history of social scientific inquiry has been punctuated by calls for the need to identify people's meaning and definitions of the situation and to take the actor's perspective. Criminological and deviance research, for example, changed shape as a result of attention to the previously neglected symbolic nature of action and the significance of subjective meaning in making sense of what "actors" do. The subject of research (the criminal offender, in this case) came to be seen not merely as an object of investigation on a par with a molecule, a chemical compound, or biological organism but rather as a person with inside knowledge and first-person perspective—that is, with information that the researcher needs to know and can attain only with the subject's cooperation. This change substitutes an appreciation for the actor's perspective in place of attempts to understand the causes of deviance from only the investigator's point of view (Matza, 1969).

While nonquantitative, open-ended interviewing (i.e., account data) has enjoyed some limited acceptance, it is controversial within the mainstream social scientific context with its behaviorist and information-processing leanings. Here, an experimental approach has been traditional. George Kelly (1955), the psychotherapist who introduced Personal Construct Theory, articulated a presumably common suspicion: that a sensible solution to the problem of acquiring relevant information about people might be to ask them for it. This goes against cardinal principles of positivist social science but embraces what is arguably the crucial difference between physical and social science: the subject matter of social science can think like the scientists themselves and has the will to change at least some of the laws that its investigators might apply to it.

This controversy rests on different assumptions, research values, and theories that researchers hold. Assumptions that stress "behavior as caused" lessen the significance of accounts, whereas assumptions that much of behavior is goal-directed and that goals are a matter for individual choice suggest greater importance for an account methodology. If we see behavior as governed by laws affecting us all, then the individual's insights are obviously less relevant than if we see behavior as under autonomous control and varying with the individual's intentions.

The positivist approach (traditional for social science) trains against finding out about people by asking them. Indeed, the very idea of studying interpersonal interaction "scientifically" has been to avoid doing this; precise and systematic procedures filter out people's own explanations and stories, their representations of what they experience and perceive as going on. The trouble with accounts is that they are interpretative and, by the criterion of orthodox methodological procedures, non-verifiable.

Nevertheless, none of these objections sufficiently overrides the argument that the study of social interaction should include people's feelings and inner experience if it is to get to the heart of what matters. Harré and Secord (1972) propose the crucial role of accounting thus:

> At the heart of the explanation of social behavior is the identification of meanings which underlie it. Part of the approach to discovering them involves the obtaining of accounts—the actor's own statements about why he performed the acts in questions, what social meanings he gave to the actions of himself and others. (p. 9)

Seen in this light, accounts are more than method: they inform transactions between people and the process of being in human society. Studies based on this position include Harré's (1984) and Sabini and Silver's (1982). The work of these scholars represents an emergent paradigm that includes the concept of people as agents whose intentions and actions are mediated by their interpretation of events and settings (see Backman, 1979).

Within these newer traditions in social inquiry, a study of interpersonal interaction without reference to accounts would seem as unthinkable as medical research without access to anatomy, or astronomy without a telescope. These newer approaches have moved on from accounts as simply an extra method to confirm and extend data obtained by other means, and they draw attention to accounts as a sine qua non in the explanation of social behavior. That there are these different positions for the importance of accounts adds complicated layers to the theoretical arguments for use or nonuse of accounts as a method. However, there is room for various positions in the large interdisciplinary field here that has always courted various methodologies.

The Common Research Problem

We have looked at various purposes and problems associated with accounts as a methodology. Let us look now at how these issues might manifest themselves in an investigation springing from this volume's shared research problem, the conflict between Michael and Cathy Stone, which was witnessed by their long-term friends, the Millers.

Accounts from these participants would most typically be obtained in unstructured interviews with open-ended questions such as the following: "Would you tell me about your marriage?"; "What is your view of your friends' relationship?"; "This is a study about conflict between couples. I'm interested in anything you can tell me of relevance". Follow-up questions and probes, similarly open-ended, might be required at lulls in the flow of words or if the respondent has touched on an issue of special relevance where expansion would be appropriate. Instead of interviews, accounts are sometimes obtained in group settings where a goal is to discuss shared experiences (e.g., Weber et al., 1987). Alternatively, participants might be asked to provide an account in writing on a given topic (e.g., all four parties might be asked to reflect on the argument and then to provide independent descriptions of what occurred).

Yet, returning to the extract given, would a researcher wanting account data be able to treat the Stones' argument itself as an account or narrative? It lacks the components of a "well-formed narrative" (Gergen & Gergen, 1987) and the various attributions and explanations included in the excerpt are not ideal accounts, if only because of their brevity. However, it could still qualify: both Cathy and Michael do begin to give some account of themselves, and this is just an extract (in the full version some of the four participants might proceed to provide lengthier explanations or appraisals or stories, and so on, all of which we include as instances of the collective term *accounts*.)

The fact that the excerpt is dialogue does not rule it out. The rapid exchange of conversation appears to be the antithesis of relating an account, wherein one person speaks and others listen. However, stories and explanations always have a conversational context. In this case, an account is requested when a friend, Holly Miller, asks her hosts a question about how they manage, and the Stones respond. This informally parallels the pattern of a researcher asking a couple how they manage their household. Much accounting, in its social role, is achieved jointly (Shotter, 1984, 1987). Discussing accounts as a research tool can give the impression that they are tangible, detachable products, but accounting as an ongoing process for negotiating meaning and as social rhetoric is more typically embedded in conversation (Gergen & Gergen, 1987; Shotter, 1987).

An example of research where dialogues were the vehicle for accounts is Hollway's (1989) work on subjectivity and gender identity. Describing this research and its methodology, she writes:

> "Enjoying myself talking to people who wanted to talk to me did not feel like data gathering. It is only now that I can look at it quite the other way round and say that I succeeded in forging a valuable method: that is, to talk with people in a such a manner that they felt able to explore material about themselves and their relationships, past and present, in a searching and insightful way. (p. 11)

The dinner-party incident, on the face of it, is a naturally occurring interpersonal interaction. As such, it is free from researcher-reactivity and procedural-reactivity; in other words, accounts have not been affected by the presence of a researcher or by constraints of a situation set up for research. But for the incident to be used as data, someone had to have collected it as such. Was one of the people at this dinner party a participant–observer with a tape recorder or a notebook? Or were they all team members in a research project where participants and instigators get together as collaborators? One possibility is for researchers to involve participants as collaborators and then—to complete the intersubjectivity of this role-sharing—to themselves enter into the study as participants (e.g., Hollway, 1989; Wilkinson, 1987).

An Account for What?

The use of accounts with regard to the common research problem of this text, the interaction between the Stones, depends upon the concerns of the investigation and why the researcher is making use of accounts.

A major distinction for the investigation of social interaction is between studies that concern the *topic* (marriage, conflict, housework, etc.) and those concerning *construction of meaning* (explanation, reasoning, cognition, etc.). For instance, perhaps the researcher is investigating some aspect of marital relationships, such as dual-career couples or marriage after 5 years (i.e., topics). Or perhaps the interest is in cognitive issues or social representation, for instance, negotiation of meaning, conceptions of relationship, implicit commonsense theories (i.e., issues that lend themselves to a study of the construction of meaning). An example from Mansfield and Collard (1988) will conveniently serve to illustrate the two contrasting directions that these suggest. With regard to running a home, first they note that "who does, or does not do, the chores is a bone of contention in modern marital relationships" and, second, they observe "few [couples] discuss arrangements . . . explanations for the allocation of household chores may actually be post hoc justifications for the way things happen to work out . . . " (p. 121). Both points are made within the context of their research interest in the quality and experience of couple relationships, but their second observation, concerning explanations and justifications, could equally be a matter for cognitive psychology or one of several fields of academic inquiry addressing problems of meaning and knowledge and where the nature of the relationship is of superfluous concern.

A researcher investigating a particular topic would invite Cathy and Michael to address this topic in their accounts: Cathy and Michael, after all, are the experts on naming the activities that they enjoy best together, what they argue about, and who usually does the shopping. They are less likely to be able to help explicitly with more abstract and remote issues surrounding the construction of meaning, and therefore the chosen topic for their account may be fairly arbitrary. Their accounts would be analyzed for instances of something they had not addressed directly—for example, use of different concepts, the extent of personal versus situational attributions.

Thus, what for one researcher is a methodological problem may be the phenomenon of interest for another. Research about attraction and partner choice that included Cathy's and Michael's accounts would need to address reliability problems arising from memory limitations and attributional biases. Present dissatisfaction with the relationship is likely to dampen recall of happier times; Michael might have a much better memory for detail; and both of them could be biased in attributing mistakes that they have made to circumstances beyond their control. However, if the point is to conduct research into memory effects or attribution differences, then their accounts could provide valuable examples of these phenomena, to be compared with others from a participant population.

The foregoing comparison between topic and consruction of meaning might also be termed a distinction between *what* and *how,* or between content and process. In the study of social problems this is a division that can cause investigators to don different hats, and the dinner party excerpt suggests issues belonging to both sides of this divide. Thus, the topic orientation (the *what* or content) could lead to getting accounts from the Millers and the Stones and other couples on, say, "what we fight about," "changes in our relationship," "our dual-career marriage." The construction of meaning orientations (the *how* or process) indicates accounts sought out to reveal, for example, errors of logic, ordinary explanations of cause and responsibility, cognitive scripts and schemas, social persuasion processes—that is, accounts in which the actual topic of discourse does not matter primarily. For example, the investigator might be interested in comparing insider (the Stones) and outsider (the Millers) constructions of a social event (the argument) or in how interdependence (as may occur over 5 years of married life) affects attributions of cause and responsibility for personal behavior.

In studies focusing on topic, the subject matter of accounts can be expected to elucidate research findings (e.g., in-depth case studies for an investigation of married life after 5 years; a corpus of accounts to be used in a typology of arguments) and may even constitute the sum data. Such accounts may be treated something like the evidence of witnesses in a courtroom (the Stones lived through it; the Millers saw it happen). However, it is important that the problematic aspects of accounts discussed earlier be allowed for at each stage of the study: Are they lying or mistaken? Were they asked fair questions and are they sufficiently at ease on the witness stand to tell their story?

In studies focusing on construction of meaning, accounts become samples or exhibits. They show instances of the phenomenon being studied, and this is why they are of value, not because of their credibility or lack of it. For example, extracts from accounts by Cathy and Michael may reveal that they have different scripts for domestic chores, Cathy's being much more thorough and detailing daily repetitive tasks about which Michael's script is vague. Or their accounts might each contain far more negative attributions about their partner than about themselves; the discrepancy must call the accuracy of each into question, but again, this would not detract from their value in a study comparing attributions of discontented and contented couples.

Getting People to Give Their Account

Accounting openly requires conditions of safety and trust, especially when intimate relationships are being discussed. Why should the Stones trust an investigator with details of their private life, and will they understate negative aspects if only because people tend to present themselves in a favorable light? Suppose the Stones' verbal fight became violent; why should the Millers breach the confidentiality of their friendship with the Stones by giving an account of what they saw and what they know about the relationship, or even if they are not close, why risk the loss of goodwill?

To minimize these obstacles, it may be appropriate to tell the participants what the research is about. Advising participants of the research rationale and objectives can be, first, reassuring and, second, motivating if the research issue interests or concerns them. For instance, the dinner party foursome might care sufficiently about the high divorce rate to cooperate in research into relationship repair. Participants may find that the research is of some personal value to them, for instance, in terms of self-growth (Wilkinson, 1981) or airing grievances and reaching understanding (Weber et al., 1987), and this in itself will motivate cooperativeness. Also, participants tend to be more motivated when they are involved not as subjects but as colleagues.

However, in many cases it may be important that participants do not know what the research is about. Revealing the issue of investigation can introduce "demand characteristics." If a participant knows the researcher's hypothesis, it is likely to influence the way in which she or he completes the task. Suppose comparison of wives' and husbands' perspectives is at issue; the participants might consciously or otherwise alter their accounts to support whatever view they hold about sex differences. Temporary deception or concealment of the purpose might be necessary to avoid the risk of either conforming with or sabotaging the researcher's goals.

As is often the case, the Millers and the Stones may be asked to tell their story in an interview setting. Where their own views and personal experience are sought, and especially if detail and in-depth reflection are required, such an interview needs to be conducted with great care, in conditions likely to elicit an unhampered, forthcoming account. Clearly, the interviewer should avoid revealing his or her own assumptions and value judgments. Questions should be open, that is, ones that do not suggest what the answer might be and that are general enough to invite a full and free response rather than a specific and limited one.

More tricky is avoidance of commonly held biases. In the sample research problem of the Stones, for example, the quarrel is about domestic chores, a topic so centered on conventional sex-role divisions of responsibility that it hardly makes sense to speak to both partners about it in the same language. Mansfield and Collard (1988) discuss how they were careful to ask the same questions of both men and women, sometimes with puzzled reactions.

> It may seem strange to the respondent if he or she discovers they are being asked identical questions. For example, in order to discover "who does what in the home," if the interviewer asks wives one set of questions based on

traditional notions about their domestic behaviour, and their husbands a different set, also in accordance with their domestic performance, then it might be thought that the interviewer shared the assumptions that certain tasks were always performed by women, and others exclusively by men. . . . It was hoped that this approach would preclude automatic responses in line with traditional views. Nevertheless . . . this was challenged by some couples [who suspected] a bias on our part toward perceiving them as two separate individuals rather than a married pair. (p. 38)

Thus, participants can be alienated by procedures they do not understand, and investigators not only need to avoid bringing their own assumptions into procedures but also need to be sensitive to any that respondents bring. Similarly, precautions in interpreting account data should include a verification procedure such as a follow-up interview containing further questions about issues not clear or discussion of what was said to clarify and extend the content and to provide a further opportunity to address the original questions.

Suppose Cathy and Michael are interviewed separately for their version of the dinner party incident and then an account is requested from James and Holly Miller, each on different occasions. It is feasible that the first participant will talk to the others about what was said and that their subsequent accounts will be influenced. Perhaps James sympathizes with Michael because he remembers similar rows or perhaps one of the Millers is infatuated with one of the Stones; such circumstances could be reasons for offering a confirmatory explanation when their turn comes to assist with the research.

Interviewing parties jointly is no solution because each is likely to influence what the other says simply by being present. Mansfield & Collard (1988) experimented with joint and separate interviews in a pilot study. Interviewing partners together yielded what they describe as "consensus accounts in which one spouse took the lead . . . and then sought confirmation from the other [thus negotiating] an 'official' version" (p. 44). However, in separate interviews on different occasions, "it was clear that the partner who was interviewed last had already been primed by the other, with the unsatisfactory result that those interviews had the feel of prepared statements" (p. 44). Separate but simultaneous interviews were decided upon, resulting sometimes, in cases where no other rooms were available, in perching on the edge of the bathtub to listen to a respondent. For the same reasons, Blumstein and Schwartz (1983) also did their share of "bathtub interviews"!

An alternative way to avoid reactivity-effects is to obtain accounts in situations that are conducive to privacy and honesty. Burnett (1986) contacted participants by letter only and obtained accounts in the form of "letters to a confidant." This procedure simulated conditions of trust and openness and discouraged the censoring of content that can occur in more vulnerable public conditions, for instance, when an unfamiliar researcher rather than a trusted friend requests appraisal of a personal relationship. A letter-writing procedure (or, similarly, a diary-procedure; see Chapter 8) might be more suitable than interviewing for a research question of potential embarrassment to the Millers and the Stones (e.g., what feelings the three others evoke in each participant).

The Millers are likely to have a different perspective on the Stones' implied marital difficulties, and Cathy and Michael, in this excerpt at least, indicate they each now view their past and present in dissimilar terms. Such differences in perspectives are symptomatic of the subjectivity of narratives and accounts. This does not make all accounts equally unreliable, however. Suppose Michael packed his suitcase and left home that night, and all four are later asked why. The Stones can report on the row that preceded this event, and Cathy can explain how the dispute escalated later on into a runaway argument, perhaps offering her interpretation of what Michael was thinking and feeling as he grabbed his suitcase; but clearly it is Michael who is in the best position to explain his departure, because it was his decision and his emotions and reasoning that led to it.

That there are such differences between various accounts of the same phenomenon poses some issues of investigative interest (Duck & Sants, 1983; Fincham, 1985; Chapter 3, this volume). A number of personal-relationship researchers have remarked on the contrasts between accounts obtained from respective partners (e.g., Blumstein & Schwartz, 1983; Weiss, 1975.) Mansfield & Collard (1988) refer to "his and her narratives"; experiences and interpretations differ so that "it can appear as if there are two different relationships cohabiting in one marriage" (p. 39). Yet some couples see themsleves as a unit and are therefore likely to underplay differences when in each other's hearing.

The Stones have 5 years to look back on. Their current perspective is likely to play tricks on their memory, perhaps coloring the emotional quality of what they recall (Miell, 1987), perhaps highlighting similar occasions of conflict and dissatisfaction. With regard to accounts, Shotter's (1987) cautions regarding the psychologist's fallacy and ex post facto reporting are relevent here. When people look back on an event, their construction will be influenced by subsequent occurrences. Therefore, the meaning imbued to event A is taken partly from event B, which occurred later. However, at the time of event A, without the hindsight from event B, that same construction was not possible. It is unlikely that a person looking back on A will avoid utilizing the extra sense derived from B to interpret A, yet they are unlikely to be aware of this fallacy in any claim they consequently make.

An example of such ex post facto reasoning is indicated by Mansfield and Collard (1988):

The researcher has to enter the biography of a respondent at a chosen point. . . . When married people discuss their courtship . . . they are bound to be affected by the knowledge that they are discussing their own route to married life. Thus, for example, when a bride remembers a disagreement in the early days of courting, her account of it is almost certain to differ from the one she would have given nearer the time it actually happened [and] her story of a disagreement with a boy she was only dating will be very different from one about a disagreement during courtship with the man she actually married. And this is not simply a matter of selective memory operating through rose-tinted spectacles. . . . The meaning for her of these events is bound to be coloured to some extent by their different contexts. (pp. 35–36)

Other methodological aspects of retrospective reporting are discussed in detail by Metts, Sprecher, and Cupsch in Chapter 9 of this volume.

Conclusion

Collecting accounts can be regarded as a variant or extension of interviewing as a method, but it is a less orthodox procedure for disciplines with an experimental background. In an interdisciplinary investigation of social interaction there is plenty of scope for the gains that can be achieved by widening access to data in this way. Developments in social science, including paradigm changes and more sophisticated data analysis procedures, suggest even more promise for a method that is gaining in respectability. Many complications remain to challenge the researcher. However, to a large extent the difficulties and complexities of it as a method are those that beset each person's attempt to represent his or her view and to attain meaning in life. In circular fashion, what we learn about accounting as a pheonmenon (Burnett et al., 1987) extends appreciation of accounting as a method. Understanding, interpretation, self-ascription and whatever individuals try to address in giving accounts make demands on the insights and comprehension of account-recipients. Thus, accounting as a method is problematic, just as is accounting as a personal and social event.

References

Antaki, C. (1987). Performed and unperformable: A guide to accounts of relationships. In R. Burnett, P. McGhee, & D. D. Clarke (Eds.), *Accounting for relationships: Explanation, representation and knowledge* (pp. 97–113). London: Methuen.

Antaki, C., & Fielding, G. (1981). Research on ordinary explanations. In C. Antaki (Ed.), *The psychology of ordinary explanations of social behaviour* (pp. 27–55). London: Academic Press.

Armistead, N. (1974). Experience in everyday life. In N. Armistead (Ed.), *Reconstructing social psychology* (pp. 115–132). Harmondsworth, Middlesex, England: Penguin.

Backman, C. W. (1979). Epilogue: A new paradigm? In G. P. Ginsburg (Ed.), *Emerging strategies in social psychological research* (pp. 289–303). Chichester, UK: Wiley.

Bell, R. R. (1981). *Worlds of friendship*. London: Sage.

Blumstein, P., & Schwartz, P. (1983). *American couples: Money, work, sex*. New York: Morrow.

Bott, E., (1957). *Family and social network*. London: Tavistock.

Burnett, R. (1986). *Conceptualization of personal relationships*. Unpublished doctoral dissertation, University of Oxford.

Burnett, R. (1987). Reflection in personal relationships. In R. Burnett, P. McGhee, & D. D. Clarke (Eds.), *Accounting for relationships: explanation, representation and knowledge* (pp. 74–93). London: Methuen.

Burnett, R., McGhee, P., & Clarke, D. D. (Eds.). (1987). *Accounting for relationships: Explanation, representation and knowledge*. London: Methuen.

Carey, P. (1989) *Oscar and Lucinda*. London: Faber and Faber.

De Waele, J-P., & Harré, R. (1979). Autobiography as a psychological method. In G. P. Ginsburg (Ed.), *Emerging strategies in social psychological research* (pp. 177–224). Chichester, UK: Wiley.

Duck, S. W. (1982). A topography of relationship disengagement and dissolution. In S. W. Duck (Ed.), *Personal relationships: Vol. 4. Dissolving personal relationships* (pp. 1–30). London: Academic Press.

Duck, S. W., & Sants, H. (1983). On the origin of the specious: Are personal relationships really interpersonal states? *Journal of Social and Clinical Psychology, 1*, 27–41

Fincham, F. D. (1985). Attributions in close relationships. In J. H. Harvey & G. Weary (Eds.), *Attribution: Basic Issues and Applications* (pp. 203–234). London: Academic Press.

Gergen, K. J., & Gergen, M. M. (1987). Narratives of relationship. In R. Burnett, P. McGhee, & D. D. Clarke (Eds.), *Accounting for relationships: Explanation, representation and knowledge* (pp. 269–288). London: Methuen.

Harré, R. (1984). *Personal being*. Cambridge, MA: Harvard University Press.

Harré, R., & Secord, P. F. (1972). *The explanation of social behaviour*. Oxford: Blackwell.

Harvey, J. H., Turnquist, D. C., & Agostinelli, G. (1988). Identifying attributions in oral and written explanations. In C. Antaki (Ed.), *Analysing everyday explanation* (pp. 32–42). London: Sage.

Hollway, W. (1989). *Subjectivity and method in psychology: Gender, meaning and science*. London: Sage.

Hudson, L. (1972) *The cult of the fact*. London: Cape.

Kelly, G. A. (1955). *The psychology of personal constructs*. New York: Norton.

Mansfield, P., & Collard, J. (1988). *The beginning of the rest of our life: A portrait of newly-wed marriage*. London: MacMillan.

Matza, D. (1969). *Becoming deviant*. Englewood Cliffs, NJ: Prentice-Hall.

Miell, D. E. (1987). Remembering relationship development: Constructing a context for interactions. In R. Burnett, P. McGhee, & D. D. Clarke (Eds.), *Accounting for relationships: Explanation, representation and knowledge* (pp. 60–73). London: Methuen.

Rapoport, R., & Rapoport, R. (1971). *Dual-career families*. Harmondsworth, Middlesex, England: Penguin

Roiser, M. (1974). Asking silly questions. In N. Armistead (Ed.), *Reconstructing social psychology* (pp. 101–114). Harmondsworth, Middlesex, England: Penguin.

Rubin, L. B. (1983). *Intimate strangers*. New York: Harper & Row.

Sabini, J., & Silver, M. (1982). *Moralities of everyday life*. Oxford: Oxford University Press.

Scott, M. B., & Lyman, S. M. (1968). Accounts. *American Sociological Review, 33*, 46–62.

Semin, G. R., & Manstead, A. S. R. (1983). *The accountability of conduct: A social psychological analysis*. London: Academic Press.

Sheehy, Gail (1982). *Pathfinders*. New York: Morrow.

Shotter, J. (1981). Telling and reporting: Prospective and retrospective uses of self-ascriptions. In C. Antaki (Ed.), *The psychology of ordinary explanations of social behavior* (pp. 157–181). London: Academic Press.

Shotter, J. (1987). The social construction of an 'us': Problems of accountability and narratology. In R. Burnett, P. McGhee, & D. D. Clarke (Eds.), *Accounting for relationships: Explanation, representation and knowledge* (pp. 225–247). London: Methuen.

Vaughan, D. (1987). *Uncoupling: How relationships come apart*. New York: Vintage.

Weber, A. L., Harvey, J. H., & Stanley, M. (1987). The nature and motivations of accounts for failed relationships. In R. Burnett, P. McGhee, & D. D. Clarke (Eds.), *Accounting for relationships: Explanation, representation and knowledge* (pp. 114–133). London: Methuen.

Weiss, R. S. (1975) *Marital Separation*. New York: Basic.

Wilkinson, S. (1981). Personal constructs and private explanations. In C. Antaki (Ed.), *The psychology of ordinary explanations of social behaviour* (pp. 205–219). London: Academic Press.

Wilkinson, S. (1987). Explorations of self and other in developing relationships. In R. Burnett, P. McGhee, & D. D. Clarke (Eds.), *Accounting for relationships: Explanation, representation and knowledge* (pp. 40–59). London: Methuen.

Chapter 8

Diaries and Logs

STEVE DUCK

When a biographer, full of hope, obtained sole rights of access to the diaries of King George V of England on his death in 1936, the biographer's expectation was that he would gain insight into the monarch's views of the powerful and significant persons with whom the king had been acquainted during 25 years on the English throne. The diaries would produce a unique perspective on world events during a period that covered the First World War, the Great Depression and the Russian Revolution, in which King George's cousin (and look-alike) Tsar Nicholas, had been executed. Instead, the biographer found that each year's diary petered out around January 10th, after 9 days of banal entries such as "Rainy," "Snow again today," and "Cold."

Nonetheless, daily or regular reports have long been recognized as useful, if sometimes eccentric, records of both momentous and trivial events and experiences but have only recently been recognized as having value to the social scientist in the quest for tools to understand social interaction. Found by chance or through the research effort of individuals, such regular reports in diaries can be analyzed; they are social artifacts that have their own validity and usefulness as historical records. Indeed, interesting work has been done explaining the unstructured, casual personal diaries, personal letters, and journals kept by the unremitting recordist with a view either to posterity or to enhanced personal recall, or merely to "ventilation" at a time of trouble (e.g., Rosenblatt, 1983; Mamali, 1989).

Although a social scientist can apply his or her skills to such casual artifacts, much more useful are the self-reported data of subjects whose recording has been intentionally prompted to address a question that a researcher has in mind. For one thing, it is clear that if diaries are to be used in a way that encourages subjects to produce more interesting data than King George V did, then the diaries must be structured, regularized, and made to bear on the issues in which the investigator has an interest. Also, if the experimenter's intent is to obtain an accurate or representative survey of the normal experience of the subjects, then such data should be gathered regularly and frequently, not just on the whim of the subject or when the subject feels that there is something particular to be described. Finally, if the data are to have maximum value for social science, then they have to be in a format that can be used in, and compared across, different situations.

The traditional "Dear Diary . . ." or ship's logs are thus not what is meant in this chapter. Nor is meant here the inculcation of persons to take up diary writing, letter writing, or other similar techniques, which have been successfully used by other researchers on a variety of populations from adolescents upwards (e.g., Brydon, 1982; Mamali, 1989). Finally, this chapter does not deal with logged diarylike records of behavior in naturalistic settings, such as are often used in very sophisticated coding studies with children (e.g., Sants, 1984). Instead of any of these possibilities, the present chapter deals with self-reported interaction logs structured by an experimenter with an interest in specific sorts of social interaction or interpersonal behavior.

Two Diary Log Methods Compared

Figures 8.1 and 8.2 depict two diary log report forms dealt with in this chapter. From Figures 8.1 and 8.2 it can be seen that diary logs ask subjects to report on certain selected facts about their interaction and also to record some of their judgments about the qualities of the interaction that they have been involved with. The diary log in Figure 8.1, the Rochester Interaction Record (RIR), was pioneered and developed by Wheeler and Nezlek (1977) and is a basic record of the social participations that the subject reports. It is mostly concerned with factual information about the time and place of the interaction, number of partners present, length of interaction, and so forth and includes some evaluative scales about the interaction. The Iowa Communication Record (ICR) is shown in Figure 8.2 and was introduced by Duck and Rutt (1988) 11 years after the RIR appeared. It further requires subjects to go into details about the processes of their social interaction itself, especially the communication and conversations that occurred. To that end, subjects are required to give their estimates of the impact of such conversations on the future of their relationships with the persons in the interaction. I will now briefly consider each record in turn.

Date _____ Time _____ A.M. ___ Length ___ hrs ___ mins

P.M. ___

Initials ___ ___ ___   If more than 3, others:

Sex   ___ ___ ___   # of females _____ # of males _____

Intimacy:		superficial	1 2 3 4 5 6 7	meaningful
I disclosed:		very little	1 2 3 4 5 6 7	a great deal
Other disclosed:		very little	1 2 3 4 5 6 7	a great deal
Quality:		unpleasant	1 2 3 4 5 6 7	a great deal
Satisfaction:	less than expected		1 2 3 4 5 6 7	more than expected
Initiation:		I initiated	1 2 3 4 5 6 7	other initiated
Influence:	I influenced more		1 2 3 4 5 6 7	other influenced more
Nature:	Work	Task	Pastime	Conversation	Date

FIGURE 8.1. The Rochester Interaction Record (RIR). From *"Loneliness, Social interaction and sex roles"* by L. Wheeler, H. T. Reis, and J. Nezlek, 1983, *Journal of Personality and Social Psychology, 45*, pp. 943–953. Copyright 1983 by the American Psychological Association. Reprinted by permission.

THE ROCHESTER INTERACTION RECORD

The institution and development by Wheeler & Nezlek (1977) of the Rochester Interaction Record (RIR) has stimulated much interest in records of social participation and their correlates, antecedents, and consequences. Using the RIR, Wheeler, Nezlek, Reis and their colleagues have illuminated several aspects of social interaction. For instance, physically attractive persons seem to experience social participation differently from the less attractive, in that their social participation rates are higher and judged more enjoyable (Reis, Nezlek, & Wheeler, 1980). Furthermore, lonely people have unusual patterns of social interaction, and these are coupled with unusual beliefs about those participations, especially since lonely people tend to denigrate interactions and *see* them as less rewarding than do nonlonely persons, even when both types of person are reporting similar levels or frequencies of interaction (Reis, Wheeler, Kernis, Spiegel, & Nezlek, 1985). Finally, men and women experience social participation in different ways, with women being rated more enjoyable partners and more significant interactants by almost everyone (Reis, Senchak, & Solomon, 1985). Thus, if we map out social participation and pay close attention to the patterns that can be found, we start to get a glimpse of some important differences that characterize the social worlds of subjects of different genders, levels of social involvement, or social attractiveness.

IOWA COMMUNICATION RECORD

Please describe your communication activities. Use one page for each conversation. A conversation is considered to be talk with one other person for 10 minutes or more.

Your I.D.: _____ **Age:** ____ **Sex:** M or F (circle one)

1. Date of Interaction:

   _____   _____
   mo.   day

2. Time of Interaction:

   _____   AM or PM
   hour   (circle one)

3. Length of Interaction:

   _____   _____
   hour   min

4. Description of Interactional Partner:
   M or F (circle one)

   _____   _____
   Initials   Age

5. Length of time you have known partner in years
   and months:

   _____   _____
   year   mo.

6. How would you describe the nature of your relationship? (circle one):

1	2	3	4
Stranger	Acquaintance	Friend	Best Friend

5	6	
Boyfriend/ Girlfriend	Relative	Other: _____

7. What type of communication? (circle one)

1	2	3
Face-to-face	Long-distance telephone	Local telephone

8. Would you consider the interaction public or private? (circle one and state place)

1	2	
Public	Private	_____
		Where

9. Were others present?   Yes or No

10. What was the role of talk? Indicate the extent to which you agree with the following:

    This was talk just for talk's sake.

1	2	3	4	5	6	7	8	9
Strong agreement							Strong disagreement	

FIGURE 8.2. The Iowa Communication Record (ICR).

Main purpose of talk was to accomplish some task. (Such as gaining information to complete a project, or solve a problem.)

| 1 | 2 | 3 | 4 | 5 | 6 | 7 | 8 | 9 |

Strong agreement   Strong disagreement

Main purpose of talk was to facilitate some social objective. (Such as talk surrounding sports activity or party.)

| 1 | 2 | 3 | 4 | 5 | 6 | 7 | 8 | 9 |

Strong agreement   Strong disagreement

Main purpose of talk was to facilitate the relationship. (Such as talk to become better acquainted or resolve differences.)

| 1 | 2 | 3 | 4 | 5 | 6 | 7 | 8 | 9 |

Strong agreement   Strong disagreement

11. Describe the main topic of talk: _____

_____

12. Were there other topics?   Yes   or   No   If yes, indicate the number of topics you think were addressed in the talk: _____

_____

13. What were you doing *right before* the conversation occurred? (circle one or more)

Working	Eating	Driving	Study
Childcare	Housework	Watching TV	Reading
Listening to music	Talking to someone else		

_____
other

14. Were you involved in any activities *during* the conversation? Yes   or   No

If yes, please indicate which of the above:

_____

15. What did you do *after* the conversation (as above)? _____

_____

16. Was the interaction *planned* or *unplanned?* (circle one)

17. If planned, indicate the extent to which you were looking forward to the meeting:

| 1 | 2 | 3 | 4 | 5 | 6 | 7 | 8 | 9 |

Looking forward to meeting   Dreading meeting

18. Who initiated the talk (circle one):

| You | Partner | Seemed mutual | Accidental | Not clear |

FIGURE 8.2. (cont.)

19. Who seemed to control the conversation; for example, who decided topics of talk?

   You   Partner   Seemed mutual   Accidental   Not clear

20. Who made moves to end the conversation?

   You   Partner   Seemed mutual   Accidental   Not clear

21. Describe the quality of communication:

1	2	3	4	5	6	7	8	9
Relaxed								Strained

1	2	3	4	5	6	7	8	9
Impersonal								Personal

1	2	3	4	5	6	7	8	9
Attentive								Poor listening

1	2	3	4	5	6	7	8	9
Formal								Informal

1	2	3	4	5	6	7	8	9
In-depth								Superficial

1	2	3	4	5	6	7	8	9
Smooth								Difficult

1	2	3	4	5	6	7	8	9
Guarded								Open

1	2	3	4	5	6	7	8	9
Great deal of understanding								Great deal of misunderstanding

1	2	3	4	5	6	7	8	9
Free of communication breakdowns								Laden with communication breakdowns

1	2	3	4	5	6	7	8	9
Free of conflict								Laden with conflict

22. Indicate the extent to which you think the talk was interesting:

1	2	3	4	5	6	7	8	9
Interesting								Boring

23. Indicate the extent to which you came away satisfied with the interaction:

1	2	3	4	5	6	7	8	9
Satisfied								Not satisfied

24. How valuable was this conversation to you for your life *right now*?

1	2	3	4	5	6	7	8	9
Extremely important								Not important at all

25. How valuable was this conversation for your future?

1	2	3	4	5	6	7	8	9
Extremely important								Not important at all

FIGURE 8.2. (cont.)

26. Indicate the extent to which this talk resulted in a change of your *attitude:*

-3	-2	-1	0	+1	+2	+3
Negative change			No change		Positive change	

27. Indicate the extent to which this talk resulted in a change of your *behavior:*

-3	-2	-1	0	+1	+2	+3
Stopped behavior			No change		Increased behavior	

Describe behavior change: _____

_____

28. Indicate the extent to which this talk changed your *thinking* or *ideas?*

0	1	2	3	4	5	6	7	8	9
No change								Great change	

Describe change in thinking/ideas: _____

_____

29. Indicate the extent to which this talk resulted in a change of your *feelings?*

-3	-2	-1	0	+1	+2	+3
Negative change			No change		Positive	

Describe change in feelings: _____

_____

30. indicate the extent to which this talk resulted in a change of your *relationship:*

-3	-2	-1	0	+1	+2	+3
Much more distant			No change		Much more close	

31. Indicate the extent to which this talk changed your *attraction* toward partner:

-3	-2	-1	0	+1	+2	+3
Great decreased attraction			No change		Greatly increased attraction	

32. On an average day how many people do you talk to? _____

33. Out of the total amount of time you spend conversing per week, what percentage of that time do you think is spent talking with this person? _____ %

34. How intimate was the interaction?

1	2	3	4	5	6	7	8	9
Not really intimate							Very intimate	

35. How intimate is the relationship, by and large?

1	2	3	4	5	6	7	8	9
Very intimate							Not really intimate	

36. How satisfied are you with the realtionship as a whole?

1	2	3	4	5	6	7	8	9
Very dissatisfied							Very satisfied	

THANK YOU!

FIGURE 8.2. (cont.)

The RIR opened up many new avenues of research and began to focus scholars on the importance of the daily routine behaviors that make up everyday life. Before the RIR was created, we really knew very little about these mundane details that are, for all of us, an extremely large part of life as we live it and experience it psychologically. Beyond such pioneering of the geography of daily life, the RIR was also used by a number of researchers to test hypotheses about relationship development; further uses remain to be added and developed as researchers apply such techniques to issues in social support, health, loneliness, daily stress, and a variety of other topics in social interaction research (see Berg & Piner, 1990, and Bolger, DeLongis, Kessler, & Schilling, 1989, for examples of such applications).

However, the RIR does not give any close scrutiny to the means of the communication through which social interaction is carried on; nor does it attend to the memories for communication that embody and ultimately represent those interactions and conversations in the minds of the persons who have them (Duck & Pond, 1989a). Indeed, the RIR seems to relegate communication, speech, and the oil of everyday life (namely, talk) to the role of mere channels through which social participation is accomplished, rather than as something that impacts on and moderates social interaction. Thus, while the RIR provides a valuable starting point from which to create a descriptive and theoretical base for understanding social interaction, the general approach clearly needs to be extended to include communication directly if we are to gain an understanding of the mechanisms and processes that provide the engine for interactive social behavior and interpersonal activity.

THE IOWA COMMUNICATION RECORD

The Iowa Communication Record (ICR) is a structured self-report form on which respondents record their recollection of conversations. It is derived from a theoretical context in which talk or discourse is seen as an important symbolic representation of people's lives to themselves and others, rather than as a mere channel or duct for individual cognitive activity to be conveyed to the world at large (Duck & Pond, 1989a). It focuses on the communicative elements of the encounter, thus implicitly treating discourse as something more than a simple instrumental conduit for thought, and recognizes that discourse has dynamics and a system all of its own, just as communication departments have known for years.

Subjects are, of course, asked to report on such matters as the day of the week, date, time, and length of the interaction; the nature of the partner with whom it was held (e.g., sex, age of partner); and the type of relationship (stranger, acquaintance, friend, best friend, lover/boyfriend/girlfriend, relative). However, the emphasis falls on a variety of measures of the subject's recollection of the conversational content of the interaction and on subjective measures of the conversation's quality, purpose, and impact on the relationship (Duck & Rutt, 1988). The full record includes sets of questions about the conversational context, that is to say, questions concerning the partners' activities immediately preceding, during, and after conversation. As can be seen from Figure 8.2, these activities include such items as watching TV, studying, and eating a meal.

The ICR consists of 36 questions or rating scales and generally takes about 20 minutes to complete on the first occasion, but it is completed much more rapidly after that, once subjects get used to it. Subjects completing the ICR, as do subjects completing the RIR, report that it is a meaningful and involving task that they take seriously—a report borne out by checks on the reliability of some of the subjects' responses on "factual" matters, such as the number of persons spoken with during a week; these responses typically yield reliability coefficients of above .95 and often as high as .99, despite the fact that in some studies the subjects are reporting over a 7-week time span (Duck & Rutt, 1988; Duck, Rutt, Hurst & Strejc, in press; Duck, Cortez, Hurst, & Strejc, 1989). The ICR typically breaks into nine factors, of which the most reliable, interpretable, and important are *Communication Quality, Change* brought about by the interaction, and *Impact* of the interaction (Duck et al., in press). The ICR is a long instrument that is initially complex to fill out and difficult to analyze, but it also gives us very detailed information about the communications that occurred.

The ICR thus retains some of the measures of "quantitative" aspects of interaction that are included in the RIR but also incorporates some direct measures of communicative elements of the interaction and measures of "qualitative" perceptions of the interaction. The RIR is quite short, which gives it some advantages over the ICR (such as ease of administration and analysis) and also some disadvantages (such as lower levels of detailed information about the encounters).

On the face of it, both instruments are rather similar conceptually and have essentially the same goals. However, there is a key difference found in the implicit treatment given to talk in social interaction. As we shall see below, such differences can be dismissed as mere methodological detail, or we can look further beneath the surface and see important theoretical assumptions in each method that ultimately make them quite different, as argued in general terms, in Chapter 1 of this book.

Appropriate Uses of Diary Logs

Even in the loose terms of the description above, it is evident that diary logs have a number of appropriate research uses and some inherent problems. It may not be immediately apparent that they also, at base, have some fairly radical assumptions that have not yet been fully discussed and understood in the wider scholarly community. Such assumptions are based on the fact that we are dealing with reports of subjective experiences, personal feelings, and phenomenal representations. We are essentially asking what each person sees from his or her own vantage point, and because the perspective of that vantage point (experience of a relationship) is itself a subjective experience, two persons in the same interaction can nevertheless legitimately report it in different ways in some respects, since they are reporting not only "facts" about it, but also their *experience* of it. Diaries will thus at some point face us with the issue of differences between interactants in perception and recall of what were, objectively, the same events (Duck, 1990). Thus, while we would expect subjects to agree about such matters as where they met and who was there with them, there is no justification for the expectation that subjects will have felt precisely the same way about what happened, what they discussed, whether they got a fair shake, and so on. With this in mind, therefore (and also reminding ourselves of the issue of the Stones' quarrel), we can look at some approriate uses for such diaries in the study of interaction.

Many scholars, such as Hinde (1979), have noted that much of the good botanical, biological, anthropological, and ethological work began with careful and systematic entry of phenomena in diaries, logs, or report formats that identified matters that later became subjects of theoretical debates and interpretations. A good descriptive base has traditionally been a hallmark of science from the crude days of alchemy to later times. By contrast, studies of social interaction have tended to leap straight into theoretical explanation for events specially observed in the laboratory on the basis of the experimenter's belief that such events are instructive or theoretically valuable. As was written over 10 years ago:

> The regular and naturally-occurring patterns of social behaviour are very poorly logged, let alone understood. We have failed to build up precisely those detailed records of normal patterns of social activity that would help us to identify the regularities that need to be explained and to assess the extents to which laboratory-based methods actually reflect those real-life regularities and frequently-occurring events. Perhaps, by focussing on striking behaviour, laboratory studies actually exaggerate the contours of life, to which our theories are therefore more likely to give unrepresentative prominence. (Duck, 1980, p. 232).

Clearly essential at some point in scientific work is some detailed geographical and topographical knowledge of the everyday events that we social scientists seek to explain by our theories. Otherwise, we may get too far from the reality that they are supposed to represent. Researchers' observation of subjects' daily behaviors is, however, often tedious and too time-consuming to be acceptable or practical whereas recording—especially unreactive or surreptitious recording—of daily behavior can get researchers into ethical quicksands. On the other hand, a method whereby the subjects themselves *regularly* record their own behavior has some advantages. For example, the subjects can do the self-reporting in their own time at their own convenience (subject to some experimenter-imposed contraints, perhaps). The subject can report what is actually felt while it is still "hot," no invasive measurement techniques are involved, the flow of the interaction is not interrupted, and subjects are not observed by anyone external to the interaction while it is occurring.

On the other hand, simple free recall is constrained by the experimenter's formatting of questions and the only data are based on the subject's interpretation of what occurred, from his or her own perspective, without benefit of being able to check any other observer's reports of what happened. However, such diary techniques are not *inherently* incapable of being used in ways that deal with these points. Recently, Duck and Pond (1989b) have conducted studies where subjects interact while being observed and recorded and *then* fill out their diary log, which can then be compared to the logs produced by other observers (along with the log from the interaction partner, of course).

LONGITUDINAL STUDY

Work using diary logs seems initially to be most useful, then, as a provider of records of the routines of life and as an indicator of the character of cross-sections or slices of a person's "average day." A more advanced use of such work has even been to explore the development of relationships over extended periods of time. Longitudinal studies have been carried out with the RIR to explore the ways in which reports of social interaction change as relationships develop (e.g., Baxter & Wilmot, 1986; Duck & Miell, 1982, 1986). Such work significantly propels the technique out of the context of its development by applying the RIR to longer-term relationships than those originally studied (which were quite deliberately chosen to be relatively isolated short interactions not particularly embedded in any context of relational change).

The RIR has proved very useful in this new context and has identified behaviors and attitudes to interaction in the long term that were previously absent from theories of relationship development. For instance, Miell (1984) showed that persons' daily reports/experiences of their relationships are quite markedly at variance with the long-term recollections of the course of those relationships. Long-term retrospective or prospective graphs of development are nevertheless often represented by subjects as a smooth stylized curve even when day-to-day development was experienced quite roughly.

This longitudinal work adds to our understanding of some of the dynamics of relationships and raises interesting new research questions (about, for instance, the psychological processes by which rough experiences are transmuted into smooth, stylized reports). It also extends our knowledge beyond the isolated social interactions studied out of relational context and creates the potential for studies of particular interactions in context (such as in the case of the Stones, in this volume's sample research problem) and the whole gamut of issues about creation of relationships, their development, and decline (Duck, 1988). Thus, longitudinal studies create another corner of the pictorial canvas that the RIR so interestingly began to sketch out. Although several later workers, such as Baxter, Wilmot, Duck, and Miell, happened to have interests in communication, they used the RIR as their research tool. Now that the ICR has also been developed, we can add the ICR as an auxiliary to investigate the communicative characteristics and dynamics of growing, stable, and disengaging relationships and thus capture information about the ways in which conversation changes in, and affects the experience of, relating.

EXPERIENCE IN PERSPECTIVE

The consideration that diary logs assess *experiences* of relating brings us to another appropriate, but so far underdeveloped, aspect of diary logs. Experiences are had by individuals; individuals have their own (often—but not always—unique) ways of interpreting events, and these are subject to change, though unfortunately we do not yet fully understand whether, how, or why such change may be systematic in relationships. If we were to record the Stones' feelings and reports of their tiff at different times, for example, we may find that the topic is "hot" and involving at one time but is regarded at another time as merely an amusing example of the sorts of things that they willingly put up with in each other or even as an example of the way in which they maturely deal with conflict. Individuals' beliefs about interactions are undoubtedly subject to change and "recontextualization," but such issues have rarely been studied carefully and are a clear case where daily diaries could be used to unravel some of the enigmas.

Individuals' probable perspectival differences bring us to a deep theoretical issue in the use of diary logs: the matter of different perspectives on the interaction and the relationship, including the matter of the different perspectives that the same person can take of a given interaction as time goes by. As has already been suggested, there are a number of complex philosophical and epistemological assumptions underlying the use of the ICR. (These are not necessarily explicated by workers who use the RIR, although I feel that this is a tool so similar to the ICR that some of the same arguments can be made for it.) The major assumption is that when we come to determine the nature of relationships, we shall be dealing with a phenomenological issue as well as a behavioral one (Duck, 1990). That is to say, relationships exist only partly because the partners involve themselves in complex, enmeshed interactional sequences of behaviors within an encounter and also—a different point—in *related* sequences of interactions. Another important feature of relationships' existence stems from the fact that the partners *think* they are in a relationship and *see* the sequence as such. As Hinde (1979) indicated, there is a difference between a sequence of interactions and a relationship, although a relationship requires that there be a series of interactions lying beneath it. The difference was claimed by Duck and Sants (1983) to depend on the psychological attitude that the partners held towards their interactions or, to put it another way, the relationship existed in part because the partners developed a sense of "being in a relationship." To put this yet another way, a relationship is partly a mental construction; it is partly a set of beliefs held by partners about the nature of their interactions.

If this argument is accepted, then the use of diary logs is a necessary tool in our development of an understanding of both relationships per se and social interactions in relational context, since we need to get a clearer picture of the mental processes through which people construct this sense of being in a relationship. For example, it is as naive to assume that reports about a given interaction are "accurate" without thinking what this means, as it is to assume that a person's accounts of a given interaction will always be the same and will be unaffected by other aspects of his or her life. Thus, it is no surprise that people change their views of, for example, their first meeting as a result of changes in the emotional interior of the relationship (Duck & Miell, 1986). Also, we can reasonably assume that changes in a person's reported perspective reflect the operation of psychological processes that are functional for the development of the relationship, as when persons construct a history of their first encounter as a part of building the relationship—an account that serves to bind the relationship together and to produce a shared story of the origin of their togetherness. An account of their first meeting is very likely to change its character if ever the couple splits up, and in the subsequent version different characteristics of the partner are likely to be highlighted, featured, and "explained" (Weber, Harvey, & Stanley, 1987).

For important theoretical reasons it is also necessary to see how subjects' *recall* of communication influences their approach to those interactions by providing opportunities to recapitulate, ponder, or plan for the future (Miell, 1987). The theoretical reasons are that subjects are likely to recall conversations in ways that set the scene for future interactions: recall of interactions is not a purely historical enterprise but is also a way of delineating the essence of the relationship and making a statement about its future form. The Stones' views of their conflict would give us some insight into their respective projected futures for their relationship. However, repeated explorations of diary logs can be used to examine the way in which a person's construction of an event differs from one time to the next as a result of the person's individual goals or relational needs at the time of measurement.

For the sample research problem considered by contributors to this book, there would be some value in gathering data, using diary logs, from the Millers as well as the Stones, but there are also good reasons for expecting the resulting four sets of data to be complex and intriguing, rather than simple replicas of one another. This is more likely to be true in the case of the ICR than the RIR, since the ICR takes a greater number of qualitative assessments of the interactions than does the RIR. But in both cases the subject is required to spend some time recording the pseudo-objective or "factual" features of interactions. In the ICR subjects also provide indications of the communicational mechanisms by which they achieve their goals. In the context of the interaction between Cathy and Michael Stone, using diary logs would be especially important. In studying (even rapid) recall of argument we are likely to be presented with dramatic evidence that two partners to an interaction disagree about the occurrences in the interaction. For instance, Gottman (1989) has frequently reported that couples not only do not agree about who started a conflict but may also disagree about the point in time when it started, the precipitating event, and the ways in which the whole event can be segmented into parts. Each person construes the experience in different ways, then, not only in terms of blame or guilt but also in terms of the ways in which the flow of experience can be broken up. Such perspectival differences probably occur in *all* interactions, but we should especially be aware of this in the context of conflicts. However, it will be important for future researchers to establish the main dimensions along which divergent perspectives arise and to determine empirical relationships between particular elements of conflict and these divergences (e.g., to determine whether the main influence on different perspectives is to be found in perceived quality of interaction or in its control).

There is, then, an interesting issue here about the conceptualization of relationships from interaction, and it bears on the points made in Chapter 1 concerning the relationship between method of measurement on the one hand and "theory" on the other (namely, that the two are interdependent). If we are interested in finding out something of what goes on in subjects' minds during the whole process of argument and conflict, then part of our ultimate long-term purpose would be to study the changes that occur over time in perspective on, or recall of, conversation as a function of personality variables, perspective of the observer, communicative circumstances, or relational events. Thus, the study of the relationship of *recall* by one subject to another's recall might be one of our objectives—an objective that could easily be incorporated in our study of the argument between the Stones, with the Millers as witnesses, and of their four views of "the events" here.

The question of bias in recall, therefore, becomes a matter of investigation, rather than an assumption, and it cautions critics to wait until they have actual data before we embark on any discussion of the alleged problems, biases, or errors in retrospective data, such as are collected through the RIR and ICR. Assumptions of bias are more often made than proved, and the system through which such bias might arise, the form that it might take, or the precise shape of the influence that it might have on recall are all rather poorly understood, despite the frequency and miasmatic nature of the accusations against such data. As Duck and Rutt (1988) argued, "at present, researchers too readily accept the claim to bias without having systematic evidence of the nature of the alleged biases, their dynamics, or their exact effects." Thus, once again, the interdependence of theory/"story" on the one hand and measurement on the other is clearly evident (cf. Chapter 1). We should approach data collection with cautious skepticism about the "reality" with which we are dealing, particularly since the "reality" of an argument, such as the Stones', is a dramatic instance where the discrepancy between viewpoints is the essence of the case. I also believe that researchers need to carefully consider the effect of different observers' perspectives on relationships in order to clarify exactly what relationships *are* when they are represented partly in behavior and partly in mental representations that people carry around with them (Duck, 1990). It is hard to decide exactly what "objective" reality would be in a relationship, since we are accessing subjects' *perceptions* or reality and work has not yet been done with diary logs to establish the status of these data relative to other perspectives on reality (such as "objective" observers' perspectives). Future research on the nature of relational reality will provide many opportunities for careful thought about this issue (see Chapter 3), and many chances to develop the use of diary log methods.

Some Potential Methodological Problems with Diary Methods and Some That Aren't . . . or Not Simply Methodological Anyway

Like all methods, diary logs have certain pitfalls and problems that need to be balanced against the disadvantages by the potential user. The deciding factor about this balance is a question of what one wishes to learn by using the method. Diaries cannot tell the researcher about factors (such as blood pressure or point in the circadian rhythm) the subjects cannot directly experience but that may nevertheless influence their activity or the way they feel. Yet it is possible, and I think desirable, to understand the ways in which diary reports are influenced by such unseen influences.

The major problem with diary reports is subjective forgetfulness. Despite an instruction to fill out the report sheets regularly and promptly, subjects do not always do this and data are lost. Conversely, the instruction to attend to interactions (so that they can be later recalled) may make subjects unduly self-conscious and aware of their behavior so that it becomes disrupted or subject to strain.

Other major research questions, for any method, concern the issues of reliability and validity. In the case of diary methods, especially the ICR, these issues are not merely routine methodological issues but verge on the substantive as we confront the very nature of the data that we are collecting through their use, since subjective recall of experience may be inherently, but meaningfully, "unreliable." Built into any test of reliability, for instance, is a social scientific "theorette" that assumes stability in the measured phenomenon (Duck, 1990; in press) and also assumes that a proper measure will assess that stability. Thus, for example, a researcher might assume that a measure of children's friendships will show the same friendship nominations on two successive occasions of measurement. Those measures that yield virtually the same results each time are thus regarded in the social scientific community as successfully measuring this supposedly stable external universe of measured phenomena. But what if the very phenomenon itself is NOT stable? What if, for example, instead of stability, the very essence of children's friendship nominations at some ages is their fluidity or *instability*? In that case, researchers who struggle to create a reliable measure are rigorously missing the point about the phenomenon that they seek to study. So it is, I believe, with some of the data from relationship studies (Duck, 1990; in press), and especially with recall of events in relationship encounters. Part of what characterizes relationship events, particularly quarrels, arguments, or conflicts, is *change* in the participants' views of what happened. An essential part of the whole experience is reflecting on what occurred and trying to explain it (Burnett, 1987); such reflection occasions change or variation in opinions and recollections (Antaki, 1987). Thus, a researcher who attempts rigorous assessment of reliability in the data, gathered by a self-report diary instrument, about a conflict is probably missing a very interesting point about the conduct and experience of conflict. Nor are data on the beginning of a relationship "reliable": Duck and Miell (1986) showed that persons' recollections of their first meeting change as they create a relationship and that these changes are systematically related to their creation of a sense of unity and togetherness. In other words, partners change their recollections to suit their present individual and relational needs. The issue of reliability for diary log data is thus not the simple one that it appears, particularly when the diaries are applied to interactions in continuing relationships, rather than to isolated social events.

The question of validity is also an interesting and ramified one in this context. If we ask one question (Do the diary logs validly tap personal experiences of relational events?), there is no simple answer—but it would probably be yes. If we ask the other—more popular but possible naive—

question (Do diary logs validly tap relational events?), any answer would be erroneous because of the mistaken beliefs implicit in such a question. The reason is that, as argued elsewhere (Duck, 1990; in press), data from the assessment of a relationship are not simply based on "what happens" (indeed, it would be interesting if some scholar could actually define what that means) but on what people *experience* as happening, and, of course, one person's experiences may differ from another's even in the same situation or at the same event.

The real questions for research are not whether one person (including the outside observer) is likely to be right in his or her assessment of a relationship or an interaction and why but what system of psychological factors accounts for the differences in perceptions. That is a higher-order issue but one that the apparent low-level matter of validity brings to point. In the area of research on social interaction, particularly ongoing interactions such as the Stones', the matters of validity and reliability have to be approached with a caution founded on an understanding of the model of phenomena that is implicitly endorsed by the very questioning of reliability and validity (cf. Chapter 1).

Application to the Stones' Argument

The use of diary logs for the study of the interaction between Cathy and Michael Stone does not require any additional information about the situation or the subjects unless we are interested in either one of two things: (1) the perceptions of the quarrel in its relational context (e.g., answers to questions about the individual psychological environments in which the quarrel arose) or (2) the changes in perception and evaluation of the quarrel that occur over time. In each of these cases, our interests would require a broader contextual background that related specifically to the conflictive interaction.

If our interests as researchers are in the conflictive interaction itself, it is enough that an interaction occurred and that the subjects feel that it was significant and required some kind of reaction from them. Indeed, those who have used the ICR (e.g., Duck et al., in press) give subjects only general instructions, urging them to complete ICR reports of "significant social interactions" during the relevant time period. (Some studies have used a 7-week time period and others as little as a part of a single day.) Subjects are instructed to complete reports as soon as possible after the interaction. On the basis of the lead of Wheeler and Nezlek (1977) and modified to emphasize communication, an interaction is normally defined as an encounter (of any length) with another person in which the participants attend to one another, converse (whether face-to-face or by telephone), and adjust their behavior in response to one another. Examples given by both RIR and ICR users at this point stress that behaviors such as sitting next to someone on the bus or in class do not count, nor do mere exchanges of greetings, unless conversation occurs and the subject feels that the encounter is significant. Obviously, the Stones and the Millers meet these criteria.

Subjects are typically unconstrained as to length of interaction selected, the day of the week that they select, or the time of day of the interaction. Clearly, in the case of the Stones' interaction some of these instructions would be irrelevant or distracting and the interaction over dinner would be the simple focus of the diary report.

It is possible that different experimenters would disagree as to whether the whole dinner would count as an interaction for study or whether just the argumentative exchange itself would be the specified topic of the diary log. If the dinner as a whole is considered the basis for the study, then the analysis would look for systematic changes in the views of the interaction provided by the different observers over time. If the argument itself is all that counts, then some contextual data would be lost. Furthermore, we would have to specify when the argument began, possibly overriding the two (or four) subjects' own personal judgments of what was the cause of the argument and what demarcated its beginning.

A researcher applying diary methods to the argument between the Stones might look for differences between each person's "story" of where the argument began. Another approach may involve looking at the ways in which such differences resolve themselves with the perspective of hindsight and continued interaction. The effect of time is one reason it would be useful to gather data over a period of interaction that extends beyond the actual argument itself. For example, a researcher may wish to know which dimensions of arguments are most predictive of sustained malice and hurt in conflicted couples, or he or she may want to establish early signs through which conflict resolution can be encouraged. A researcher may want to discover the relationship of gender perspectives to representation of conflict or the relationship between physiological reactions and perceptions of conflict. With suitable modifications to procedures, such issues can be readily addressed by ICR logs.

Finally, the researcher interested in the present argument between the Stones may well want to assess the basis for the Stones' different perceptions of their household activities, which led to the original complaint from Cathy. For instance, who does, over a period of time, report doing the most housework or cooking? How do the Stones' perceptions of their partner's effort on these chores match up with their own reports of those behaviors? Such questions could be answered in part by having subjects record, on the ICR, the time that they spend doing housework. This would allow us to begin to get a picture of the relationship between their individual reports of their working efforts, their perceptions of their own and the partner's efforts, and their beliefs about those respective efforts.

As argued above, we can also expect the partners in a relationship to hold mildly, or perhaps wildly, different assessments of some elements of the relating that occurs. Subjects are human beings after all, and agreement with others is not a necessary condition of humanity! The dimensions of difference and the systematic organization of such differences are of considerable interest to the social science researcher and can be tapped using the ICR. Finally, it will be useful in the future for researchers to use diary log methods to try to understand the ways in which different observers of an interaction reach their judgments and conclusions about it. In the case of relationships this is particularly important since perspectives and feelings are a very large part of relating. Certainly the matter of differences in perspectives and the ways in which they arise are fascinating problems for future workers on relationships. I am hopeful that the use of ICR techniques will uncover many present mysteries in social interaction, including these. There is much to be learned beyond the assessment a person might make that a given January day was "cold."

References

Antaki, C. (1987). Performed and unperformable: A guide to accounts of relationships. In R. Burnett, P. McGee, & D. Clarke (Eds.), *Accounting for Relationships*. London: Methuen.

Baxter, L. A., & Wilmot, W. (1986). Interaction characteristics of disengaging, stable and growing relationships. In R. Gilmour & S. W. Duck (Eds.), *Emerging field of personal relationships* (pp. 145–160). Hillsdale, NJ: Erlbaum.

Berg, J. H., & Piner, K. (1990). Social relationships and the lack of social relationships. In S. W. Duck, *Personal Relationships and Social Support* (R. Silver, Ed.; pp. 104–121).

Bolger, N., DeLongis, A., Kessler, R. C., & Schilling, E. A. (1989). Effects of daily stress on negative mood. *Journal of Personality and Social Psychology*.

Brydon, C. F. (1982, July). *Interviewing adolescent friends: A progress report*. Paper for Social Science Research Council Grant HR 2891. London.

Burnett, R. (1987). Reflection in personal relationships. In R. Burnett, P. McGee, & D. Clarke (Eds.), *Accounting for Relationships*. London: Methuen.

Duck, S. W. (1980). Personal relationships research in the 1980s: Towards an understanding of complex human sociality. *Western Journal of Speech Communication 44*, 114–119.

Duck, S. W. (1988). *Relating to Others*. Open University (UK) and Dorsey/Brooks/Cole/Wadsworth, Belmont CA.

Duck, S. W. (1990). Relationships as unfinished business: Out of the frying pan and into the 1990s. *Journal of Social and Personal Relationships, 7*, 5–28.

Duck, S. W. (in press). The role of theory in relationship loss. In T. L. Orbuch (Ed.), *Ending close relationships* (in press). New York: Springer.

Duck, S. W., Cortez, C. A., Hurst, M., & Streje, H. (1989). Recalled communication parameters of successful and unsuccessful first dates as a function of loneliness. Manuscript under review.

Duck, S. W., & Miell, D. E. (1982). Charting the development of personal relationships. Paper presented to Second International Conference on Personal Relationships, Madison, WI.

Duck, S. W., & Miell, D. E. (1986). Charting the development of personal relationships. In R. Gilmour & S. W. Duck (Eds.), *Emerging field of personal relationships* (pp. 133–144). Hillsdale, NJ: Erlbaum.

Duck, S. W., & Pond, K. (1989a). Friends, Romans, countrymen, lend me your retrospective data: Rhetoric and reality in personal relationships. In C. Hendrick (Ed.), *Review of Social Psychology and Personality: Vol 10. Close Relationships* (pp. 3–29). Newbury Park: Sage.

Duck, S. W., & Pond, K. (1989b). Different perspectives on interaction. Manuscript in preparation, University of Iowa.

Duck, S. W., & Rutt, D. (1988). The experience of everyday relational conversations: Are all communications created equal? Paper presented at the annual convention of the Speech Communication Association, New Orleans.

Duck, S. W., Rutt, D., Hurst, M., & Strejc. H. (in press). Some evident truths about conversation in everyday relationships: All communications are not created equal. *Human Communication Research*.

Duck, S. W., & Sants, H. K. A. (1983). On the origin of the specious: Are personal relationships really interpersonal states? *Journal of Social and Clinical Psychology 1,* 27–41.

Gottman, J. M. (1989). Address on receipt of the International Network on Personal Relationships Berscheid & Hatfield Award. *INPR Newsletter, 3*(2), 8–11.

Hinde, R. A. (1979). *Towards understanding relationships* London: Academic Press.

Mamali, C. (1989, May). Epistolary communication and relationships. Paper presented to the International Network on Personal Relationships Conference, Iowa City.

Miell, D. E. (1984). Cognitive and communicative strategies in developing relationships. Unpublished doctoral dissertation, University of Lancaster, England.

Miell, D. E. (1987). Remembering relationship development: Constructing a context for interaction. In R. Burnett, P. McGee, & D. Clarke (Eds.), *Accounting for Relationships* (pp. 60–73). London: Methuen.

Reis, H. T., Nezlek, J., & Wheeler, L. (1980). Physical attractiveness and social interaction. *Journal of Personality and Social Psychology, 38,* 604–617.

Reis, H. T., Senchak, M., & Solomon, B. (1985). Sex differences in the intimacy of social interaction. Journal of *Personality and Social Psychological,* 48, 1204–1217.

Reis, H. T., Wheeler, L., Kernis, M. H., Spiegel, N., & Nezlek, J. (1985). On specificity in the impact of social participation on physical and psychological health. *Journal of Personality and Social Psychology, 48,* 456–471.

Rosenblatt, P. (1983). *Bitter, bitter tears: Nineteenth century diarists and twentieth century grief theories*. Minneapolis: University of Minnesota Press.

Sants, H. K. A. (1984). Conceptions of friendship, social behaviour, and school achievement in six-year-old children. *Journal of Social and Personal Relationships*, *1*, 293–309.

Weber, A., Harvey, J. H., & Stanley, M. A. (1987). The nature and motivations of accounts for failed relationships. In R. Burnett, P. McGhee, & D. Clarke (Eds.), *Accounting for Relationships* (pp. 114–133). London: Methuen.

Wheeler, L., & Nezlek, J. (1977). Sex differences in social participation. *Journal of Personality and Social Psychology*, *35*, 742–754.

Chapter 9

Retrospective Self-Reports

SANDRA METTS
SUSAN SPRECHER
WILLIAM R. CUPACH

Description of the Method

At the risk of being simplistic, we might argue that there are two kinds of data in the world of the social sciences: those that are observed directly by the researcher and those that are reported to the researcher. Our task in this chapter is to examine a particular type of reported data, retrospective self-reports, and the traditional methods used to collect such data. Although some of our remarks may be relevant to other sources of retrospective data such as diaries, logs, and accounts, we direct the reader to Chapters 7 and 8 for more detailed information about these techniques.

For the purposes of this chapter, we consider retrospective data to include reports of recollected behavior, experience, events, and affect, as well as global assessments of affective/psychological states and typical behavior based on accumulations of previous experiences and knowledge. Although there is a degree of subjectivity in all self-reports, some retrospective data are expressly subjective (e.g., amount of love felt in a relationship) whereas other retrospective data are relatively more objective (e.g., how often the husband did the dishes over the past week).

Uses and Abuses of Retrospective Data

Data obtained from retrospective descriptions of interaction and other relational phenomena are sometimes indicted as being a pragmatic but inferior substitute for observations of actual behavior. In reality, such an indictment should not be directed toward retrospective data per se but toward inappropriate uses of the data.

Although retrospective data are appropriate for many research questions on interaction and other relational phenomena, they will not provide the researcher with an objective measure of actual interactional behavior (i.e., what was said, how it was said, or how often). In this case, observational data (particularly with audio and/or video recording) or self-reported data recorded immediately in diaries and logs are more appropriate. Retrospective reports of interaction are necessarily subjective reconstructions. Such reconstructions vary in accuracy and objectivity as a function of emotional arousal level (Sillars & Scott, 1983), contextual and temporal factors, memory expectancies, and recall mode (e.g., Stafford, Burggraf, & Sharkey, 1987). Certainly interactional information is stored in memory and can be retrieved, but the type of information recalled from a conversation is more likely to be (1) the "gist" of the conversation rather than verbatim messages, (2) verbal rather than nonverbal behaviors, (3) one's own messages rather than partner's, and (4) the presence or absence of specific statements rather than frequencies of occurrences of behaviors (Benoit & Benoit, 1988). Thus, interaction information can be recognized and/or recalled but at a more general and impressionistic level than would be provided by verbatim recordings.

The same sort of leveling effect and recall biases make retrospective data less useful than other methods (e.g., diaries and logs) for representing the subtle changes and transitions experienced in relationships (Duck, 1990; Duck & Pond, 1989; Duck & Sants, 1983). Retrospective data generally represent the endpoints of change or transition rather than the process itself. In fact, the endpoint or current state of a relationship tends to act as a framework through which previous relationship events are interpreted and emotional fluctuations are stabilized (see Miell, 1987). In short, retrospective data do not provide information that is amenable to tests of accuracy or veridicality.

There are several research questions, however, for which retrospective data are appropriate. First, retrospective data are appropriate for occasions when researchers wish to study *individual and jointly created relationship histories,* including, for example, critical events and turning points (Baxter & Bullis, 1986), why people made a marriage commitment (Surra, Arizzi, & Asmussen 1988), how and why people deceived relational partners (Metts, 1989), and how and why people enacted breakups (Cupach & Metts, 1986).

Retrospective self-report data are also appropriate when researchers are interested in the *meanings that people ascribe to their own and others' behaviors during communication episodes.* For example, the "perlocutionary" force of messages (i.e., what "counts as" affection, insult, play, self-disclosure, etc.) and what will be interpreted as appropriate responses are not so much inherent in the message as they are negotiated from the private culture of a relationship (Bradac, 1983; Hopper, Knapp, & Scott, 1981). Self-report data allow researchers to understand the role of individual belief systems and attributions in the process of assigning meaning. Self-report data also allow researchers to assess the extent to which partners ascribe similar meanings to behaviors, episodes, and events—or perceive that they do.

Finally, retrospective data are appropriate when researchers are interested in *participants' attitudes, emotions, and perceptions of relationship qualities.* These covert variables can be examined in relation to each other or examined as antecedents, consequences, or contexts for observed behaviors. For example, relational quality (including satisfaction, happiness, and adjustment) has been perhaps the most frequently researched topic on marriage and other close relationships (Adams, 1988; Baxter, 1988). Variables such as love, liking, and trust have also been examined frequently, particularly in dating relationships.

Methods for Collecting Retrospective Data

RESEARCH DESIGNS

The most commonly used design for collecting retrospective data is the *cross-sectional design* that has only one data collection point. Data are collected through a survey that may include questions about the past, present, and future. Although cross-sectional designs do not explicitly include the time dimension within the data collection procedure, they are often used to draw time-related conclusions, including the effects of antecedent variables on consequent variables and how relationship phenomena (e.g., satisfaction) change over age groups, relationship stages, and the family life cycle. Caution must be exercised, however, in interpreting temporal or causal associations from cross-sectional designs.

Two other types of designs incorporate time more directly and thus are more appropriate for examining temporal and developmental issues. In the *longitudinal design,* retrospective data (as well as concurrent data) are obtained from individuals or couples on two or more separate occasions over a period of time. Longitudinal designs have been used to examine determinants of relationship breakups or other relationship change, the effects of antecedent variables on consequent variables, and how relationships or participants' perceptions of the relationship change over time. One of the most well known longitudinal studies in personal relationships research is the Boston Dating Couples Study conducted by Rubin and his colleagues (e.g., Hill, Rubin, & Peplau, 1976).

In the *retrospective design,* information is collected from individuals or couples on a single occasion about relationship phenomena for several earlier stages of the relationship. In this way, a cross-sectional design is actually used to derive "longitudinal" data. The Retrospective Interview Technique (Huston, Surra, Fitzgerald, & Cate, 1981) represents a good illustration of this design. Through personal interviews (typically lasting 2 hours), individuals are asked to recall several aspects of their relationship, usually from the beginning to its current state (e.g., newly married, dissolved). The specific information that the subjects are asked to recall varies, but in most studies a graph (e.g., "chance of marriage," "chance of divorce") is plotted for the history of the relationship. This trajectory to a particular endpoint is typically then divided into discrete stages or periods, and subjects are asked to complete scales or other measures for each period and/or turning point. Data collected in this way are used to address several research issues, including developmental trends in relationship variables (e.g., conflict), how intercorrelations among relationship variables change with increases or decreases in commitment, and attributions made about significant changes in the relationship. Although only this design is referred to specifically as a "retrospective" design, retrospective data can be obtained in all three designs.

DATA COLLECTION

Retrospective data can be collected through face-to-face interviews, telephone interviews, self-administered questions, or a combination of these methods. Self-administered protocols (through the mail or to a captive group) are popular because of their efficiency and because they are appropriate for the lengthy scales and other measurement instruments often used. Although face-to-face interviews are often more expensive and time-consuming than self-administered surveys, they are justified for questions that require detailed and/or complicated answers (e.g., the Retrospective Interview Technique) or for groups that cannot read (e.g., small children).

The telephone interview has not been used as frequently as the other two modes of data collection in research on interpersonal interaction. Recently, however, Schmidt and Cornelius (1987) employed telephone interviews in a study of self-disclosure. Indeed, the telephone offers several unique advantages that may lead to its increased use. For example, with computer-assisted telephone interviewing (CATI) researchers can use the computer to randomly select, dial, interview, and record responses from respondents. The telephone interview has also been used to screen potential participants for eligibility before they participate in a mailed survey or face-to-face interview (e.g., Krokoff, 1987) and as a method of data collection for follow-up surveys (e.g., Adams, 1987).

The protocols used for soliciting retrospective data can exhibit a variety of forms. For example, verbal reports of cognitive processes and conversations can be elicited through recognition, prompted (cued) recall, or free (unassisted) recall (see Benoit & Benoit, 1988; Greene, 1988). Specific questions can be either open-ended (possible response options are not provided) or closed-ended (possible response options are provided).

Constructs can be measured by only one item or by several, usually in the form of a scale or index. Single items should be avoided in the measurement of complex variables because they are frequently less reliable and it is more difficult to discern their reliability. Although longer scales and indices are generally preferred, precautions have to be taken in how they are used. For example, several scales/indices included in one questionnaire may exceed the limits of subject attention and motivation.

Detailed methodological considerations are beyond the scope of this chapter. However, several reference materials carefully examine the merits and techniques of questionnaire design (e.g., Babbie, 1973; Sudman & Bradburn, 1982), modes of gathering data (e.g., Dillman, 1978; Groves & Kahn, 1979), sampling (e.g., Kish, 1965; Sudman, 1976), psychometrics (Nunnally, 1978) and survey research in general (e.g., Babbie, 1973; Schuman & Kalton, 1985).

Advantages of Retrospective Self-Report Methods

Regardless of the specific design or protocols used, retrospective self-report (RSR) methods have both practical and theoretical advantages.

PRACTICAL ADVANTAGES

Because RSR methods fall under the more general rubric of survey research, they provide researchers certain advantages. One major advantage is that they offer a relatively easy and efficient way to obtain data. This advantage accrues at several stages in the research process. First, it can be relatively easy to design a RSR instrument, particularly if previously developed and validated scales are used. Several scales and indices are available to the interpersonal interaction researcher (e.g., see Baxter, 1988; Harvey, Hendrick, & Tucker, 1988; Sabatelli, 1988; Tardy, 1988a, 1988b). Second, data collection can be conducted quickly, particularly if the questionnaire is self-administered and the sample is a captive group (e.g., college students). Third, the preparation and analysis of the data can be straightforward if the questions are closed-ended and standardized.

Occasionally, the researcher does not even have to conduct a new investigation in order to obtain retrospective data. Secondary data analysis refers to analyzing census data or data collected earlier by another researcher or organization for a different purpose. For example, data from the General Social Surveys conducted by the National Opinion Research Center (NORC) have been used by several researchers to explore issues on marriage and the family (e.g., Palisi & Ransford, 1987).

Compared to experimental and observational methods, survey methods in general, and RSRs in particular, also provide researchers wide latitude in sampling procedures. Some samples are convenient (nonprobability), such as college students from intact classes, volunteers who respond to ads, and readers of a periodical. Other samples are representative (probability), in which participants are selected randomly from a specific population (geographic location or group). For example, Krokoff (1987) describes how a sample of married couples from a specific location was chosen on the basis of numbers selected randomly from a telephone directory. (However, see also Bell, 1989, and Krokoff, 1989, for a discussion of the advantages and disadvantages of using random digit dialing instead).

THEORETICAL ADVANTAGES

The practical advantages of RSR methods are complemented by their important theoretical advantages. RSR methods enable researchers to measure and analyze a broad domain of private experience that contributes to their use in theory building and testing.

A primary theoretical advantage of the RSR and other self-report methods is that they offer access to a wide diversity of interaction contexts. Self-report is sometimes the only method that can be used to obtain information on behaviors that are private to individuals and/or relational partners and not generally accessible through direct observation (e.g., sexual behaviors), or behaviors that might occur unpredictably or infrequently (e.g., arguments, deception). Consequently, RSRs allow researchers to study a wider range of situations than alternative methods.

A second advantage of the self-report, and particularly the RSR, is that it allows researchers to explore the complex, multidimensional nature of relationship/interaction constructs and the multicausal nature of the phenomena. (By contrast, only a few variables can be manipulated in the experiment.) Recent theoretical models of personal relationships have stressed taking into account several types of causes in understanding the development, maintenance, and termination of personal relationships (e.g., Kelley et al., 1983).

Problems That Can Limit the Validity of Retrospective Self-Report Data

The biases and limitations of human judgment are well documented (e.g., Nisbett & Ross, 1980). When participants are asked about their past experiences, they may not be able to remember, particularly if they are asked about experiences from the distant past or things that are not very salient. By their nature, RSRs are subject to the vagaries of memory and information-processing capabilities.

Participants may also not be able to engage in the mental processes demanded by certain questions in RSRs. In a classic paper on social cognition, Nisbett and Wilson (1977) provided evidence that people usually report on their cognitive processes without any true introspection. For example, if participants are asked to indicate why they behaved in a particular way in their interactions with others, they may not know. In such cases, they may rely on implicit causal theories provided by the culture to explain their response. Although Nisbett and Wilson were describing research in experimental social psychology, Berger (1980) and Duck and Sants (1983) have provided similar critiques of research on interpersonal interaction and personal relationships, arguing that researchers often attribute more self-awareness to social actors than is warranted.

In addition to recall problems, a number of systematic perceptual biases can be manifested in certain types of data generated from RSRs. These biases include the following: (1) the classic fundamental attribution error, in which there is a tendency to underestimate the impact of external factors and overestimate the impact of personality characteristics when explaining the behavior of others (Ross, 1977); (2) the negativity effect, in which negative information is given more weight than other information in making judgments (Kanouse & Hanson, 1972); (3) egocentric bias, in which people are less aware of their relational partner's behaviors and feelings than of their own (Christensen, Sullaway, & King, 1983; Ross & Sicoly, 1979); and (4) social desirability, in which respondents attempt to present a positive and socially appropriate self-image (Crowne & Marlowe, 1960). These biases are exacerbated and compounded by flaws in research procedures, such as ambiguously worded questions, and characteristics of interviewers such as gender and race that may introduce error into survey responses.

Paradoxically, perceptual biases may be magnified in interpersonal relationships as they become more intimate. Sillars (1985; Sillars & Scott, 1983) has convincingly argued that there are situations in which intimate relationships promote and sustain perceptual biases, such as in the presence of strong positive or negative emotions, during emotionally expressive conflicts, and during highly stressful interactions. Traditionally, these perceptual biases have been considered error variance. However, memory biases, and the changes in perceptions over time, can be of intrinsic theoretical interest (e.g., Duck & Pond, 1989).

Some of the threats to the validity of RSR data can be mitigated by the researcher. For example, Ericsson and Simon (1980) suggest that verbal reports are more likely to be accurate when they access short-term memory. Respondents generally are better able to answer questions that pertain to events that are specific, objective, and recent, rather than general, subjective, and temporally distant. Response biases such as social desirability can be minimized by the careful construction of forced-choice response formats (e.g., Kilmann & Thomas, 1977) or by measuring the propensity of respondents to manifest a social approval motive in their self-reports and controlling for it statistically (Crowne & Marlowe, 1960; Edmonds, 1967). Directions to the questionnaire are also an important way to reduce biases. For example, Cannell, Miller, and Oksenberg (1981) encourage the researcher to provide clear instructions that emphasize completeness and accuracy and that include a purpose to the study. While careful construction of RSR protocols is essential to maximizing the utility of self-report data, awareness of the limitations intrinsic to RSRs is necessary for researchers to properly qualify the "meaning" of their data.

In sum, RSRs are a widely used and versatile technique for studying interpersonal interaction and relationships. RSRs permit the assessment of private events and cognitions not amenable to direct observation by the researcher, allow multivariate study of complex phenomena, and offer a relatively easy and efficient way to obtain data. Limitations of RSRs include the inability to measure interaction directly, the inability to capture the processual nature of interactions and relationships, and the perceptual biases attendant on self-reports.

The Use of Retrospective Self-Reports to Study Interpersonal Conflict

RSR methods may appear to be an unlikely approach to the study of interaction, particularly complicated relational conflict as illustrated in the sample interaction between Cathy and Michael Stone. Traditionally, conflict has been studied with experimental (e.g., the prisoner dilemma games) and quasi-experimental designs (e.g., hypothetical scenarios and role-playing) and observational methods. However, the study of conflict need not be confined to these methods. Conflict is a phenomenon whose origin and consequences extend beyond the level of the episode. Any particular conflict episode is embedded within a larger system of rules, roles, norms, rituals, expectations, and interpretive filters known as the "relational culture" (Wood, 1982). RSR methods are an ideal vehicle for gaining access to relational cultures and the meanings ascribed to the events occurring within those subjective worlds.

In this section of the chapter, we offer several possible approaches to the study of conflict using RSR methods. To the extent that the Stones' dialogue is representative of other conflict episodes in their relationship and representative of the conflict episodes of other couples, we can use it as an exemplar to study three general aspects of conflict: perceived causes, management, and relational antecedents and consequences.

CAUSES OF CONFLICT

One of the obvious applications of RSR methods to episodes like that between Cathy and Michael Stone is to answer the question, *What do couples perceive to be the causes of their conflict?* This question can be answered with two levels of data. For some purposes, researchers may be interested simply in "topics" (terms and phrases) that couples associate with their conflict episodes (e.g., household responsibilities, lack of affection or attention, disagreement over spending money, lack of communication, etc.). For other purposes, researchers may be interested in more complex notions of what couples argue about. Watzlawick, Beavin, and Jackson (1967) noted that all messages have a content and a relational dimension. Thus, conflict, for example, can be focused on either dimension—determining which movie to see or who has the right to decide which movie to see. Concerns about how partners define themselves and their relationship are common "issues" embedded within topics. Thus, in episodes like that of the Stones, the topic of performing household tasks entails several issues, such as how the distribution should be determined, what relational meaning is associated with not performing a task (e.g., "You don't care if I'm tired; you don't love me"), whether the strain is temporary or continuing ("It's so busy at work, I need your help"), and so forth.

Identifying prominent or typical "issues" is a more difficult research endeavor than determining prominent or typical "topics." Issues can be subtle, implicit, complicated, and ego-involving. Respondents may be unwilling or unable to articulate issues and trace them across topics. For these reasons, open-ended, free-recall questions will not serve well for eliciting a couple's perception of conflict issues. If a researcher-generated list of issues cannot be provided to respondents, researchers may be able to elicit salient issues through cued-recognition tasks. For example, a couple's own or hypothetical conflict episodes can be presented to the couple (separately or together) for their analysis.

Conflict "topics" can be fairly easily studied through both interview and self-administered questionnaires. In-depth interviews conducted with a small number of participants is an effective means for identifying all conflict topics that exist in a particular population (e.g., Gottman, 1979). Self-administered questionnaires using preselected lists of topics or open-ended questions might be used when a large sample is necessary in order to investigate factors associated with conflict topics. For example, Argyle and Furnham (1983) compared married couples to other relationship types (e.g., siblings, coworkers, neighbors) on a number of topics likely to cause conflict. Zietlow and Sillars (1988) used a cross-sectional design to compare topic salience in early marriages and long-term marriages.

Finally, RSR methods can be used to assess the congruence in partners' interpretation of what causes their conflict. A common approach in the literature is to compare partners on summary measures of how often they believe a topic or issue causes conflict or how likely it would be to cause conflict (how potent for self and partner). For example, Harvey and Wells (presented in Harvey, Wells, & Alvarez, 1978) gathered both questionnaire and interview data from 36 unmarried couples. They found that subjects were not only inaccurate in assessing how potent certain issues were to their partner but they were also consistently egocentric in predicting patterns for their partner that were similar to their own ratings (also see Sillars, Pike, Jones, & Murphy, 1984). A less common, but certainly useful, approach is asking partners to consider the same conflict episodes (taped by the researcher or reconstructed by the couple) and to identify what each believes to be the cause or focus of the conflict. This technique clarifies differences in how partners are interpreting the same events by minimizing variance due to differences in recall.

CONFLICT MANAGEMENT

A second general type of question that RSR methods can be used to address is, *How do partners perceive they manage conflict episodes, both in terms of individual behaviors and in terms of dyadic patterns?*

Individual Conflict Behaviors

The question of how individuals perceive that they manage conflict can be addressed from two perspectives. The first assumes that people develop characteristic responses to conflict and employ them with little variation across situations and interactional partners (Hocker & Wilmot, 1985; Sternberg & Dobson, 1987). When people report what they "typically" do in recollected conflict situations or would "most likely" do in hypothetical situations, they are reporting their perception of their conflict style. Several scales have been developed and used widely to study behavioral predispositions in conflict episodes (e.g., Brown, Yelsma, & Keller, 1981; Kilmann & Thomas, 1977; Rahim, 1983; Sternberg & Soriano, 1984).

The second perspective on individual behaviors during conflict assumes that situational variables moderate the strength of personal conflict styles. A number of variables amenable to RSR methods can be explored as correlates of perceived strategy use/selection: demographic and personality variables such as gender (e.g., Berryman-Fink & Brunner, 1987; Kelley et al., 1978), relational variables such as satisfaction (e.g., Canary & Cupach, 1988) or type of relationship (e.g., Fitzpatrick & Winke, 1979), and cognitive processes such as causal attributions (Fincham & Bradbury, 1987; Sillars, 1980).

Both approaches typically begin by providing respondents with a list of tactics (specific communication behaviors), each followed by response scales measuring frequency or likelihood of use. These tactics are factor analyzed to yield a smaller set of strategies (global communication plans). Fitzpatrick and Winke (1979), for example, began their investigation of conflict with the 44 tactics from the Kipnis (1976) Interpersonal Conflict Scale. Factor analysis of the responses to these items indicated five underlying conflict strategies: manipulation, non-negotiation, emotional appeal, personal rejection, and empathic understanding.

Management Patterns of the Dyad

Although we can say with certainty that conflict will arise in any system composed of interdependent persons, we cannot assess the impact or conduct of that conflict without knowledge of the system itself. As a number of scholars have noted, family systems differ in their ability and willingness to deal with conflict (Olson, Sprenkle, & Russell, 1979; Peterson, 1983).

RSR methods are a common approach to measuring a couple's predisposition toward engaging or not engaging in conflict. Questionnaires have been developed, for instance, to measure the extent to which people have relatively stable beliefs that conflict should be avoided in relationships (Eidelson & Epstein, 1982). Questionnaires have also been developed to assess the extent to which couples exhibit internal norms regarding the open expression of conflict. Fitzpatrick's (1988) Relational Dimensions Index illustrates this in items such as the following: "We try to resolve our disagreements immediately" and "We are likely to argue in front of friends or in public places" and "If I can avoid arguing about some problems, they will disappear" (p. 260). Based on typal analysis of responses to these and other Likert-type items, couples are arrayed on the dimensions of ideology, interdependence, and communication in order to identify couple types (Independent, Separate, and Traditional). Fitzpatrick's work confirms an association between couple type and conflict occurrence (e.g., Traditional couples tend to avoid conflict while Independent couples tend to engage in open and expressive conflict).

RELATIONAL ANTECEDENTS AND CONSEQUENCES OF CONFLICT

RSR methods can also be used to address questions concerned with how conflict is situated in the dynamics of the larger relational culture. Conflict and relationship changes exert reciprocal influences and invite such questions as, *How does the level of conflict change over relationship stages?* and *How is conflict related to relationship qualities such as love, satisfaction, and stability?*

The retrospective design has been used in several studies to address both of these questions. Typically, the Retrospective Interview Technique is conducted with individuals or couples who have reached a particular relationship stage (e.g., marriage, breakup). Respondents are asked to call to mind specific previous stages in their relationship and then to complete a battery of scales for each stage. Most commonly the scales include the Braiker and Kelley (1979) self-administered scales to measure conflict/negativity, maintenance, ambivalence, and love, and occasionally other scales, for previous stages of their relationship. The Retrospective Interview Technique has been used to assess the relationship between conflict and other variables across a variety of relationship stages—for example, married couples reflecting on courtship stages (Braiker & Kelley, 1979), divorced individuals reflecting on dissolution stages (Kelly, Huston, & Cate, 1985; Ponzetti & Cate, 1987), and dating couples reflecting on their sexual involvement though several stages of courtship (Christopher & Cate, 1985).

Longitudinal designs have also been used, although less frequently, to determine patterns of conflict across stages of relationships. For example, in a longitudinal study of 38 couples who had just started to date, Berg and McQuinn (1986) found no change in the level of conflict (measured by the Braiker & Kelley scale) over a 4-month period. Conflict also did not predict final relationship status. Felmlee, Sprecher, and Bassin (1990) likewise found that conflict was not a significant predictor of the rate of premarital breakups.

Conclusion

This chapter provided an overview of the use, advantages, and limitations of retrospective self-reports and illustrated their applicability to one specific research area, interpersonal conflict. RSRs are also appropriate for many other topics in the general research areas of interpersonal interaction and close relationships. RSRs provide unique access to information about relational participants' concurrent and retrospective feelings and thoughts and their perceptions of how they behaved in the past.

Researchers of interaction and close relationships are pragmatic, as are other social scientists, and sometimes choose the RSR method primarily because it can be an easy and efficient way to obtain data. However, it is time for us to move beyond simple RSR designs and make more complex designs the rule rather th.⁣ the exception. That is, we need to more often conduct longitudinal studies, collect data from both partners of the couple, obtain probability samples, and study populations other than undergraduate students and middle-class professional couples. Furthermore, researchers should try, as often as possible, to consider using the RSR in combination with another method to address a particular research question. With these improved aspects of the RSR, we will be able to add significantly to knowledge and theory about conflict and other areas of close relationships.

References

Adams, B. N. (1988). Fifty years of family research: What does it all mean? *Journal of Marriage and the Family, 50,* 5–17.

Adams, R. G. (1987). Patterns of network change: A longitudinal study of friendships of elderly women. *The Gerontologist, 27,* 222–227.

Argyle, M., & Furnham, A. (1983). Sources of satisfaction and conflict in long-term relationships. *Journal of Marriage and the Family, 45,* 481–493.

Babbie, E. (1973). *Survey research methods.* Belmont, CA: Wadsworth.

Baxter, L. A. (1988). Dyadic personal relationships: Measurement options. In C. H. Tardy (Ed.), *A handbook for the study of human communication: Methods and instruments for observing, measuring, and assessing communication processes* (pp. 193–228). Norwood, NJ: Ablex.

Baxter, L. A., & Bullis, C. (1986). Turning points in developing romantic relationships. *Human Communication Research, 12,* 469–493.

Bell, R. A. (1989). A comment on Krokoff's "Recruiting representative samples for marital interaction research." *Journal of Social and Personal Relationships, 6,* 231–234.

Benoit, W. L., & Benoit, P. J. (1988). Factors influencing the accuracy of verbal reports of conversational behavior. *Central States Speech Journal, 39,* 219–232.

Berg, H. J., & McQuinn, R. D. (1986). Attraction and exchange in continuing and noncontinuing dating relationships. *Journal of Personality and Social Psychology, 50,* 942–952.

Berger, C. R. (1980). Self-consciousness and the adequacy of theory and research into relationship development. *Western Journal of Speech Communication, 44,* 93–96.

Berryman-Fink, C., & Brunner, C. C. (1987). The effects of sex of source and target on interpersonal conflict management styles. *Southern Speech Communication Journal, 53,* 38–48.

Bradac, J. J. (1983). The language of lovers, flovers, and friends: Communicating in social and personal relationships. *Journal of Language and Social Psychology, 2,* 141–162.

Braiker, H. B., & Kelley, H. H. (1979). Conflict in the development of close relationships. In R. L. Burgess & T. L. Huston (Eds.), *Social exchange in developing relationships* (pp. 135–168). New York: Academic Press.

Brown, C. T., Yelsma, P., & Keller, P. W. (1981). Communication-conflict predisposition: Development of a theory and an instrument. *Human Relations, 34,* 1103–1117.

Canary, D. J., & Cupach, W. R. (1988). Relational and episodic characteristics associated with conflict tactics. *Journal of Social and Personal Relationships, 5,* 305–326.

Cannell, C. F., Miller, P. V., & Oksenberg, L. (1981). Research on interviewing techniques. In S. Leinhardt (Ed.), *Sociological methodology* (pp. 389–437). San Francisco: Jossey-Bass.

Christensen, A., Sullaway, M., & King, C. (1983). Systematic error in behavioral reports of dyadic interaction: Egocentric bias and content analysis. *Behavioral Therapy, 5,* 129–140

Christopher, F. S., & Cate, R. M. (1985). Premarital sexual pathways and relationship development. *Journal of Social and Personal Relationships, 2,* 271–288.

Crowne, D. D., & Marlowe, D. (1960). A new scale of social desirability independent of psychopathology. *Journal of Consulting Psychology, 24,* 349–354.

Cupach, W. R., & Metts, S. (1986). Accounts of relational dissolution: A comparison of marital and non-marital relationships. *Communication Monographs, 53,* 311–334.

Dillman, D. A. (1978). *Mail and telephone surveys: The total design method.* New York: Wiley.

Duck, S. W. (1990). Relationships as unfinished business: Out of the frying pan and into the 1990s. *Journal of Social and Personal Relationships, 7,* 5–28.

Duck, S. W., & Pond, K. (1989). Friends, Romans, countrymen, lend me your retrospections: Rhetoric and reality in personal relationships. In C. Hendrick (Ed.), *Review of social behavior and personality: Vol. 10. Close relationships* (pp. 17–38). Newbury Park: CA: Sage.

Duck, S. W., & Sants, H. (1983). On the origin of the specious: Are personal relationships really interpersonal states? *Journal of Social and Clinical Psychology, 1,* 27–41.

Edmonds, V. H. (1967). Marriage conventionalization: Definition and measurement. *Journal of Marriage and the Family, 29,* 681–688.

Eidelson, R. J., & Epstein, N. (1982). Cognition and relationship maladjustment: Development of a measure of dysfunctional relationship beliefs. *Journal of Consulting and Clinical Psychology, 50,* 715–720.

Ericsson, K. A., & Simon, H. A. (1980). Verbal reports as data. *Psychological Review, 87,* 215–251.

Felmlee, D., Sprecher, S., & Bassin, E. (1990). The dissolution of intimate relationships: A hazard model. *Social Psychology Quarterly, 53,* 13–30.

Fincham, F. D., & Bradbury, T. N. (1987). Cognitive processes and conflict in close relationships: An attribution-efficacy model. *Journal of Personality and Social Psychology, 53,* 1106–1118.

Fitzpatrick, M. A. (1988). *Between husbands & wives: Commication in marriage.* Newbury Park, CA: Sage.

Fitzpatrick, M. A., & Winke, J. (1979). You always hurt the one you love: Strategies and tactics in interpersonal conflict. *Communication Quarterly, 27,* 3–11.

Gottman, J. M. (1979). *Marital interaction: Experimental investigations.* New York: Academic Press.

Greene, J. O. (1988). Cognitive processes: Methods for probing the black box. In C. H. Tardy (Ed.), *A handbook for the study of human communication: Methods and instruments for observing, measuring, and assessing communication processes* (pp. 37–66). Norwood, NJ: Ablex.

Groves, R. M., & Kahn, R. L. (1979). *Surveys by telephone: A national comparison with personal interviews.* New York: Academic Press.

Harvey, J. H., Hendrick, S. S., & Tucker, K. (1988). Self-report methods in studying personal relationships. In S. W. Duck, D. F. Hay, S. E. Hobfoll, W. Ickes, & B. Montgomery (Eds.), *Handbook of personal relationships* (pp. 99–113). New York: Wiley.

Harvey, J. H., Wells, G. L., Alvarez, M. D. (1978). Attribution in the context of conflict and separation in close relationships. In J. H. Harvey, W. Ickes, R. F. Kidd (Eds.), *New directions in attribution research* (Vol. 2, pp. 235–260). Hillsdale, NJ: Erlbaum.

Hill, C., Rubin, Z., & Peplau, L. A. (1976). Breakups before marriage: The end of 103 affairs. *Journal of Social Issues, 32,* 147–168.

Hocker, J. L., & Wilmot, W. W. (1985). *Interpersonal conflict.* Dubuque, IA: Wm. C. Brown.

Hopper, R., Knapp, M. L., & Scott, L. (1981). Couples' personal idioms: Exploring intimate talk. *Journal of Communication, 31,* 23–33.

Huston, T. L., Surra, C. A., Fitzgerald, N. M., & Cate, R. M. (1981). From courtship to marriage: Mate selection as an interpersonal process. In S. W. Duck & R. Gilmour (Eds.), *Personal Relationships: 2. Developing Personal Relationships* (pp. 53–88). London: Academic Press.

Kanouse, D. E., & Hanson, L. R. (1972). Negativity in evaluations. In E. E. Jones, D. E. Kanouse, H. H. Kelley, R. E. Nisbett, S. Valins, & B. Weiner (Eds.), *Attribution: Perceiving the causes of behavior* (pp. 1–16). Morristown, NJ: General Learning Press.

Kelley, H. H., Berscheid, E., Christensen, A., Harvey, J. H., Huston, T. L., Levinger, G., McClintock, E., Peplau, L. A., & Peterson, D. R. (1983). Analyzing close relationships. In H. H. Kelley, E. Berscheid, A. Christensen, J. H. Harvey, T. L. Huston, G. Levinger, E. McClintock, L. A. Peplau, & B. R. Peterson (Eds.), *Close relationships* (pp. 20–67). San Francisco, CA: Freeman.

Kelley, H. H., Cunningham, J. D., Grisham, J. A., Lefebvre, L. M., Sink, C. R., & Yablon, G. (1978). Sex differences in comments made during conflict within close heterosexual pairs. *Sex Roles, 4,* 473–492.

Kelly, C., Huston, T. L., & Cate, R. M. (1985). Premarital relationship correlates of the erosion of satisfaction in marriage. *Journal of Social and Personal Relationships, 2,* 167–178.

Kilmann, R. H., & Thomas, K. W. (1977). Developing a forced-choice measure of conflict-handling behavior: The MODE instrument. *Educational and Psychological Measurement, 37,* 309–325.

Kipnis, D. (1976). *The power-holders.* New York: Academic Press.

Kish, L. (1965). *Survey sampling.* New York: Wiley.

Krokoff, L. J. (1987). Recruiting representative samples for marital interaction research. *Journal of Social and Personal Relationships, 4,* 317–328.

Krokoff, L. J. (1989). Recruiting representative samples for marital interaction research: A reply to Bell. *Journal of Social and Personal Relationships, 6,* 235–238.

Metts, S. (1989). An exploratory investigation of deception in close relationships. *Journal of Social and Personal Relationships, 6,* 159–179.

Miell, D. E. (1987). Remembering relationship development: Constructing a context for interactions. In R. Burnett, P. McGhee, & D. Clarke (Eds.), *Accounting for relationships: Explanation, representation and knowledge* (pp. 60–73). London: Methuen.

Nisbett, R., & Ross, L. (1980). *Human inference: Strategies and shortcomings of social judgment.* Englewood Cliffs, NJ: Prentice-Hall.

Nisbett, R. E., & Wilson, T. D. (1977). Telling more than we know: Verbal reports on mental processes. *Psychological Review, 84,* 231–259.

Nunnally, J. C. (1978). *Psychometric theory.* New York: McGraw-Hill.

Olson, D. H., Sprenkle, D. H., & Russell, C. (1979). Circumplex model of marital and family systems. I: Cohesion and adaptability dimensions, family types and clinical applications. *Family Process, 18,* 3–28.

Palisi, V. J., & Ransford, H. E. (1987). Friendship as a voluntary relationship: Evidence from national surveys: *Journal of Social and Personal Relationships, 4,* 243–259.

Peterson, D. R. (1983). Conflict. In H. H. Kelley, E. Berscheid, A. Christensen, J. H. Harvey, T. L. Huston, G. Levinger, E. McClintock, L. A. Peplau, & D. R. Peterson (Eds.), *Close relationships* (pp. 360–396). New York: Freeman.

Ponzetti, J. J., Jr., & Cate, R. M. (1987). The developmental course of conflict in the marital dissolution process. *Journal of Divorce, 10,* 1–15.

Rahim, M. A. (1983). A measure of styles of handling interpersonal conflict. *Academy of Management Journal, 26,* 368–376.

Ross, L. (1977). The intuitive psychologist and his shortcomings: Distortions in the attribution process. In L. Berkowitz (Ed.), *Advances in experimental social psychology* (Vol. 10, pp. 173–220). New York: Academic Press.

Ross, M., & Sicoly, F. (1979). Egocentric biases in availability and attribution. *Journal of Personality and Social Psychology, 37,* 322–336.

Sabatelli, R. M. (1988). Measurement issues in marital research: A review and critique of contemporary survey instruments. *Journal of Marriage and the Family, 50,* 891–915.

Schmidt, T. O., & Cornelius, R. R. (1987). Self-disclosure in everyday life. *Journal of Social and Personal Relationships, 4,* 365–373.

Schuman, H., & Kalton, G. (1985). Survey methods. In G. E., Lindzey & E. Aronson (Eds.), *Handbook of social psychology* Vol. 1, (pp. 635–697). New York: Random House.

Sillars, A. L. (1980). Attributions and communication in roommate conflicts. *Communication Monographs, 47,* 180–200.

Sillars, A. L. (1985). Interpersonal perception in relationships. In W. Ickes (Ed.), *Compatible and incompatible relationships* (pp. 277–305). New York: Springer.

Sillars, A. L., Pike, G. R., Jones, T. S., Murphy, M. A. (1984). Communication and understanding in marriage. *Human Communication Research, 10,* 317–350.

Sillars, A. L., & Scott, M. D. (1983). Interpersonal perception between intimates: An integrative review. *Human Communication Research, 10,* 153–176.

Stafford, L., Burggraf, C. S., & Sharkey, W. F. (1987). Conversational memory: The effects of time, recall mode, and memory expectancies on remembrances of natural conversation. *Human Communication Research, 14,* 203–229.

Sternberg, R. J., & Dobson, D. M. (1987). Resolving interpersonal conflicts: An analysis of stylistic consistency. *Journal of Personality and Social Psychology, 52,* 794–812.

Sternberg, R. J., & Soriano, L. J. (1984). Styles of conflict resolution. *Journal of Personality and Social Psychology, 47,* 115–126.

Sudman, S. (1976). *Applied sampling.* New York: Academic Press.

Sudman, S., & Bradburn, N. (1982). *Asking questions: A practical guide to questionnaire design.* San Francisco, CA: Jossey-Bass.

Surra, C. A., Arizzi, P., & Asmussen, L. A. (1988). The association between reasons for commitment and the development and outcome of marital relationships. *Journal of Social and Personal Relationships, 5,* 47–63.

Tardy, C. H. (1988a). Interpersonal evaluations: Measuring attraction and trust. In C. H. Tardy (Ed.), *A handbook for the study of human communication: Methods and instruments for observing, measuring, and assessing communication processes* (pp. 269–283). Norwood, NJ: Ablex.

Tardy, C. H. (1988b). Self-disclosure: Objectives and methods of measurement. In C. H. Tardy (Ed.), *A handbook for the study of human communication: Methods and instruments for observing, measuring, and assessing communication processes* (pp. 323–346). Norwood, NJ: Ablex.

Watzlawick, P., Beavin, J., & Jackson, D. D. (1967). *Pragmatics of human communication: A study of interactional patterns, pathologies, and paradoxes.* New York: Norton.

Wood, J. T. (1982). Communication and relational culture: Bases for the study of human relationships. *Communication Quarterly, 30,* 75–83.

Zietlow, P. H., & Sillars, A. L. (1988). Life-stage differences in communication during marital conflicts. *Journal of Social and Personal Relationships, 5,* 223–246.

Chapter 10

Discourse

KAREN TRACY

In the past decade, a new area of scholarly inquiry has emerged as a center of intellectual energy. This area, cutting across traditional disciplinary lines, has come to be known as discourse analysis. That this new approach has become influential is evidenced by the emergence of new journals focusing on discourse (e.g., *Discourse Processes, Journal of Language and Social Psychology, Research on Language and Social Interaction, Text*) and by publication of many discourse-focused books (e.g., Coupland, 1988; Craig & Tracy, 1983; de Beaugrande, 1980; Ellis & Donohue, 1986; Haslett, 1987; Kreckel, 1981; Levinson, 1983; Stubbs, 1983) as well a four-volume handbook devoted to the area (vanDijk, 1985). The diversity of interests, approaches, and commitments existing within discourse analysis is large; nevertheless, two common threads run through this work.

The first thread is a commitment to the study of connected texts. The connected text might be as short as two sentences or as long as a book; it might be oral or written; interactive or monologic. This commitment to connected text stands in contrast to research practices of equating language study with the study of sentences and of examining words, sentences, and single utterances out of their textual and social context. The second thread running through discourse approaches is a concern with the function of language—a concern with how people use language to accomplish social purposes.

My purpose in this chapter is to illuminate and critique discourse analytic approaches that contribute to the study of interpersonal interaction.

With this goal in mind, five relatively distinct ways to approach or use discourse can be discerned: (1) ethno-methodological, (2) formal/structural, (3) culturally-focused, (4) discourse processing, and (5) discourse and identity. These approaches differ with regard to whether discourse is seen as data selected or constructed to answer a theoretically derived question or whether discourse is the starting point from which a researcher generates questions and theoretical distinctions; whether one should only use naturally occurring texts or whether one may construct examples and use discourse produced in a laboratory setting; whether and how discourse data should be used with other kinds of data (e.g., interviews, contextual information); what role, if any, there is for quantification; and what the most appropriate systems of recording and transcribing discourse are. Table 1 overviews the positions of each of the five approaches with regard to these issues.

For each of the approaches I will identify the kinds of substantive questions the approach is most suited to answering, provide research examples, explain the positions taken toward the issues outlined in Table 10.1, and suggest some research questions the discourse approach might raise about the Cathy and Michael Stone scenario.

Discourse Analytic Approaches

ETHNOMETHODOLOGICAL

Of the various approaches to discourse, ethnomethodology—also called conversation analysis—differs the most radically from traditional research methods. Arising out of the work of sociologists Sacks and Schegloff (Sacks, Schegloff, & Jefferson, 1974; Schegloff, Jefferson, & Sacks, 1977; Schegloff & Sacks, 1973), conversation analysis is concerned with explicating the practices social actors use to understand, and exhibit understanding of, everyday discourse. Like most sociological approaches, conversational analysis (CA) is interested in social structure. But in contrast to traditional sociological approaches, which locate structure at the level of roles and institutions, CA locates it in interaction.

An example of this approach is Pomerantz's (1988) work on information seeking. The study begins by identifying two general features of information-seeking: (1) a person's purpose in seeking information is relevant to the recipient's determining what to give and the manner in which to give it; and (2) both speakers' and recipients' knowledge levels are relevant to information seeking. Because of these general features of information seeking, Pomerantz argues, speakers often use a question that is a "candidate answer" to provide the recipient a model of the kind of answer that

TABLE 10.1 Criteria Differentiating Approaches to Discourse

Criteria	Approaches				
	CA	FS	CF	DP	D&I
Starting point for research	Discourse	Theory	Discourse	Theory	Discourse
Text type studied	Natural	Constructed /natural	Natural	Constructed	Constructed /natural
Transcription detail	High	Moderate	High	Low	Moderate
Reliance on nontext information	No	Yes	Yes	Yes	Yes
Role for quantification	None	None	Limited	Major	Limited

Note. CA stands for Ethnomethodology (Conversation Analysis); FS for Formal/ Structural; CF for Culturally Focused; DP for Discourse Processing; D&I for Discourse and Identity.

would be appropriate. For example, the questions "And have you been treated all right by the police?" and Was Tom home from school ill today?" presuppose the recipient's answer in ways that a differently worded question (e.g., "How did the police treat you?" and "Why was Tom absent today?") would not. Thus, through presenting and analyzing naturally occurring examples, Pomerantz describes a previously unidentified device that everyday communicators use routinely in seeking information.

The kinds of communicative behaviors analyzed using a CA approach include, for example, fault finding (Morris, 1988), story telling between intimates (Mandelbaum 1987, 1989), and breaking up with a dating partner over the telephone (Hopper & Drummond, in press). Conversational analytic studies can be found across a variety of journals but much of the work is located in a few edited volumes (Atkinson & Heritage, 1984; Beach, 1989; Button & Lee, 1987; Schenkein, 1978).

The hallmarks of conversation analytic work are a commitment to naturally occurring discourse; usage of a particularly detailed transcription system; an inductive, antitheoretical stance; a strong reliance on the conversational text; and an avoidance of nondiscourse data (participant interviews) or predetermined category information (e.g., gender) that is unavailable in the interaction itself.

In contrast to more traditional research methods, the relationship between "doing conversational analysis" (i.e., engaging in the research activity) and writing a research report is a fuzzy one. A centerpiece of conversational analytic activity is the "work session." Work sessions involve an individual or a group of people getting together to listen/view a segment of taped interaction that has been carefully transcribed. Taped segments are initially selected because they are interesting in some general way. After repeated listenings, attempts are made to analyze the discourse. This involves having people articulate their intuitions about what a speaker is doing in a particular utterance and then grounding the intuition in textual features. The actual research paper, then, arises when an investigator has a connected set of insights into an everyday practice or practices (see Hopper, Koch, & Mandelbaum, 1986 for a more detailed overview of the method). Good conversation analytic work identifies and describes plausible accounts for general discourse practices.

With regard to the Stone scenario, our sample research problem, CA would begin by transcribing the audiotaped discussion between Cathy and Michael. Such a transcript might look like the following:

C: We:: kin entertain (0.4) cuz *I* do it all.
M: hhh she's right about the dinner, yuh wouldn't wanta eat *my* cookin (0.5) so::: I ju::ss don't cook.
C: yuh *don't* cook, yuh *don't* clean, yuh don't do *laun*dry.

Transcription of a 30-minute audiotape using the transcript notation developed by Gail Jefferson (Atkinson & Heritage, 1984) would take a researcher roughly 20 hours. Generally, too, this kind of labor is not farmed out to others because the process of transcribing is seen as a valuable first part of acquainting a researcher with his or her data. Following transcription of the tape and multiple listenings to sections of it, the investigator would begin to focus in on what seemed to be interesting conversational practices noted in the tape—for instance, how a conversant turns a criticism into a joke. On the basis of studying the part of the Cathy–Michael exchange where Michael appears to do just that, the investigator would then seek out other instances of this, perhaps from the same tape but from other discourse data as well. Then, after looking at a number of instances, the researcher would formulate how that activity is accomplished. If there were enough interesting permutations in how criticism gets turned into a joke, this issue might become the focus of a paper; if it were not interesting and complex enough to stand alone, it might become the basis of a section in a larger paper focused on, for instance, deflecting criticism.

Many traditional researchers have been skeptical of the value of conversation analysis. The questions that animate CA studies—How is conversation organized? How do people accomplish ordinary activities?—are not seen as the "right" questions for researchers to ask (Sharrock & Anderson, 1987). From the vantage point of mainstream communication and social psychology, the "right" questions are ones that involve formulation and testing of broad-based theories. This difference in starting point, between theory and situated practice, puts CA and mainstream approaches at extreme loggerheads. And, while other discourse approaches do not use "theory" as the starting point for research, none rejects its usefulness as forcefully as does CA.

Conversation Analysis departs the most radically of the discourse approaches from traditional social science assumptions; as such, it offers an interesting and clearly demarcated alternative to mainstream interpersonal approaches. And, while CA will speak most forcefully to interpersonal researchers dissatisfied with mainstream methods, it offers something important to everyone. In particular, the ability to observe and describe interesting features of discourse, a skill that CA hones, is invaluable to traditional researchers in the theory invention and hypothesis formulation phases.

FORMAL/STRUCTURAL*

Discourse is used quite differently in formal structural approaches than is the case with CA. Whereas CA begins inductively with the discourse, formal structural approaches (FS) begin with theoretical formulations and models. Within this approach, discourse is used to exemplify and test a model. For instance, in a paper that proposed a model of how utterances are styled to constrain what follows, Sanders (1984) provided the following discourse example:

(a)   S: I was thinking of staying home and maybe sitting down with
            something to read this evening.
       H: I hoped we'd go see the new Bergman film.
(b)   S: I really need to stay home and relax with a book tonight.
       H: I hoped we'd go see the new Bergman film. (p. 164)

This example, which includes the same response (H's) to two different ways of formulating a desire to stay home is used to illuminate how formulation form constrains what can reasonably follow. Discourse examples, then, are selected or created to illuminate the model.

---

*The names used to reference these five approaches vary in the degree to which they are established labels. "Ethnomethodological" ("CA") and discourse processing are common labels; "Formal/structural," "Culturally focused" and "Discourse and Identity" are my labels. I have chosen these descriptive labels over others that would tie an approach closely to a particular discipline (e.g., anthropological linguistics vs. culturally focused).

FS approaches*, extend the methods of linguistics. In a nutshell, the procedures include (1) identifying a set of basic categories of discourse and (2) specifying how the categories are linked or sequenced in the specific discourse type. The test of the model lies in its ability to account for all forms of the discourse type that people would routinely interpret as coherent at the same time that it does not produce anything people would judge to be incoherent. People's intuitions about what are reasonably likely sequences, then, are an important resource of FS approaches. Another example of this approach is seen in Jacobs and Jackson's (1989) modeling of conversational argument. In their work, examples of naturally occurring discourse, either tape-recorded or written down shortly after occurring, are used to illuminate a model.

While the degree of detail used in transcribing varies enormously with individual researchers, it is generally less detailed than seen in CA (cf. Labov & Fanshel, 1977). As numerous discourse analysts (e.g., Craig & Tracy, 1983) have pointed out, there is no "right" way to transcribe. A researcher's purpose will determine which and how many particulars need to be recorded. In general, the more deductive and theoretically motivated one's research approach, the more license a researcher has to transcribe broadly; the more inductive one's approach, the more important it is to record a larger number of particulars (pronunciation, pausing, stress, overlap, nonfluencies, etc.). Thus, in contrast to CA, FS researchers begin theoretically and, a priori, are willing to ignore certain kinds of discourse detail (see Brown & Levinson, 1978, 1987, and Sanders, 1987, for other formal/structural examples).

If we considered the Stone scenario from a FS approach, we might begin by reviewing prior ideas about conversational disagreement and posit a model of the basic discourse units in conversational disagreement. In this case, we would use an extended example from the Michael and Cathy dialogue to illuminate and support the predicted disagreement model. Another way to proceed, illustrated in Newell & Stutman's (1988) work on social confrontation, includes a somewhat larger inductive component. In this study, strangers role-played different relationships (roommate, boyfriend/girlfriend) and one person confronted another over an incident. These taped interactions, along with the prior theory, were used to refine a model of the various trajectories of social confrontation. Applying this to the Stone

---

*Levinson (1983) labels what I call Formal/Structural approaches as "discourse analysis." Because most other authors do not use the term in this narrow way, neither do I. This highlights the problem of terminological confusion that exists. Terms are used in both broad and narrow ways. Another term, "conversation analysis," is also used in these two ways; this term is used either to identify anyone who is interested in analyzing conversation or to reference the ethnomethodological approach. In contrast to "discourse analysis," however, "conversation analysis" has come to be more strongly associated with the particular research approach.

scenario, we might ask individuals to initiate a confrontation with their spouse, tape-record their interaction, and then use this as a data base to test out our models.

The value of good FS research is its ability to provide an overarching framework that explains many particulars; FS approaches also provide direction regarding where to start research. The limitation of this approach is that FS models and theories often are formulated at levels of abstraction that gloss over important interactional activities.

CULTURALLY FOCUSED

A third approach to discourse, illustrated in the anthropological linguistic work of Gumperz and his students (1982a; 1982b), gives attention to the ways in which the interpretation and production of discourse varies with persons' cultural group membership. An example of this approach is seen in Tannen's (1984) analysis of a Thanksgiving dinner conversation among six friends. The thesis of her work is that each person has a conversational style, a characteristic way of talking, that works well when talking with others of a similar style but which can lead to interactional difficulties when the other's style is different. While everyone's conversational style is unique, large chunks of a person's style are shared with others who have similar ethnic, family, and class backgrounds. Tannen's study supports these claims by drawing upon several kinds of data. First and foremost is the conversational data. Through close analysis of the dinner conversation, Tannen concretizes and illustrates the idea of conversational style. In addition to the discourse data, background information about the participants—their occupation, region of origin, sex, nationality—as well as information gained through participant interviews is used to support the claims. Interviews involve playing excerpts from the interaction to participants and asking them questions about what they meant or what they thought another conversant meant. Then, by combining the interview results with the conversational data, Tannen makes a case for how the six friends have different styles and how the friends with the most dissimilar styles experience the most misunderstandings and moments gone awry. Other examples of culturally focused discourse research include Gumperz's (1982a, 1982b) work on discourse strategies and Katriel's (1986) study of "dugri" speech, a style of speaking common in Israel that involves speaking straight to the point.

Much like FS and CA approaches, culturally focused discourse analysis tends to be nonquantitative, although it is not necessarily so. Tannen (1984), for instance, used simple tables that summarized the frequency of conversational features such as amount of talking, frequency of story telling, and frequency of topic introduction to support her claims about con-

versational style. The use of numbers for selected purposes stands in contrast to CA's philosophical commitment to avoid them—Conversational
Analysts believe counting anything requires a researcher to treat instances as
the "same," therein overlooking the particular ways in which they are
different.

Similar to conversation analysis, culturally focused research proceeds
inductively. But whereas CA is uninterested in data other than the text,
culturally focused approaches make use of a variety of other resources. Not
uncommonly, when culturally based discourse researchers get together
with CA researchers, an argument ensues as to whether using other data
besides the discourse is an advantage or a limitation. As with many such
methodological arguments, there is often a failure to consider the important
ways in which the motivating question of each research approach is fundamentally different. If one's main interest is in explicating conversational
structure within a culture, as is true of CA, textual data is the strongest kind
there can be. However, if one is interested in contrasts between cultures and
in more generally describing the ways in which discourse practices are
culturally rooted, then use of many kinds of data will build a stronger case
than relying solely on the text.

In approaching the sample scenario of the Stone interaction, culturally
based researchers might start from the premise that gender is a culture
where we learn rules of interaction (Maltz & Borker, 1982). Given the
relatively transparent fact that men and women can experience discomfort
in their communication with each other, we might consider how men's and
women's production and interpretation of criticism and confrontation
might be following different cultural logics. Stated more broadly, we might
begin with the assumption that different cultures have different expectations
about who should criticize whom, how, and over what in any well
functioning relationship. To study this issue we would observe men and
women like the Stones in confrontational situations, interview them about
their own and their attributed meanings, and look at instances of actual
criticism. By making connections among these different types of data, we
would try to illuminate the different cultural logics at work.

Good culturally based discourse analysis provides a vivid sense of the
ways in which a myriad of communicative practices are culturally differentiated. It does so by making understandable how and why activities such as
confrontation, friendly talk, or getting intimate are organized differently in
different ethnic, national, or gender groups. From the vantage of communicative practice, the value of understanding and having knowledge of
different ways of handling a situation are inestimable. Not only does such
knowledge increase a person's ability to understand another and potentially
minimize problems, it also gives people an alternative map for action. Like
CA, although in not quite as marked a way, culturally focused research is
not especially interested in formulating broad theories; to the degree that a

researcher sees this goal as the central one, the value of culturally based discourse analysis will be seen as limited.

DISCOURSE PROCESSING

The fourth approach, discourse processing (DP), is interested in the modeling and experimental testing of theories about how text is comprehended and, to a lesser degree, produced. Most centrally, discourse processing is an extension of cognitive psychological interests and methods. It does, however, also include a commitment to computer simulations of natural language processes. Similar in both of these strands of discourse processing is a focal concern with the mind and human reasoning procedures (see, for instance, Bower & Cirilo, 1985, and Schank & Burstein, 1985). Neither of the approaches ignores the text, but because studying text comprehension is complicated and all texts are assumed to have similarities, there has been a tendency to select noninterpersonal discourse. Nonetheless, while much of the work has had a noninteractive focus, interactive spoken discourse has received some attention.

Two studies (Kellermann, Broetzmann, Lim, & Kitao, 1989; Turner & Cullingford, 1989) assessing and simulating knowledge structures for initial-acquaintance conversations illustrate the DP approach and demonstrate its value to interpersonal scholars (see also Daly, Weber, Vangelisti, Maxwell, & Neel, 1989; Harris, Lee, Hensley, & Schoen, 1988). Drawing on Schank's idea of a memory organization packet (MOP) as a theoretical starting point, the Kellermann study poses two research questions: (1) What is the nature of the cognitive structures that guide initial interaction conversations? and (2) How closely does actual conversational discourse reflect the hypothesized initial interaction cognitive structure?

To answer the first question, participants in the Kellerman study were surveyed and asked to list the first 20 acts that would occur in a typical initial interaction. Surveys were coded to produce a general model of the content and sequence of initial interaction. Stated somewhat differently, decontextualized general expectations about what topics people talk about and the order in which they usually occur—that is, what the researchers got from the surveys—were used to provide evidence of people's knowledge structures. The second question Kellermann and associates answered by coding videotapes of unacquainted dyads who conversed for 5 minutes. Discourse was coded to see if it corresponded with the typical knowledge structures generated in the first part of the study. "Discourse" then is oriented to in rather different ways than was seen in the other approaches. A survey provides people's generalized knowledge about one kind of discourse; then, conversational discourse is coded to test a hypothesis about the cognitive knowledge structures underlying the production of discourse.

Turner and Cullingford (1989) also focus on conversational MOPs, but rather than testing their existence, they seek to use them to build a computer simulation designed to handle the opening dialogue of initial interaction. Their goal is to produce a program that will generate what we recognize as normally polite conversation. A research "success" gives evidence that the knowledge representation used to design the simulation is an adequate, although perhaps not the only, account of people's discourse-processing capacities.

Discourse processing seeks to develop broad-based theories: it begins with theory, it works deductively, it is usually quantitative, and it frequently uses constructed texts. Its desired research goals and starting assumptions differ markedly from CA and culturally-focused research. As an approach to discourse, it shares the most in common with the formal/structural approaches. Both types of approach are interested in broad-based theories and proceed deductively. Both types of approach recognize the need to take account of text features and the comprehending mind; they differ, however, with regard to which is given more attention. This difference in emphasis co-occurs with, and perhaps causes, different attitudes toward quantification. It is not at all convincing to draw conclusions about discourse processing based on two or three persons' interpretation of a text. But it can be relatively convincing that a model has captured the existing structure of a type of text if one has demonstrated its correspondence with several well-chosen examples.

How would a discourse-processing researcher approach the study of the sample scenario involving Cathy and Michael Stone? One way might be to attempt to build a model of memory that simulated a person's attitudes and knowledge of a content-specific area—for instance, how husbands and wives should divide labor at home—that could be used to develop a computer program for carrying on a coherent conversation on the topic. Such attempts have already been made for political exchanges (e.g., Schank & Burstein, 1985). A second approach would be to investigate how people's memory of conversations is influenced by relational knowledge schemas or expectations. In this case researchers would bring participants into a lab, vary the expectation in some way, have the subjects converse, record the conversation, code it, bring participants back in a week or two, ask them to recall the conversation, and test whether the expectation manipulation influenced conversational memory in the hypothesized manner.

Although the substantive questions posed by discourse-processing researchers are not typically central ones for researchers interested in interpersonal relationships, this approach's preference for theory-motivated, deductive, quantitative research offers a starting point similar to the majority of current social psychological and communicative research. As such, interpersonal researchers should find the goals and assumptions undergirding the discourse-processing orientation one of the easiest to understand and give assent to. Perhaps the most significant limitation of this approach is that the concern for general principles of discourse processing leads DP research away from consideration of those texts—intimate, elliptical, relationally and contextually embedded talk—that would be most interesting to interpersonal researchers.

DISCOURSE AND IDENTITY

The last approach to discourse explores relationships between the use of particular discourse features and socially important outcomes (e.g., being judged a reasonable, fair, or intelligent person) or antecedents (e.g., different social roles). While there is considerable diversity within this approach, particularly with regard to the value of quantitative methods, there is a shared interest in understanding how discourse creates, manifests, and challenges both valued and disvalued identities. Thus, discourse is valued, not in and of itself as some researchers would argue for (see Hopper, 1988), but because it provides a way into the social identities people claim and attribute to others.

Let me offer two examples of the discourse and identity (D & I) approach. The first is seen in McLaughlin and Cody's work on accounts, a device used when a communicator has engaged in inappropriate behavior (Cody & McLaughlin, 1985; McLaughlin, 1984; McLaughlin, Cody, & Rosenstein, 1983). In this work, a large number of account sequences are collected. In one study (McLaughlin, Cody, & O'Hair, 1983) participants were asked to recall an account sequence—reporting, where they could, the exact words used. After completing the task, participants filled out scales that gave information about the relationship in which the accounting occurred (its intimacy), subsequent consequences of the situation, and several other factors. In another study (McLaughlin, Cody, & Rosenstein, 1983) participants conversed with a stranger in a laboratory setting where they had been provided a general list of topics they could talk about. Following the taping and transcribing of the conversations, account sequences were coded for type of offense, type of reproach, account strategy, and evaluation type. Then, using statistical analysis, conclusions were drawn about relationships between, for instance, types of accounts and whether or not they would be accepted/honored by the party to whom they were directed. McLaughlin & Cody's work, then, helps us understand which kinds of discourse forms co-occur with desired identities (being seen as reasonable, believable) and which with undesired ones (being seen as inappropriate or unbelievable).

A second example of the D & I approach is illustrated in the work of Nikolas and Justine Coupland and their colleagues (Coupland, Coupland, Giles, & Henwood, 1988; in press). Their research reports come out of studying videotaped interaction between 40 dyads of old–young, old–old, and young–young women. Participants who had not met previously were asked to "get to know one another"; interaction was videotaped for 8 minutes and later transcribed in detail. The specific issue focused on in each paper is different, but all concern ways in which age-identity is displayed or oriented to by a partner. In one study interested in understanding younger people's goals in intergenerational talk, a second kind of discourse data is used. Young people, different from the dyadic participants, listen to pieces of the earlier-taped conversations between a young and older person. Then the young people are interviewed in a focus group to elicit reactions to the conversation. These interviews are taped and subsequently analyzed as another source of discourse to give evidence of how young people think about older people and how they think older people should be talked to (see Burke, 1986, and Tracy, 1989, in press, for other examples).

Within the D & I approach, the value of quantifying language phenomena are debated. On the one side are arguments against quantifying that highlight the cost of simplification. People's talk, Potter and Wetherell (1987) argue, is always adapted to the nature of a local occasion. To quantify requires a researcher to treat talk features at a general category level, ignoring the way individual talk examples differ and the way in which specific talk is situationally adapted. To lose this quality of discourse is to lose what is most interesting.

On the other side (Tracy, 1989) is the argument that the central substantive question—What discourse features typically co-occur with specific social judgments?—demands some kind of quantitative evidence. Both of these positions have merit. In the section to follow, I sketch out a new methodology—the laboratory case study—that allows for attention to patterns of likelihood in a way that does not generalize beyond the context inappropriately.*

The laboratory case study is not the only way D & I researchers might approach the Stone scenario; there are several. Because much of my own research is concerned with D & I questions and because I think the current methodological forms, from conversational analysis to experimental study, make assumptions poorly suited to discourse and identity kinds of questions, I offer the laboratory case study as a first attempt to design a more appropriate method.

---

*In another article (Tracy, 1989) I labeled this new method a "naturalistic experiment." Both names—*naturalistic experiment* and *laboratory case study*—suggest a blend of qualitative and quantitative methods but differ regarding which they imply is primary. After some consideration I have decided that *laboratory case study* more accurately reflects the method's underlying logic; this method, while it possesses elements of laboratory approaches, is a modification of case study logic.

The Laboratory Case Study

If a D & I researcher were to carry out a laboratory case study with the Stone scenario, the first step would be to pose an interesting question, one that inquired about links between specific kinds of discourse and identity concerns. A possible question, for instance, might be, What discourse features relate to one spouse feeling that the other spouse has represented him or her fairly in reporting a mutual conflict? Given this question, we would bring 30 married couples into an interview session and audio- or videotape them. At the interview spouses would be asked to think of a conflict they had with their partner they would feel comfortable discussing. Each spouse would be asked to describe the conflict. After one spouse's description, the other would be asked if he or she would add or modify it in any way. In addition, after the interview, spouses would fill out scales evaluating how fairly they felt they represented the conflict and how fairly they felt their spouse represented the conflict. Then drawing upon some or all of the three kinds of data—(1) extensions of the spouse's account, (2) self-rating of fairness, and (3) rating of other's fairness—the interviews would be divided into different groups. For example, we might divide conflict accounts into the 15 fairest and the 15 unfairest, as rated by one spouse of the other. If we had reason to believe that the role "husband" or "wife" influenced that judgment process, we might separate spouse accounts by role. Then, after transcribing and carefully studying the two "piles," we would try to formulate the features that led to high and low attributions of fairness. While the discourse features that would be given attention might be influenced by theories about conflict and disagreement, the theories would be background for the largely inductive nature of the study. Through careful study of the transcribed interaction, the researcher would identify the discourse features that co-occurred with the judgments that the spouse was fair or unfair in his or her descriptions of a conflict.

The logic of the laboratory case study, then, is to attempt in the particular case studied to account for the variation in a particular identity—related judgment. This approach is a laboratory one because it puts numbers of people in a relatively similar situation—in this case, talking about a marital conflict to a stranger who has no prior information about either individual or the dyad—rather than observing the accounts in natural conversational settings (i.e., with friends and family, where they typically arise). It is a laboratory approach because judgments capable of being coded or scaled are collected from relevant others. It is a laboratory approach because it is centrally interested in drawing conclusions about how two things, discourse features and identity judgments, relate.

While the laboratory case study has many laboratory features, it is primarily a case study. Like most case studies it is interested in the complexities of the particular case. For the hypothetical case described thus far, the researcher would be interested in describing the discourse features that led a group of middle-class, American married couples to see their partner as fair when their partner was asked to describe a marital conflict to a stranger in an interview situation.

A laboratory case study begins by focusing on an everyday kind of interaction. This everyday situation then, is justified as deserving of study because of its problematic nature for interactants (see Tracy, 1990 for a discussion of situation problematicity). To justify this example study, for instance, we could point to the ubiquitous concern people have about being treated fairly in their relationships; we would also highlight the way in which representing one's own side in a conflict can be at odds with the desire to be perceived as fair by one's partner. While fairness includes more than how one person talks about another, how people carry out this activity is clearly going to be important. In sum, while a laboratory case study may speak to theoretical interests, traditionally conceived, its main justification is the real-world importance and interest value of the relationship being studied.

In contrast to CA, which begins with instances of everyday discourse, the laboratory case study seeks to simulate a situation in which multiple participants deal with the "same" situation in the ways that are routinely available in everyday life. Similar to the discourse-processing perspective, the laboratory case study is interested in the relationship between discourse and something else. However, no simple principles of generalizability are expected to operate. In fact, it is considered quite likely that the set of discourse features that co-occur with attributions of fairness would change if the participants were not American or middle-class, were talking to a friend, were allowed to co-construct the account, and so forth. While generalizability is not straightforward, it is possible. In essence, it is assumed that in-depth knowledge of an interesting complex case will have implications for others.

Unlike much inductive research, there is a role for quantification in the laboratory case study. It is, however, different from what is seen in most statistically based research. In large measure, the aims and logic of inferential statistics are at odds with the laboratory case study. Where research using inferential statistics begins with either hypotheses or a priori research questions; the laboratory case study begins inductively. Where research using inferential statistics seeks to generalize relationships that occurred in the sample to a theoretical population, the laboratory case study sees "theoretical populations" as, at best, trivially present. For instance, a researcher could treat the 30 husband–wife accounts as a pilot study in which the features inductively identified are treated as hypotheses for the "real" study. But the value in doing this is undercut if one's theoretical population is seen to be no more extensive than one's selected case, in this instance, middle-class, American married couples being interviewed by a stranger about their conflicts. If a researcher thinks people produce discourse in a highly situation-adapted manner, as I and most D & I researchers do, then it is to be expected that the configuration of discourse features that occur with particular social judgments will change when an aspect of the situation changes. Thus, the logic of generalization that is part of statistical testing is incompatible with the laboratory case study. In addition, if one is interested in unique ways of talking that co-occur with social judgments, statistics can offer no help.

In sum, the laboratory case study is a hybrid method that seeks to bring together two methodologies. Whether this method will be judged a viable solution to the competing goals of naturalism and control, induction and deduction, and qualitative description and quantification remains an open question until we have more research examples (see Tracy & Eisenberg, in press, for a preliminary example). My hope is that the laboratory case study will enable D & I scholars to better answer some of the research questions that most intrigue them.

Conclusions

This chapter has considered five ways in which discourse is used as data. As with most classification systems, the five-part system offered here simplifies what is actually occurring. Besides individual studies that bridge categories (for instance, for a bridge between formal/structural and discourse-processing approaches, see van Dijk & Kintsch, 1983), researchers draw upon discourse data to make theoretical critiques. For instance, Potter & Wetherell (1987) criticize the inappropriate simplicity of traditional models of attitude through analyzing conversations in which speakers from a dominant social group express attitudes about a minority group.

As I argue elsewhere (Tracy, 1988), different approaches to the study of discourse, such as those discussed in this chapter, make markedly different assumptions about what is worth knowing and what a researcher should be willing to trade off in the knowledge-seeking process. These issues must be confronted by any researcher in deciding to use discourse as data. While I have tried to highlight the advantages of each approach, I have, admittedly, given more attention to the inductive ones (ethnomethodological, culturally focused, discourse & identity). I have done this to correct what I see as an overemphasis on deductive methods and because I think understanding of interpersonal interaction can be advanced by starting with the particulars of talk.

References

Atkinson, J. M., & Heritage, J. (Eds.). (1984). *Structures of social action: Studies in conversation analysis.* Cambridge: Cambridge University Press.

Beach, W. (Ed.). (1989). Sequential organization of conversational activities. Special issue of *Western Journal of Speech Communication, 52.*

Bower, G. H., & Cirilo, R. K. (1985). Cognitive psychology and text processing. In T. A. Van dijk (Ed.), *Handbook of discourse analysis: Vol. 1. Disciplines of discourse* (pp. 71–105). London: Academic Press.

Brown, P., & Levinson, S. (1978). Universals in language usage: Politeness phenomena. In E. N. Goody (Ed.), *Questions and politeness: Strategies in social interaction* (pp. 56–310). Cambridge: Cambridge University Press.

Brown, P., & Levinson, S. (1987). *Universals in language usage: Politeness phenomena.* Cambridge: Cambridge University Press.

Burke, J. A. (1986). Interacting plans in the accomplishment of a practical activity. In D. G. Ellis & W. A. Donohue (Eds.), *Contemporary issues in language and discourse processes* (pp. 203–222). Hillsdale, NJ: Erlbaum.

Button, G., & Lee, J. R. E. (Eds.). (1987). *Talk and social organisation.* Clevedon, England: Multilingual Matters.

Cody, M. J., & McLaughlin, M. L. (1985). Models for the sequential construction of accounting episodes: Situational and interactional constraints on message selection and evaluation. In R. L. Street & J. N. Cappella (Eds)., *Sequence and pattern in communicative behaviour* (pp. 50–69). London: Edward Arnold.

Coupland, N. (1988). Introduction: Towards a stylistics of discourse. In N. Coupland (Ed.), *Styles of discourse* London: Croom Helm. (1–19).

Coupland, N., Coupland, J., Giles, H., & Henwood, K. (1988). My life in your hands: Strategic and discoursal processes in the management of elderly self-disclosure in intergenerational talk. Paper presented at Temple University's Ninth Annual Conference on Discourse Analysis, Philadelphia.

Coupland, N., Coupland, J., Giles, H., & Henwood, K. (in press). The consonance and conflict of goals in intergenerational talk. In K. Tracy (Ed.), *Understanding face-to-face interaction: Issues linking goals and discourse.* Hillsdale, NJ: Erlbaum.

Craig, R.. T., & Tracy, K. (Eds.). (1983). *Conversational coherence: Form, structure and strategy.* Beverly Hills: Sage.

Daly, J. A., Weber, D. J., Vangelisti, A. L., Maxwell, M., & Neel, H. (1989). Concurrent cognitions during conversations: Protocol analysis as a means of exploring conversations. *Discourse Processes, 12,* 227–244.

de Beaugrande, R. (1980). *Text, discourse and process: Toward a multidisciplinary science of text.* Norwood, NJ: Ablex.

Ellis, D. G., & Donohue, W. A. (1986). *Contemporary issues in language and discourse processes.* Hillsdale, NJ: Erlbaum.

Gumperz, J. J. (Ed.). (1982a). *Language and social identity.* Cambridge: Cambridge University Press.

Gumperz, J. J. (1982b). *Discourse strategies.* Cambridge: Cambridge University Press.

Harris, R. J., Lee, D. J., Hensley, D. L., & Schoen, L. M. (1988). The effect of cultural script knowledge on memory for stories over time. *Discourse Processes, 11*, 413–422.

Haslett, B. (1987). *Communication: Strategic action in context*. Hillsdale, NJ: Erlbaum.

Hopper, R. (1988). Speech, for instance: The exemplar in studies of conversation. *Journal of Language and Social Psychology, 7*, 47–64.

Hopper, R., & Drummond, K. (in press). Emergent goals at a relational turning point. The case of Gordon and Denise. *Journal of Language and Social Psychology*.

Hopper, R., Koch, S., & Mandelbaum, J. (1986). Conversation analysis methods. In D. G. Ellis & W. A. Donohue (Eds.), *Contemporary issues in language and discourse processes* (pp. 169–186). Hillsdale, NJ: Erlbaum.

Jacobs, S., & Jackson, S. (1989). Building a model of conversational argument. In B. Dervin, L. Grossberg, B. J. O'Keefe, & E. Wartella (Eds.), *Rethinking communication: Vol. 2. Paradigm exemplars* (pp. 153–171). Newbury Park, CA: Sage.

Katriel, T. (1986). *Talking straight: Dugri speech in Israeli Sabra culture*. London: Cambridge University Press.

Kellermann, K., Broetzmann, S., Lim, T., & Kitao, K. (1989). The conversation MOP: Scenes in the stream of discourse. *Discourse Processes, 12*, 27–62.

Kreckel, M. (1981). *Communicative acts and shared knowledge in natural discourse*. London: Academic Press.

Labov, W., & Fanshel, D. (1977). *Therapeutic discourse: Psychotherapy as conversation*. New York: Academic Press.

Levinson, S. C. (1983). *Pragmatics*. Cambridge: Cambridge University Press.

Maltz, D. N., & Borker, R. A. (1982). A cultural approach to male-female miscommunication. In J. J. Gumperz (Ed.), *Language and social identity* (pp. 195–216). Cambridge: Cambridge University Press.

Mandelbaum, J. (1987). Couples sharing stories. *Communication Quarterly, 35*, 144–170.

Mandelbaum, J. (1989). Interpersonal activities in conversational storytelling. *Western Journal of Speech Communication, 53*, 114–126.

McLaughlin, M. L. (1984). *Conversation: How talk is organized*. Beverly Hills: Sage.

McLaughlin, M. L., Cody, M. J., & O'Hair, H. D. (1983). The management of failure events: Some contextual determinants of accounting behavior. *Human Communication Research, 9*, 208–224.

McLaughlin, M. L., Cody, M., & Rosenstein, N. E. (1983). Account sequences in conversation between strangers. *Communication Monographs, 50*,102–125.

Morris, G. H. (1988). Finding fault. *Journal of Language and Social Psychology, 7*, 1–26.

Newell, S. E., & Stutman, R. K. (1988). The social confrontation episode. *Communication Monographs, 55*, 266–285.

Pomerantz, A. (1988). Offering a candidate answer: An information-seeking strategy. *Communication Monographs, 55*, 360–373.

Potter, J., & Wetherell, M. (1987). *Discourse and social psychology*. Newbury Park, CA: Sage.

Sacks, H., Schegloff, E. A., & Jefferson, G. (1974). A simplest systematics for the organization of turn taking for conversation. *Language, 50*, 696–735.

Sanders, R. E. (1984). Style, meaning, and message effects. *Communication Monographs, 51*, 154–167.

Schank, R., & Burstein, M. (1985). Artificial intelligence: Modeling memory for language understanding. In T. A. van Dijk (Ed.), *Handbook of discourse analysis: Vol. 1. Disciplines of discourse* (pp. 145–166). London: Academic Press.

Schegloff, E. A., Jefferson, G., & Sacks, H. (1977). The preference for self-correction in the organization of repair in conversation. *Language, 53,* 361–382.

Schegloff, E. A., & Sacks, H. (1973). Opening up closings. *Semiotica, 8,* 289–327.

Schenkein, J. (Ed.). (1978). *Studies in the organization of conversational interaction.* New York: Academic Press.

Sharrock, W., & Anderson, B. (1987). In G. Button & J. R. E. Lee (Eds.), *Talk and social organisation* (pp. 290–321). Clevedon, Avon: Multilingual Matters.

Stubbs, M. (1983). *Discourse analysis: The sociolinguistic analysis of natural language.* Chicago: University of Chicago Press.

Tannen, D. (1984). *Conversational style: Analyzing talk among friends.* Norwood, NJ: Ablex.

Tracy, K. (1988). A discourse analysis of four discourse studies. *Discourse Processes, 11,* 243–259.

Tracy, K. (1989). Conversational dilemmas and the naturalistic experiment. In B. Dervin, L. Grossberg, B. J. O'Keefe, & E. Wartella (Eds.), *Rethinking communication: Vol. 2. Paradigm exemplars* (pp. 411–423). Newbury Park, CA: Sage

Tracy, K. (1990). The many faces of facework. In H. Giles & W. P. Robinson (Eds.), *Handbook of Language and Social Psychology* (pp. 209–223). New York: Wiley.

Tracy, K., & Eisenberg, E. M. (in press). Giving criticism: A multiple goals case study. *Research on Language and Social Interaction.*

Turner, E. H., & Cullingford, R. E. (1989). Using conversation MOPs in natural language interfaces. *Discourse Processes, 12,* 63–90.

van Dijk, T. A. (Ed.). (1985). *Handbook of discourse analysis, Vol. 1–4.* London: Academic Press.

van Dijk, T. A., & Kintsch, W. (1983). *Strategies of discourse comprehension.* New York: Academic Press.

Chapter 11

Behavioral Observation

ALAN L. SILLARS

In this chapter, I consider basic issues and design options in observational research on interaction processes. More specifically, my focus is on collecting, rather than analyzing, observational data. Interaction analysis methods are described thoroughly in several other sources (e.g., Bakeman & Gottman, 1986; Poole, Folger, & Hewes, 1987; Sackett, 1978; Tardy, 1988; Also Part III, this volume). The phrase *observational research* applies to studies that collect and analyze records of interactional events from the perspective of an outside observer. The interactional record may take the form of audio or video recordings, a narrative record of events made by an observer, or interpretations and codes that are registered at the time of observation. If not done immediately, interaction records are eventually converted to qualitative summaries, ratings (e.g., of affection or responsiveness), or behavioral codes, with codes further reduced to measures of frequency (e.g., the number of head nods, questions, companionate themes, or domineering statements), duration (e.g., length of eye gaze, talk time), and sequence (e.g., the incidence of imitative motor behavior or complain-countercomplain sequences). Although experiments and self-reports also involve observation of behavior, they differ in emphasis and perspective from observational methods. In experiments the focus is on antecedent-consequent relations. The interactional events that intercede between input and output may be greatly simplified in the interests of experimental control. In observational studies interactional events are the primary focus, so there are fewer controls and behavior is more naturally instigated, with

multiple antecedents (Weick, 1968). Self-report methods differ from observational methods in terms of observer perspective (third party vs. participant) and level of abstraction. Self-reports characteristically measure more
global, less contingent, and less transitory aspects of behavior in comparison with observational measures.

Although there are several vigorous areas of observational research, a
few authors have still commented that behavioral observation is the "Cin-
derella" of the methodological family for studying relationships (James,
1983, McCarthy, 1981). Most observational studies of interaction have been
studies of unacquainted strangers (usually college students), family members, or children. Strangers appear in research on acquaintance formation
and also tend to be the population of choice in research on basic interaction
processes (e.g., turn-taking, speech convergence, conversational involvement). Within the realm of ongoing personal relationships, family interaction and parent–infant research predominate. There are few observational
studies of adult friendships or developing romantic relationships. Perhaps
these relationships are too ambiguous and fragile to permit the same
amount of intrusive observation that researchers have performed on families. There are also surprisingly few observational studies of parent–child
interactions during the middle and later years of childhood, perhaps because
observations are more difficult to arrange once children reach school age.
With older children, studies of teacher–child and child–child interaction are
far more numerous than parent–child studies (Shields, 1981).

Needless to say, all methods, observational research included, entail
trade-offs. Observational studies pose challenging validity issues, which are
considered later in this chapter. Observational studies are also difficult to
carry out. The collection, transcribing, and coding of interaction records
can be a time-consuming, expensive, and tedious effort. At the same time,
observational studies have an irreplacable function in the larger scheme of
things, which I would characterize as the study of relationships "in progress." Human relationships evolve from and are, in effect, constituted by
specific interactional behaviors. I believe that this is essentially what Watzlawick, Beavin, and Jackson (1967) mean when they suggest that communication "defines the relationship" and what Berger and Kellner (1964)
mean when they state that we "converse our way through life." Global
qualities of relationships (e.g., distress, traditionalism, nurturance, rigidity)
acquire their substance through the enactment of specific interactional
routines in particular contexts. Observational methods subject these
routines to a more rigorous and intensive analysis than they could otherwise
receive. Experimental methods are less concerned with such matters than
with isolating cause and effect relationships. Self-report methods confound
what people do with what they think they do. Although self-reports may be
enlightening in numerous respects, particularly when used in combination

with observation, they nonetheless represent subjective accounts that are more global, thematic, and selective than behavioral records.

In the following pages, I consider issues and options in observational research. Initially, I consider alternative methods for observing and simulating interaction. Later, I discuss a few central problems in observational research, focusing particularly on sampling and reactivity issues.

Designing Observational Studies

Observational design largely boils down to a set of decisions about how much and what kind of structure to impose. Observational settings vary widely in the degree of structure imposed by the researcher. Conventionally, we may think of laboratory research as "structured" and field research as "unstructured," but the actual design alternatives are far more complex (see Parke, 1979). A researcher might observe naturally occurring events unobtrusively, administer a structured task in a field setting, observe unstructured activity in a laboratory (e.g., free play between a parent and child), and so forth. Further, even highly structured observations range widely in the extent to which they reproduce elements of natural interactions. To some extent, researchers can "naturalize" structured observations by simulating an activity that is familiar to the people involved.

As a rule of thumb, I suggest that observational studies should preserve as many elements of naturally occurring behavior as possible, while still accomplishing the goals of a study. All other things being equal, unobtrusive methods (i.e., observation without participants' awareness) are preferable to obtrusive observations, naturalistic observation is desirable over interaction simulations, and structured interaction in a natural setting is preferable over structured laboratory observation. Intuitively, to the extent that the obtrusive presence of the researcher is minimized and the situation reproduces elements that are familiar to individuals (i.e., a familiar setting or task), people will reveal more personally significant and familiar patterns of behavior.

The rule of thumb stated above carries an escape clause (i.e., "all other things being equal"), because the need for realism must also be balanced against the practical constraints of observation and the need for control. Not all elements of naturally occurring interactions can or should be preserved, since they may leave an event too complex to understand (see Weick, 1968; Bavelas, 1984). Still, it is possible to eject the baby with the bath water, as in cases where the essential characteristics of interactions or relationships are sacrificed for the benefit of control. For example, interaction simulations involving randomly matched strangers have weak relevance for the study of personal relationships, because they sanitize the interaction of all gradually acquired, interdependent patterns of perception and behavior (i.e., the "relationship culture"). Although these interdependent qualities produce irregularities in the interaction, the irregularities are at the heart of most investigations into personal relationships. Similarly, emotionless games and note-passing tasks delete many of the most essential features of interpersonal conflict and communication, respectively. However, there are many difficult judgment calls about what aspects of natural interactions are important to preserve. Further, the exact point at which an acceptable trade-off between realism and control or simplicity and complexity is reached cannot be determined in a vacuum. Depending on the objectives of a study, any number of designs, ranging from laboratory-based games to naturalistic observation, may be called for.

NATURAL EVENTS AND STAGED EVENTS

The first step in observational design is to decide whether or not to create the event under investigation. That is, the research may either target naturally occurring interactions or employ "staged" events that would not occur in the same way without the researcher's intervention. The obvious solution to the many trappings of simulated interactions is to study naturally occurring events and, better still, to do so unobtrusively, where responsible ethics permit. Although clearly a minority among observational studies, there are still many examples of naturalistic observation. Naturalistic observation has been used most often with children, particularly parent–infant studies, studies of children's peer interactions, and ethological investigations of child behavior (Jones, 1972). Children are typically observed in homes, preschools, playgrounds, or classrooms. Predictably, most unstructured, naturalistic observation of parent–child interaction occurs when the child is still immobile and interactions are easier to track (Lytton, 1971). Family interactions have also been observed during shopping trips (Brown, 1979), dinnertime (Dreyer & Dreyer, 1973), television viewing (Lull, 1980), and varied activities throughout the home (Kantor & Lehr, 1975; Steinglass, 1979). Other forms of naturalistic observation include the monitoring of professionally-oriented interactions, such as therapeutic, employment, or physician interviews (e.g., Street & Buller, 1988); observations in institutional or organizational settings, such as a natural decision-making groups (Poole & Roth, 1989); and analyses of existing tapes and transcripts, such as radio interviews (Sherblom & Van Rheenen, 1984) and recorded divorce-mediation sessions (Donoghue, in press).

Both natural and staged observations entail trade-offs. Naturalistic observations are most desirable for their realism. Any form of observation will affect behavior if the observer's presence is known; however, habituation to the researcher should be faster with naturalistic observation than if the event is staged. In part, this is because people experience less confusion about how they should behave if the event and context are very familiar. Naturally occurring events also command the participants' attention in a way unlike staged observations. In naturalistic observations the main business at hand is to shop, play, prepare meals, negotiate a divorce, and so forth. The fact that these events have a structure apart from the researcher diminishes the effect of the researcher's presence. When people have other concerns to attend to, they engage in less self-conscious second-guessing about what the researcher is after.

Although naturalistic observations are desirable for their realism, the range of situations that can be observed without intervention is limited, due to norms regarding privacy and decorum in public encounters. Limitations on the types of events that can be observed without intervention threaten the validity of conclusions about, say, intimate conflict or parental discipline that are based on the sort of behavior that is normally open to public inspection. Of course, restrictions on the observability of behavior are greatest for unobtrusive methods. Although it is possible to observe family conflict in shopping malls and "state of the relationship" talks in restaurants, their occurrence is not regular enough for the purpose of research, and ethical problems are encountered in the use of personal information without subjects' awareness. Further, the very fact that personal conversations take place within earshot suggests that the remarks do not issue from a cross section of individuals but, rather, from individuals with relaxed privacy norms and permeable relationship boundaries. While unobtrusive observations are the most limiting, even intensive observations of natural interactions may elicit a "houseguest" effect (i.e., the house is prepared for inspection, the family becomes less business-like or punitive and more fun loving, decisions and conflicts are postponed). Interaction simulations, if they are sufficiently involving, provide a more efficient means of observing private behaviors such as marital conflict, because the behavior is directly elicited by the structure of the task.

The other limitation of naturalistic observation is also a strength, depending on the researcher's objective. Naturally occurring behavior is unfocused and chaotic by comparison with behavior on a structured task. Conversations rapidly shift topic, people come and go, discussions are interrupted by phone calls and small emergencies, and numerous other irregularities occur. The ability of unstructured observation to attend to this chaos is a strength if the researcher is concerned with the natural ecology of interaction. On the other hand, the lack of standardization in naturalistic observation can make comparisons between subject groups tenuous, due to the large number of uncontrolled nuisance variables. Comparing conversations that are of unequal length, dissimilar content, different physical locations, and different constituencies is like comparing apples and

artichokes, unless length, content, location, and constituency are the qualities of interest.

A final limitation of naturalistic observation, which applies mainly to
unobtrusive observation, is that it provides little flexibility for combining
observations with self-reports. Although internal states such as affect may
be inferred from overt behavior, the range of covert responses that can be
safely inferred is very small.

SIMULATING INTERACTION

Parent–infant simulations are usually very straightforward. Most typically,
parents are invited to engage in unstructured or semi-structured play in a
play lab (e.g., Stafford, 1987). Interactions with older children may involve
a more structured game, such as "pin the tail on the donkey" (Yarrow &
Waxler, 1979) or joint manipulation of an Etch-a-Sketch toy (Hess &
Shipman, 1965). Interaction simulations involving strangers are also easy to
contrive. Individuals may be asked to discuss controversial topics or everyday problems (O'Keefe & Shepherd, 1989), to informally interview the
other person (Kellerman, 1986), to discuss suggested topics typical of initial
interactions, such as "things about your hometown" (McLaughlin, Cody,
Kane, & Robey, 1981), or simply to hold an informal, get-acquainted
conversation (Duncan & Fiske, 1977). These instructions are likely to work
fine if the researcher is interested in the initial stages of acquaintance or in
elements of interaction that can be observed in any discussion. However, if
the interest of the researcher is in something more intimate and threatening,
such as higher-level self-disclosure or conflict, realistic simulations involving strangers are more difficult to devise for the simple reason that strangers
do not ordinarily engage in these behaviors. Researchers would be well
advised to regard most interaction simulations between strangers as acquaintance studies. Efforts to study influence, power, conflict, or intimate
disclosure among strangers may lack realism because subjects are more
concerned with politeness and uncertainty reduction than the researcher's
agenda.

Numerous studies have simulated conflict, decision making and problem solving within intimate couples and families. Here, the main challenge
in arranging simulations is to make the task sufficiently involving. A
number of approaches have been devised, including games, role plays,
conflict-generating tasks, discussion of family members' own conflicts, and
interview schedules (see Riskin & Faunce, 1972). Some tasks suggest a
devious imagination on the part of the researchers. Among the games used
to study family interaction is the "ball and pusher" task (Hamblin, 1958),
employed in SIMFAM (simulated family interaction; see Straus & Tallman,
1971), which resembles shuffleboard; families are required to infer the

method of scoring from red and green lights flashed for positive and negative scores. Families are told that "the problem to be solved is to figure out how to play this game" (Straus & Tallman, p. 388). Similarly, Reiss (1971) has had families arrange cards with nonsense syllables printed on them (e.g., "VSPFMK") to assess whether they could extract implicit principles of stimulus organization. Games require the participants to master a novel situation and, consequently, they are more appropriate to the study of problem solving or creativity than, conflict. An advantage of games is that it is relatively easy to involve whole families, including children. Lack of realism and generality of game-playing behavior are the biggest potential limitations, since games only vaguely resemble other situations a family may face. At best, game behavior represents low-key problem solving, not problem solving under duress.

In role play simulations, family members are asked to act out a hypothetical but common scenario. For example, they might be asked to plan an activity for the Fourth of July (Levinger, 1963), decide how to spend $300 received as a gift (Kenkel, 1963), or load a large crate painted to represent a station wagon (Straus, 1964). In the more elaborate role plays used by Raush, Barry, Hertel and Swain (1974), Gottman (1979), and Wittman and Fitzpatrick (1986), spouses were given explicit roles designed to directly induce conflict. For example, in one improvisation, the husband has decided to surprise his wife with an anniversary dinner at their favorite restaurant, while the wife has spent half a day preparing a special dinner at home (Raush et al., p. 57–58); inexplicably, the husband has paid in advance. In another scenario, the wife wants to be close and make love, whereas the husband wants to complete some "activity of his choosing" without being interrupted (Gottman, 1979, p. 137). Conflict-generating tasks include the Color Matching Test (Goodrich & Boomer, 1963; Ryder & Goodrich, 1966), the Revealed Differences Technique (Strodbeck, 1951; Mishler & Waxler, 1968), and the Inventory of Marital Conflicts (Olson & Ryder, 1970). In both the Color Matching Test and Inventory of Marital Conflicts spouses are duped into disagreements by conflicting information provided by the researcher. In the Color Matching Test, spouses each have a display of colors that they attempt to match with other colors presented to them. Spouses are asked to agree on the best match. Conflict is created by the fact that the two color displays are numbered differently. In the Inventory of Marital Conflicts, spouses read and discuss 18 vignettes describing typical marital conflicts. In 12 of the vignettes the husband receives a description that is highly sympathetic to the male in the story, whereas the wife receives a description that is sympathetic to the female, thus creating conflict when the couple is asked to mutually determine responsibility for the problems. The Revealed Differences Technique is more straightforward. Here, family members separately complete a questionnaire that, though varying from study to study, may include opinions about reference

families, everyday situations, or values. Subsequently, differences in their
separate answers are revealed and members are asked to discuss and resolve
these differences. A similar approach used by Ting-Toomey (1983) was
based on disagreements expressed on a marital adjustment scale.

Role plays and conflict-generating tasks are more precise than many
methods in eliciting the behavior of interest and they provide a standardized
stimulus for the purpose of comparing couples or families. However, both
types of tasks cause people to disagree about things that they might not
normally disagree on and cause them to express their disagreement whether
they normally would or not. Role plays in which people are assigned
specific feelings, thoughts, and behaviors have the added problem that
people are required to become actors. To their credit, researchers usually
prepare and coach role play participants in order to make the simulations as
realistic and involving as possible. Still, people may or may not feel comfortable about the role assigned. Although people may be encouraged to
"act themselves," they have limited freedom to do so. Since some people
are undoubtedly more comfortable with role plays than others, the method
potentially yields a "psychology of exhibitionists' personal relationships"
(McCarthy, 1981, p. 38).

The approach recommended by Glick and Gross (1975), among others,
is to have people discuss issues that occur in their own relationships. A
number of studies, particularly recent ones, have adopted this approach
(e.g., Burggraf & Sillars, 1987; Fitzpatrick, 1988; Krokoff, Gottman, &
Roy, 1988; Noller, 1985). This approach should be most successful at
eliciting the involvement of participants and reducing the reactivity of
observation because the stimulus has known personal relevance. A few
studies suggest that couples manipulate their style of interaction more
readily when discussing hypothetical conflicts rather than their own conflicts (see Harvey, Christensen & McClintock, 1983). A potential disadvantage to having couples discuss their own conflicts is that the topic of
discussion will not be sufficiently standardized for comparisons across
couples. To overcome this problem, studies have had couples rate the
severity of different conflicts beforehand (e.g., Burggraf & Sillars, 1987;
Krokoff et al. 1988) or simply select a serious conflict (Fitzpatrick, 1988) so
that the salience of conflicts is standardized somewhat. Since the emphasis
of most studies is on the style rather than the content of interaction, the
salience of an issue is probably a more important source of variation than its
content.

Finally, researchers have simulated couple interactions by having them
respond to a series of interview questions. Rogers, Courtright, and Millar
(1980) taped in-home discussions in response to questions about how the
couple decided to marry, how they deal with disagreements, and other
matters. Since the questions do not all involve conflict or suggest a problem
to be resolved, the procedure is more appropriate for studying dimensions
of marital communication that are common to all interactions. In this case,

the researchers investigated aspects of "relational communication" that were presumed to be quite general.

Subtle differences in instructions may affect the nature of discussions. Many conflict tasks ask couples to speak for a specified period of time or to resolve their disagreements, thus limiting opportunities for conflict avoidance. When couples are told to discuss issues for as long as they like without specific instructions to resolve, they rarely mention possible solutions or request behavior changes from their partner (Sillars & Kalbfleisch, 1989, p. 181), and avoidance behaviors (e.g., topic shifts, denial, and equivocation) are extremely common (Sillars, Wilmot, & Hocker, in press). A colleague and I have suggested that the extent to which couples explicitly manage and resolve conflicts or decisions is a central dimension of couple communication styles (Sillars & Kalbfleisch, 1989). Some couples manage decisions and conflicts proactively, self-reflectively, and explicitly. Others may allow decisions and relationship changes to evolve incrementally with minimal explicit discussion. Thus, if couples are told to resolve conflicts or are otherwise given minimal opportunity for conflict avoidance, a more explicit and confrontive style of communication may appear in simulations than in their natural interactions. Of course, instructions to resolve conflict may be necessary if the research is concerned with explicit negotiation of relationship change (e.g., Gottman, 1979).

A few remaining factors may affect the realism of interaction simulations. First, interactions may be staged either in a laboratory setting or in a natural setting, usually the home. Setting up simulations in the home increases the likelihood of irregularities in the data. Some families more than others will successfully isolate themselves from interruptions and noise, depending on privacy norms, family size, and living conditions. However, this trade-off may be easily compensated by increased realism in home observations. The laboratory adds a host of unfamiliar elements to the already strange experience of being observed. As we might expect, people seem to behave more spontaneously when observed at home. In two studies that compared the same task conducted in two settings, marital interaction was more emotional (O'Rourke, 1963) and negative (Gottman, 1979) at home than in the laboratory. Similarly, Moustakas, Sigel, and Schalock (1956) reported that mothers showed greater hostility, less interaction, less helping and more restrictive and forbidding behavior at home than in a playroom laboratory, suggesting that the laboratory evokes more constrained and socially desirable behavior. While observation in a natural setting may be preferred, as a next best alternative researchers may create a "naturalized" laboratory environment, such as a simulated living room or playground (e.g., Raush et al., 1974). In its unaltered state the typical university or institutional laboratory, with its one-way mirror, stiff furniture, glaring fluorescent lights, bare walls, and other moonscape qualities, is indeed an imposing environment in which to hold a conversation.

A second factor that may produce a more or less intimidating observational setting is the method of recording observations. Research on this subject is inconclusive. Some studies suggest, as we might expect, that the reactivity of observation is increased when the observer or recording instrument is more immediate and obvious (e.g., the camera or tape recorder is clearly visible vs. hidden). However, these effects are not very robust (see Weick, 1968; Wiemann, 1981). Wiemann suggests that behaviors not under the conscious control of individuals (e.g., nonverbal anxiety cues) are least affected by the method of observation and most effects are confined to the initial period of observation. For at least some behaviors, however, the most obtrusive recording methods, such as videotaping with the camera visible, are likely to increase reactivity. Attribution studies indicate that pointing a camera at people alters their focus of attention and makes them more objectively aware of their own behavior (Duvall & Hensley, 1976; Taylor & Fiske, 1978).

My colleagues and I have administered the same marital communication task using both video recording in a laboratory setting and audio recording at home (see Burggraf & Sillars, 1987). In addition, the home recordings were self-administered according to detailed instructions given to couples. We cannot strictly compare the two methods because of differences in samples, coders, and other factors. Still, there is clearly a different "feel" to the data sets, as the self-administered audio recordings intuitively appear more spontaneous and realistic than the video recordings. There was also considerably more confrontational behavior in the audio recordings. An effect of observation was still evident; for example, people would occasionally talk to the tape recorder rather than to each other, but this type of self-consciousness was diminished in comparison with the videotapes. Having couples self-administer the discussion task further removes the observer from the immediate context and may contribute to realism. However, it also carries liabilities; for example, inaudible tapes and irregularities (e.g., phone call interruptions) are more common.

Along with video recording, direct observation is also quite obtrusive unless people have an extended period to acclimate to the observer. If an observer is immediately present, people may also try to interact with the observer. Naturally, if nonverbal behaviors are very important, then video recording or direct observation is mandated. Direct observation is used more with naturalistic observation than with simulations because of the need to record environmental cues and to follow the interaction as it changes setting. Alternatively, recording devices can be placed in multiple locations (e.g., Christensen, 1979; Kantor & Lehr, 1975). Christensen (1979) has devised an automated recording system that simplifies in-home observation and appears relatively nonreactive (Christensen & Hazzard, 1983). The system utilizes two microphones inconspicuously placed in high-interaction areas of a home and activated at random 15-minute intervals during periods when family members are most likely together. The fact that family members do not know when the recorder is on may reduce reactivity.

As a general guideline, researchers should opt for the least obtrusive and structured task that is necessary to accomplish the purpose of the research. Where possible, interaction simulations should utilize topics that are familiar and personally salient, with minimal guidance from the researcher about how to conduct the discussion. However, a more structured task may be needed to observe events like compliance gaining (Witteman & Fitzpatrick, 1986), which otherwise would not occur with enough regularity. Similarly, video cameras and laboratory observations are not desirable options unless the need to observe nonverbal behaviors or to standardize observations are at a premium in a particular study.

Problems in Observational Research

SAMPLING

Although sampling issues are not unique to observational research, representative samples are generally more difficult to achieve and sampling practices are far less adequate in observational studies than in surveys. There are two respects in which sampling is problematic in observational studies. First, less accessible subject groups are underrepresented in observational studies. Second, behaviors tend to be sampled from a narrow range of contexts. The effect of these sampling biases is to threaten the generalizability of results to all persons and contexts intended.

Sampling of People

The vast majority of observational studies use convenience sampling; that is, they recruit subjects based on their availability rather than utilizing random sampling procedures. Consequently, studies overrepresent individuals who are affiliated with university communities, clinical programs, communication workshops, and other organizations that are easily accessible. These individuals are typically young, white-collar and well educated (Krokoff, 1987). Observational research on couples neglects such groups as blue-collar couples (Krokoff, Gottman, & Roy, 1988) and middle-aged or elderly couples (Zietlow & Sillars, 1988). This presents a threat to the generalizability of research on marital communication because the young, white-collar couples who predominate in most communication studies are less traditional, more expressive, and more sensitive to the quality of communication in marriage than older couples and blue-collar couples (Krokoff et al., 1988; Zietlow & Sillars, 1988). Only slightly less obvious is the bias that occurs due to self-selection. Couples may be attracted to interaction studies owing either to crisis or to a strong interest in communication, thereby exaggerating overrepresentation of expressive, introspective, and communication-oriented couples (Krokoff et al., 1988). Kirby and Davis (1972) found that, out of a randomly generated sample of households, those who agreed to participate in research on couple communication counseling (and who actually followed through) were more likely to have separated for a marital problem than couples who declined to participate after an initial interview. Participants also came more from higher social class groups. Thus, self-selection may create social class biases similar to most convenience samples.

Although sampling problems occur in all interaction research, it is especially difficult to recruit a representative sample in observational research due to the inconvenience and intrusiveness of observation. The most ambitious and successful sampling strategy for marital research that I am aware of is that by Krokoff (Krokoff, 1987; Krokoff et al., 1988). Krokoff followed a three-step procedure that included random telephone interviews, a letter sent to obtain interested couples from the telephone sample, and an informational home meeting with couples prior to scheduling an observational session. Krokoff achieved good rates of participation and a sample that was far more representative of the U.S. general population than comparable studies. Further, the dropout rate was not strongly related to marital happiness or demographics. Another element of the recruitment effort, which should not be overlooked, is that Krokoff paid couples ($n = 120$) $100 each for their participation—a fair, but nonetheless higher than usual, sum. We can only assume that the fee was a stronger incentive for lower-income individuals, thus counteracting the usual tendency to underrepresent such people. Thus, Krokoff's research speaks to the need for strong grant support. For the "make ends meet" researcher, quota sampling (see Babbie, 1989) might provide a reasonable next best alternative for ensuring representativeness in terms of demographic groups.

Behavioral Samples

The behavioral sample refers to the behaviors that are recorded for a particular individual, dyad, or group. Just as the sample of individuals may or may not be representative of the population of individuals, the behavioral record may or may not provide a representative sample of an individual or dyad's normal patterns of behavior (i.e., their behavioral "repertoire"). As in the case of subject samples, both the size and diversity of the behavioral sample may affect representativeness.

The size of the behavioral sample does not normally present a problem in interaction studies. In one sense, the problem can be too many observations. Interaction studies may record several thousand or more behaviors, making statistical procedures overly powerful if the behavior or "act," rather than the individual or dyad, is treated as the unit of analysis (Cappella, 1980, p. 133; Hamilton & Hunter, 1985). However, even if a large number of behaviors are recorded, some behaviors of vital interest to the researcher may be too irregular or infrequent to provide a reliable baseline. For example, Yarrow and Waxler (1979) found it difficult to sample such sporadic or impulsive behaviors of children as tantrums and aggression. In addition, if interaction sequences are of interest, then a larger behavioral sample is needed. For example, if seven conflict behaviors are observed (e.g., "confront," "deny," "analyze," "joke"), there are 49 possible two-act sequences and 343 possible three-act sequences. Although the most common two-act sequences could be analyzed with a moderate behavioral sample, a titanic sample would be needed to analyze all possible three-act sequences, particularly since some sequences are likely to be very infrequent.

Increasing the length of the observation period increases the stability of observations, as Yarrow and Waxler (1979) have demonstrated. Based on observations of nursery school play, these researchers found dramatic fluctuations in children's social behavior from one time period to the next. Considerable stability in behavioral estimates was observed only when the period of observation was increased from 10- or 20-minute intervals to an hour or longer. Unfortunately, if the observation is very detailed, increasing the length of the observation period may not be a practical option. Gottman (1979), whose system for analyzing interaction is only moderately involved, estimates that a single hour of interaction requires 28 hours to transcribe and code.

While the size of the behavioral sample is an occasional difficulty, the diversity of the behavioral sample is a more basic concern. Most observation takes place in one narrowly specialized context. Few studies consider how the behaviors in question vary with the context of observation, and studies that observe a cross section of typical interaction contexts are rare (Kantor & Lehr, 1975; Steinglass, 1979; Yarrow & Waxler, 1979).

The limited scope of most observational research seems more attributable to practical constraints than to disregard for the importance of context. Observational studies of interaction typically trade breadth for depth. Direct observation makes detailed analysis of behavior possible; however, since observation is laborious and expensive, practical constraints inhibit the variety of situations that are considered. The more encompassing the study, the more the researcher risks being overwhelmed by the scope and expense of data analysis. Self report methods can more economically assess responses across a variety of situations.

While it may be legitimate and necessary to restrict the scope of observational studies, it is still important to consider how limited sampling of behavioral contexts may have affected the research. One bias suggested by the situations chosen for study, particularly in couple and family re-search, is that the situations usually elicit disagreement and conflict. The sort of encounters that are lighthearted, affectionate, or mundane are not well represented. Further, the context in which most observation takes place is some sort of staged communication event in which individuals are instructed to solve a problem, make a decision, or discuss some matter together. Important as they are, these focused interaction situations do not resemble the bulk of everyday interactions. Most interactions are routine, brief, and centered around other activities (e.g., doing the laundry, getting ready for work, watching television). Since routine interactions are in-vestigated in only a small number of naturalistic studies, the literature as a whole may overrepresent explicit, focused interactions and underestimate the extent to which individuals discuss issues and make decisions implicitly, indirectly, or incrementally. Steinglass (1979), who had participant observ-ers follow spouses from room to room in their homes, found that family members seemed to behave automatically much of the time and engaged in very little explicit decision making. Decision making that occurred pro-gressed at a leisurely pace without the pressure to achieve closure created by laboratory encounters. Blood (1958) found that family members were sel-dom even together in the same room except at dinner. Thus, the literature on couples and whole families seems to overrepresent "boardroom-style" interactions and neglects the sort of brief, unfocused, and variable encount-ers that dominate daily interactions.

REACTIVITY OF BEHAVIOR

Behavior is reactive to the extent that it is changed by observation. For example, people may behave in a more inhibited or socially desirable manner in the presence of an observer (see Harvey et al., 1983). In my own experience, the single concern that causes the most suspicion about interac-tion research is that the people studied might be unnaturally affected by observation. This, is, of course, a legitimate concern. Unless the study is completely unobtrusive, the effect of observation is undeniable. However, this does not make observation meaningless. Even the most contrived performances may indicate something of interest. For example, the be-havior may indicate how subjects perceive social desirability, how com-petent they are at enacting a socially desirable style, how stringently they maintain the privacy of personal matters, how freely they express disagree-ment in public, and so forth. Still, it is necessary to anticipate the likely effects of observation and to take these into account.

Some behaviors are presumably more reactive than others. Behaviors that are under the conscious control of individuals and that reflect directly on self-presentation are most likely to be reactive. For example, Roberts and Renzaglia (1965) found that positive statements about self increased and negative disclosures decreased when clients in counseling interviews were aware of being recorded. Behaviors that occur at a low level of awareness or that are difficult to fake are less apt to be affected by observation than behaviors that are consciously monitored and easily manipulated (see Wiemann, 1981). Nonverbal behaviors are less directly monitored and less easily manipulated than verbal communication. Thus, conflictual couples might express hostility nonverbally even if they suppress conflict verbally (Pike & Sillars, 1985). In addition, interactive behaviors, particularly between people who have an established relationship, are less apt to be reactive than individual behaviors, owing to the way people elicit and constrain one another's behavior during interaction. Certain behaviors (say, a particular tone of voice or mention of a sensitive topic) may cue a familiar sequence of interaction, which is governed by implicit "rules" and mindless interactional habits. Thus, individuals sometimes appear to "forget" they are being observed, even in the intimidating presence of a videocamera. Even if they fail to reach this level of spontaneity, behaviors are constrained by the collaborative nature of interaction. For example, it is difficult to engage in conflict denial or to joke about a sensitive matter without the partner's participation. In conflict studies the most socially desirable style of communication is to openly confront conflict in an objective and mutually supportive fashion. One has to assume that individuals in a communication study are aware of such demand characteristics and will try to fulfill them. However, the most socially desirable style proves difficult to sustain unless it is well practiced. Some married couples in conflict studies initiate a socially desirable style of communication but quickly become argumentative or withdrawn, since even their best efforts at communication evoke criticism and hurt feelings (Sillars et al., in press). Although people may not always behave as they do in communication studies, they are still constrained by their normal repertoire of interaction styles.

Reactivity and the Sample Scenario

The dialogue involving Cathy and Michael Stone, described at the beginning of this volume, illustrates several points about the effects of observation on interaction. Although this is a fairly uninhibited discussion, we can nonetheless assume that it is colored by observation. Indeed, the most revealing thing about the conversation is that it occurs in the presence of an audience.

Although they may not be the best dinner partners, Cathy and Michael are model research participants. They say what is on their minds, even in the company of observers. Some couples (or individual spouses) actually appear to relish participation in research as a forum in which to express themselves. The dinner conversation provides essentially the same sort of

forum in this example, since the conversation appears to be staged for the
benefit of the dinner guest the Millers. Cathy and Michael assign an observer's role to their guests by speaking directly to one another and providing
no opportunity for the Millers to participate or interfere. Remarkably,
Cathy's complaints about having to "do it all" plainly demonstrate that she
is aggravated about having to prepare the dinner that the Millers are now
eating. In this episode at least, Cathy shows little susceptibility to social
desirability pressures.

Cathy and Michael are a typical modern couple: dual income, egalitarian (in thought if not in deed), expressive, and introspective. Both the fact
that they argue in front of friends and the way they argue indicate that they
value openness and are not highly constrained by social propriety. The
latter part of the conversation, particularly, shows that Cathy and Michael
analyze themselves as a couple and freely engage in self-disclosure (e.g.,
segments #09, 10, and 12). Whereas Cathy and Michael reveal a great deal
about themselves in a short time, other couples give a much less direct
account of themselves, either because they guard their privacy and public
image or because the relationship seems simple and transparent, with little
to discuss (Sillars & Kalbfleisch, 1989). In other words, relationship culture
is partly revealed by whether observed behavior appears inhibited or concealed. Cathy and Michael demonstrate an introspective and com-
munication-sensitive relationship with relaxed privacy standards.

This is also a case in which the reactivity of behavior is diminished by
the collaborative nature of interaction. Throughout the conversation,
Michael shows concern for saving face and he consistently tries to minimize
the conflict issue. If Michael alone were to describe the conflict over
housework he would probably present a much less dire state of affairs than
envisioned by Cathy. However, Cathy blocks Michael's attempts to avoid
and minimize the conflict, causing Michael to try several alternative conflict
strategies in quick succession. Michael attempts to deflect the first criticism
by joking ("You wouldn't want to eat my cooking . . . "). When Cathy
persists, he tries several approaches, including a weak counterattack
("Come on—that's not fair"); a question ("Like the cat box?"), which could
be serious or sarcastic depending on unspecified shared context; a limited
admission ("I do occasionally do them [dishes]—but not enough"); and
disclosive, self-analytic remarks ("Sometimes I think about how I'd do
them more often probably if you weren't around"). Michael evidently
would rather not have this conversation just now. However, Cathy's persistence forces him to acknowledge the conflict and to search (un-
successfully) for a style of conflict engagement that appeases Cathy and
preserves face. Thus, much more about the relationship is revealed through
the interplay of speakers than a single individual would provide.

If this episode was observed as part of a study on marital conflict, it
would not be possible to determine if the observed style of interaction is

broadly representative of the couple's interactions. In other situations, Cathy and Michael may argue continuously, with Cathy maintaining her role as the disgruntled aggressor; the couple may confine their arguments to the subject of housework; or they may argue about different matters in different ways, perhaps shifting roles or adopting a more symmetrical (i.e., attack–attack rather than attack–defend) or problem-focused (rather than personality-focused) pattern of interaction. Although it is not possible to tell how representative their style of interaction is from a small excerpt, it is clear that the issue has come up before. Even if Cathy hadn't mentioned in segment #09 that "we've talked about this before," the conversation appears rehearsed at various points. Cathy has obviously thought about the conflict a great deal, particularly that afternoon while preparing the dinner, as she acts with little immediate provocation and produces a list of complaints, rather than an isolated criticism ("You don't cook, you don't clean, you don't do laundry!"). Michael, although he tries to deflect the criticism in various ways, expresses no surprise at the attack and even indicates through admissions of responsibility that a half-hearted consensus is already in place. Thus, the interaction observed is apparently not an isolated occurrence. Although we cannot determine exactly how often Cathy and Michael behave this way, it can be safely inferred that the observed behavior constitutes an important part of the couple's conflict repertoire.

Different couples might behave very differently from the Stones in this same situation. Similarly, people respond to research simulations in a multitude of ways. In conflict studies some couples argue aggressively, some analyze and problem solve, some vacillate between engagement and withdrawal, and others are polite to a fault. Each of these adaptations to the research context demonstrates something of interest about the couple, including their interpretations of appropriate behavior and the extent of their communication repertoire.

Conclusion

Observational methods are particularly adept at describing interactional behaviors that shape (i.e., develop, affirm, or change) relationships. Observational studies subject these behaviors to intensive analysis, typically with an untimate interest in the connection between molecular and molar qualities of relationships (e.g., the behavioral components of interpersonal competence or interactional causes of marital distress). While observational methods provide a more sensitive gauge of detailed interactional events than other methodologies, observation also poses troublesome validity problems.

One problem is that naturally occurring interactions are spontaneous, and spontaneity is fragile. By having to isolate and structure an event sufficiently for observation, the essence of spontaneous interaction may be lost. Further, the researcher or researcher's surrogate (the tape recorder) forms an undeniable part of the social context, and this transforms dyadic relationships into at least triadic ones. It is difficult for people to carry on even an ordinary conversation when the event is being scrutinized by a team of scientists. The difficulty is compounded severalfold when the conversation itself is hard to pull off, for example, if the topic elicits embarrassment or disagreement.

The problems associated with observation should be taken seriously but not to the point of discouraging use of observational methods. Although observation changes behavior, it often does so in ways that are predictable and informative. In this respect, the limitations of observational methods are not basically different from those of social science research generally. Any attempt to study an event changes it, by either artificially creating or structuring the event, by influencing the self-presentation of participants, by omitting context (such as adjacent, unrecorded scenes), or by selective coding and interpretation. Since these limitations are inherent in all research on social interaction, observational designs should be judged by whether they produce acceptable distortions (which can be anticipated and factored into conclusions about the data), not by the ability to provide a completely sanitized view of people "as they really are." While I have suggested that more naturalistic observations should be the method of first choice, all other things being equal, even highly contrived observations have the potential to contribute theoretically important and coherent results. Contrived behavior may reveal interpretations of social desirability, the permeability or privacy of relationships, the breadth of interaction repertoires, or responses to novel situations. Although different approaches to observation are not equivalent, the utility of a given method is clearly seen only within the context of a particular research program, including its own objectives and constraints.

References

Babbie, E. (1989). *The practice of social research* (5th edition). Belmont, CA: Wadsworth.

Bakeman, R., & Gottman, J. M. (1986). *Observing interaction: An introduction to sequential analysis.* Cambridge: Cambridge University Press.

Bavelas, J. B. (1984). On "naturalistic" family research. *Family Process, 23,* 337–341.

Berger, P., & Kellner, H. (1964). Marriage and the construction of reality. *Diogenes, 46,* 1–24.

Blood, R. O. (1958). New approaches in family research: Observational methods. *Marriage and family living, 20,* 47–52.

Brown, B. W. (1979). Parents' discipline of children in public places. *Family Coordinator, 28*, 67–71.

Burggraf, C. S., & Sillars, A. L. (1987). A critical examination of sex differences in marital communication. *Communication Monographs, 54*, 276–294.

Cappella, J. N. (1980). Talk and silence sequences in informal conversations I. *Human Communication Research, 6*, 130–145.

Christensen, A. (1979). Naturalistic observation of families: A system for random audio recordings. *Behavioral Therapy, 10*, 418–422.

Christensen, A., & Hazzard, A. (1983). Reactive effects during naturalistic observation of families. *Behavioral Assessment, 5*, 349–362.

Donoghue, W. A. (in press). *Communication, marital dispute, and divorce mediation*. Hillsdale, NJ: Erlbaum.

Dreyer, C. A., & Dreyer, A. S. (1973). Family dinner-time as a unique behavior habitat. *Family Process, 12*, 291–301.

Duncan, S., & Fiske, D. W. (1977). *Face-to-face interaction: Research, methods, and theory*. Hillsdale, NJ: Erlbaum.

Duvall, S., & Hensley, V. (1976). Extensions of objective self-awareness theory: The focus of attention-causal attribution hypothesis. In J. H. Harvey, W. J. Ickes, & R. F. Kidd (Eds.), *New directions in attribution research* (Vol. 1, pp. 165–198). Hillsdale, NJ: Erlbaum.

Fitzpatrick, M. A. (1988). *Between husbands and wives: Communication in marriage*. Beverly Hills: Sage.

Glick, B. R., & Gross, S. J. (1975). Marital interaction and marital conflict: A critical evaluation of current research strategies. *Journal of Marriage and the Family, 37*, 505–512.

Goodrich, D. W., & Boomer, D. S. (1963). Experimental assessment of modes of conflict resolution. *Family Process, 2*, 15–24.

Gottman, J. M. (1979). *Marital interaction: Experimental investigations*. New York: Academic Press.

Hamblin, R. L. (1958). Leadership and crisis. *Sociometry, 21*, 322–335.

Hamilton, M. A., & Hunter, J. E. (1985). Analyzing utterances as the observational unit. *Human Communication Research, 12*, 285–294.

Harvey, J. H., Christensen, A., & McClintock, E. (1983). Research methods. In H. H. Kelley (Eds.), *Close relationships* (pp. 449–485). New York: Freeman.

Hess, R. D., & Shipman, V. (1965). Early experience and socialization of cognitive modes in children. *Child Development, 36*, 869–886.

Jones, B. N. (Ed.). (1972). *Ethological studies of child behavior*. London: Cambridge University Press.

Jones, S. C. (1973). The psychology of interpersonal attraction. In C. Nemeth (Ed.), *Social psychology: Classic and contemporary integrations*. Chicago: Rand McNally.

Kantor, D., & Lehr, W. (1975). *Inside the family: Toward a theory of family process*. New York: Harper & Row.

Kellerman, K. (1986). Anticipation of future interaction and information exchange in initial interaction. *Human Communication Research, 13*, 41–75.

Kenkel, W. F. (1963). Observational studies of husband–wife interaction in family decision making. In M. B. Sussman (Ed.), *Sourcebook in marriage and the family* (pp. 144–156). Boston: Houghton Mifflin.

Kirby, M. W., & Davis, K. E. (1972). Who volunteers for research on marital counseling? *Journal of Marriage and the Family, 34,* 469–473.

Krokoff, L. J. (1987). Recruiting representative samples for marital interaction research. *Journal of Social and Personal Relationships, 4,* 317–328.

Krokoff, L. J., Gottman, J. M., & Roy, A. K. (1988). Blue-collar and white-collar marital interaction and communication orientation. *Journal of Social and Personal Relationships, 5,* 201–221.

Levinger, G. (1963). Supplementary methods in family research. *Family Process, 2,* 357–366.

Lull, J. (1980). The social uses of television. *Human Communication Research, 6,* 197–209.

Lytton, H. (1971). Observational studies of parent–child interaction: A methodological review. *Child Development, 42,* 651–684.

McCarthy, B. (1981). Studying personal relationships. In S. W. Duck & R. Gilmour (Eds.), *Personal relationships: 1. Studying personal relationships* (pp. 23–46). New York: Academic Press.

McLaughlin, M. L., Cody, M. J., Kane, M. L., & Robey, C. S. (1981). Sex differences in story receipt and story sequencing behaviors in dyadic conversations. *Human Communication Research, 7,* 99–116.

Mishler, E. G., & Waxler, N. E. (1968). *Interaction in families: An experimental study of family processes and schizophrenia.* New York: Wiley.

Moustakas, C. E., Sigel, I. E., & Schalock, M. D. (1956). An objective method for the measurement and analysis of child–adult interaction. *Child Development, 27,* 109–134.

Noller, P. (1985). Negative communications in marriage. *Journal of Social and Personal Relationships, 2,* 289–301.

O'Keefe, B. J., & Shepherd, G. J. (1989). The communication of identity during face-to-face persuasive interactions: Effects of perceiver's construct differentiation and target's message strategies. *Communication Research, 16,* 375–404.

Olson. D. H., & Ryder, R. G. (1970). Inventory of Marital Conflicts (IMC): An experimental interaction procedure. *Journal of Marriage and the Family, 32,* 443–448.

O'Rourke, J. F. (1963). Field and laboratory: The decision-making behavior of family groups in two experimental conditions. *Sociometry, 26,* 422–435.

Parke, R. D. (1979). Interactional designs. In R. B. Cairns (Ed.), *The analysis of social interactions: Methods, issues, and illustrations* (pp. 15–35). Hillsdale, NJ: Erlbaum.

Pike, G. R., & Sillars, A. L. (1985). Reciprocity of marital communication. *Journal of Social and Personal Relationships, 2,* 303–324.

Poole, M. S., Folger, J. P., & Hewes, D. E. (1987). Analyzing interpersonal interaction. In M. E. Roloff & G. R. Miller (Eds.), *Interpersonal processes: New directions in communication research* (pp. 220–256). Beverly Hills: Sage.

Poole, M. S., & Roth, J. (1989). Decision development in small groups: IV. A typology of group decision paths. *Human Communication Research, 15,* 323–356.

Raush, H. L., Barry, W. A., Hertel, R. K., & Swain, M. A. (1974). *Communication, conflict and marriage.* San Francisco: Jossey-Bass.

Reiss, D. (1971). Varieties of consensual experience: II. Dimensions of a family's experience of its environment. *Family Process, 10,* 28–35.

Riskin, J., & Faunce, E. E. (1972). An evaluative review of family interaction research. *Family Process, 11,* 365–455.

Roberts, R. R., & Renzaglia, G. A. (1965). The influence of tape recording on counseling. *Journal of Counseling Psychology, 12,* 10–16.

Rogers, L. E., Courtright, J. A., & Millar, F. E. (1980). Message control intensity: Rationale and preliminary findings. *Communication Monographs, 47,* 201–219.

Ryder, R., & Goodrich, D. (1966). Married couples' response to disagreement. *Family Process, 5,* 30–42.

Sackett, G. P. (Ed.), (1978). *Observing behavior: Vol. 2. Data collection and analysis methods.* Baltimore: University Park Press.

Sherblom, J., & Van Rheenen, D. D. (1984). Spoken language indices of uncertainty. *Human Communication Research, 11,* 221–230.

Shields, M. M. (1981). Parent–child relationships in the middle years of childhood. In S. W. Duck & R. Gilmour (Eds.), *Personal relationships: 2. Developing personal relationships.* New York: Academic Press.

Sillars, A. L., & Kalbfleisch, P. J. (1989). Implicit and explicit decision-making styles in couples. In D. Brinberg & J. Jaccard (Eds.), *Dyadic decision making* (pp. 179–215). New York: Springer.

Sillars, A. L., Wilmot, W. W., & Hocker, J. L. (in press). Communication strategies in conflict and mediation. In J. Wiemann & J. A. Daly (Eds.), *Communicating strategically: Strategies in interpersona communication.* Hillsdale, NJ: Erlbaum.

Stafford, L. (1987). Maternal input to twin and singleton children: Implications for language acquisition. *Human Communication Research, 13,* 429–462.

Steinglass, P. (1979). The Home Observation Assessment Method (HOAM): Real-time naturalistic observation of families in their homes. *Family Process, 18,* 337–354.

Straus, M. A. (1964). Measuring families. In H. T. Christianson (Ed.), *Handbook of marriage and the family* (pp. 335–400). Chicago: Rand McNally.

Straus, M., & Tallman, I. (1971). SIMFAM: A technique for observational measurement and experimental study of families. In J. Aldous (Eds.), *Family problem solving: A symposium on theoretical, methodological, and substantive concerns* (pp. 381–438). Hinsdale, IL: The Dryden Press.

Street, R. L., & Buller, D. B. (1988). Patients' characteristics affecting physician–patient nonverbal communication. *Human Communication Research, 15,* 60–90.

Strodbeck, F. L. (1951). Husband–wife interaction over revealed differences. *American Sociological Review, 16,* 468–473.

Tardy, C. H. (1988). Interpersonal interaction coding systems. In C. H. Tardy (Ed.), *A handbook for the study of human communication: Methods and instruments for observing, measuring and assessing communication processes.* (pp. 285–300). Norwood, NJ: Ablex.

Taylor, S. E., & Fiske, S. T. (1978). Salience, attention, and attribution: Top of the head phenomena. In L. Berkowitz (Ed.), *Advances in experimental social psychology* (Vol. 11). New York: Academic Press.

Ting-Toomey, S. (1983). An analysis of verbal communication patterns in high and low marital adjustment groups. *Human Communication Research, 9,* 306–319.

Watzlawick, P., Beavin, J., & Jackson, D. D. (1967). *Pragmatics of human communication: A study of interactional patterns, pathologies, and paradoxes.* New York: Norton.

Weick, K. E. (1968). Systematic observational methods. In G. Lindzey & E. Aronson (Eds.), *The handbook of social psychology* (Vol. 2, pp. 357–451). Reading,
MA: Addison-Wesley.

Wiemann, J. M. (1981). Effects of laboratory videotaping procedures on selected
conversational behaviors. *Human Communication Research, 7,* 302–311.

Witteman, H., & Fitzpatrick, M. A. (1986). Compliance-gaining in marital interaction: Power bases, power processes, and outcomes. *Communication Monographs,
53,* 130–143.

Yarrow, M. R., & Waxler, C. Z. (1979). Observing interaction: A confrontation
with methodology. In R. B. Cairns (Ed.), *The analysis of social interactions:
Methods, issues, and illustrations* (pp. 37–65). Hillsdale, NJ: Erlbaum.

Zietlow, P. H., & Sillars, A. L. (1988). Life stage differences in communication
during marital conflicts. *Journal of Social and Personal Relationships, 5,* 223–245.

Chapter 12

Experimentation

CHARLES H. TARDY
LAWRENCE A. HOSMAN

More than any other methodology, the experiment divides scholars of social behavior. Some writers see this method as the plague of the social sciences; according to this viewpoint, experiments require a simplistic and reductionistic view of humans. Other scholars hold the experiment to be the only method capable of producing scientifically useful generalizations. Experiments allow investigators to be objective by removing bias and preconception from the observation of human behavior. This chapter, however, does not purport to reconcile or adjudicate these two viewpoints. Both have flaws and merits. Rather, we will strive to introduce the issues and concepts on which these arguments are based. Understanding the fundamental ideas is a prerequisite for appropriate use of the experimental method to study social interaction.

Nature of Experimentation

Before discussing the use of experiments to study social interaction, basic terms, concepts, and principles must be explained. First, the use of the term experiment is quite imprecise because there are many types of *experiments*. Campbell and Stanley (1966) in their seminal monograph distinguish between pre-experiments, true experiments, and quasi-experiments based on the study's design. *Pre-experiments* are simple comparisons between groups of people. For example, a study that compares the interaction of marital couples before and after a counseling or training session would be pre-experimental. The introduction of a control group, that is, a group of couples who did not go to the counseling session, and the random assignment of couples to either the control or the treatment group would constitute a *true experiment*. A *quasi-experiment* refers to a study that allows comparisons between groups but no random assignment of subjects. For example, if the researcher had observed a couple interacting once a month for 6 months prior to and following the training session, this design would be quasi-experimental.

Another prominent distinction is between field and laboratory experiments. *Laboratory experiments* are those in which subjects are recruited and asked to report to a particular location (e.g., a laboratory) for participation. *Field experiments* are those in which people are not informed of the experimenter's observations; people's responses to a situation that has been contrived by the experimenter are observed. For example, in Harrell's (1978) study people on a campus were observed as an experimenter's assistant either revealed or concealed her name when asking for directions to a building. This chapter will refer to all of these types of experiments but will focus on the true experiment conducted in the laboratory.

Several more terms must be understood by the reader. *Dependent variable* refers to that which is observed or measured by the investigator. Dependent variables change as a function of, and are therefore dependent upon, changes in the variables manipulated by the experimenter. The field experiment by Harrell, 1978, (mentioned in the previous paragraph) used the length of answer given to the question asked by the experimenter's assistant as the dependent variable. Attitude scales, self-reports of communication behavior, objectively measured speech traits such as rate of speech have all been used as dependent variables. Generally, the experiment is designed to observe and explain variation in dependent variables.

Independent variables are features over which the experimenter has control. Independent variables are antecedent to, and therefore considered independent of, the dependent variables. For example, the inclusion or exclusion of the requester's name constituted the independent variable in the field study by Harrell (1978). Though the experimenter always controls the independent variable by deciding what constitutes the variable, he or she may not always be able to manipulate the independent variable. When studying stable individual difference factors such as personality or gender, the independent variable is called an *organismic variable*. Regardless of whether the independent variable is organismic or nonorganismic, the experiment typically ascertains if the independent variable affects or causes change in the dependent variable.

Two concepts are important for assessing experiments: reliability and validity. *Reliability* refers to the stability or internal consistency of the observation of the dependent variable. Validity is of many types. *Validity of the dependent variable* concerns the interpretation of the observation. The degree to which the observation measures what it is intended to measure is its validity. Validity also applies to the design of the study. Doubts about the conclusion that the independent variable actually affected the dependent variable(s) are related to *internal validity*. For example, a claim that some agent other than the independent variable caused the observed difference indicts the study's internal validity. *External validity* refers to the generalizability of the findings from the study to people and situations that have not been studied. Concerns about the ability to replicate the findings with different subjects (for example, non–college students in Harrell's 1978 field study) relate to external validity. As will be seen later in this chapter, concerns of internal and external validity influence choices made by the experimenter during the design of a study.

Two threats to a successful study are noise and bias, two forms of error. *Noise* refers to variability in dependent variables that is uncontrolled or random. For example, a study that uses male and female subjects may produce noise in the dependent variable because of differences in their responses. A way to control this noise might be to use only male or only female subjects (see Archer, Berg, & Runge, 1980; Berg & Archer, 1982). However, the use of only one sex introduces *bias,* variance that is systematic. That is, the use of only female subjects may bias the findings and limit the conclusion such that it may be generalizable only to female subjects.

Thus, an experiment involves two fundamental operations: (1) manipulation of independent variables, and (2) measurement of response, in terms of dependent variables. Social interaction can constitute either type of variable. Some studies manipulate a component of social interaction, for example, message strategy, and observe its effect, for example, compliance gaining. Other studies may manipulate some variable, for example, room decoration, and examine its effects on social interaction, for example, intimacy of responses.

TRADITIONAL USES OF EXPERIMENTATION

As this book demonstrates, a variety of research methods are available for the study of social interaction, each having its particular advantages. Experiments are used for three primary purposes. One purpose is control. Experimental control allows the investigator to rule out alternative explanations of research findings. In a tightly controlled experiment, if two sets of groups differ on some hypothesized dimension, for example, amount of interaction (dependent variable), one can plausibly argue that it was the experimental manipulation that produced the difference and not some irrelevant factor that may have varied systematically between the two groups. Properties that are associated with the independent variable in uncontrived settings may be eliminated. For example, an experiment that uses written transcripts of interruptions to examine the effects of this speech behavior on perceptions of politeness removes the possibility that the speaking voice quality is the source of subjects' perceptions. Thus, the experiment allows the researcher to reduce, if not eliminate, alternative explanations for the relationship between the specified variables.

Experiments also allow researchers to control variables that would occur randomly or systematically in other types of studies, for example, in those employing ethnomethodology. Thus, whereas a study of natural language use might have to wait for the occurrence of specific types of dialogue, experiments may produce the dialogue and solicit subjects' responses to it. In so doing, the experiment has the luxury of selecting which features accompany the independent variable. For example, the experimenter could specify that the dialogue was produced by a female speaker or that the dialogue was produced by a couple experiencing marital discord. In contrast, the natural study of language use would merely note if the speaker was male or female and might not be capable of ascertaining other information, for example, the marital harmony of the couple producing the dialogue. Hence, the experimenter gains considerable control over the variables studied.

A second purpose, closely related to the first, is to make cause-and-effect claims. By conducting a well-designed experiment, one can infer that a change in or manipulation of an independent variable produced a change in a dependent variable. The ability to make such claims is dependent upon experimental control. Experimental control gives the experimenter confidence that the manipulation produced changes in the dependent measures. As the degree of control decreases, so does confidence that the experimental manipulation produced the changes in the dependent measure.

The experiment also is used to address phenomena that cannot be addressed any other way. The experiment can be used to assess phenomena that are beyond the means of either the subject to produce or of an observer to directly note. For example, people are not consciously aware of many of their behaviors or of the motivations or causes of those behaviors. People do not, for example, realize that they change the rate of their speech to match the rate of the person with whom they are talking (Street, 1988). To simply ask people if they do would not produce scientifically useful results. Also, scientists may be interested in relationships between social interaction and outcomes that may not be observable. For example, no matter how much training and time is spent, a passive observer cannot detect the effect of an intimate revelation on the blood chemistry of the discloser (Pennebaker, Kiecolt-Glaser, & Glaser, 1988). Consequently, the only way to make such a determination would be to reproduce the behavior of interest in a context in which responses can be measured.

ASSESSMENT CONSIDERATIONS

We should note that the uses and principles of experimentation discussed thus far are not reflected in all experiments. As in any human endeavor, some experiments are good and some are not. What distinguishes between them? Two criteria are useful in evaluating experiments.

The minimization of sources of internal invalidity is the first criterion. One goal of experiments is to state precisely the variables that affect the dependent variable(s). If there are alternative explanations, the experiment has not accomplished its goal. Campbell and Stanley (1966) detail numerous threats to internal validity. The more of these sources that are eliminated, the better the experiment.

A second goal is the maximization of external validity. The investigator hopes that his or her findings are generalizable to contexts other than the one studied. This is perhaps the most frequent criticism of experiments. Procedures that operationalize independent and dependent variables such that they reflect the ways the phenomena occur outside the laboratory are preferred.

Researchers must balance a paradoxical tension between the two criteria, the minimization of sources of internal invalidity and the maximization of external validity. Steps to increase the internal validity reduce the external validity and vice versa. By increasing control over a variable in order to reduce noise, the researcher may inadvertently make that experimental variable unlike the natural phenomenon the experiment hopes to duplicate. For example, using transcripts of dialogue may increase internal validity by eliminating voice quality as a potential causal variable but it also reduces external validity by making the experiment less similar to conversation as it occurs outside the experiment. There is no simple solution to the resolution of these issues. One reasonable guide for resolving this dilemma suggests emphasizing internal validity during the initial stages of an idea's investigation and external validity in the later stages. Preference is thus given to producing limited generalizations with confidence, and then systematically assessing the scope of the generalization. Another guide suggests that research with important implications for practice or application should be more concerned with external validity. For example, a heart disease prevention campaign study might be more concerned with detecting some effect of the campaign rather than with its ability to isolate the specific feature, for example, advertisements or personal contacts, that produced the effect. Such factors as these should be considered as the investigator resolves the balance between internal and external validity.

Special Concerns in Studying Social Interaction Experimentally

In studying social interaction by means of experimental methods, the interaction can be treated as either an independent or dependent variable. The next two sections will explore the issues involved in conducting experimental research in each instance.

SOCIAL INTERACTION AS AN INDEPENDENT VARIABLE

When social interaction is treated as an independent variable, the experimenter asks the question: "What effects do variations in social interaction have?" In order to use the experimental method effectively, certain issues must be addressed. The important aspects of interaction that are to be manipulated must first be selected, and then dimensions potentially affected must be identified.

The aspects of social interaction that can be manipulated are quite varied. Studies have explored the effects of powerful and powerless speech styles (Erickson, Lind, Johnson, & O'Barr, 1978), of different types of topic changes (Planalp & Tracy, 1980; Tracy, 1982), and of self-serving utterances (McLaughlin et al., 1985) and different ways of reciprocating self-disclosure (Bradac, Hosman, & Tardy, 1978; Morton, 1978). All of these studies have as a common feature the manipulation of some aspect of social interaction.

Also important is the identification of relevant dependent variables. The investigator asks: "What effects will the independent variable produce?" The dependent measures could include assessments of impression formation, communicative competence (Wiemann, 1977), speaker credibility (McCroskey & Young, 1981), speech evaluation (Zahn & Hopper, 1985) or dialect perception (Mulac, 1975) and so forth.

When using social interaction as an independent variable, several special concerns arise. First, the investigator desires to generalize the results beyond the specific message(s) or stimulus materials that constitute the independent variable. As scholars Jackson and Jacobs (1983) point out, when only a single example of discourse constitutes the manipulation, the results are potentially limited to that particular example of social interaction. Using multiple examples of discourse increases the generalizability of the results.

Second, a researcher must decide where to obtain the messages being used to manipulate the independent variables (Bradac, 1988). The experimenter could either construct original messages (Bradac et al., 1978) or use actual messages that have been altered to produce the experimental manipulation (Zahn, 1989; O'Barr, 1982). The first alternative allows a high degree of internal validity since the researcher includes only those variables of interest; it has the disadvantage of possibly not reflecting aspects of actual discourse. The second alternative ensures that the messages reflect actual discourse, but also means that the researcher loses some control because extraneous variables may occur and be confounded with theoretically important variables.

Third, the researcher must decide how to present the messages. Messages could be presented in a written (Bradac et al., 1978; Hawkins, 1988; Hosman, 1987, 1989; Zahn, 1989), an aural (Erickson et al., 1978; Jones & Gordon, 1972), or a videotaped mode (Chaikin & Derlega, 1974; Town & Harvey, 1981). Each entails trade-offs. Written messages allow the investigator to control for extraneous nonverbal or speech characteristics, such as speech rate, that might influence a message's evaluation. This strength is also its liability, since important nonverbal features cannot be handled well in a written mode.

Aural messages have the advantage of providing messages more typical of social interaction than the written mode and of allowing the manipulation of nonverbal features. The inclusion of these additional aural features introduces the possibility of confounding these features with the social interaction properties of theoretical interest. For example, aural messages allow subjects to identify quickly the gender of the speaker (Lass, Hughes, Bowyer, Waters, & Broune, 1976) and this gender identification may influence subjects' evaluations of the variables of interest.

Videotaped messages have the advantage of presenting to subjects messages as they would be commonly processed, with the full range of verbal and nonverbal cues available. Though clearly enhancing the external validity of the messages, this full range of verbal and nonverbal cues presents the possibility of one or several of the cues being confounded with the variables of theoretical interest. For example, the physical attractiveness or ethnic identity of a speaker may influence the evaluation of the speaker's message.

There are no easy resolutions of the trade-offs between methods of presentation (for a more extensive discussion of these issues, see Bradac, 1986). Research exploring different presentation methods has produced conflicting results (O'Barr, 1982; Vinson & Johnson, 1989). If aural or videotape methods of presentation are chosen, the messages should be presented, where possible, using a "matched guise" technique, a procedure in which one speaker presents the same message in different ways, for example, one with a Welsh accent and another with an English accent. This allows the researcher to control for idiosyncratic aspects of a communicator's speech that might affect the results.

SOCIAL INTERACTION AS A DEPENDENT VARIABLE

Social interaction can also be studied as a dependent variable. In this case the researcher asks, What changes in independent variables affect social interaction. If this approach is chosen, the experimenter selects independent variables expected to affect social interaction and decides what aspects of interaction may be affected by the manipulated variables.

Research using this approach has manipulated a number of different types of variables in order to assess their effects on social interaction. Shaffer and Ogden (1986) manipulated whether subjects expected to interact in the future with a stranger and observed its impact on self-disclosure. Berg and Archer (1982) investigated whether the goals of an interactant affected reciprocity of self-disclosure. Berger and Kellerman (1989) told subjects to be either evasive or open in a conversation with a stranger and explored what effect these goals had on the ways in which they interacted.

Three general characteristics of such research can be noticed: (1) this research often uses confederates who are trained by the experimenter to exhibit particular behaviors that are expected to affect a naive subject's communication behavior; (2) subjects are given a goal or instructional set and are then allowed to interact; (3) the social interaction is recorded in some manner and subsequently analyzed.

These three characteristics produce special concerns. One concern is whether the confederates behave both consistently with the manipulation and naturally. If a confederate is instructed to brag about himself or herself, for example, then the researcher must ensure that bragging occurs and that it appears natural. If multiple confederates are used, then the researcher must determine whether all of the confederates behave similarly.

A second concern is whether the method of recording interaction will affect subjects' performances. It is possible that audiotaping or videotaping the interaction may affect the interaction process. Although very little research bears on this issue, one study (Wiemann, 1981) found that videotaping did not affect conversational behaviors out of conscious awareness.

Experiments can be used to study social interaction either by assessing the effects that manipulations of messages have on dependent measures or by exploring the effect that experimental manipulations have on interaction. Each use of experimentation has special considerations that must be addressed by the researcher.

Strengths and Weaknesses of Experimentation

Although experiments are used frequently, they have been widely assailed by critics (Harré & Secord, 1973; McGuire, 1973; Totman, 1985). We do not propose to deal at length with these issues, but several seem particularly important to address in the context of using experiments to study social interaction. First, critics argue that laboratory experiments are artificial: because the experimental setting is not natural and subjects realize they are being studied, the subjects behave differently. Experimenters have been sensitive to these charges, and the nature of experimentation has evolved. Attempts have been made to decrease the artificiality of the experimental setting. For example, Tracy (1989; see also Chapter 10, this volume) uses the naturalistic experiment to study social interaction. She describes it as involving the analysis of "free-form responses in relation to the standardized situations, reported goals, and [self- and third-party] evaluations" (p. 422). In addition, researchers have used field experiments more frequently to study social interaction in order to reduce the artificiality of their research (Rubin, 1975).

Second, experiments are criticized because they make impoverished ontological assumptions about people. Critics argue that subjects are viewed as passive reactors in a communication situation. Furthermore, researchers are not interested in subjects' interpretation of events. This view is changing, however. Some experimenters view subjects as active participants in the social interaction process and have begun to explore the goals communicators have, how they construct messages, and how they interpret situations. For example, Sanders (1987) used experiments to study how people interpret utterances. Various cognitive approaches to social interaction (Kellerman & Lim, 1989; Planalp, 1989) have been developed, and some experiments analyze subjects' verbal reports (Ericsson & Simon, 1984). Thus, researchers using the experimental method do not necessarily adhere to a view of people that is essentially reactive and passive.

Third, and most commonly, experiments are criticized for lacking external validity, generalizability, or ecological validity. Byrne's (1971) attraction paradigm has, for example, drawn the ire of many critics for this reason. However, it was subsequent *experimental* research that revealed the limitations of the initial studies (e.g., Sunnafrank, 1983). The issue of generalizability is, then, an empirical one and has been the subject of much research. Literature reviews of this topic (Berkowitz & Donnerstein, 1982; Dipboye & Flanagan, 1979; Mook, 1983) consistently note that generalizability is a problem of specific experiments, not an inherent problem of the experimental method. Subsequent research will show some initial experiments to have and others not to have external validity. Though the investigator's ingenuity and concern for internal validity will influence the apparent external external validity of his/her experiment, only through further research will the issue be resolved.

Finally, experiments are not appropriate for all stages of research but are most appropriate for a specific stage. The initial investigation of a topic or problem should be descriptive (Cappella, 1987). Variables must be identified and their interrelationships specified. Experiments seek to verify relationships, not conceptualize variables, and they require the researcher to ignore many facets of social interaction. If the topic being investigated is new, the experiment quite likely will prematurely restrict the investigator's observations. Consequently, experiments are generally not appropriate for exploratory research.

In short, experiments do have limitations. But to suggest that experiments inherently involve stark, sterile laboratory environments where subjects act as "robots" producing results inapplicable to the real world oversimplifies the current state of experimentation, a methodology whose evolution addresses its limitations.

Case Study of the Stones

To further illustrate the use of experimentation in studying social interaction, the following two sections of this chapter will apply the method to the sample interaction of this volume, the argument between Cathy and Michael Stone. The research problem will be analyzed first by exploring the interaction as an independent variable and then by examining the interaction as a dependent variable.

SOCIAL INTERACTION AS AN INDEPENDENT VARIABLE

Why would the experimental method be employed to study interaction as an independent variable? The primary reason would be to determine the consequences of various aspects of the conversation. The method assumes that the variables of interest would have the same effect on subjects vicariously experiencing the conversation as it would have on the actual participants. To assume otherwise would be to deny the external validity of the experiment.

In applying the experimental method to the research problem, two general issues arise. First, what aspects of the interaction between the Stones would be important to manipulate? Second, what should the dependent variables be?

The interaction between the Stones would serve as the stimulus material that would contain the experimental manipulation(s). Using an experimental method necessitates determining which aspects of the argument would be fruitful to manipulate. One feature noticeable in the argument (a feature that has been the source of previous research) is interruptions. For example, in the Stone transcript Cathy interrupts her husband, while the opposite never occurs. Are there any effects due to the interruptions always being produced by the wife? Several studies (Dindia, 1987; Kennedy &

Camden, 1983) have investigated whether there are gender differences in interruption behavior in mixed-sex dyads but have not pursued how people evaluate different patterns of interruption behavior. That is, do people evaluate men who interrupt women differently from women who interrupt men? Previous research, then, suggests that the experiment could examine interruptions as the independent variable.

The Stones' dialogue is, by itself, inadequate to constitute the manipulation of the independent variable. In the argument Cathy always interrupts Michael. Also needed is an argument where Michael interrupts Cathy. This could be done by using the same text, deleting Cathy's interruptions, and inserting ones for Michael or by simply assigning Michael's lines to Cathy and Cathy's lines to Michael. Both procedures create two arguments differing only in terms of who interrupts whom.

Two additional issues should be addressed before the two messages would be ready for use. One concern would be with the method of presenting the argument. As indicated previously, messages could be written, aural, or videotaped. Written messages might be difficult to employ here because interruptions are indicated by brackets in a written transcript and subjects might not understand their use or might not understand where they occur. In this case an aural message might be preferred because it provides some control over extraneous variables but also requires that subjects only listen for interruptions rather than read them.

A second concern would be whether subjects perceive the differences in the two messages. For the experiment to have internal validity any differences found between the two messages would have to be attributed to the manipulation of interruptions. This could be determined by pretesting the messages in order to assess whether subjects perceive Michael to be interrupting more in his message than he is in the other message and whether a corresponding perception holds true for Cathy.

Once the above concerns are addressed, the dependent variables become of concern. What effects can be reasonably expected to accrue from manipulation of the independent variables? What variables are suggested by relevant theory? In this instance the experiment might focus on perceptions of perceived sociability, authoritativeness, or powerfulness. After the dependent measures are selected, the experiment could then be conducted.

We previously advanced two criteria by which experiments can be evaluated. One called for the minimization of sources of internal invalidity. In this example two steps were taken to eliminate the problem. First, the messages were constructed so that the only systematic difference between them was who interrupted whom. All other aspects were held constant. Second, in order to ensure that the messages were perceived to differ in the intended way, they were also pretested. The use of aural messages, however, introduces at least one potential source of internal invalidity. It may be that the male and female voices used to represent Cathy and Michael may differ systematically in ways that would be related to the dependent variables. For example, the female voice may sound more pleasant than the male voice, regardless of the content. This possibility should be eliminated by pretesting messages spoken by several speakers and finding two that do not differ significantly on these other characteristics.

A second criterion advocated the maximization of external validity. As noted earlier, experimentation always involves a trade-off between internal and external validity. The proposed experiment is weak in external validity in three areas. First, using aural messages reduces the range of nonverbal cues, especially facial expressions, present in the conversation. These additional nonverbal cues might modify the results found in a study using only aural cues. Second, the results may not generalize to other types of arguments, such as ones between coworkers or strangers. Since the information contained in the description of the setting notes that the Stones are married, the results may generalize only to that setting; this possibility could be explored by another experiment. Third, the results may not generalize beyond the particular sample argument used as the stimulus material. The results might not be the same if another argument from another couple was used instead. This problem can be minimized by using multiple dialogues as stimulus materials. This study has one feature that enhances its external validity: rather than contriving an argument that may not bear a resemblance to a "real" argument, the experimenter adapted an actual argument, thus ensuring that the interaction bears some resemblance to a naturally occurring conversation

SOCIAL INTERACTION AS A DEPENDENT VARIABLE

Let us assume the sample dialogue emanated from a study in which social interaction constituted the dependent variable. Cathy and Michael's would be only one of many conversations studied. Separately or as a couple, the Stones constitute only one of the sample of subjects. The experiment would examine the effects of some variable on the dialogue produced by the subjects. Whether these are manipulated and how they are observed would determine the type of experiment. Consequently, before proceeding, the type of experiment, the independent variables, and the dependent variables should be specified.

The Stone's dialogue could generate many dependent variables. Objective measures could be derived (such as length of utterances, pause durations, and rate of speech) or meaning-centered categories (such as self-disclosure, agreement, and disagreement) could also be identified. For purposes of continuity with the preceding analysis of interaction as the independent variable, let us presume that this study used interruptions as the primary dependent variable. The study would be concerned with the effect of some independent variable on interruptions in couples' conversations. Again, many independent variables would be candidates for study. Do newlyweds interrupt more than couples who have been married for 2 or more years? Do dissatisfied couples interrupt more than satisfied couples? However, studies addressing these questions would not constitute true experiments, since subjects would not be randomly assigned to conditions. The experimenters might be interested in studying the nature of marital communication as it occurs privately. Do couples communicate differently when observers are present than when observers are absent? The independent variable in this hypothesized study might be the context of the conversation: public or private. Half of the married couples in this study, let us presume, were asked to audio-record a conversation as it occurred while in the presence of two close friends, while the other half were to record a conversation while alone. In this case the researchers would be attempting to ascertain the effect of context on interruptions.

In order to assess the hypothetical experiment examining the effect of context on interruptions, let us examine the criteria indentified earlier. The first consideration was internal validity. The experiment should eliminate plausible alternative explanations for the observed effects. One threat to this experiment could be the use of the recording device. If the recorder affected dialogue in one context, for example, private, but not the other, then the findings could be attributable to this factor. This could be a particularly salient concern in the present study because the recorder may make the "private" condition a public one. The presence of the recorder would remind the subjects that other people will be attending to their conversation, and the subjects may unintentionally act as they would in a setting where the observers are actually present. The experimenter can sometimes guard against such threats by having subjects complete a self-report measure that validates the manipulation, for example, one with questions such as "How private was the context in which this conversation occurred?" A pretest could also be used to validate the assumption that the private condition would not be affected by the presence of the recorder. If neither is conducted by the researcher and no differences were observed between public and private conversations, then the presence of the recorder could account for the finding and would be considered a plausible alternative to the conclusion that the two situations are in fact not different. However, if differences between the conditions are observed, there would be no threat to internal validity since the alternative explanation would be inconsistent with the data.

Let us specify the contexts and subjects we would hope to generalize to and then note limitations or threats to the study's external validity. First, we suggest the results would be generalizable to subjects similar in age and socioeconomic status to the Stones. Krokoff (1987) describes procedures that can be used to obtain representative samples of married couples (cf.

Bell, 1989; Krokoff, 1989). Second, we suggest the results would be generalizable to conversations that take place in the presence of close friends. Conversations in the presence of acquaintances or strangers may or may not evidence the same patterns yielded in this study. Someone might contend that the mere presence of the tape recorder may make the experimental conditions so different from private and public conversations that are not recorded that the results could not be generalized beyond the laboratory setting. Though the available evidence would not support this argument, this possibility cannot be completely discounted. Other types of research could be conducted that would triangulate with the present study to eliminate this possible explanation.

Conclusions

From this review a picture emerges of the experiment as a method with clear strengths and limitations. Accounting for these assets and deficits during the planning of a study will ensure the appropriate use of the experiment to study social interaction. With reasoned use, the experiment will be recognized neither as a scourge of the social sciences nor a panacea for all research problems.

References

Archer, R. L., Berg, J. H., & Runge, T. E. (1980). Active and passive observers' attraction to a self-disclosing other. *Journal of Experimental Social Psychology, 16,* 130–145.

Bell, R. A. (1989). A comment on Krokoff's "Recruiting representative samples for marital interaction research." *Journal of Social and Personal Relationships, 6,* 231–234.

Berg, J. H., & Archer, R. L. (1982). Response to self-disclosure and interaction goals. *Journal of Experimental Social Psychology, 18,* 501–512.

Berger, C. R., & Kellerman, K. (1989). Personal opacity and social information processing: Explorations in strategic communication. *Communication Research, 16,* 314–351.

Berkowitz, L., & Donnerstein, E. (1982). External validity is more than skin deep: Some answers to criticisms of laboratory experiments. *American Psychologist, 37,* 245–257.

Bradac, J. J. (1986). Threats to generalization in the use of elicited, purloined, and contrived messages in human communication. *Communication Quarterly, 34,* 55–65.

Bradac, J. J. (1988). Language variables: Conceptual and methodological problems of instantiation. In C. H. Tardy (Ed.), *A handbook for the study of human communication: Methods and instruments for observing, measuring, and assessing communication processes* (pp. 301–322). Norwood, NJ: Ablex.

Bradac, J. J., Hosman, L. A., & Tardy, C. H. (1978). Reciprocal disclosures and language intensity: Attributional consequences. *Communication Monographs, 45,* 1–14.

Byrne, D. (1971). *The attraction paradigm.* New York: Academic Press.

Campbell, D. T., & Stanley, J. C. (1966). *Experimental and quasi-experimental designs for research.* Chicago: Rand McNally.

Cappella, J. N. (1987). Interpersonal communication: Definitions and fundamental questions. In C. R. Berger & S. H. Chaffee (Eds.), *Handbook of communication Science* (pp. 184–238). Newbury Park, CA: Sage.

Chaikin, A. L., & Derlega, V. J. (1974). Liking for the norm-breaker in self-disclosure. *Journal of Personality, 42,* 117–129.

Dindia, K. (1987). The effects of sex of subject and sex of partner on interruptions. *Human Communication Research, 13,* 345–371.

Dipboye, R. L., & Flanagan, M. F. (1979). Research settings in industrial and organizational psychology: Are findings in the field more generalizable than in the laboratory? *American Psychologist, 34,* 141–150.

Erickson, B., Lind, E. A., Johnson, B. C., & O'Barr, W. M. (1978). Speech style and impression formation in a court setting: The effects of "powerful" and "powerless" speech. *Journal of Experimental Social Psychology, 14,* 266–279.

Ericsson, K. A., & Simon, H. A. (1984). *Protocol analysis: Verbal reports as data.* Cambridge: MIT Press.

Fitzpatrick, M. A. (1988). *Between husbands and wives: Communication in marriage.* Newbury Park, CA: Sage.

Harré, H., & Secord, P. F. (1973). *The explanation of social behaviour.* Totowa, NJ: Littlefield, Adams.

Harrell, W. A. (1978). Physical attractiveness, self-disclosure, and helping behavior. *Journal of Social Psychology, 104,* 15–17.

Hawkins, K. (1988). Interruptions in task-oriented conversations: Effects of violations of expectations by males and females. *Women's Studies in Communication, 11,* 1–20.

Hosman, L. A. (1987). The evaluational consequences of topic reciprocity and self-disclosure reciprocity. *Communication Monographs, 54,* 420–435.

Hosman, L. A. (1989). The evaluative consequences of hedges, hesitations, and intensifiers: Powerful and powerless speech styles. *Human Communication Research, 15,* 383–406.

Jackson, S., & Jacobs, S. (1983). Generalizing about messages: Suggestions for design and analysis of experiments. *Human Communication Research, 9,* 169–181.

Jones, E. E., & Gordon, E. M. (1972). Timing of self-disclosure and its effects on personal attraction. *Journal of Personality and Social Psychology, 24,* 358–365.

Kellerman, K., & Lim, T. S. (1989). Conversational acquaintance: The flexibility of routinized behaviors. In B. Dervin, L. Grossberg, B. J. O'Keefe, & E. Wartella (Eds.), *Rethinking communication: Vol. 2. Paradigm exemplars* (pp. 172–187). Newbury Park, CA: Sage.

Kennedy, C. W., & Camden, C. T. (1983). A new look at interruptions. *Western Journal of Speech Communication, 47,* 45–58.

Krokoff, L. J. (1987). Recruiting representative samples for marital interaction research. *Journal of Social and Personal Relationships, 4,* 317–328.

Krokoff, L. J. (1989). Recruiting representative samples for marital interaction research: A reply to Bell. *Journal of Social and Personal Relationships, 6,* 235–238.

Lass, N. J., Hughes, K. R., Bowyer, M. D., Waters, L. T., & Broune, V. T. (1976). Speaker sex identification from voice, whispered, and filtered isolated vowels. *Journal of the Acoustical Society of America, 59,* 675–678.

McCroskey, J. C., & Young, T. J. (1981). Ethos and credibility: Its measurement after three decades. *Central States Speech Journal, 32,* 24–34.

McGuire, W. J. (1973). The yin and yang of progress in social psychology: Seven koan. *Journal of Personality and Social Psychology, 26,* 446–456.

McLaughlin, M. L., Louden, A. D., Cashion, J. L., Altendorf, D. M., Baaske, K. T., & Smith, S. W. (1985). Conversational planning and self-serving utterances: The manipulation of topical and functional structures in dyadic interaction. *Journal of Language and Social Psychology, 4,* 233–251.

Mook, D. G. (1983). In defense of external invalidity. *American Psychologist, 38,* 379–387.

Morton, T. L. (1978). Intimacy and reciprocity exchange: A comparison of spouses and strangers. *Journal of Personality and Social Psychology, 36,* 72–81.

Mulac, A. (1975). Evaluation of the speech dialect attitudinal scale. *Speech Monographs, 42,* 184–189.

O'Barr, W. M. (1982). *Linguistic evidence: Language, power, and strategy in the courtroom.* New York: Academic Press.

Pennebaker, J. W., Kiecolt-Glaser, J. K., & Glaser, R. (1988). Disclosure of traumas and immune function: Health implications for psychotherapy. *Journal of Consulting and Clinical Psychology, 56,* 239–245.

Planalp, S. (1989). Relational communication and cognition. In B. Dervin, L. Grossberg, B. J. O'Keefe, & E. Wartella (Eds..), *Rethinking communication: Vol. 2. Paradigm exemplars* (pp. 269–279). Newbury Park, CA: Sage.

Planalp, S., & Tracy, K. (1980). Not to change the topic but . . .: A cognitive approach to the management of conversation. In D. Nimmo (Ed.), *Communication yearbook 4* (pp. 237–258). New Brunswick, NJ: Transaction.

Rubin, Z. (1975). Naturalistic studies of self-disclosure. *Personality and Social Psychology Bulletin, 2,* 260–263.

Sanders, R. E. (1987). *Cognitive foundations of calculated speech: Controlling understandings in conversation and persuasion.* Albany, NY: State University of New York Press.

Shaffer, D. R., & Ogden, J. K. (1986). On sex differences in self-disclosure during the acquaintance process: The role of anticipated future interaction. *Journal of Personality and Social Psychology, 51,* 92–101.

Snyder, M. (1979). Self-monitoring processes. In L. Berkowitz (Ed.), *Advances in experimental social psychology* (Vol. 12, pp. 85–128). New York: Academic Press.

Street, R. L., Jr. (1988). Communication style: Considerations for measuring consistency, reciprocity, and compensation. In C. H. Tardy (Ed.), *A handbook for the study of human communication: Methods and instruments for observing, measuring, and assessing communication processes* (pp. 139–161). Norwood, NJ: Ablex.

Sunnafrank, M. J. (1983). Attitude similarity and interpersonal attraction in communication processes: In pursuit of an ephemeral influence. *Communication Monographs, 50,* 273–284.

Totman, R. (1985). *Social and biological roles of language: The psychology of justification*. London: Academic Press.

Town, J. P., & Harvey, J. H. (1981). Self-disclosure, attribution, and social interaction. *Social Psychology Quarterly, 44,* 291–300.

Tracy, K. (1982). On getting the point: Distinguishing "issues" from "events," an aspect of conversational coherence. In M. Burgoon (Ed.), *Communication yearbook 5* (pp. 279–301). New Brunswick, NJ: Transaction.

Tracy, K. (1989). Conversational dilemmas and the naturalistic experiment. In B. Dervin, L. Grossberg, B. J. O'Keefe, & E. Wartella (Eds.), *Rethinking communication: Vol. 2. Paradigm exemplars* (pp. 411–423). Newbury Park, CA: Sage.

Vinson, L., & Johnson, C. (1989). The use of written transcripts in powerful and powerless language research. *Communication Reports, 2,* 16–21.

Wiemann, J. M. (1977). Explication and test of a model of communicative competence. *Human Communication Research, 3,* 195–213.

Wiemann, J. M. (1981). Effects of laboratory videotaping procedures on selected conversation behaviors. *Human Communication Research, 7,* 302–311.

Zahn, C. J. (1989). The bases for differing evaluations of male and female speech: Evidence from ratings of transcribed conversation. *Communication Monographs, 56,* 59–74.

Zahn, C. J., & Hopper, R. (1985). Measuring language attitudes: The speech evaluation instrument. *Journal of Language and Social Psychology, 4,* 113–123.

PART III

METHODS FOR DATA ANALYSIS

Chapter 13

Content Analysis

LESLIE A. BAXTER

Content analysis is perhaps the oldest of the methods for data analysis examined in this volume. Krippendorff (1980) dates the systematic application of the method back to the 18th century when Swedish scholars and clergy analyzed a collection of nonorthodox hymns called the "Songs of Zion" to determine whether the songs blasphemed the doctrines of the Swedish State Church. However, most modern social scientists associate the origin of the method with the analysis of propaganda during the Second World War and with the publication in 1952 of Berelson's now classic book on the subject. Berelson (1952, p. 18) defined content analysis as "a research technique for the objective, systematic, and quantitative description of the manifest content of communication." Central to Berelson's definition was a focus on manifest, as opposed to latent, content, that is, content features that could be categorized with little or no interpretation by the coder. Berelson differentiated substance content features from form content features, the former referring to what was communicated and the latter referring to how it was communicated.

An example of manifest content analysis relevant to conflict interaction has been suggested by Bavelas, Rogers, and Millar (1985). Observing that many conflicts display avoidance and distancing as well as confrontation, these researchers suggested use of Wiener and Mehrabian's (1968) construct of "nonimmediacy," where "nonimmediacy" is marked by surface language features that convey distancing (e.g., reference to "you and I" rather than to "we" or reference to "those events" in contrast to "these events"). The sample conflict interaction studied in this text, between Michael and Cathy Stone, could be coded for its surface features of immediacy and nonimmediacy, with the proportion of nonimmediacy to immediacy indicators serving as an index of distancing from the other in the conflict. Reference to "we" in the first utterance, for example, rapidly changes into a series of nonimmediacy references to "I" and "you."

Although Berelson's (1952) definition of content analysis is still widely accepted (Kaid & Wadsworth, 1989), an alternative perspective on content analysis has been advanced by Krippendorff (1980). Krippendorff (p. 21) conceived of content analysis as "a technique for making replicable and valid inferences from data to their context." He argued that content analysts should not restrict themselves to summarizing surface features of messages but should instead interpret the meaning of content. A focus on the meaning of content would, according to Krippendorff (1980, p. 7), allow content analysis to "pursue more seriously than it has in the past what is involved in the claim to analyze something that is recognizably symbolic as a symbolic phenomenon."

Krippendorff's (1980) assessment of manifest content analysis may be a candidate for Berelson's (1952, p. 128) reference to the "silly dichotomization between analyses based on 'mere frequencies' as against 'real meanings.'" In point of fact, a manifest content analysis is not lacking in value simply because it entails the counting of surface features of content. If surface features such as linguistic cues of "immediacy" and "nonimmediacy" serve to predict and explain conflict behavior, their study is warranted. On the other hand, if a researcher is interested in a richer understanding of the meanings of the content, manifest content analysis will not be as enlightening as what I shall call interpretive content analysis.

Based on the conclusion that manifest and interpretive content analyses are different methods appropriate to different research goals, the remainder of this chapter concentrates on interpretive content analysis. Three reasons justify this decision. First, interpretive content analysis is more complex than manifest content analysis, because the act of interpretation potentially makes problematic the reliability with which coders categorize units and the validity of the resulting categorizations. Second, I agree with Krippendorff's claim that the complete analysis of symbolic content cannot ignore that which is key to symbolic phenomena—namely, meaning.

The third reason for concentrating on interpretive content analysis is that the method illustrates the "cross-pollination" of perspectives articulated by Montgomery and Duck (Chapter 18) in this volume. Interpretive content analysis and the methods defined as "qualitative" are coding operations that share in common the translation of one set of meanings into another. Content analysis is the process by which the researcher represents one set of meanings in terms of a second system of symbols, the coding categories to which numerical representations are ultimately assigned. With the exception of the requirement that coding categories must receive numerical transformation, the coding operation of interpretive content analysis is remarkably similar to qualitative methods that, like mapmaking, entail the systematic reduction and translation of raw social data into other symbolic forms (Werner & Schoepfle, 1987a).

If interpretive content analysis is to do justice to communication as a symbolic phenomenon, adequate researcher attention must be given to the reliability and validity of the coding categories. Quite simply, an interpretive content analysis stands or falls on the adequacy of its categories and their application. I argue in the following paragraphs that interpretive content analysis frequently can be faulted on these grounds and that users of interpretive content analysis could productively turn to qualitative methods for insights into the coding of meanings. The next section challenges the false dichotomy between qualitative methods and content analysis, discussing a number of areas related to reliability and validity in which content analysts might benefit from their qualitative cousins. The final section discusses five qualitative techniques of particular relevance to interpretive content analysis.

Issues Related to Reliability and Validity

This section discusses four areas of possible "cross-pollination" from qualitative methodology to interpretive content analysis: (1) the role of analytic induction in the derivation of coding categories, (2) the significance of the semantic relationship in determining what is meaningful to code, (3) the importance of validation through representational validity, and (4) the value of unitizing content into semantic units.

Users of interpretive content analysis could benefit significantly by drawing upon the literature of qualitative methodology in order to systematize the process of deriving coding categories. Unfortunately, too many users of content analysis appear to display the stance taken by Krippendorff (1980, p. 76) in his comment that how categories are defined is an "art" about which little is or can be known. Given this attitude, it is not surprising that researchers applying interpretive content analysis methods often fail to report the method by which coding categories are derived and the coding unit to which they are applied. Instead, the coding categories suddenly materialize in "Results" sections of research articles with insufficient attention to their development and use.

A substantial body of work in qualitative methodology challenges the perception that coding activity is an intuitive art that cannot be understood and systematized (e.g., Lofland & Lofland, 1984; Manning, 1987; Spradley, 1979, 1980; Strauss, 1987; Werner & Schoepfle, 1987a, 1987b). Despite variations in specific qualitative techniques, the qualitative derivation of categories relies on the methodology of *analytic induction* (Bulmer, 1979). As Jackson (1986) has observed, analytic induction is not a method in the sense of a specific technique or procedure but, rather, a methodology in the sense of a logic or way of reasoning about the claims generated from one's data. Analytic induction involves not only discovery of categories but the testing of them within the falsification mode: the researcher inductively derives a working hypothesis (in this instance, coding categories) from a subsample of the data, then proceeds to test the hypothesis against additional data cases. Data cases that cannot be described by the coding categories constitute a failure of the hypothesis and the necessity for the researcher to revise the hypothesis. Unlike traditional quantitative hypothesis-testing, both the derivation and revision of the hypothesis occur during the process of the study.

A study of conflict among married couples by Sillars, Weisberg, Burggraf, and Wilson (1987) provides an illustration of analytic induction in practice. The researchers sought to derive a set of content themes by which to categorize couple conflicts. Couples were provided with a list of topics to discuss, each representing an issue common to marital conflict. The couples discussed the topics, and the transcripts of the discussions were broken down into units that captured the "core propositions stated by each person on each topic" (p. 505). The propositions were placed on cards that two of the researchers independently sorted into inductively-derived categories. The researchers then discussed the differences in their categories and "through a process of discussing and resorting, eventually arrived at an agreed-upon set of categories" (p. 506). This process of analytic induction produced 11 total categories, including references to togetherness, references to situational constraints on individual choices, and references to the individuals' personality characteristics.

Analytic induction is a necessary but not sufficient factor in generating categories that do justice to the meaning of symbolic phenomena. Work in ethnoscience and cognitive anthropology provides insight into meaningful categorization by introducing the concept of the *semantic relationship*. One of the first systematic investigations of semantic relationships was done by Casagrande and Hale (1967) among the Papago Indians of the Southwest United States. In their endeavor to understand the meanings operative in their informants' language use, these researchers observed that all definitions were structured as two or more folk terms linked together through a finite number of semantic relationships. A number of sets of semantic relationships have been advanced, but Spradley's (1979, p. 111) list of posited universal semantic relationships is helpful for our purposes:

1. Strict Inclusion X is a kind of Y
2. Spatial X is a place in Y; X is part of Y
3. Cause–Effect X is a cause/result of Y
4. Rationale X is a reason for doing Y
5. Location for X is a place for doing Y action
6. Function X is used for Y
7. Means–end X is a way to do Y
8. Sequence X is a step/stage in Y
9. Attribution X is an attribute/characteristic of Y

A given cultural domain (Y) is meaningful when one understands the web of semantic relationships that links the domain with other domains (X). For example, the meaning of the domain known as "interpersonal conflict" consists of a set of semantic relationships that probably includes at least these semantic relations: (1) *Inclusion:* "Xs are kinds of interpersonal conflict"; (2) *Attribution:* "Xs are characteristics of interpersonal conflict"; (3) *Sequence:* "Xs are stages in interpersonal conflict"; and (4) *Means–End:* "Xs are ways to do interpersonal conflict." Someone can be said to have "full understanding" of what interpersonal conflict "means" to the extent that he or she has woven a complete web of its relevant semantic relationships. The set of "Xs" that defines a given semantic relationship is the category set of an interpretive content analysis.

Because semantic relationships are key to meaning, their systematic analysis is the linchpin to any interpretive coding endeavor. Although treatments of qualitative analysis distinguish a number of analytic approaches from one another, five of which are discussed in the next section, the various techniques share in common the analytic centrality of the semantic relationship (for a detailed treatment, see Werner & Schoepfle, 1987a, 1987b).

The criterion by which to determine the validity of the categorizations in an interpretive content analysis should correspond to that employed by qualitative researchers in assessing interpretations of social phenomena. Qualitative researchers strive to capture "the native's point of view" (Geertz, 1973). Just as the qualitative researcher strives for an interpretation to which speech community members would respond "That's right, but I hadn't thought of it that way" (Carbaugh, 1988, xiv), the user of interpretive content analysis should ask whether his or her categorizations capture adequately the symbolic meanings of the content. The "native's point of view" shows remarkable conceptual similarity to *representational validity*. This form of validation refers to whether one's categorizations capture the conventional meanings that would be ascribed to the content by members of the speech community (Folger, Hewes, & Poole, 1984).

Researchers can mistakenly use forms of validation more appropriate to manifest content analysis in applying interpretive content analysis

methods. The relational communication coding schemes have been a focused object of criticism in terms of representational validity. Such coding
schemes categorize interpersonal interaction by control function; typical is
the Rogers and Farace (1975) scheme that categorizes acts as bids for
dominance ("one-up acts"), submission ("one-down acts"), or neutrality
("one-across" acts). Although the coding scheme has demonstrated adequate forms of traditional validity (Rogers & Millar, 1982), it has been
criticized because evidence is lacking that would demonstrate that the
coding categories of dominance, submission, and neutrality reflect the
conventionalized or shared meanings of control by native speakers of the
culture (Folger & Poole, 1982). In a published debate over the question of
the validity of the relational coding schemes, Folger and Poole (1982)
basically took the position that coding schemes such as that by Rogers and
Farace (1975) were interpreting interactional meanings and thus should be
held to the standard of representational validity. Rogers and Millar (1982)
disagreed with this position, arguing that relational coding schemes code
behavioral functions, not meanings. Without taking a position one way or
the other in this particular debate, it is simply worth noting that neither side
to the debate challenged the value of traditional forms of validity when
meanings were not at issue and the value of representational validity when
the content analyst claimed to interpret meanings of symbolic phenomena.

Any adequate content analysis application must also address the content units that are to be categorized, that is, the issue of unitizing. Reliability
demands explicit and clear description of the parsing rules by which the
content data are unitized, and validity requires meaningfulness in such
unitizing (Folger et al., 1984). However, unitizing is often mentioned by
content analysts only when the coding unit is at the manifest level, for
example, the word, the sentence, the utterance. Even in instances in which
the unit is defined, separate reliability indices are rarely reported for the
separate judgments of unitizing and categorizing, thereby confounding how
content is parsed with how it is classified (Folger et al., 1984). The unitizing
question is a relatively straightforward matter with units defined at a
manifest level. However, coding operations that seek to make sense of
symbolic meanings need to employ *semantic units* rather than units defined
through grammatical or other arbitrary surface feature markers.

Depending on the particular semantic relationship that the researcher
wishes to classify, the semantic unit can be defined as that content segment
that delimits an instance of the semantic relationship. For example, if one
were interested in the semantic relationship of Function with regard to the
ways (X) in which people verbally manage conflict (Y), one would search
the data until encountering a content segment that could be interpreted as a
complete instance of the relationship "X is used for Y." In the Michael–
Cathy exchange (in the sample research problem of this volume), for
example, one might identify the last sentence of utterance #05 ("You either,

you choose to ignore these things, don't you"). as an instance of Mindreading, that is, statements that attribute feelings, attitudes or motives to the other party (Gottman, 1979). A second independent coder might parse the same content segment as an instance of an "X," in which case the two coders would display high unitizing reliability. However, if the second coder interpreted this content unit not as Mindreading but as an instance of another category type, the two would have low categorizing reliability. Depending on the loquacity of a given interactant and the complexity of the particular semantic relationship under study, a semantic unit could range from a single word to a complete utterance.

The first section of this chapter has addressed at a general level the ways in which qualitative methodology holds relevance for the interpretive content analysis method. The next section of the chapter presents selected qualitative techniques that hold potential relevance for users of interpretive content analysis.

Using Qualitatively Enhanced Content Analysis: Selected Approaches to This Text's Sample

Qualitative researchers have developed five analytic methods of particular relevance to interpretive content analysis: (1) domain analysis, (2) taxonomic analysis, (3) componential analysis, (4) thematic analysis, and (5) sequential analysis (for detailed explanations of these approaches see Spradley, 1979, 1980, and Werner & Schoepfle, 1987a, 1987b). These five methods provide an organizing framework by which to categorize types of interpretive content analyses.

DOMAIN ANALYSIS

Domain analysis, the simplest approach, involves a description of a given category of meaning or domain through a relevant semantic relationship. That is, the researcher is seeking to define the set of Xs that are kinds of Y, parts of Y, causes of Y, effects of Y, reasons for doing Y, ways to do Y, and so forth. Holland and Skinner (1987) illustrate the Strict Inclusion semantic relationship applied to the domain of gender types. These researchers interviewed a sample of men on the types of women they perceived and interviewed a sample of women on the types of men they perceived. For each type generated, informants were asked to describe the type. A rich and colorful domain of "Xs" was generated in completing the semantic relationship "X is a kind of man/woman," including, among others, "jock," "stud," "hunk," "wimp," and "guy" as kinds of men and "slut," "bitch," "airhead," and "libber" as kinds of women.

Although interviewing is a frequently employed research strategy for purposes of conducting a domain analysis, alternative strategies exist. Researchers interested in describing kinds of men/women from the "native's point of view" could gather together same-sex groups for focus group discussions on the opposite sex or could record naturally occurring conversations in which the opposite sex is the topic. The researchers then would analyze the discussions or conversations for purposes of identifying all of the terms used to describe kinds of men and kinds of women. In order to maximize representational validity, people similar to the interactants should be asked to identify the kinds of men and women represented in the talk.

If the data set consisted of marital conflict interaction, the first task of the researcher interested in doing a domain analysis would be a determination of the domain and the semantic relationship to be studied. Many possibilities obviously exist. One researcher might be interested in a Strict Inclusion domain analysis of kinds of conflict episodes. The domain in this instance would be conflict episodes, and the semantic unit would be an entire interaction episode of which the entire exchange between Michael and Cathy Stone would be one instance. The set of conflict episodes could be transcribed and presented to a group of persons who would be asked to sort the transcripts into piles, with each pile representing a kind of conflict episode.

The Strict Inclusion semantic relationship could be examined with respect to a different domain as well. If one were interested in the domain of marital complaints, for example, people could be presented with transcripts of the conflict interactions and asked to identify each segment that captured a kind of complaint.

Other semantic relationships hold interesting research possibilities. A researcher interested in the semantic relationship of Sequence for the domain of conflict episodes would be seeking an understanding of the stages of marital conflict interactions. Informants could be presented with one or several transcripts of conflict from one's data sample and asked to parse the episode(s) into the stages they perceived. A researcher interested in examining the Means–End semantic relationship with respect to the domain of conflict management strategies might present transcripts of marital conflicts to informants and ask them to identify all of the different ways in which spouses handle conflict.

Regardless of the particular domain and semantic relationship under study, the researcher is obligated to seek understanding from the informant perspective, not the researcher perspective. Such a commitment to representational validity is based on the assumption that one is seeking an understanding of meanings.

TAXONOMIC ANALYSIS

Taxonomic analysis concentrates on the internal structure of elements within a given domain. It maps which elements are subsets of other elements, evidencing at a generic level the Spatial semantic relationship of which elements are parts of other categories. Taxonomic analysis is employed whenever a researcher is seeking to determine whether redundancy in meaning exists among his or her set of domain analysis elements; the method is a natural sequel to domain analysis, particularly when the number of elements in a domain is large.

A study by Douglas (1987) of the ways interactants test the other party's affinity in initial interactions illustrates a taxonomic analysis. At the initial stage of the research, interviewers queried male and female informants about all of the things they did to find out how much someone of the opposite sex liked them in initial encounters, that is, a domain analysis on the semantic relationship of Means–End. After a corpus of 101 affinity-seeking strategies was generated in this manner, the interviewers, who were from the same speech community as the informants, sorted the strategies into more general category types, producing eight general affinity-seeking categories: confronting, withdrawing, sustaining, hazing, diminishing self, approaching, offering, and networking. At the next stage of taxonomic analysis, two judges were provided with each of the initial 101 strategies together with descriptions of the eight inductively-derived categories. These judges sorted the strategies into the eight generic categories with inter-judge agreement of .90. During a final stage, designed to determine representational validity, three examples from the initial pool of 101 strategies that represented each category type were presented to informants drawn from the same population as the initial interview informants. These informants were asked to sort the examples into like-kind clusters, with no suggestion from the researcher as to the number of categories or their type. The pooled sorting data were submitted to a cluster analysis statistical procedure to determine the appropriate number of clusters by which to capture the informants' sorts. The cluster analysis replicated the eight general categories that had been inductively derived from the interviews, thereby demonstrating that the eight categories captured the types of affinity-seeking strategies from the "native's point of view." The initial pool of 101 strategies was thus reduced to an eight-category taxonomy.

To illustrate a taxonomic analysis with the Michael–Cathy conflict interaction data, suppose that a researcher were interested in the Rationale semantic relationship and sought to examine the attributional reasons people give for their own behavior and their partner's behavior during marital conflict. If the data set were composed of transcripts of marital conflict interaction, the research goal would be the inductive derivation of all of the types of reasons expressed in the interaction. The researcher would derive all of the types of reasons contained in the sample and seek to validate their taxonomic organization by submitting them to informants who could be asked to sort reasons into like kind. A perusal of the Michael–Cathy exchange produces the following set of reasons: "You wouldn't want to eat my cooking" as a reason for not cooking (utterance #02); "You choose to ignore these things" as an attributed reason for why Michael didn't assist in household chores (utterance #05); a full load at work as a reason for being particularly bothered that Michael didn't do housework over the summer (utterance #05); looseness [in standards] as a reason for reacting to how housework is done (utterance #09); the presence of Cathy as a reason for why Michael doesn't do more housework (utterances 11 and 12); not thinking about housework as a reason for not noticing that it needs to be done (utterance #12). Clearly, over a number of conflict episodes, the list of specific reasons would be enormous, and a researcher might reasonably wonder if a smaller number of types captures the domain of reasons. Specific reasons expressed during interaction could be printed on cards and given to informants who were like the married couples from whom the conflict interactions were obtained. These informants would be asked to sort the expressed reasons into piles, with each pile capturing a different type of reason. The frequencies with which cards were sorted into the same piles could be used as quantitative data for input into a cluster analytic procedure. Note that in this example I parsed the Michael–Cathy interaction using the reason as a semantic unit. It would be advisable in the actual research study to ask informants to identify the initial reasons from the stream of interaction, thereby ensuring that the corpus of reasons was informant-based.

COMPONENTIAL ANALYSIS

Componential or semantic feature analysis asks the analytic question, What binary features distinguish categories from one another? That is, what are the characteristics that sort out which elements in a given category are equivalent and which are different? The analytic technique exemplifies at the generic level the semantic relationship of Comparison, that is, X is defined with respect to the similarity or contrast with Y (Casagrande & Hale, 1967). The technique is integrally related to taxonomic analysis, because the decision to group elements together calls for judgments of sameness/difference. Componential analysis makes explicit the implicit judgments of comparison that informants use in deriving taxonomies. In its focus on binary contrast features, componential analysis displays its intellectual roots in structuralism. Structuralism seeks to identify the underlying pairs of binary oppositions that constitute the structural codes or grammars of meaning in texts (Berman, 1988; Eagleton, 1983).

Conville (1988) provides a good illustration of the analytic search for binary semantic features. He analyzed a case study of the language accounts provided by a husband and wife to describe the transitions in their relationship. From a close reading of the accounts, Conville inferred four basic kinds of stages in their relationship's transitions: (1) Anticipation concerning the couple's relocation to a new city; (2) Separation related to the distancing that occurred in the couple following the move; (3) Discovery, a stage in which both spouses realized how much they missed their partner; and (4) Reconciliation. After identifying these stages, Conville sought the underlying semantic oppositions by which the spouses made sense of their relationship's transition across these four stages. Three underlying binary oppositions were identified in the language accounts of the pair: affect (positive–negative); intimacy (close–distant); and time perspective (past–future). The husband experienced the anticipated move positively whereas the wife experienced the move negatively. Both spouses agreed in describing the Separation phase as distant and the Reconciliation phase as close. The husband's discovery of how much he missed his wife was rooted in reminiscence about the past whereas the wife's discovery of how much she missed her husband was framed in future-directed thinking. Although Conville's study was not directed toward generalizing binary oppositions across a sample of couple accounts, it nonetheless illustrates the essential elements of a componential analysis. The study is closely tied to the language of one's informants and seeks to locate the binary semantic dimensions by which meaning is organized.

A more quantitative illustration of componential analysis is provided in the second study described by Holland and Skinner (1987) in their examination of cultural gender types. The researchers took a sample of the terms used by informants to describe members of the opposite sex and asked a separate sample of informants to sort a card deck containing the gender terms. The sorting data were submitted to multidimensional scaling analysis, with a three-dimensional solution emerging for types of men and for types of women. Informant explanations of why they sorted terms as they did were used as a basis of inferring labels for the underlying dimensions in the multidimensional space. Males determined sameness and difference among types of women along three semantic dimensions: high-status sexual companions (e.g., "foxes") versus low-status sexual companions (e.g., "whores"); overdemanding and unlikable women (e.g., "bitches") versus likable and undemanding women (e.g., "sweetheart"); and sexually repulsive women (e.g., "dykes") versus sexually attractive women (e.g., "dolls"). Females made sense of the domain of types of men using three different underlying semantic oppositions: men who use their maleness for selfish purpose (e.g., "playboys") versus men who do not (e.g., "guys"); ineffectual and unlikable men (e.g., "jerks" and "nerds") versus effectual and likable men (e.g., "boyfriends"); and men for whom sexuality is important to their identity (e.g., "gays") versus men for whom sexuality is unimportant to their identity (e.g., "nerds").

The specific binary contrast features that describe conflict interactions depend on the particular domain under investigation. Nonetheless, their investigation would be guided by a common research question: What are the underlying binary semantic pairs by which informants categorize two elements as similar or different? The question on its surface appears to have much in common with semantic differential methodology (Osgood, Suci, & Tannenbaum, 1957). However, componential analysis is based on inductive analysis of unstructured informant language rather than researcher-determined semantic pairs that are provided to respondents as stimuli for reaction.

THEMATIC ANALYSIS

Thematic analysis is the most complex of the qualitative techniques of relevance to interpretive content analysis, because the researcher's interpretations are based on a holistic analysis. In order to perform a thematic analysis, the researcher must perform analyses on more than one domain. Once several domains have been interpreted, the researcher asks how the meaning domains are similar, that is, the semantic relationship of Synonymy (Casagrande & Hale, 1967). Themes are threads of meaning that recur in domain after domain.

Baumgartner's (1988) participant observation study of dispute management in an American suburb illustrates a thematic analysis. Baumgartner's investigation involved several domain analyses, including, in part, types of conflicts in families, types of conflicts among friends, types of conflicts among neighbors, ways to manage conflicts over obligations, and ways to manage conflicts over control of material possessions. She interviewed people both formally and informally about conflicts in their lives and about their knowledge of the conflicts in the lives of their friends and neighbors. She also directly observed conflicts and disputes whenever possible during her year-long investigation. Across various domains of analysis, all of which related to the broad question of how people in one American suburb managed conflicts in their lives, Baumgartner observed a pattern or theme that she labeled moral minimalism, that is, "efforts to deny, minimize, contain, and avoid conflict" (p. 127). In contrast to a pervasive characterization of the American culture as violent and aggressive, Baumgartner concluded that the dominant theme of the American suburbs is a moral order of minimalism that manifests itself not only in limited conflictual interaction but in limited interactions of connectedness as well.

On its face, the Michael–Cathy conflict stands in marked contrast to Baumgartner's theme of moral minimalism. The conflict, despite an attempt at conciliation by Michael in his admission that his housework contribution is insufficient (utterance #08), is quite confrontational in nature. The discrepancy between this conflict episode and Baumgartner's analysis may rest with the comprehensiveness of Baumgartner's work in contrast to the isolated incident represented by the Stone exchange. In "real time," the entire Michael–Cathy episode probably is completed in about a minute. We are not given any information about whether their guests, the Millers, defined the eruption between Michael and Cathy as an embarrassing incident, nor are we given information about whether Michael and Cathy enacted remedial repair work, which one would expect after performing a social transgression. Such contextual information would be a part of a holistic analysis such as that undertaken by Baumgartner.

SEQUENTIAL ANALYSIS

The first four analytic approaches share in common a static, structural approach to meaning. In its focus on the semantic relationship of Sequence (X is a stage or step in Y) and the temporal quality inherent in the Cause-Effect semantic relationship, sequential analysis addresses temporal meaning.

A study by Lee (1984) illustrates a sequential analysis of premarital relationship dissolution. A close interpretation was given to 24 case histories of breakups. Using the method of analytic induction, Lee derived five stages of dissolution: Discovery of Dissatisfaction, Exposure, Negotiation, Resolution, and Transformation. Each stage could be further delimited in terms of which party served as an agent of action during the stage, the expression of dissatisfaction or desired action, and the time length or latency of the stage. Lee then validated this sequential model in 112 interviews with relational parties who retrospectively described their relationship's dissolution.

Sequential analysis of conflict interaction can take at least three forms. If a researcher were interested in studying individual styles of conflict management, the sequence of interest would be the string of utterances expressed by the person. Such a sequential analysis might, for example, differentiate someone whose style is to begin an argument with an exaggerated claim but who subsequently moderates that claim from someone who begins with understatement but escalates demands as the conflict proceeds. A second form of sequential analysis, and the form most frequently found in the interaction coding literature (Tardy, 1988), focuses on the sequence of exchanges between parties, that is, what follows what between interacting parties. The third form of sequential analysis examines the sequence of conflict episodes, examining the sequential pattern of types of conflict enactments across a relationship's history, for example, whether emotionally charged conflict episodes are followed by enactments that are more emotionally controlled.

Conclusion

It would be remiss to close the chapter with the implication that interpretive content analysis is a nonproblematic method by which to study meaning. Although certainly better than manifest content analysis in capturing latent meanings, the method is subject to at least three fundamental criticisms that set the boundary conditions for its usefulness. First, in its assumption that meanings can be categorized, content analysis trivializes the complex interaction process by which meaning is constructed (Sigman, Sullivan, & Wendell, 1988). If the researcher seeks to understand the process by which meaning is constructed, a method such as conversation analysis would probably be more appropriate (see Chapter 10). Second, in counting particular instances of content as the same category of meaning, content analysis ignores the emergence of unique meanings in the immediacy of the local context and the interactional moment (Sigman et al., 1988). The study of localized and emergent meanings would probably be better suited to participant observation or conversation analysis methods than to interpretive content analysis. Third, the typical interpretive content analysis application considers only isolated semantic relationships for isolated domains of meaning and thereby lacks the "thick description" that many regard as essential to meaningful understanding (Geertz, 1973). When one is seeking to understand the gestalt of a culture's code of meaning, rather than seeking to understand selected domains of meaning for selected symbolic phenomena, participant observation methods (see, e.g., Chapters 7 & 8) would be more appropriate than interpretive content analysis.

This chapter has attempted to draw qualitative methods and interpretive content analysis closer together both conceptually and in practice. I have argued that this synthesis is a natural one based on the fact that the approaches share in common the activity of categorizing or coding. If users of content analysis are to analyze content as a symbolic phenomenon, as Krippendorff (1980) has urged, they could benefit from the body of work in qualitative methodology. These methods, and their logic of analytic induction, provide potential users of interpretive content analysis with systematic ways to describe domains of meaning in symbolic content.

References

Baumgartner, M. P. (1988). *The moral order of a suburb*. New York: Oxford University Press.

Bavelas, J. B., Rogers, L. E., & Millar, F. E. (1985). Interpersonal conflict. In T. A. van Dijk (Ed.), *Handbook of discourse analysis: Vol. 4. Discourse analysis in society* (pp. 9–26). New York: Academic Press.

Berelson, B. (1952). *Content analysis in communication research*. New York: The Free Press.

Berman, A. (1988). *From the new criticism to deconstruction*. Chicago: University of Illinois Press.

Bulmer, M. (1979). Concepts in the analysis of qualitative data. *Sociological Review, 27,* 651–671.

Carbaugh, D. (1988). *Talking American: Cultural discourses on Donahue*. Norwood, NJ: Ablex.

Casagrande, J. B., & Hale, K. L. (1967). Semantic relations in Papago folk definitions. In D. Hymes & W. E. Bittle (Eds.), *Studies in southwestern ethnolinguistics* (pp. 165–196). The Hague: Mouton.

Conville, R. L. (1988). Relational transitions: An inquiry into their structure and functions. *Journal of Social and Personal Relationships, 5,* 423–437.

Douglas, W. (1987). Affinity-testing in initial interactions. *Journal of Social and Personal Relationships, 4,* 3–15.

Eagleton, T. (1983). *Literary theory: An introduction*. Minneapolis: University of Minnesota Press.

Folger, J. P., Hewes, D. E., & Poole, M. S. (1984). Coding social interaction. In B. Dervin & M. J. Voigt (Eds.), *Progress in communication sciences (Vol. 4,* pp. 115–162). Norwood, NJ: Ablex.

Folger, J. P., & Poole, M. S. (1982). Relational coding schemes: The question of validity. In M. Burgoon (Ed.), *Communication yearbook 5* (pp. 235–248). New Brunswick, NJ: Transaction.

Geertz, C. (1973). *The interpretation of cultures*. New York: Basic Books.

Gottman, J. M. (1979). *Marital interaction: Experimental investigations*. New York: Academic Press.

Holland, D., & Skinner, D. (1987). Prestige and intimacy: The cultural models behind Americans' talk about gender types. In D. Holland & N. Quinn (Eds.), *Cultural models in language and thought* (pp. 78–111). New York: Cambridge University Press.

Jackson, S. (1986). Building a case for claims about discourse structure. In D. G. Ellis & W. A. Donohue (Eds.), *Contemporary issues in language and discourse processes* (pp. 129–148). Hillsdale, NJ: Erlbaum.

Kaid, L. L., & Wadsworth, A. J. (1989). Content analysis. In P. Emmert & L. Barker (Eds.), *Measurement of communication behavior* (pp. 197–217). New York: Longman.

Krippendorff, K. (1980). *Content analysis: An introduction to its methodology*. Beverly Hills: Sage.

Lee, L. (1984). Sequences in separation: A framework for investigating endings of the personal (romantic) relationship. *Journal of Social and Personal Relationships, 1,* 49–73.

Lofland, J., & Lofland, L. H. (1984). *Analyzing social settings: A guide to qualitative observation and analysis* (2nd ed.). Belmont, CA: Wadsworth.

Manning, P. K. (1987). *Semiotics and fieldwork* (Sage University Paper Series on Qualitative Research Methods, Vol. 7). Newbury Park, CA: Sage.

Osgood, C. E., Suci, G. J., & Tannenbaum, P. H. (1957). *The measurement of meaning.* Chicago: University of Illinois Press.

Rogers, L. E., & Farace, R. V. (1975). Analysis of relational communication in dyads: New measurement procedures. *Human Communication Research, 1,* 222–239.

Rogers, L. E., & Millar, F. (1982). The question of validity: A pragmatic answer. In M. Burgoon (Ed.), *Communication yearbook 5* (pp. 249–257). New Brunswick, NJ: Transaction.

Sigman, S. J., Sullivan, S. J., & Wendell, M. (1988). Conversation: Data acquisition and analysis. In C. H. Tardy (Ed.), *A handbook for the study of human communication* (pp. 163–192). Norwood, NJ: Ablex.

Sillars, A. L., Weisberg, J., Burggraf, C. S., & Wilson, E. A. (1987). Content themes in marital conversations. *Human Communication Research, 13,* 495–528.

Spradley, J. P. (1979). *The ethnographic interview.* New York: Holt, Rinehart & Winston.

Spradley, J. P. (1980). *Participant observation.* New York: Holt, Rinehart & Winston.

Strauss, A. L. (1987). *Qualitative analysis for social scientists.* New York: Cambridge University Press.

Tardy, C. H., (1988). Interpersonal interaction coding systems. In C. H. Tardy (Ed.), *A handbook for the study of communication* (pp. 285–300). Norwood, NJ: Ablex.

Werner, O., & Schoepfle, G. M. (1987a). *Systematic fieldwork* (Vol. 1). Newbury Park, CA: Sage.

Werner, O., & Schoepfle, G. M. (1987b). *Systematic fieldwork* (Vol. 2). Newbury Park, CA: Sage.

Wiener, M., & Mehrabian, A. (1968). *Language within language: Immediacy, a channel in verbal communication.* New York: Appleton-Century-Crofts.

Chapter 14

Analyzing Categorical Data

ROGER BAKEMAN

A segment of a discussion between Michael and Cathy Stone, a married couple, serves as a common example throughout this book. For simplicity, the sample is very brief, consisting of just 13 turns of talk—7 for the wife and 6 for the husband. The discussion occurs at a dinner party and is played out in front of long-term friends, another married couple. It constitutes what readers of this book would probably call a sample of marital (or, more broadly, interpersonal) interaction.

Attempts to study interpersonal interaction, like that between Cathy and Michael Stone, can proceed through one or more of four stages or levels. No one level is necessarily or inherently superior to any other, and the four levels are postulated here as a heuristic device, useful for framing the material presented in this chapter. These four levels, each of which can provide opportunities for scholarly activity, are the following:

1. Selection
2. Qualitative Interpretation
3. Measurement
4. Quantitative Interpretation

Consider *selection* with respect to the present example. Why were Michael and Cathy Stone selected to be observed? Why not some other married couple, or why not an unmarried opposite-sex or same-sex couple (see Blumstein & Schwartz, 1983). Why not several different kinds of couples? Again, why was dinnertime conversation recorded, not some other kind? Probably good answers to all of these questions could be provided, but they would need to reference the research question that motivated selection of the source material in the first place.

No matter what the question, selection of source material (including decisions related to settings, subjects, recording methods, etc.) provides the foundation on which all subsequent analysis rests. In fact, selection may be the only level utilized, as it is in such documentary films as Frederick Wiseman's *Titticut Follies* and *Highschool* and Errol Morris's *Vernon, Florida*. These films rely solely on selection—of people, places, situations, lighting, camera angles, and so forth. The directors rarely speak in their own voices, rarely make their interpretations of the selected material public.

It is the very absence of overt and explicit *qualitative interpretation* that gives these films their distinctive quality, that distinguishes them from scholarly attempts at explication and understanding. Qualitative interpretation, which I have called here a level-two endeavor, is an ancient human activity. Certainly it is part of what for centuries has been called humanistic studies, although some modern names for the enterprise include ethnomethodology, participant observation, or plain old-fashioned journalism. Some of its better known practitioners include Robert Coles (1967), Erving Goffman (1962), Oscar Lewis (1961), and Susan Sheehan (1982).

At its best, qualitative interpretation represents lively intelligence and informed sensibility—and at its worst it seems simply ill-informed, self-contained, self-indulgent, and dull. But this variability of product is both the great glory and profound trap of qualitative interpretation. How do we know if work is good? How do we judge? How do we train practitioners? And how do we respond to the criticism that the authors viewed phenomena from a certain preconceived point of view, a point of view that unduly colored or biased their reports and their interpretations?

Partly to escape from this criticism, there have been attempts over the past few centuries to remove interpretation from the subjective realm. This can be viewed as part of an increasing reliance on methods regarded as scientific or as part of the increasing dominance of approaches compatible with bourgeois professionalism. In either case, the trend has been towards an increased reliance on quantification, on *measurement* of phenomena of interest—the third level identified earlier.

Measurement has a number of merits. Chief among them is the greater objectivity it provides, an insulation of data from personal bias. In fact, only at this level is it possible to talk of data instead of source material because, by definition, data are what result from measurement. Videotapes or transcripts by themselves are not data, only source material waiting to be transformed into data by measurement. Quantification has its pitfalls (e.g., measuring instruments necessarily limit what phenomena are considered), but normally it allows us to discount the personal qualities of the measurer and to expect reproducible results from trained and professional coders under similar circumstances. It is difficult to judge qualitative interpretations without also judging the interpreter, but the data that result from measurement are seldom acclaimed or discounted on the basis of the personal qualities of the measurer.

The fourth and final level identified earlier is *quantitative interpretation*. This level presupposes measurement. With techniques of statistical and logical analysis, the intent is to wrest meaning and interpretation from raw data. This activity is the stock in trade of work that is usually characterized as scientific and empirical, and reports of such work form the bulk of articles published in established journals.

Although the title of this chapter, "Analyzing Categorical Data," suggests an explication primarily of third- and fourth-level activities, at least two major limitations should be noted. First, as the title states, only categorical (or nominal) data are considered here. For such data, measurement consists of assigning categories (like male/female, friendly/unfriendly, etc.), and quantification begins by noting the simple frequencies with which the various instances of each category occur. Second, the material presented in this brief chapter should be viewed as introductory. I plan to pursue a quite limited goal, demonstrating a few simple ways that measurement and quantitative interpretation could be applied to material like Michael and Cathy Stone's sample of interpersonal interaction. I will also describe one potential problem (the problem of "independence") and will provide a number of references so that interested readers can pursue the matters discussed here further (one of the more informative and readable introductions to the analysis of categorical data is Kennedy, 1983; also helpful is Upton, 1978, and a standard basic reference is Bishop, Fienberg, & Holland, 1975).

Measuring Behavior: From Codes to Counts

The measuring instrument for the sort of observational studies discussed here is the *coding scheme*. In its simplest manifestation a coding scheme consists of a list of mutually exclusive and exhaustive categories or codes. That is, only one code can be applied to each event coded and the scheme contains some code for all possible events.

The event is basic, and defining exactly what constitutes an event is one of the first orders of conceptual business when planning an observational study. Events could consist of 1-minute time periods occurring at random times over successive days (Parten, 1932), successive, brief time-intervals in sequence (Bakeman & Brownlee, 1980), or successive turns of talk (Dorval & Eckerman, 1984; Gottman, 1980; Hauser et al., 1984). For the present example, the turn of talk as defined in the transcript might serve as the basic "unit" or event coded, although some investigators might want to further subdivide turns into smaller units (e.g., a single turn might be viewed as containing more than one "thought").

Just as there is no single generic event that can be applied automatically in all situations, so too there is no single generic coding scheme that is appropriate for all situations. Always, the appropriate unit to use for any given study, as well as the appropriate coding scheme to categorize those units, depends on the research questions that motivate the study. These questions need to fit the codes as hand to glove. For example, some time ago Hops, Patterson, and their associates defined a Marital Interaction Coding System (Hops, Willis, Patterson, & Weiss, 1971). The basic scheme, in various modified and elaborated versions, has seen service in a number of studies. As an example, useful for the present discussion, I will define a simplified version, consisting of five codes intended to capture the function of successive turns of talk in problem-centered conversation between spouses like Cathy and Michael Stone. These codes are the following:

1. Complains
2. Emotes
3. Approves
4. Empathizes
5. Negates

They seem well suited, indeed designed, to investigate how couples deal with complaints in their conversation and whether negative comments, once begun, tend to be self-perpetuating, resulting in what is termed negative-reciprocity (Cousins & Power, 1986).

Still, how are coding schemes like the one just described developed in the first place? I find it convenient to think of coding scheme development as a level-two activity. Qualitative interpretation is important, indeed essential, for practitioners of behavioral measurement. As Rosenblum (1978) noted some time ago, "At the beginning, the observer must simply watch, allowing individual subjects to arise as separate entities in the group and behavior patterns to emerge against the background of initially amorphous activity" (p. 17).

In other words, even quantitative researchers should not eschew the level of qualitative interpretation. As a first step they should invest their talent, their experience, their understanding of the phenomena under consideration, and their informed sensibility in the process of code development, which can be viewed as a level-two activity. In one sense, what is viewed as end product for a qualitative researcher is pilot study for a quantitative researcher. Consider the present example. Ideally, the investigator begins with a series of relatively well-defined questions in mind.

Conversations between various kinds of couples in various situations are required to answer those questions, and so the investigator acquires transcripts of such conversations. These are read and discussed with colleagues and associates, with as few preconceptions as possible but with the questions underlying the investigation firmly in mind. Codes are suggested and refined on successive readings (or hearings or viewings, depending on the medium used to capture the source material; see Chapter 13).

With a refined code catalogue firmly in hand, the investigator can move the study to a new level—the third, or measurement, level. Individuals and situations are selected for observation, and the events observed are coded using the codes defined in the coding scheme. Behavior can be observed live or—better, because of the possibility for replay—on audio- or videotape. For the present example, assuming the five codes given earlier, the data would consist of sequences of codes. These codes would represent the functions that trained coders assigned to each successive turn of talk, and although only a segment of conversation is given here, we can assume that for an actual study many such segments would be coded and that some segments might represent different kinds of couples perhaps observed in different situations. (For additional discussion of code development and recording, as well as discussion of the crucial topic of coder agreement or reliability, see Bakeman & Gottman, 1986.)

2 × 2 TABLES: A PROCRUSTEAN APPROACH

Among the more interesting questions for which observational data of the sort described here are appropriate are those dealing with sequential process. Imagine that the present investigation was motivated by a desire to determine whether, and how, particular research factors affect negative reciprocity. (Possible research factors include a couple's status, which could be coded as distressed or not, and social context, which could be coded as observed with others present or not.) First we would need to assess negative reciprocity separately for the various couples observed. My recommendation is that all sequential descriptive measures needed to answer particular research questions be cast initially in the form of 2 × 2 tables—in a manner that would satisfy Procrustes, that hospital Greek highwayman of legend who, by either chopping or stretching, ensured that all guests would fit his iron bed.

The appropriate event for addressing questions of sequential process is not the single event coded initially but adjacent pairs of events. In other words, shifting our focus to sequential concerns requires a new definition for the event investigated, but no new coding. Given the present coding scheme, we would first form a 5 × 5 table. Rows and columns would be labeled with the five codes; rows would represent the antecedent event, columns the consequent one. Next we would examine each successive pair of adjacent codes and would add a tally to the appropriate cell of the initial 5 × 5 table.

For example, using the five codes of the Marital Interaction Coding Scheme introduced earlier (recall that 1 = Complains, 2 = Emotes, 3 = Approves, 4 = Empathizes, and 5 = Negates), the 13 turns of talk in the example segment could be coded as follows:

$$1 \ 3 \ 1 \ 5 \ 1 \ 4 \ 2 \ 4 \ 2 \ 3 \ 5 \ 3 \ 5$$

(I make no claim that this is a reasonable coding for the example segment; in order to determine that, we would need complete definitions for the codes, not just the words provided here. We would also need to demonstrate observer reliability.) This segment of 13 turns of talk consists of 12 transitions. We can regard transitions as events in their own right, and can visualize these 12 transition events as follows. Imagine a two-event "window" (represented here with parentheses) moving through the sequence, first enclosing events 1 and 2, then events 2 and 3, then events 3 and 4, and so forth as follows:

$$(1 \ 3) 1 \ 5 \ 1 \ 4 \ 2 \ 4 \ 2 \ 3 \ 5 \ 3 \ 5$$
$$1 (3 \ 1) 5 \ 1 \ 4 \ 2 \ 4 \ 2 \ 3 \ 5 \ 3 \ 5$$
$$1 \ 3 (1 \ 5) 1 \ 4 \ 2 \ 4 \ 2 \ 3 \ 5 \ 3 \ 5$$

The transitions between the five possible codes are tallied in a 5 × 5 table. If we let the first code of the transitional pair determine the row and the second determine the column, then the first window would result in a tally being added to the cell in the first row and third column; the second window, to the cell in the third row and first column, and so forth. The cells in the resulting 5 × 5 table would indicate how often each particular transition occurred—how often, for example, Empathizes followed Complains, or how often Negates followed Negates.

Even a simple 5 × 5 table contains 25 possible transitions, not all of which may be of interest. To avoid being swamped, following every significant transition (some of which may be due to chance) like so many will-o'-the-wisps, I strongly recommend that investigators commit themselves to a manageable number of questions and represent each with a 2 × 2 table. Consider the issue of negative reciprocity—the tendency for negative turns to be reciprocated. The appropriate 2 × 2 table would be formed by collapsing the 5 × 5 table: rows and columns would still represent antecedent and consequent events, but now both antecedent and consequent events would be categorized simply Negates or Non-Negates and the two rows and two columns would be labeled accordingly.

This Procrustean approach has at least two major advantages. As already noted, it ensures that data analysis is guided by research questions. Presumably, those questions are limited in number, which should prevent us from drifting in a sea of analyses, awash in potential type I error. Moreover, techniques for dealing with 2 × 2 tables are generally well understood and a number of well-known statistics, such as chi-square, can be derived from them. These statistics assess the relation or association between the row and column variable and, in common with other statistics of association, are of two kinds: those that describe the magnitude of the association and those that assess its statistical significance.

Statistics that assess significance, like chi-squares or (for the 2 × 2 case) its square root, z, are probably better known, but for the present purposes I want to give equal weight to statistics that describe the magnitude of the relation. Perhaps the best known of these—better known to epidemiologists than sociologists and better known to sociologists than psychologists—is the *odds ratio* (Kleinbaum, Kupper, & Morgenstern, 1982). Imagine, for example, that our transcript included 211 turns of talk and that 10 of the 210 transitions were from Negate to Negate, 20 from Negates to Non-Negates, 30 from Non-Negates to Negates, and the remaining 150 from one Non-Negates code to another. These tallies are arranged in the following 2 × 2 table:

Consequent:

		Negates	Non-Negates
Antecedent:	Negates	10	20
	Non-Negates	30	150

We could label the four cells of the 2 × 2 table *a, b, c,* and *d* as follows (and label rows A, not-A and columns B, not-B for generality):

Consequent:

		B	Not-B
Antecedent:	A	a	b
	Not-A	c	d

Then the odds ratio is defined as:

$$\text{Odds ratio} = \frac{a/b}{c/d} \qquad (1)$$

The numerator represents the odds that a consequent event will be B, as opposed to Not-B, if the antecedent is A. In this case, the odds that the consequent event after Negate will again be Negate is 10 divided by 20, or 1:2, which equals 0.5. Similarly, the denominator represents the odds that a consequent event will be B, as opposed to Not-B, if the antecedent is not-A. For the present example, this value is 30 divided by 150, or 1:5, which equals 0.2. The odds ratio is then the ratio of these two odds: 10:20 divided by 30:150, or 1:2 divided by 1:5, or 0.5 divided by 0.2, which equals 2.5. In other words, the odds that the consequent event will be Negate are 2.5 times greater if the antecedent event is Negate instead of some other event—a value that suggests negative reciprocity.

The odds ratio is a useful descriptive statistic and can have a clear and concrete meaning. Moreover, it can be tested for significance. Probably the easiest way to determine its significance is simply to compute the standard chi-square for the table. If there is no association between row and column variables, then the odds ratio will be 1. Values from 1 to infinity indicate a positive association whereas values from 0 to 1 indicate a negative relation. A significant chi-square indicates that the observed deviation from 1 is unlikely if there really is no relation between the row and column variable. For the present example, the value of chi-square is 4.63, $df = 1$, $p < .05$.

A useful variant of the odds ratio is Yule's Q—for which –1 indicates a negative association; zero, no association, and +1, positive association (see Kennedy, 1983). In terms of the 2 × 2 cell labeling given previously, Yule's Q is defined as:

$$\text{Yule's Q} = \frac{ad - bc}{ad + bc} \qquad (2)$$

If for the example given above we had labeled the rows Non-Negates and Negates, instead of Negates and Non-Negates, the odds ratio would have been 0.2 divided by 0.5, which equals 0.4 (instead of 0.5 divided by 0.2, which equals 2.5); yet both would have indicated the same strength of association. This problem is avoided by the more symmetric Yule's Q, whose value for this example would have been +0.429 or –0.429, depending on whether the top row was labeled Negates or Non-Negates.

SEQUENTIAL TALLIES: INDEPENDENT IN ANY SENSE

As long as we make no tests or claims for the statistical significance of the odds ratio or Yule's Q, the independence of the sequential transitions on which these descriptive statistics is based is not an issue. However, imagine the following scenario: a researcher carefully and reliably codes hundreds of successive turns of talk and begins to look for sequential patterns in the data only to be told by a colleague that such an enterprise is doomed. After all, turns of talk are all strung together. Presumably, preceding turns influence subsequent ones. Thus, successive turns are not independent, and this violates the assumption of independence, or so claims the colleague.

This is only a slight parody of statements I have heard. But statements like it, I think, reflect an unfortunate confusion, a conflating of two senses of the word "independence." First, there is the issue of *sampling independence*. For example, only if successive coin tosses are independent, like tickets independently sampled from an urn, and only if the probability of a head is as specified by our null hypothesis, can we determine the exact sampling distribution for the number of heads in N tosses. And only if we know the exact sampling distribution do we have a basis for accepting or rejecting the null hypothesis.

Second, there is the issue of *empirical independence*. Adjacent events may or may not be associated in fact, but that is an empirical matter—although it is usually the matter of primary concern to researchers. However, we should not assume that sequences lacking empirical independence will also lack sampling independence. The two matters, to coin a phrase, are independent. Thus, it makes no sense to claim that because subsequent events are in fact affected by antecedent ones, sampling independence has been violated for that reason alone.

It is worthwhile to reflect for a moment on what sampling independence means. The traditional model concerns drawing tickets from an urn (with replacement). Each successive draw is said to be independent if it is unaffected by the previous draw. For example, if other tickets were connected by slender threads to the ticket we drew and we were required to select one of those connected tickets on the next draw, sampling independence would be violated. To be independent, the probabilities for selecting various kinds of tickets on the next draw can in no way be conditional on the particular ticket just selected. Sticky tickets (to use the typical historical example) or sticky balls (to use the typical current textbook example) are not allowed.

Sampling independence is thus a procedural matter. As Marascuilo and Serlin note in their text *Statistical Methods for the Social and Behavioral Sciences* (1988), statistical independence means one measurement can in no way influence any other measurement. In the context of sequential analysis this means that coders are sufficiently trained so that when they assign a code to one event, they consider only the event at hand and are not influenced by their coding of the previous event. It may turn out that subsequent events are indeed affected by preceding ones, but, as previously noted, that is a matter of empirical independence—and the very matter sequential analysis is designed to explore. Sampling independence, on the other hand, can be reasonably assumed if subsequent codings are not affected by previous ones.

For example, if the null hypothesis predicted equal occurrences for the five codes listed earlier, then a chi-square comparing observed to expected frequencies could be computed. The sampling distribution—that is, the probability distribution for this chi-square assuming that the null hypothesis is true—is based on the assumption of sampling independence, and applying a probability value to the computed chi-square in this case would likely not be controversial. After all, the argument that each code assignment is unaffected by other assignments—which is analogous to saying that tickets are not connected by slender threads—seems reasonable.

An attempt to discern sequential patterns in these same data, however, could be controversial. For example, suppose we want to know whether complaining is followed by empathizing more often than the base rates for these two codes would predict. As recommended earlier, first we would construct a 2×2 table. The rows are labeled Complains and Non-Complains for the antecedent and the columns are labeled Empathizes and Non-Empathizes for the consequent event. Then successive pairs of codes are categorized and a tally placed in the appropriate cell. By passing our moving "time window" over the data—by tallying transitions—overlapping pairs of the original events (events 1–2, 2–3, 3–4, etc.) are categorized and tallied. And when overlapping pairs are categorized, the assumption of sampling independence seems to be violated. The second code of the current pair becomes the first code of the next pair. Thus, the first code of the following pair is constrained (as though connected by slender threads).

This apparent lack of sampling independence when coding overlapping pairs of events need not cause immediate despair. One solution would be to tally only nonoverlapping pairs (events 1–2, 3–4, 5–6, etc.). Because the assignment for each pair is not constrained by the prior one, sampling independence is not violated. This situation is equivalent to drawing a series of tickets that have, in effect, two-digit codes on them. But there is a practical price: in order to tally the same number of pairs, twice as many events would need to be coded. However, after tallying the first nonoverlapping series (1–2, 3–4, etc.), we could tally a second nonoverlapping series (2–3, 4–5, etc.). The sum of these two independent series is the same as the tallies for the overlapping series. This interesting fact caused Bruce Dorval and me to suspect that the sampling independence argument against the use of overlapping series might be more apparent than real.

Whatever the merits of this suspicion, the consequences of tallying adjacent pairs can be subjected to empirical test. We carried out Monte Carlo simulations using series of random codes, series that modeled the null hypothesis of no association between adjacent codes (Bakeman & Dorval, 1989). If the results of the simulations for both overlapped and nonoverlapped methods of assessing association were indistinguishable from what would be expected by chance, then the practice of using overlapping tallies would be supported. But if not, then the alternative position—that the violation of sampling independence inherent in the overlapped method is a fatal flaw—would be upheld and we would conclude that this practice, which I recommended earlier, should be abandoned.

We generated two sets of 100,000 different sequences and for each we tallied 500 overlapping and 500 nonoverlapping pairs into a 2×2 table. For each table we computed a chi-square and, because its distribution is more familiar, the square root of chi-square or z, which with one degree of freedom should be distributed approximately normally. In effect, we were testing for an association between Complains and Empathizes, knowing that for these data that association (or any other) was nonexistent.

As it turned out, none of the distributions we produced deviated significantly from the normal. In particular, the percentage of scores whose absolute values were greater than 2, which for normally distributed scores would be 4.56%, was for nonoverlapped versus overlapped series 4.59% versus 4.48% for one set of 100,000 trials and 4.68% versus 4.53% for another set we ran. Thus z scores derived from the non-overlapped method were normally distributed, as they should be. But in addition, z scores derived from the overlapped method were also normally distributed. Thus, a practice that appeared objectionable on formal grounds—tallying overlapping pairs—turned out to be empirically inconsequential. Not only is it reasonable to compute measures of association like the odds ratio for antecedent–consequent transitions, but tests of significance for the distribution of those tallies seem warranted as well.

PARALLEL SEQUENTIAL INTERVALS: CROSS INFLUENCES

At least one qualification should be noted. The preceding discussion of independence assumed data that consisted of a single stream of coded events, but data can take other, more complex forms. One relatively common form—one that has received perhaps the lion's share of methodological attention—consists of parallel streams of pairs of coded intervals or events (see, e.g., Allison & Liker, 1982; Iacobucci & Wasserman, 1988). For example, the two streams might consist of a wife's and a husband's behavior and the behavior might be gaze, coded as looking at or not looking at the partner in successive 5-second intervals.

Typically, the research question in such cases concerns whether there is cross dependence between the sequential behaviors of the members of the dyad. However, there may well be sequential dependence within the behavior of the interacting individuals, which could bias the test for dependence between the behaviors of the two individuals. Garner, Hartmann, and Mitchell (1982), using Monte Carlo techniques, simulated the effect on the chi-square statistic of various levels on serial dependence or auto-dependence and concluded that the chi-square test should not be used inferentially when levels of serial dependence exceed an absolute value of 0.5 and that inferential tests should be used only with caution when moderate levels of serial dependence are present. One solution, suggested by Gardner and associates, is to simulate the distribution of the chi-square statistic that would obtain for the level of serial dependence noted in the data, assuming no cross-dependence, and then compare the observed chi-square against this distribution. Note, however, that issues of the effects of various kinds of dependence on a chi-square computation only arise if that chi-square is to be used inferentially—that is, if we wish to assign it a probability value.

BEYOND THE ODDS RATIO: LOG-LINEAR MODELS

Occasionally our interest may focus solely on a single case, like the case of Cathy and Michael Stone. The recommendation I make here is that specific research questions be listed and 2×2 tables constructed for each. In this way we can answer, for example, whether negative reciprocity characterizes this couple. If so, the odds ratio for the 2×2 Negates by Negates table would be significantly larger than 1. Not all questions, of course, neatly fit the Procrustean bed of a 2×2 table. For example, we might want to know if spouses differ in their tendency to empathize with complaints. This would require two 2×2 Complains by Empathizes tables, one for each spouse. The difference between them could then be tested using log-linear modeling techniques, which is the statistical approach most worth mastering if one is concerned with categorical data arranged in contingency tables.

A simple example can give some sense of how a log-linear analysis might proceed. First I will present an analysis of a 2×2 Complains by Empathizes table and then an analysis of a $2 \times 2 \times 2$ spouse by Complains by Empathizes table. The first analysis tells us whether empathizing follows complaining more often than chance would suggest and the second analysis tells us whether spouses vary, with one spouse more likely to empathize with complaints than the other. There is nothing complex about the first analysis. Indeed, it can be accomplished using the sort of chi-square tests usually taught in introductory statistics courses. But the second analysis requires a log-linear approach, and as an aid to understanding that approach, it is useful to recast the first analysis in log-linear terms.

For the first analysis, imagine that 100 transitions were coded, that 36 of them began with a complaint, that 42 ended with an empathizing statement, and that 26 of the transitions consisted of a complaint followed by empathizing. These observed counts suggest that empathizing is more likely to follow a complaint than a noncomplaint. The odds that a transition will end in empathizing, given that it began with a complaint, is 26:10, which equals 2.60, whereas the odds that a transition will end in empathizing, given that it began with something other than a complaint, is 16:48, which equals 0.333. Thus the odds ratio for this contingency table is 2.60 divided by 0.333, which equals 7.80.

It appears that there is a relation between complaining and empathizing, but as always, we want to know if this apparent effect is statistically significant. In order to determine this, we first postulate a series of four hierarchical models. Each successive model is more complex than the preceding one; that is, it consists of more terms and imposes more constraints on the cell frequencies. Each model generates expected counts for the four cells of the contingency table. Normally, two matters concern us: whether the counts generated by a particular model fit the observed ones, which is indicated by a small and insignificant chi-square, and whether the term (or terms) added at a particular step results in a significant change in fit, which is indicated by a large and significant change in chi-square between steps.

The four models are shown in Table 14.1 and their associated chi-square statistics are given in Table 14.2. As a first step, if we know only the number of transitions and were asked to "model" the cell frequencies, the best we could do with this limited information would be to guess that half of the transitions were from Complains and half to Empathizes. Because this model only takes the total number of transitions into account and nothing else, it is often called the null model, symbolized as [0], a zero in brackets. This model is also called the equiprobable model because it necessarily generates equal frequencies in each cell (see Panel A, Table 14.1).

The second model assumes knowledge of the antecedent variable (Complains vs. Non-Complains) and hence constrains the first row to contain 36, and the second row 64, tallies. The columns, however, are not constrained and so the tallies are divided evenly between columns 1 and 2. (See Panel B, Table 14.1.) Because this model takes into account the row totals (Complains vs. Non-Complains) represented in the margins of the 2 × 2 table, I have called it the Com Marginal Model and have represented it symbolically with [C].

The third model assumes knowledge both of the antecedent and consequent variables. It assumes that both row and column marginal totals are known. In other words, in addition to knowing that 36 transitions began with a complaint, we also know that 42 ended with empathizing. This additional information allows us to refine our guesses. Taking both row and

TABLE 14.1. Cell Tallies Generated by Four Hierarchic Log-Linear Models for the *Complains* by *Empathizes* Contingency Table

(A) Equiprobable

	Empathizes		
Complains	Yes	No	
Yes	25	25	50
No	25	25	50
	50	50	100

(B) Com Marginal

	Empathizes		
Complains	Yes	No	
Yes	18	18	36
No	32	32	64
	50	50	100

(C) Com + Emp Marginal

	Empathizes		
Complains	Yes	No	
Yes	15	21	36
No	27	37	64
	42	58	100

(D) Com × Emp

	Empathizes		
Complains	Yes	No	
Yes	26	10	36
No	16	48	64
	42	58	100

Note. Expected counts for the Com + Emp Model are rounded to the nearest whole digit.

column marginal totals into account, we would expect the 36 marginal tallies in row 1, and the 64 in row 2, to be distributed into the cells like the column marginal totals—that is, with a 42:58 ratio. These considerations generate the expected cell frequencies shown in Panel C of Table 14.1. Because this model takes into account marginal totals for both the Complains and Empathizes dimensions of the table, I have called it the Com + Emp Marginal Model and have represented it symbolically with [C] [E].

The expected cell frequencies generated by the third model are those used for the traditional chi-square test of independence, which tests whether the row and column factors are independent, or for the chi-square test for homogeneity of proportions, which tests whether the distribution of the counts in one row is essentially the same as the distribution in another row. Students are usually taught to compute expected cell frequencies from the

TABLE 14.2. Analysis of the *Complains* by *Empathizes* Contingency Table

		Total		Change	
Step	Model	χ^2	df	χ^2	df
1	[0], Equiprobable	33.44	3		
2	[C], Com Marginal	23.11	2	10.33	1
3	[C] [E], Com + Emp Marginal	21.09	1	2.02	1
4	[C] [E] [CE], Com × Emp	0.0	0	21.09	1

observed row and column marginals and from the grand total. Thus, for a 2 × 2 table, the expected value for the upper left cell is the column 1 total multiplied by the row 1 total divided by the grand total, the upper right cell is the column 2 total multiplied by the row 1 total divided by the grand total, and so forth. But this is simply another way of computing the expected cell frequencies generated by this model.

The fourth and final model assumes knowledge not just of the row and column totals for the independent and dependent variables but also knowledge of the frequencies in the four cells formed by crossing these two variables. For a 2 × 2 table, this fourth model generates cell frequencies identical to those observed. (See Panel D, Table 14.1). Such a model is called a saturated model and the scores generated by it necessarily fit the observed perfectly. Because this model, in addition to marginal totals for both the Complains and Empathizes dimensions, takes the cross-classification of the cells by these dimensions into account, I have called it the Com × Emp Model and have represented it symbolically as [C] [E] [CE].

Because each successive model after the null adds a term—first [C], then [C] [E], then [C] [E] [CE]—it makes sense to represent the fourth model as a series of three terms. Still, I should mention that the fourth model is usually represented simply as [CE]. Scores that satisfy the [CE] constraint—scores that reflect the actual Complains by Empathizes cross-classification—necessarily satisfy the [C] and [E] row and column marginal constraints as well. Thus, once the fourth model has been represented with [CE], it is redundant to add [C] and [E] to it. For that reason, and in the interest of simplicity, [CE] is usually presented by itself in the log-linear literature.

How well the scores generated by each of these four models fit the observed data can be assessed with a chi-square statistic. Recall that the formula for the standard Pearson chi-square, summing over cells, is:

$$\chi^2 = \Sigma \; \frac{(\text{observed} - \text{expected})^2}{\text{expected}} \tag{3}$$

Applying this formula to the cell frequencies shown in panels A–D of Table 14.1 results in the values for chi-square shown in Table 14.2. The value of chi-square at each step indicates how well the expected scores for the model defined at that step fit the observed scores, and the change in chi-square from step to step indicates how important the term or effect or constraint added at that step is. Naturally, the chi-square for Step 4 for the [C] [E] [CE] model is zero because the expected values are identical to the observed ones. The only model that fits these data is the saturated model. Adding the [CE] term—the term that indicates that complaints are associated with empathizing—results in a significant change in chi-square.

All four steps are presented here for the sake of completeness and to illustrate how a log-linear analysis might proceed, but in practice an investigator faced with a two-dimensional contingency table, as for this first analysis, would only compute chi-square for the third model. This model, often called the independence or homogeneity of proportions model, assumes that cell frequencies reflect their marginal totals, nothing more. If this model fails—that is, if it generates scores quite discrepant from those actually observed, which is reflected in a chi-square significantly different from zero—then we reject this model and accept the only one remaining— the full or saturated model; and we conclude that the two dimensions of the contingency table are not independent or that the proportions reflected in the rows are not homogeneous. This, in fact, is the substantive result usually desired by researchers. For the present example, we conclude that empathizing follows complaining significantly more often than their base rates would suggest.

An analysis of three-dimensional tables follows the same logic. Imagine that for 50 of the 100 transitions shown in Table 14.1 the husband responded to the wife, whereas for the other 50 the wife responded to the husband. Imagine further that the observed counts were those shown in Table 14.3. One series of five of the more complex models possible is given in Table 14.4. The [S] term constrains cell frequencies to reflect the spouse marginals (husband vs. wife responded to spouse's complaint). Similarly, the [C] and [E] terms constrain cell frequencies to reflect the Complains and Empathizes marginals, whereas the [SC], [SE], and [CE] terms constrain cell frequencies to reflect the indicated cross-classification—spouse by complain for [SC], and so forth. Finally, the [SCE] term represents the saturated

TABLE 14.3. Cell Tallies Generated by Saturated Model for the Spouse by *Complains* **by** *Empathizes* **Contingency Table**

[S] [C] [E] [SC] [SE] [CE] [SCE] or Saturated Model

Wife complains	Husband empathizes			Husband complains	Wife empathizes		
	Yes	No			Yes	No	
Yes	14	6	20	Yes	12	4	16
No	10	20	30	No	6	28	34
	24	26	50		18	32	50

Note. The cell frequencies generated by the saturated model are identical to the observed cell frequencies.

TABLE 14.4. Analysis of the Spouse by *Complains* by *Empathizes* Contingency Table

Step	Model	Total χ^2	df	Change χ^2	df
1	[S][C][E]	23.87	4		
2	[S][C][E][SC]	22.79	3	1.07	1
3	[S][C][E][SC][SE]	22.00	2	0.80	1
4	[S][C][E][SC][SE][CE]	1.32	1	20.67	1
5	[S][C][E][SC][SE][CE][SCE]	0.0	0	1.32	1

model and constrains the cell frequencies to be identical with those observed.

A log-linear analysis of a $2 \times 2 \times 2$ contingency table is analogous to a 2×2 factorial analysis of variance. In the present case, the dependent variable—the variable we want to explain—is represented by the Empathizes dimension, and the independent variables are represented by the spouse and Complains dimensions. If there is a main effect for spouse—that is, if husbands and wives empathize at different rates—then the [SE] term should account for a significant change in chi-square. Similarly, if there is a main effect for complaints—that is, if empathizing is more likely given that the antecedent was a complaint—then the [CE] term should account for a significant change in chi-square. Finally, if the association between complaining and empathizing is different for husbands and wives—that is, if the spouse and Complains variables interact—then the [SCE] term should account for a significant change in chi-square.

The current analysis indicates that both husbands and wives were likely to respond to complaints with empathizing. The Step 4 model (Table 14.4) was the first model to fit the data: this model added the [CE] term, which represents a main effect of complaining on empathizing, and accounted for a significant decrease in chi-square from the previous model. However, the Step 5 model, although it also fit the data, did not account for a significant decrease in chi-square. This model added the [SCE] term; if it had been significant, it would have indicated a significant interaction between spouse and complaining on empathizing. In any event, it was not signficiant, and so we conclude that the association between complaining and empathizing was not different for husbands and wives—one was not more likely than the other to empathize with his or her spouse's complaints.

These comments concerning log-linear analysis have been extremely brief and limited. For example, I have not mentioned how expected counts are generated for other than two-dimensional models (computer programs are necessary), nor I have mentioned that there is more than one way to compute chi-square (Pearson and likelihood ratio). For a somewhat longer introduction to log-linear techniques, especially as they apply to the study of interaction, see Bakeman, Adamson, & Strisik (1989), and for a readable and informative basic text, see Kennedy (1983).

BEYOND THE ODDS RATIO: REGRESSION MODELS

The analyses presented in the previous section focused on a single case. Often, however, in the interests of generalization, we wish to analyze whether specified research factors exert effects on various groups of cases. For example, we might sample two kinds of couples—those who report marital distress and those who do not—and we might hypothesize that on average greater negative reciprocity will characterize the distressed couples. Happily, learning about techniques for answering questions like these is part of the standard statistical training social scientists almost always receive. An understanding of regression models in general, which subsume such techniqes as t-tests or simple analyses of variance, is all that is required. (For an excellent and readable introduction to multiple regression, see Cohen & Cohen, 1983.)

For the present example, the criterion or dependent measure is the odds ratio. If Negates follows Negates exactly at its base rate predicted level, its value will be 1. Higher values indicate greater negative reciprocity, a greater probability that Negates turns will follow other Negates turns. Thus a categorical approach—coding turns of talks, tallying transitions, computing an odds ratio—provides a score that is then analyzed using standard and widely understood techniques like analysis of variance and/or multiple regression.

One technical note should be added: the odds ratio or Yule's Q should be used for this purpose, not chi-square or z. The odds ratio and Yule's Q indicate the strength of the association: their magnitude is not affected by the total number of tallies in the 2×2 table. Chi-square and z, on the other hand, indicate statistical significance and will, for the same degree of association, be larger the greater the number of tallies in the table. This matters if the number of transitions tallied is different for different subjects (couples, families, etc.). In earlier writing I recommended using z scores for this purpose (Bakeman & Gottman, 1986), but that was not sound advice.

Actually, there is another even simpler possibility for analyzing criterion scores. The criterion score could be reduced to a plus/minus dichotomy. If the odds ratio is above 1, the z-score will be above zero. In either case, a plus sign is assigned the criterion and a minus otherwise. Then simple sign tests could be used to assess the significance of various sequences (see, e.g., Bakeman, Adamson, Konner, & Barr, in press). If negative reciprocity characterizes a group of subjects, for example, then significantly more of the signs than the 50% expected by chance should be pluses.

Summation

As a number of articles, books, and book chapters attest, methods for studying interpersonal interaction can be made very complex indeed. In this chapter I have attempted an opposite tack, running the risk of making matters far too simple. I have suggested that studies of interpersonal interaction can be located on, or can progress through, any of four different levels. I have stressed some very simple approaches to measurement and quantitative interpretation, and I have tried to provide some references to more thorough treatments for dealing with the categorical data that typically result from attempts to quantify or code interaction. For better or worse, I have avoided the more technical literature that often engrosses specialists on the frontiers of their fields.

As noted earlier, qualitative approaches are important during the pilot phase of quantitative work, especially during code development. And I should add that once quantitative studies have identified typical patterns, qualitative material can be used to illustrate those patterns, a strategy that is used to excellent effect in *American Couples* (Blumstein & Schwartz, 1983). At their best, quantitative studies stand as a bulwark against bias, but qualitative studies can greatly enrich numeric understanding.

References

Allison, P., & Liker J. (1982). Analyzing sequential categorical data on dyadic interaction: A comment on Gottman. *Psychological Bulletin, 91,* 393–403.

Bakeman, R., Adamson, L. B., Konner, M., & Barr, R. G. (1990). !Kung infancy: The social context of object exploration. *Child Development, 61,* 794–809.

Bakeman, R., Adamson, L. B., & Strisik, P. (1989). Lags and logs: Statistical approaches to interaction. In M. H. Bornstein & J. Bruner (Eds.), *Interaction in human development* (pp. 241–260). Hillsdale, NJ: Erlbaum.

Bakeman, R., & Brownlee, J. R. (1980). The strategic use of parallel play: A sequential analysis. *Child Development, 51,* 873–878.

Bakeman, R., & Dorval, B. (1989). The distinction between sampling independence and empirical independence in sequential analysis. *Behavioral Assessment, 11,* 31–37.

Bakeman, R., & Gottman, J. M. (1986). *Observing interaction: An introduction to sequential analysis.* New York: Cambridge University Press.

Bishop, Y. M. M., Fienberg, S. R., & Holland, P. W. (1975). *Discrete multivariate analysis: Theory and practice.* Cambridge, MA: MIT Press.

Blumstein, P., & Schwartz, P. (1983). *American couples.* New York: Morrow.

Cohen, J., & Cohen, P. (1983). *Applied multiple regression/correlation analysis for the behavioral sciences.* Hillsdale, NJ: Erlbaum.

Coles, R. (1967). *Children of crisis: A study of courage and fear.* Boston: Little Brown.

Cousins, P. C., & Power, T. G. (1986). Quantifying family process: Issues in the analysis of interaction sequences. *Family Process, 25,* 89–105.

Dorval, B., & Eckerman, C. O. (1984). The development of conversation. *Monographs of the Society for Research in Child Development, 49* (No. 2).

Gardner, W., Hartmann, D. P., & Mitchell, C. (1982). The effects of serial dependence on the use of χ^2 for analyzing sequential dyadic interactions. *Behavioral Assessment, 4,* 75–82.

Goffman, E. (1962). *Asylums: Essays on the social situation of mental patients and other inmates.* Chicago: Aldine.

Gottman, J. M. (1980). *Marital interaction: Experimental investigations.* New York: Academic Press.

Hauser, S. T., Powers, S. I., Noam, G. G., Jacobson, A. M., Weiss, B., & Follansbee, D. J. (1984). Family contexts of adolescent ego development. *Child Development, 55,* 195–213.

Hops, H., Willis, T. A., Patterson, G. R., & Weiss, R. L. (1971). Marital Interaction Coding System, Eugene, OR: University of Oregon and Oregon Research Institute (order from ASIS/NAPS, Microfishe Publications, 305 E. 46th St., New York, NY 10017).

Iacobucci, D., & Wasserman, S. (1988). A general framework for the statistical analysis of sequential dyadic interaction data. *Psychological Bulletin, 103,* 379–390.

Kennedy, J. J. (1983). *Analyzing qualitative data: Introductory log-linear analysis for behavioral research.* New York: Praeger.

Kleinbaum, D. G., Kupper, L. L., & Morgenstern, H. (1982). *Epidemiologic research: Principles and quantitative methods.* New York: Van Nostrand Reinhold.

Lewis, O. (1961). *The children of Sanchez: Autobiography of a Mexican family.* New York: Random House.

Marascuilo, L. A., & Serlin, R. C. (1988). *Statistical methods for the social and behavioral sciences.* New York: Freeman.

Parten, M. B. (1932). Social participation among preschool children. *Journal of Abnormal and Social Psychology, 27,* 243–269.

Rosenblum, L. A. (1978). The creation of a behavioral taxonomy. In G. P. Sackett (Ed.), *Observing behavior: Vol. 2. Data collection and analysis methods* (pp. 15–24). Baltimore: University Park Press.

Sheehan, S. (1982). *Is there no place on earth for me?* Boston: Houghton Mifflin.

Upton, G. J. G. (1978). *The analysis of cross-tabulated data.* New York: Wiley.

Chapter 15

Analyzing Interdependence in Dyads

DAVID A. KENNY
DEBORAH A. KASHY

I am he as you are he as you are me and we
are all together
John Lennon and Paul McCartney,
I Am the Walrus

People in dyadic social interaction coordinate their thoughts, feelings, and behaviors. At the extreme, this coordination represents a merging of two people into one. The two people transcend their own identities and become something together that never was before. Researchers studying interpersonal relationships attempt to understand this trenscendence. This chapter represents one more attempt to increase understanding of what is such a fascinating but difficult topic to study.

Interdependence is a topic that has many names. When speaking of attitudes it is called *agreement* or *similarity*, when speaking of affect it is called *reciprocity* or *compensation*, and when speaking of nonverbal behavior it is called *synchrony*. Related terms are *understanding*, *empathy*, and *intersubjectivity*.

The chapter begins by making a distinction between the two major types of interdependence: within- and between-dyad. It then shows how interdependence complicates the analysis of data. The next section discusses how interdependence can be measured and how it can be handled in statistical analyses. Finally, we will describe how overall interdependence can be partitioned into different types of interdependence. Throughout, we have attempted to present a nontechnical but thorough description of the issues involved. Sources that provide the specific details are cited whenever possible. We will, throughout the chapter, make allusions to Cathy and Michael Stone, the couple whose dinnertime scenario serves as the sample research problem of this volume.

Types of Interdependence

Interdependence can be conceptualized in two different ways. Two persons' behaviors can be interdependent sequentially. That is, Michael may say something negative to Cathy, and then during her next conversational turn she may say something negative to him. This will be referred to as *within-dyad interdependence*. Within-dyad interdependence is measured over time for a single dyad.

The second type of interdependence is measured, in general, at one point in time and across dyads. A questionnaire concerning marital satisfaction administered separately to husbands and wives would be one possible measure that would be subject to this type of interdependence. What we will call *between-dyad* interdependence assesses the degree to which marital satisfaction scores for wives are related to marital satisfaction scores for husbands.

A given behavior can be interdependent one way and not the other. Consider two different illustrations of this in the literature. First, there appears to be evidence that self-disclosing behaviors are interdependent between and not within dyads (Dindia, 1988). That is, across relationships, if one member of a dyad discloses to a large extent, the other member also discloses to a large extent. However, within any single relationship, if one person discloses to his or her partner, there is little increase in the probability that the partner will immediately respond in kind. As a second example, it seems that length of an utterance is negatively correlated within a dyad, but positively correlated between dyads (Cappella, 1981). Thus, within a conversation, utterances of a long duration are commonly followed by short utterances. However, the *average* length of a person's turn across the entire conversation is highly correlated with the average length of his or her partner's turn. So between dyads utterances are positively correlated, and within dyads they are negatively correlated.

At first blush it would seem that the most important type of interdependence is within-dyad. It captures very clearly the cycle of negativity that is apparent in the Stones' interaction. It is certainly the case that by observing the sequence of social interaction important insights can be made.

However, as Ned Mueller (personal communication, 1980) has pointed out, there is an implicit behavioristic bias in much within-dyad research. It views social interaction as a tit-for-tat type of experience. Michael is negative to Cathy and then Cathy is negative to Michael. One person's behavior serves as a stimulus for the next person's behavior. While this approach provides an important perspective, human beings are more complex. Michael may be negative toward Cathy, but Cathy may lie in wait for 10 years before she retaliates. We have relational bank accounts that are not often evened up in 5-second intervals but, rather, over a much longer period of time. Reciprocity may be more evident in the long run than in the short run. Therefore, between-dyad interdependence is important to study too.

Between- and within-dyad interdependence examine totally different questions and should not be confused. As stated earlier, one type of interdependence does not imply the other. So one of the first questions that an investigator should ask is what type of interdependence it is that she or he is studying. Although some theories specify the type of interdependence that is to be studied, they typically do not.

In the remainder of this chapter, we will consider only between-dyad interdependence. We do this for two related reasons. First, between-dyad interdependence is the area that the first author has investigated most extensively. Second, within-dyad interdependence is discussed in Chapters 5, 14, and 16. Our omission of within-dyad interdependence is not meant to imply that between-dyad interdependence is any more important than within-dyad interdependence.

Interdependence and the Statistical Assumption of Independence

Interdependence implies that the score of one person on a given variable is correlated with the score of that person's partner on the same variable. If person is treated as the unit in the statistical analysis and the interdependence is ignored, then the independence assumption is likely to be violated. Because virtually every commonly used inferential statistical technique requires the independence of observations, interdependence creates a statistical problem.

Sadly, interdependence is often treated merely as a statistical nuisance and not as something interesting in its own right. Many researchers are not at all interested in interdependence, but they are forced to confront it because of statistical complications.

Imagine a pair of researchers who are interested in sex differences in the expression of negative affect. They hypothesize that males express less negative affect than females. They record 50 interactions of which the

Stones' is but one example. They then test whether there is, in fact, a sex difference by comparing the proportion of negative statements that males utter to the proportion of negative statements that females utter. The researchers forget about interdependence (if one person is negative, it is likely that the other person is also negative), and they use person, not dyad, as the unit of analysis. Using statistical jargon, the researchers use an independent groups t-test when they should have used a matched pairs test. However, their real error is not statistical but, rather, conceptual. Although they are not primarily interested in reciprocity of negative affect, they still should take the time to see if such interdependence does, in fact, exist; they would probably learn something about what is going on between the dyads as well as how to analyze their data.

Because of complications that arise as a result of interdependence and the feeling that it is a problem to be avoided as opposed to an opportunity to learn, all too often relational researchers design their studies or analyze their data in less than optimal ways. The strategies to be described in the following paragraph, while sometimes useful, retard the development of relationship science when they are the only ones used.

The first suboptimal strategy is to use confederates or phantom strangers as "interaction" partners. By having confederates, the natural give-and-take in social interaction is lost because the behavior of one of the interactants is constrained. This strategy is especially popular among social psychologists. A second strategy, commonly used in survey research, is to measure only one of the two people and then pretend that the whole picture has been described. The third less than optimal approach is to study both people but then throw out half the data. This approach is obviously wasteful both economically and scientifically. While each of these strategies eliminates the statistical problem of interdependence, each clearly loses much of the potential richness available in relational research.

To see how these approaches are less than optimal, consider the area of sex research. Would we believe the results of sex research if all the research involved surrogates or mechanical devices? While such research would be useful, it would give us a very incomplete view of human sexual response. Or, what if all sex research examined only masturbation? It seems that relationship research inherently requires the person to interact with a partner. To continue the example, research on heterosexual behavior would not be very credible if we relied only on the male's perspective; this is what we do, in essence, if we throw out one person's data.

How, then, does the reseacher solve the problem of analyzing relationship data when the statistical techniques that are commonly employed require that the data be independent? The solution involves a two-step procedure. The first step is the measurement of the degree of interdependence in the data. (The measurement of interdependence is discussed in the next section of this chapter.) If the scores are independent, then the standard data analytic techniques can be used. However, if interdependence is indicated, then alternative analytic procedures must be used. Generally, these alternative analytic procedures involve treating dyad, not person, as the unit of analysis. That is, the investigator views the "organism" that is generating the data not as the person but as the dyad, and the effective sample size is then the number of dyads, not the number of persons.

Interdependence complicates the analysis of relationship data. Yet it is that interdependence itself that defines relationships. Without interdependence neither relationships nor relationship data would exist.

The Measurement of Interdependence

Generally, interdependence is indexed by a correlation coefficient; one simply correlates one person's score with the other person's score. So if the dyads are husband and wife, the wives' scores are correlated with the husbands'. If there are other variables in the design (for instance, half of the couples are distressed and the other half are not), then these variables should be partialled out of the interdependence correlation.

A problem arises in measuring interdependence when the dyad members are indistinguishable. By indistinguishable we mean that the members cannot be consistently differentiated by any variable. For instance, married couples can be distinguished by their gender and siblings by their age; but same-sex roommates and friends are "indistinguishable." If the dyad members are not distinguishable, it becomes difficult to measure the association between their scores. Designation of one person's score as an X variable and the other person's score as a Y variable is arbitrary and improper. However, interdependence can be measured when dyad members are indistinguishable, by using the intraclass correlation (Kenny, 1990).

The relational researcher should first measure the degree of interdependence in the data. A significance test should then be performed to determine if the degree of interdependence is significant. Contrary to conventional statistical practice, the test of interdependence should be quite liberal; that is, researchers should treat data involving low levels of interdependence as nonindependent data, and instead of using the conventional .05 level of significance, the .20 level should be used. The reason for this is that if, in fact, interdependence does exist, the p values of other statistical tests will be distorted by the violation of the independence assumption. As Kenny and Judd (1986) state, violation of that assumption can sometimes lead to overly conservative tests (results that are statistically significant appear not to be) and at other times to overly liberal tests (results that are not significant appear to be). To prevent distortion of p values in subsequent analyses, a liberal test of interdependence should be used.

Analytic Procedures for Interdependent Data

In this section we will briefly discuss the statistical procedures that must be used if the data are interdependent. We presume that an initial test has already been performed and that the data are interdependent. We will illustrate the different procedures with hypothetical examples.

MEANS

A team of researchers is interested in sex differences in negative statements. In the study are 25 male–female dyads, one of which is the Stones, and members of each couple interact for 20 minutes. The number of negative statements made by each person is coded. To analyze the data properly, a paired t-test should be used. A paired or matched pairs t-test is equivalent to a repeated measures analysis of variance in which dyad is the unit of analysis. That is, each "subject," (e.g. the Stones) has two scores: the husband's and the wife's scores. So gender is the repeated measure, and dyad is the unit of analysis.

Let us say that in this study the researchers also wish to compare two different types of couples: distressed and nondistressed couples. If there is interdependence, the proper analysis is to average the two scores for each dyad and, using a standard independent groups t-test, see if means differ for the distressed couples versus the nondistressed couples. Such an analysis could also be accomplished by performing a repeated measures analysis of variance, including one between-dyad factor, distressed versus nondistressed, and one within-dyad factor, gender.

Or, the researchers might be interested in negative statements made in stranger dyads. They could redesign the study to create three dyad types: male–male, female–female, and male–female. This type of design is called a Kraemer–Jacklin design, and it should be analyzed using procedures discussed by Kenny (1988a). (Kraemer-Jacklin designs are usually not discussed at all in texts on experimental design, yet they are very important in relational research.) With such a design three questions can be answered: (1) Are males more or less negative than females? (2) Do females receive more or less negativity than males? (3) Is there more or less negativity in same- versus opposite-sex dyads? This third question can be viewed as the interaction of the previous two. Thus, the Kraemer-Jacklin design permits examination of several different perspectives on sex differences in negativity.

VARIANCES

A research team may wish to test whether husbands are more variable than wives on marital satisfaction. It may be that wives are generally happy in their marriages whereas some husbands are very happy and others are rather unhappy. The research team obtains a sample of 100 married couples and measures marital satisfaction. The researchers then compute the variance in marital satisfaction for both husbands and wives. If the data were independent, they could use the standard F test to compare the variances. But because the scores are interdependent, they should use the following test described by Kenny (1987). The sum of the husband and wife satisfaction scores is correlated with the difference between these two scores, husband minus wife. (This difference score is the signed, not the absolute, difference.) If the correlation is positive, then more variance is present in satisfaction scores for husbands than for wives. If the correlation is negative, then wives are more variable.

CORRELATIONS

Perhaps a research team wishes to determine if the correlation between the number of common interests and marital satisfaction is greater for husbands than for wives. The researchers develop a measure of common interests by having both husbands and wives choose the 10 interests from a list of 75 that are most applicable to them. The measure of common interests is the proportion of interests that the husband and wife agree upon. The research team administers this instrument to 42 couples, including the Stones, measures each couple's marital satisfaction, and then correlates the common-interest score with marital satisfaction for both husbands and wives. Thus, the researchers have two correlations and must then test whether the two correlations are significantly different from each other. The significance test that should be used is the Hotelling test with the Williams modification (Kenny, 1987).

In the aforementioned study there are three variables: husband satisfaction, wife satisfaction, and number of common interests. If the two correlations involved four different variables (say, for instance, if husband's satisfaction were correlated with husband's age and wife's satisfaction were correlated with wife's age), the Pearson-Filon test with the Stigler modification (Kenny, 1987) would be used to test whether the two correlations differ significantly.

PROPORTIONS

A research group may wish to test whether wives, more than husbands, view their marriages as an important part of their lives. They conduct one-on-one interviews with each member of 50 couples. The interviewer asks each person whether the marriage is the most important part of his or her life and calculates what percentage of the husbands and what percentage of the wives see their marriage as important. If the data were independent, the researchers could perform an ordinary chi-square test of a 2 × 2 table to determine if more wives saw the relationship as important then husbands. But since the data are not independent, the researchers must perform a McNemar test (Kenny, 1987).

The Social Relations Model

An important part of relational science is the attempt to determine the components of interdependence. In work over the past decade or so with various colleagues, the first author developed a model that allows for such a decomposition of interdependent data (Kenny, 1988b; Kenny & La Voie, 1984). Just as the atom comprises component parts, so too the concept of relational interdependence. In the social relations model interdependence can be thought of as having an individual, a dyadic, and an occasion-specific component.

That is, behavior in a two-person social interaction is assumed to be a function of four components. For example, the degree to which Paul likes Peter is assumed to be a function of how much Paul likes people in general (the actor component), how much people in general like Peter (the partner component), how much Paul uniquely likes Peter (the relationship component), and how much Paul particularly likes Peter at that moment in time (the occasion component).

The four components of two-person social interaction create three types of interdependence in the social relations model. At the individual level one can examine whether a person who likes others in general is liked by others in general. This involves correlating a person's actor component with his or her partner component. Dyadic interdependence examines whether a person who tends especially to like his or her partner is especially liked by the partner. This measure of interdependence involves correlating the relationship components. That is, returning to the example of Paul and Peter, this dyadic measure involves correlating Paul's relationship component with Peter and Peter's relationship component with Paul. Finally, we can examine whether reciprocal liking is unique to specific occasions.

In order to partition interdependence into these three types, each person must interact with multiple partners, and if occasion-specific variables are of interest, each person must interact with multiple partners under multiple situations. A typical design is a round-robin design in which each member of a group interacts with every other member of the group. In order to estimate all of these effects, group size must be at least four persons. (Other types of designs that can be used with the social relations model are discussed in Kenny, 1990.)

To appreciate the complexity of the different levels of interdependence, consider the recently completed study by Dindia, Fitzpatrick, and Kenny (1990). The researchers studied four sets of married couples and had them interact with all possible partners in a round-robin format. Thus, each person interacted with his or her spouse, three other members of the opposite sex, and three members of the same sex. One of the key variables in this study was reciprocity of self-disclosure; that is, if the husband discloses to his wife, does the wife disclose to her husband? Reciprocity in the Dindia et al. (1990) study was measured between-couples, not sequentially.

Within the Dindia et al. study (1990), reciprocity can be studied from several perspectives. First, individual reciprocity examines whether, when a particular subject discloses to all of his or her interaction partners, those interaction partners return the disclosure. Actually there are four individual reciprocity correlations: males when interacting with males, males when interacting with females, females when interacting with males, and females interacting with females. Individual reciprocity for females when interacting with males, for example, concerns whether females who disclose to males are in turn disclosed to by their male partners.

Dyadic reciprocity is also examined in the Dindia et al. (1990) study. To examine reciprocity at the dyadic level, individual-level effects (a person's tendency to disclose to all of his or her partners and the tendency for people in general to disclose to a particular person) are removed. Thus, dyadic-level effects measure the extent to which a person is especially disclosing to a particular partner. There are four types of dyadic reciprocity in the Dindia et al. (1990) study:

1. In female–female dyads, if one person is especially disclosing, does the partner reciprocate?
2. In male–male dyads, if one person is especially disclosing, does the partner reciprocate?
3. In female–male dyads in which the partners are not married, if one person is especially disclosing, does the partner reciprocate?
4. In female–male dyads in which the partners are married, if one person is especially disclosing, does the partner reciprocate?

A final type of reciprocity is occasion-specific reciprocity. If one partner discloses to a partner at a particular time (but may not be disclosing at other times), does the partner reciprocate that disclosure? Occasion-specific disclosure can be measured for the four dyad types: male–male, female–female, male–female (unmarried), and male–female (married).

Although the focus in this chapter is the degree of interdependence between two interacting people, "interdependence" can be calculated even when the two people do not interact with each other. For instance, we know that Cathy acts very negatively when she interacts with Michael. It would be interesting to determine if Sally (Michael's first wife) also interacted negatively when she interacted with Michael. By determining the interdependence of behavior between two different people interacting with the same partner, we can determine partner effects (Kenny & Malloy, 1988) within the social relations model. Sally and Cathy never interact; they each interact with Michael, however, and we can measure the degree to which the two interactions are similar, thus determining Michael's partner effect.

Conclusion

Most of the discussion of interdependence concerns positive interdependence. If Michael is negative toward Cathy, Cathy is negative toward Michael. Certainly positive correlations do deserve the extensive attention they receive, but the correlations are sometimes negative. In asymmetric dyads, especially those in which one person has much more power than the other, the interdependence may well be negative. Also, whenever there is a limited resource that must be divided by the dyad, such as time, power, or amount of housework done, it is likely that there will be negative interdependence.

Interdependence is a fundamental focus in a relational science. The assessment of interdependence establishes the fact that a relationship exists between two people. We can then assess what factors account for variation of interdependence, and we can proceed to partition interdependence, as is done by the social relations model. Relational researchers need to view interdependence as one of their primary constructs and not as a statistical nuisance.

Acknowledgment

The research on which this chapter is based was supported in part by National Science Foundation Grant BNS–8807462.

References

Cappella, J. N. (1981). Mutual influence in expressive behavior: Adult–adult and infant–adult dyadic interaction. *Psychological Bulletin, 89,* 101–132.

Dindia, K. (1988). A comparison of several statistical tests of reciprocity of self-disclosure. *Communication Research, 15,* 726–752.

Dindia, K., Fitzpatrick, M. A., & Kenny, D. A. (1990). *Self-disclosure in spouse and stranger interaction: A social relations analysis.* Unpublished paper, University of Wisconsin, Milwaukee.

Kenny, D. A. (1987). *Statistics for the social and behavioral sciences.* Chicago: Scott-Foresman.

Kenny, D. A. (1988a). The analysis of data from two-person relationships. In S. W. Duck, D. F. Hay, S. E. Hobfoll, W. Ickes, & B. Montgomery (Eds.), *Handbook of Personal Relationships* (pp. 57–77). London: Wiley.

Kenny, D. A. (1988b). Interpersonal perception: A social relations analysis. *Journal of Social and Personal Relationships, 5,* 247–261.

Kenny, D. A. (1990). Design and analysis issues in dyadic research. In C. Hendrick & M. S. Clark (Eds.), *Review of Personality and Social Psychology* (Vol. 11, pp. 164–184) Newbury Park, CA: Sage.

Kenny, D. A., & Judd, C. M. (1986). Consequences of violating the independence assumption in analysis of variance. *Psychological Bulletin, 99,* 422–431.

Kenny, D. A., & La Voie, L. (1984). The social relations model. In L. Berkowitz (Ed.), *Advances in experimental social psychology,* (Vol. 18, pp. 142–182). Orlando: Academic Press.

Kenny, D. A., & Malloy, T. E. (1988). Partner effects in social interaction. *Journal of Nonverbal Behavior, 12,* 34–57.

Chapter 16

Longitudinal Analysis

MICHAEL E. HOLMES
MARSHALL SCOTT POOLE

Time brings all things to pass.
Aeschylus

Time is the common substrate of human experience. All social phenomena unfold and change over time, and one of the best ways to understand them is to discover how they are born, develop, and terminate and the processes that drive their unfolding. This is certainly true of interpersonal interaction, which is constituted by temporal relations. Answers mean little unless preceded by questions; a conflict means different things and has different consequences at different points in a relationship. Observation and analysis of a life cycle or long-term process requires a considerable commitment of time and effort, but the required investments are repaid by a familiarity with our subject that fosters deep understanding and novel insights (see Chapter 5).

For the purposes of this chapter, longitudinal analysis is defined as identification and testing of a model or explanation that accounts for the characteristics of long series of time-ordered observations. We will consider two methods, time series analysis and phasic analysis, that enable us to describe and explain the development of processes. To describe the development of interpersonal interaction requires us either to analyze trends in the interaction or to divide it into phases or sequences of acts. The former approach results in a "graph" of the trends developing in the interaction. For example, Huston, Surra, Fitzgerald, and Cate (1981) charted the rise and fall of attraction in blossoming relationships. The latter approach results in a "map" of the interaction consisting of a series of coherent periods or functions following one on another. For example, we might chart the sequence of problem-solving phases that families engage in when working on conflict-laden tasks. In cases where we observe different developmental paths or trends for different cases, typologies may be created (e.g. Huston et al., 1981; Poole and Roth, 1989).

While descriptions of development are interesting, explanation is even more important. Three types of explanation are possible. First, we can explain development in terms of the underlying processes that generate change. For example, the sequence of phases in family problem-solving might be explained as a function of necessary steps in a logical thinking process. As the family thinks together, its communication is devoted to accomplishing these steps in the logical order. Second, when we have a typology of developmental paths or trends, we can identify the contingency variables that determine which type results. For example, if we observe two different sequences of family problem-solving behavior, one type may occur in "normal" families and another type in "troubled" families. Third, we can explain changes in interaction patterns as a function of "causal interventions" into the interaction. This type of explanation accounts for changes in developmental patterns due to "local" events rather than to the overall shape of development. For example, an escalating trend in conflict interaction might be initiated by a confrontational statement by one of the parties.

Both time series analysis and phasic analysis allow us to address these questions. Time series analysis, the traditional approach for long series of longitudinal observations, works with continuous data and fits models that indicate the patterns in series of observations and the dependencies between two or more series. Phasic analysis is designed to test models of longitudinal development based on categorical interaction codes.

Data Requirements

Longitudinal methods require a lengthy series of reliable and valid observations. In the longitudinal study of interpersonal interaction, two types of data can be used: observational data and self-reports. Observational data are codings of interaction that capture a construct of interest. The data stream can also be composed of subjects' self-reports of an attitude, emotion, or belief. For example, Huston et al. (1981) had couples rate their attraction for each other every week for a 40-week period. Because of the sensitivity of longitudinal methods to error, it is important that measures be as reliable and valid as possible. In the case of interaction coding, measures can be taken to maximize interrater reliability and to minimize problems like "coder drift" (Folger, Hewes, & Poole, 1984). Procedures are also available for assessing the validity of codings against both "objective" and "subjective" standards (Poole, Folger, & Hewes, 1986; Folger, Hewes, & Poole, 1984). In the case of self-reports, special scale-design techniques can be employed (Wohlwill, 1973). High reliability is especially important in the case of dynamic models, given the well-known problems with change scores (Cronbach & Furby, 1970).

To this point we have considered only the case where we measure a single variable. However, often research is concerned with the development and interrelation of several measures over time. Hence, our data may consist of more than one coded variable or self-report at each time point. Several of the methods discussed in this chapter permit us to study relationships between two or more variables.

The Traditional Approach: Time Series Analysis

The most common method for the analysis of long data sequences is time series analysis, a family of methods for discovering longitudinal patterns among continuous variables. A number of excellent sources describe time series analysis in general (Chatfield, 1975; Cook & Campbell, 1979; McDowall, McCleary, Meidinger, & Hay, 1979) and its application to the study of interpersonal interaction (Gottman, 1979).

Time series analysis requires at least 50 observations on one or more continuous variables. For example, we might analyze the level of antagonism, coded on a seven-point scale, reflected in a series of 50 or more statements in the Michael/Cathy conflict, this volume's sample interaction. Gottman (1979) discusses several ways of transforming the categorical variables common in interaction research into continuous variables.

Time series analysis enables researchers to address several questions: (1) Is there order in the longitudinal process or is development random? (2) Is there a general trend in development? (3) Are there cycles in the interaction? Cycles, for example, have been posited for arousal and attention in mother–child interaction (Cappella, 1981) and for competitive and conciliatory behavior in negotiations (Gulliver, 1979).

More complex relationships can also be studied, such as the following: (1) What relationships hold between two or more variables over time? For example, the relationship between level of self-disclosure and liking as friendship develops can be studied with time series methods. (2) What is the relationship between two or more interactors? Gottman (1979) defined dominance in marital interaction with a time series measure of which partner influenced the other in changing interaction patterns. (3) What is the impact of a causal intervention on the time series? The time series experiment, described by Campbell and Stanley (1966), first establishes a behavioral baseline by observing actors through a number of periods. At some point a treatment is introduced and the succeeding time series is observed. Comparison of pre- and post-time series can be used to determine experimental effects. For instance, researchers might study the impact of having a first baby on marital interaction by observing couples at 3-day intervals for 6 months prior to delivery and then for 6 months after birth.

Several caveats must be noted along with the potential of time series analysis. Time series analysis involves powerful and complex statistical techniques. These impose stringent requirements on the data, which must be measured at the interval or ratio levels, not on nominal or ordinal scales. Relatively few social scientific measures qualify as interval or ratio scales. Problems are likely to result from the use of ordinal data or from transformations of nominal data into interval or ratio scales that are not theoretically justified. Moreover, the application of complicated statistical algorithms may process our data so much that it becomes hard to tell what the results really mean. Analytical techniques that involve multiple transformations and operations may hide as much as they reveal. For example, some varieties of time series analysis involve an operation called "prefiltering," which removes certain "undesirable" variability from time series. Some writers have noted that prefiltering may cancel out such interesting properties as trend or seasonal variations. After these properties are controlled for, there is sometimes little covariation to use in testing relationships between variables or people.

Another limitation relates to the substantive meaning of time series results. Time series analysis can tell us whether the level of hostility between two actors goes through cycles over time. It can also tell us which actor's level leads the other's. However, time series methods are not well suited to deal with qualitative features of interpersonal interaction. Time series analysis is not suited for direct study of categorical constructs. For example, if we classify Cathy and Michael's conflict behavior into the categories "Forcing," "Avoiding," and "Problem-Solving," it is difficult to see how time series methods could be usefully applied without transforming these categories into a measure that loses much of their meaning. Time series methods are also not suited for the analysis of social episodes—that is, discrete, recognizable periods that make up interactions. For example, a conversation can be divided into an opening, several themes or topics, and a closing. These would be hard to identify with time series methods. Other methods, especially designed for dealing with qualitative features of interaction, are required to complement time series techniques.

An Alternative: Phasic Analysis

BASIC ASSUMPTIONS

Phasic analysis methodologies make the following three assumptions: First, *social behavior can be meaningfully described in units larger than individual acts or interacts*. Human interaction takes place in episodes that are unified periods of coherent activity that serves a particular function. Examples of such episodes are the closing of a telephone call (Albert & Kessler, 1978), a conflict (Walton, 1969), and the accounts we give for mistakes (McLaughlin, Cody, & O'Hair, 1983).

Second, *episodes cohere into larger social events*. The larger events are defined by their content (the kinds of episodes they contain) and form (the sequential structure of the episodes). The episodes that make up the larger event are phases or stages in the developmental path of the event. The phases may proceed in linear development or in cyclical patterns. An event of bounded and continuous interaction, such as a martial conflict, may progress in stages from opening to closing or be structured in cyclical phases of conflict engagement and avoidance. A larger, less clearly delineated event, such as relationship development (Knapp, 1984) or dissolution (Duck, 1982), may progress in stages marked by changing conditions of uncertainty and social penetration.

Third, *the phase structure of a social event, for example, its configuration of form and content, is the result of process dynamics that drive the shifts in behavior from phase to phase*. The dynamics that lead to change in behavior may be efficient (direct), formal (structural), or final (end-driven) causes. Knapp's (1984) staircase model of relationship stages suggests efficient causes, since at any stage the next step depends on events in the present stage. The tradition of normative models of decision making relies at least in part on formal causes or the assumption that a correct pattern of development causes a good decision. Final causes are implied in functional models in which each stage accomplishes a necessary function in the drive to the outcome of the interaction, as in Gulliver's (1979) model of negotiated disputes.

WHAT CAN PHASIC ANALYSIS TELL US?

What types of developmental paths are there? Phasic analysis can be used to test models of development in interpersonal interaction that predict types of sequences that should occur. Phase models are of two general types: unitary sequence models, which posit a uniform progression through a series of phases in a given order, and multiple sequence models, which assume that the occurrence and ordering of phases may vary (Poole, 1981). Through phasic analysis we can test whether unitary or multiple sequence models are more appropriate. For example, if we create a model of marital disputes that defines a number of possible sequences of conflict phases, we can compare that model to phase maps generated from a sample of marital disputes. If the multiple sequence model holds, we can also develop typologies of developmental paths. For example, Poole and Roth (1989) developed a typology of three varieties of group decision paths: simple unitary sequences, complex sequences, and solution-centered sequences.

What are the structural properties of longitudinal interaction? Structural properties of developmental sequences include phase cycles or repetition, breakpoints between phases (e.g., developmental transitions), complexity, and the proportions of different phase types (Poole & Doelger, 1986). For example, conflict phases may cycle between confrontative and analytic or integrative behavior. Repetitions or cycling may signal an unresolved problem driving movement from phase to phase. Breakpoints are junctures where the nature of the interaction changes suddenly, such as the precipitation of a conflict or the onset of lengthy silence. They are important because they may signal critical incidents or changes in a relationship. Complexity refers to the degree to which the developmental pattern departs from a simple unitary sequence. Among other things, high complexity may indicate that the interactors are experiencing difficulty in coordinating their behavior. It may also indicate a struggle for control. Proportions of the phase types in a sequence are important because they indicate which kinds of activity predominate in an interaction, and which kinds of activity occur infrequently.

What factors influence development? Implicit within every model of development is a theory of what causes development. For example, a unitary problem-solving sequence that posits a single progression from problem definition to conflict to solution emergence is built on the premises that behavior is governed by a necessary, logical sequence of requirements that must be met to solve a problem (hence the progression, which is governed by a formal cause) and that the interactors must work out their differences for a unifying plan of action to result (hence the conflict phase in the middle). Phasic analysis allows us to test this; if this theory does, in fact, explain family problem solving, we should find that this sequence holds for most or all family discussions.

In cases in which phasic analysis indicates several different types of developmental paths, we can identify which factors predict which types of paths. We can also test theories about the types of paths that are most effective under various circumstances. The third type of explanation, which focuses on changes in interaction patterns, is more difficult to study with phasic analysis. However, the approach can be used to pinpoint sudden shifts in development, which can then be investigated with other techniques.

CONDUCTING A PHASIC ANALYSIS

The analytical steps in phasic analysis proceed from raw interaction to coded interaction that is transformed into phase markers, mapping of phase sequences based on these markers, and clustering of phase maps into sequence types. The process is a series of incremental steps utilizing precise rules for the data transformations at each step.

Generating Phase Indicators

Step 1. Code the interaction. The starting point for phasic analysis is a series of time-ordered categorical interaction codes that index those aspects of interaction the researcher is interested in. A researcher interested in studying development of conflict must use a conflict-coding system; one interested in relational control development might use the Rogers and Farace (1975) system. The coding unit may vary: thought units, turns, or timed intervals (e.g., 1-minute periods). It is important that the codes be meaningful and systematic, and the coding must be reliable. To ensure that the codes are meaningful, it is a good idea to validate the coding system (Poole, Hewes, & Folger, 1987). Sillars' (1987) Interpersonal Conflict Interaction Coding System (ICICS) is an example of a coding system that could be used in phase analysis. Its basic categories are listed in Table 16.1. (See Sillars, Coletti, Parry, & Rogers, 1982, for a validation study of this coding system.) The ICICS will be used in the example analysis of the Michael/Cathy dispute. The phase analysis procedures can easily be adapted for use with other interaction coding systems.

Step 2. Transform coded data into phase markers. Social episodes or phases are typically defined by constellations of acts. For example, Knapp (1984) notes that "stages in the development of relationships . . . are characterized by certain systematic patterns of communication" (p. 32) and that stages can be identified by the proportion of different kinds of communicative acts. Hence, characteristic acts or interacts can serve as indicators of the larger phase to which they belong. In some cases there is a one-to-one correspondence between interaction codes and phase types. In many cases, however, the interaction coding system may contain a number of codes that indicate a given phase; for example, a researcher using the ICICS may use remarks that are supportive and remarks that accept responsibility as markers of a phase of integration. There are also cases, such as relational control coding, where one may need to use combinations of codes in an interact, rather than an act, as phase markers.

To generate the sequence of phase markers, we need a translation table that shows the codes or combinations of codes that indicate various phases. In the case of the ICICS, one approach is to use the ICICS codes to generate markers of avoidance, integrative, confrontative, and neutral conflict

TABLE 16.1. Sillars' (1987) Interpersonal Conflict Interaction Coding System

Major category	Subcategories
Analytic (AN)	AN DES—Descriptive AN DI—Disclosive AN QU—Qualifying AN SD—Soliciting Disclosure AN SC—Soliciting Criticism AN PRS—Procedural Statement AN PRQ—Procedural Question
Confrontative (CF)	CF RE—Rejection CF CR—Personal Criticism CF HI—Hostile Imperative CF HJ—Hostile Joke CF PQ—Pointed Question CF PR—Presumptive Remark CF DR—Denying Responsibility
Conciliatory (CL)	CL SU—Supportive Remark CL CN—Concession CL AR—Accepting Responsibility CL AM—Attempt at Mediation
Denial and Equivocation (DE)	DE DI—Direct Denial DE ID—Implicit Denial DE EV—Evasive Reply
Topic Management (TM)	TM TS—Topic Shift TM TA—Topic Avoidance
Noncommittal Remarks (NR)	NR NS—Statement NR NQ—Question NR AB—Abstract Remark NR PC—Procedural Remark
Irreverent Remarks (IR)	IR JO—Friendly Joking
Disagreement (DI)	DI DIS—Simple Disagreement

Note. From "Coding Manual for the Interpersonal Conflict Interaction Coding System" (Tech. Rep.) by A. Sillars, 1987. Missoula, MT: University of Montana. Reprinted by permission of the author.

phases, since these phases are congruent with the theoretical underpinnings of the ICICS code system (Sillars et al., 1982). Table 16.2 shows the translation table for the ICICS. Table 16.3 displays the coding of the Michael/Cathy dispute into the ICICS categories and the operation involved in Step 2, the transformation of the sequence of ICICS codes from the disagreement into a set of phase markers. In the case of interact-based

TABLE 16.2. ICICS Phase Marker Translation Table

ICICS major category	Phase marker value
Analytic (AN)	Neutral (NTL)
Confrontative (CF)	Distributive (DST)
Conciliatory (CL)	Integrative (INT)
Denial and Equivocation (DE)	Avoidance (AVD)
Topic Management (TM)	Avoidance
Noncommittal Remarks (NR)	Neutral
Irreverent Remarks (IR)	Integrative
Disagreement (DI)	Distributive

analysis, the translation would be considerably more complex because of the increased number of values to be assigned to phases. Based on a 16-category coding system, Poole (1981) had 256 interacts that indicated 8 basic phases (see the Appendix of that article for its translation tables).

Establishing the Phase Sequence

The methods used to develop phase maps must adhere to the law of requisite variety; that is, the chosen method must produce a map whose

TABLE 16.3. ICICS Coding of Michael–Cathy Conflict, with Translation of ICICS Codes Into Conflict Phase Markers

Turn number	ICICS code	Conflict phasemarker
1	CF CF	DST
2	IR JO	INT
3	CF CR	DST
4	CF RE	DST
5	CF CR	DST
5	CF PR	DST
6	DE EV	AVD
7	AN DI	NTL
8	CL AR	INT
9	NR NS	NTL
9	AN DES	NTL
9	AN DI	NTL
9	AN QU	NTL
10	AN DI	NTL
11	CF PR	DST
12	CL SU	INT
12	DE ID	AVD
12	AN DI	NTL
13	CF PR	DST

Note. See Table 16.1 for translation of codes.

characteristics are suitable for testing the model in question. For example, methods that cannot capture phase recycling become self-fulfilling confirmations of models that posit single occurrences of phases. Traditional fixed-interval phasic analysis and the more recently developed flexible phase mapping (Poole & Roth, 1989) differ in the kinds of phase sequence maps produced and therefore in the kinds of questions each can address. Phasic analysis has usually been accomplished through a priori divisions of the interaction into three to five segments of equal length. The distribution of phase markers across the segments is used as evidence of phase structure. For example, if we expect a problem-solving sequence of the phases orientation, information sharing, solution adoption, and action planning, we would expect phase markers indicative of orientation to be highest in the first third of the discussion, those indicative of information sharing to be highest in the second third, and so on. The fixed-interval approach is common in the study of phases in group behavior (Bales & Strodtbeck, 1951; Fisher, 1970).

The fixed-interval approach works for testing a simple, unitary model of developmental stages or phases. Unfortunately, the a priori division of an interaction into intervals of equal length presents a number of problems (Poole, 1981; Poole & Doelger, 1986). Phase recycling or breakpoints within a time interval will not be captured by the method. If data are aggregated across a number of instances, further detail is lost. Researchers cannot detect between-subject differences in development, and this precludes discovering phase typologies. The flexible phase mapping method (Poole & Roth, 1989) avoids these problems.

Flexible phase mapping procedures do not require a priori assumptions about the number of intervals to identify. They parse interaction into phases of different lengths based on shifts in functions of interaction. Flexible mapping procedures are designed to be responsive to the specific nuances of the particular discussions. If the interaction moves in a smooth and orderly fashion, only a few phases will be identified. However, if the interaction is complex and repetitive, many phases will be identified. In contrast to fixed-interval phasic analysis, flexible maps will vary in complexity, depending on the interaction. The primary advantages of this kind of phase mapping are the ability to produce a detailed phase map that describes phases of different lengths, the ability to describe phase recycling, and the ability to identify "null" or disorganized periods that do not cohere as phases.

The parsing of a sequence of phase markers into discrete phases and labeled disorganized periods is based on the assumption that phases are indicated by consecutive occurrence of a number of phase markers of the same value. The rules for parsing define the minimum conditions indicating a phase and the various conditions identifying a boundary between phases. Poole and Roth (1989) used a rule set similar to the following:

1. A phase is minimally defined as three consecutive codes that share the same phase marker value. The initial boundary of a phase is the first phase marker of the set of three.

2. A phase continues until it is terminated by the occurrence of three consecutive phase markers not of the same phase value. The terminal boundary of a phase is the last phase marker prior to the three nonmatching codes.

3. If three codes from three different phase classifications occur consecutively, the period is designated a nonorganized period, one in which no distinctive or coherent behavior can be detected with this coding system.

4. Combination phases may be defined when theoretically appropriate. In this case, combinations of several different phase markers are used to identify the complex phase. For example, if one partner in a dispute is consistently integrative to the other partner's confrontative moves, the "rule of three" might lead to assignment of a nonorganized phase value, but if a combination phase of Integration/Distribution has been defined, this interesting pattern will be captured in the phase map.

Additional rules may be devised to handle special cases. Table 16.4 shows the sequence of phase markers from the Michael/Cathy interaction mapped into phases using the aforementioned rules.

Methods for Generating Sequence Typologies

Generally, we construct phase typologies by qualitatively grouping a number of phases sequences. For example, we might group phase maps from 20 marital conflicts. This usually involves implicit comparison to a hypothesized ideal sequence or some other criterion for meaningful collections of phases. However, statistical methods are also available for comparing and grouping phase sequences. Pelz's gamma allows us to compare phase sequences on the basis of the order and separation of phases; optimal string matching methods allow cluster analysis of phase sequences.

Prior to qualitative grouping or other analysis, we might "normalize" each phase map to 100 data points for easier comparison. This is accomplished by multiplying the length of each phase (in number of phase markers) by the ratio obtained by dividing 100 by the original sequence length. The Michael/Cathy example is incomplete, so let us assume that the interaction is the beginning of a longer conflict, for which the ICICS coding produced a sequence of 200 conflict codes. The constructed 200-code sequence was mapped into conflict phases and normalized to the conflict map shown in Figure 16.1. A set of such maps would serve as the basis for generating a marital conflict typology, either through qualitative grouping, gamma analysis, or string matching. Note that the map displays a repetitive

TABLE 16.4. Parsing of Conflict Phase Markers into Phases Using Flexible Mapping Rules

Turn number	Conflict phase marker	Phase
1	DST	
2	INT	
3	DST	Distributive
4	DST	
5	DST	
5	DST	
6	AVD	
7	NTL	
8	INT	
9	NTL	
9	NTL	Neutral
9	NTL	
9	NTL	
10	NTL	
11	DST	
12	INT	
12	AVD	Null
12	NTL	
13	DST	

Note. AVD = Avoidance
DST = Distributive
INT = Integrative
NTL = Neutral

cycle of neutral and integrative interaction; there are a number of short distributive phases early in the sequence, perhaps as key issues surface, and a mixed Integration/Distribution near the two-thirds mark of the sequence.

The Goodman–Kruskal gamma statistic (Pelz, 1985) can be used to establish whether phases occur in an hypothesized order and, if not, what order they occur in. It lets us know if the phases are distinct, that is, whether the structure of the interaction is simple or complex. Gamma is a nonparametric statistic that provides a measure of the "proportion of A events that precede or follow B events" (Poole & Roth, 1989). Gamma analysis of a sequence of phase markers yields a separation score and precedence score for each type of phase. The precedence score (ranging from −1.0 to 1.0) describes the overall ordering of phase types, and the separation score (ranging from 0 to 1) describes the relative distinctness of a phase type. Table 16.5 shows the results of a gamma analysis of the normalized map of the Michael/Cathy conflict.

The higher the precedence score, the earlier in the interaction the phase occurs. So the sequence of phases indicated by the precedence scores is Avoidance, Distributive, Neutral, and Integration. However, the separa-

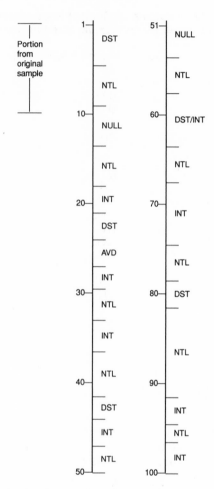

FIGURE 16.1. Normalized map of conflict interaction in Michael–Cathy dispute. This map is based on ICICS coding. See the note to Table 16.4 for translations of the phase labels.

tion scores are low, which suggests that even though the interaction generally occurs in this order, there is considerable overlap among phase types. This is not surprising, given the cycling of integrative and neutral phases mentioned earlier and the spread of short distributive phases fairly evenly throughout the sequence. The higher separation and precedence scores for Avoidance reflect the single early phase of avoidance found in the flexible phase mapping. The two properties of phase sequencing and degree of overlap can then be used in the qualitative grouping of sequences.

Optimal string matching is a way of measuring the "distance" between

TABLE 16.5. Gamma Analysis of the Normalized Conflict Phase Marker Sequence from the Michael/Cathy Example

Phase separation scores			
DST	INT	AVD	NTL
0.27	0.37	0.54	0.30
Phase precedence scores			
DST	INT	AVD	NTL
0.05	−0.37	0.54	−0.21
Phase order by precedence score			
AVD	DST	NTL	INT

Note. This map is based on ICICS coding. See the note to Table 16.4 for translations of the phase labels.

two sequences in terms of the number of insertions, deletions, and substitutions required to transform one sequence into another (Sankoff & Kruskal, 1983). Once distances between all pairs of sequences in a data set have been calculated, multidimensional scaling or clustering methods can be used to identify similar developmental sequences and establish differences between clusters.

UTILIZING DEVELOPMENTAL MAPS TO TEST HYPOTHESES

A set of developmental maps can be used to test hypotheses addressing the questions about developmental structure mentioned earlier. What are the types of developmental paths? Are they unitary or multiple? What are the structural properties of the maps? Given demographic information about the subjects, or contextual information about the interaction, what factors appear to influence development and such properties of developmental sequences as complexity, number of breakpoints, or recycling? For example, we might be interested in the association between number of years of marriage and type of developmental path in marital disputes, or the association between third-party intervention and path complexity.

CAVEATS

As noted earlier, phasic analysis is best suited for dealing with longitudinal data when the theoretical assumptions posit developmental paths of stages or phases. If a theoretical perspective posits continuous change, time series analysis is more appropriate. The kinds of analyses also underemphasize the importance of single acts or interacts as opposed to coherent phases. For example, isolated topic management moves in the Michael/Cathy dispute may exert an important influence on the conflict, but they are not captured in the maps. A similar weakness is that each type of act counts equally in the identification of phases. It is possible that one act type is more important than another in establishing a stage or phase. For example, a single strongly confrontative act may carry more weight in defining a phase of interaction than several analytic acts. There is no differentiation of this kind in the methods outlined earlier.

Phases analysis, like all content analysis, requires considerable data transformation. Each step introduces new opportunities for error. Considerable effort is required in developing or applying an appropriate coding system and in creating a set of rules for transforming interaction codes into phase markers. The cumulative effect of unreliability of coding at the individual unit level and unreliability of reclassification into phases is unclear.

Discussion

Both time series and phasic analyses offer unique opportunities to researchers. Confronted with a mass of longitudinal data, researchers are often tempted to collapse the data into some overall summary measure or reduce the analytical burden by dividing the data set into a relatively small number of segments and summarizing within each segment. Time series and phasic analyses allow researchers to take full advantage of longitudinal data. Little information need be lost through preliminary aggregation. The two methods allow identification and testing of a number of different relationships and models, ranging from the simple determination of which dyadic partner leads the relationship to complicated developmental theories. Longitudinal methods also permit stronger inferences by eliminating a number of competing explanations and possible confounds. In many cases they allow researchers to determine whether the nature of interaction changes as it progresses. Both time series and phasic analysis enable researchers to develop theories commensurate with the complexity of interpersonal interaction.

Perhaps because time is so common to all experience, we sometimes forget to figure it into our theories. Warner (Chapter 5) notes a number of reasons why this may be a regrettable oversight. If, however, we take the time to figure time in, time series and phasic analyses provide methods suitable for working with the longitudinal data necessary for exploring processes through time.

Acknowledgment

The preparation of this chapter was supported by National Science Foundation Grant N. SES-8715565 to Marshall Scott Poole and Gerardine DeSanctis. The views expressed herein are solely those of the authors and not of the National Science Foundation.

References

Albert, S., & Kessler, S. (1978). Ending social encounters. *Journal of Experimental and Social Psychology, 14*, 541–553.

Bales, R. F., & Strodtbeck, F. (1951). Phases in group problem solving. *Journal of Abnormal and Social Psychology, 46*, 485–495.

Campbell, D. T., & Stanley, J. (1966). *Experimental and quasi-experimental designs for research.* Skokie, IL: Rand-McNally.

Cappella, J. (1981). Mutual influence in expressive behavior: Adult–adult and infant–adult dyadic interaction. *Psychological Bulletin, 89*, 101–132.

Chatfield, C. (1975). *The analysis of time series.* London: Chapman & Hall.

Cook, T. D., & Campbell, D. T. (1979). *Quasi-experimental design: Design and analysis in field settings.* Boston: Houghton-Mifflin.

Cronbach, L. J., & Furby, L. (1970). How should we measure "change"—or should we? *Psychological Bulletin, 74*, 68–80.

Duck, S. W. (1982). A topography of relationship disengagement and dissolution. In S. W. Duck (Ed.), *Personal relationships 4: Dissolving personal relationships* (pp. 1–30). Academic Press: New York.

Fisher, B. A. (1970). Decision emergence: Phases in group decision making. *Speech Monographs, 37*, 53–66.

Folger, J. P., Hewes, D. E., & Poole, M. S. (1984). Coding social interaction. In B. Dervin & M. Voight (Eds.), *Progress in communication sciences* (Vol. 5, pp. 115–161). Norwood, NJ: Ablex.

Gottman, J. M. (1979). Time-series analysis of continuous data in dyads. In M. E. Lamb, S. J. Suomi, & G. A. Stephenson (Eds.), *Social interaction analysis* (pp. 207–229). Madison: University of Wisconsin Press.

Gulliver, P. H. (1979). *Disputes and negotiations: A cross-cultural approach.* Orlando, FL: Academic Press.

Huston, T. L., Surra, C. A., Fitzgerald, N. M., & Cate, R. M. (1981). From courtship to marriage: Mate selection as an interpersonal process. In S. W. Duck & R. Gilmour (Eds.), *Personal relationships 2: Developing personal relationships* (pp. 53–90). New York: Academic Press.

Knapp, M. (1984). *Interpersonal communication and human relationships.* Newton, MA: Allyn & Bacon.

McDowall, D., McCleary, R., Meidinger, E. E., & Hay, R. A., Jr. (1979). *Interrupted time series.* Beverly Hills: Sage.

McLaughlin, M., Cody, M. J., & O'Hair, D. (1983). The management of failure events: Some contextual determinants of accounting behavior. *Human Communication Research, 9,* 208–224.

Pelz, D. C. (1985). Innovation complexity and the sequence of innovating phases. *Knowledge: Creation, Diffusion, Utilization, 6,* 261–291.

Poole, M. S. (1981). Decision development in small groups: I. A comparison of two models. *Communication Monographs, 48,* 1–24.

Poole, M. S., & Doelger, J. A. (1986). Developmental processes in group decision making. In R. Hirokawa & M. S. Poole (Eds.), *Communication and group decision making* (pp. 35–62). Beverly Hills: Sage.

Poole, M. S., Folger, J. P., & Hewes, D. E. (1986). Methods of interaction analysis. In G. Miller & M. Roloff (Eds.), *Interpersonal Processes* (pp. 220–250). Beverly Hills: Sage.

Poole, M. S., Hewes, D. E., & Folger, J. P. (1987). Analyzing interpersonal interaction. In M. E. Roloff & G. R. Miller (Eds.), *Interpersonal processes: New directions in communication research* (pp. 220–256). Beverly Hills: Sage.

Poole, M. S., & Roth, J. (1989). Decision development in small groups: IV. A typology of decision paths. *Human Communication Research, 15,* 323–356.

Rogers, E., & Farace, R. (1975). Analysis of relational communication in dyads: New measurement procedures. *Human Communication Research, 1,* 222–239.

Sankoff, D., & Kruskal, J. B. (1983). *Time warps, string edits, and macromolecules: The theory and practice of sequence comparison.* Reading, MA: Addison-Wesley.

Sillars, A. (1987). Coding manual for the interpersonal conflict interaction coding system. (Tech. Rep.) Missoula, MT: University of Montana, Interpersonal Communication Department.

Sillars, A., Coletti, S. F., Parry, D., & Rogers, M. A. (1982). Coding verbal conflict tactics: Nonverbal and perceptual correlates of the "avoidance-distributive-integrative" distinction. *Human Communication Research, 9,* 83–95.

Walton, R. E. (1969). *Interpersonal peacemaking, confrontation, and third party consultation.* Reading, MA: Addison-Wesley.

Wohlwill, J. (1973). *The study of behavior development.* New York: Academic Press.

Chapter 17

Reviewing Previous Research by Meta-Analysis

BARRY H. SCHNEIDER

This chapter considers the usefulness of previous empirical studies—and techniques for reviewing and summarizing them—in understanding the dynamics of interpersonal interaction. Unassisted by a technology suitable for reviewing scientific literature, researchers may find the array of opinions and findings about any given issue to be confusing and contradictory. Clinicians, who also require an unclouded picture of relevant data bases to use as guides in prescribing treatment for any particular couple, are equally in need of credible research reviews. This chapter describes both qualitative and quantitative options that meet these needs.

The marital conflicts experienced by Michael and Cathy Stone (see Preface) will be used in some of the examples that follow. Techniques for reviewing and summarizing data will be discussed from the point of view of the following research questions: (1) Might a married couple's problems relate to the stage of their relationship? (2) Does the balance of decision making in a marital relationship affect the emergence of conflict? (3) How successful might marital therapy or relationship enhancement be in general or for this specific couple?

Is It a Phase?

A researcher trying to understand the interpersonal squabbles that arise within a marital relationship might wonder if difficulties are more frequent at a particular stage of a typical couple's relationship. This would entail reviewing and summarizing the many studies that have investigated the onset of conflict as a function of time within a relationship or as a function of new tasks (e.g., childrearing, retirement).

Let us put ourselves in the position of a reviewer examining relevant studies of this type in the *Journal of Marriage and the Family,* in which the largest number of studies on the topic have been published. Suppose we adopt as a working hypothesis the proposition that marital conflict over the life cycle of a typical marriage follows a U-shaped curve, as has often been suggested. This means that there is an initial "honeymoon" period in which there are few problems that romance cannot overshadow, followed by a peak of conflict in the middle years as the couple faces the problems of managing a family, finances, and so forth. These problems abate in the later years as new burdens become fewer and, hopefully, solutions are achieved.

Perusing the back issues in sequence, one would probably first come across a study by Bossard and Ball (1955), who asked the brothers and sisters of 440 married partners in Pennsylvania to rate the marital satisfaction of their siblings. These findings would at first glance seem supportive of the U-shaped curve hypothesis. However, some might argue that this study might be excluded because of the impact of time on the outcome. At the time the data were collected, the subjects in their 40s and 50s would have had to face the hardships of the Depression era far more than the younger and older subjects. Clearly, longitudinal data would be more trustworthy. As well, some might argue that collecting information from siblings is at best idiosyncratic and at worst unlikely to represent the true dynamics of a marriage as perceived by those directly involved.

Returning to the back issues of the journal, one would next come across a study conducted by Deutscher (1964) with 49 spouses from 31 couples. It indicated that the midcareer, postparental stage was viewed as highly problematic. This study could be tallied on the side of the U-shaped curve if—and only if—one would accept a study with so small a sample.

Another questionnaire study was conducted by Burr (1970) in the homes of 147 subjects. As in the two previous studies, a U-shaped curve emerged in the results. However, no statistical analyses were conducted on the data. Therefore, one cannot dismiss the possibility that the results occurred on the basis of chance alone.

The U-shape curve derives further support from the findings of Rollins and Feldman (1970), who studied a sample of 852 middle-class couples in Syracuse, N.Y. These findings were replicated in 1974 in a cross-sectional study of 800 couples. However, Rollins and Cannon (1974) point out that the findings, though significant and consistent with the U-shaped curve hypothesis, were statistically quite weak. Some might also argue that since the 1974 study was conducted exclusively with Mormons, results cannot be generalized beyond that culture.

Yet another study conducted by Anderson, Russell and Schumm

(1983) with 196 Midwestern couples, portrays a curvilinear U-shaped trend in marital satisfaction over the life cycle. However, these authors, like Rollins and Cannon, noted that the findings are statistically weak, accounting for 8% of the variance in marital satisfaction.

What can be summarized from this review of studies of marital satisfaction over the life cycle of a relationship? First of all, most studies are consistent with the picture of a U-shaped curve. However, serious methodological limitations and problems of interpretation could be found with many, if not all, of the studies. Therefore, a reviewer with very stringent methodological standards might dismiss most of these studies as scientifically unsound or difficult to interpret. But is it reasonable to overlook the consistency of the findings and behave as if there were no evidence at all in this area?

A more profitable approach would be to scrutinize the studies carefully, comparing differences in findings between high-quality studies and poorer ones, between more recent ones and those that are dated, and between studies that differ in their sources of information. In this particular body of literature, few such differences are immediately apparent. However, just tallying the studies *Yes* and *No* according to whether the findings resemble a U-shaped curve or not (the "vote count" method) would still not convey an accurate picture of these studies. The most accurate summary statement one might make about the aforementioned studies is that, despite their shortcomings, they provide consistent *but statistically weak* support for the U-shaped curve hypothesis. What does this mean for inferences regarding the course of marital satisfaction? This means that stage of the marital life cycle should be considered as a *partial* explanation of marital conflict among individuals in the middle stages of a relationship but that many other important explanations should be considered at the same time. A small effect evident in a series of studies should not be ignored, since it may have considerable impact on certain individuals (Rosenthal & Reubin, 1982) or be apparent only in combination with other effects on other individuals. In certain cases, other stressors might be more likely to embroil a couple in the middle years of a relationship in heated conflict whereas the effects of the same stressors might be mitigated in the earlier or later phases.

Thus, some challenges in reviewing empirical studies have already become apparent: (1) one must take into account differences in the quality of the original studies; (2) one must consider not only the direction of the findings but also their strength; and (3) clear inclusion criteria must be specified so that the reader can properly identify the scope of a review.

Decision-making Roles

The balance of decision-making power within a couple is another possible explanation for interpersonal conflict for which a considerable amount of

TABLE 17.1. Summary of Self-Report Studies

Study	Sample	Power measure[a]	Satisfaction measure	Findings[b]
Bean, Curtis, & Marcu, 1977	325 Mexican-American couples: Texas	DM scale: 5 areas	4-item MS scale	Highest MS in egalitarian marriages; lowest in wife-dominant marriages[c]
Blood & Wolfe, 1960	731 urban wives & 178 rural wives; Michigan	DM scale: 8 areas	5-item MS scale	Highest MS in egalitarian marriages; lowest in wife-dominant marriages
Buric & Zecevic, 1967	117 urban wives; Yugoslavia	DM scale: 7 areas	7-item MS scale	Highest MS when wife slightly dominant or husband very dominant; lowest when wife very dominant
Centers, Raven, & Rodrigues, 1971	776 husbands and wives including 86 couples; Los Angeles	DM scale: 8 areas from Blood & Wolfe plus 6 other areas	1-item MS scale	Highest MS in egalitarian marriages; lowest in wife-dominant marriages
Corrales, 1975	394 couples; Minnesota	DM scale: 8 areas from Blood & Wolfe	Marital Adjustment Balance Scale	Highest MS in husband-dominant marriages; lowest in wife-dominant marriages
Gray-Little, 1982	75 urban black couples; North Carolina	1. DM scale: 13 areas 2. Frequency of concessions: 2 items	10-item MS scale plus measures of positive regard and reciprocity	1. Highest MS in husband-dominant marriages; lowest in wife-dominant marriages[c] 2. Lowest overall marital quality in wife-dominant marriages[c]
Locke & Karlsson, 1952	1,352 married and divorced individuals—both male and female; Indiana and Sweden	DM scale: 6 areas	Marital adjustment scale: 29 items	Highest MA in egalitarian marriages[c]
Lu, 1952	603 couples; Chicago	Dominance-submissiveness scale: 16 items	Burgess-Cottrell scale of marital adjustment	Highest MA in egalitarian marriages

306

Study	Sample	Power measure	Satisfaction measure	Findings
Michel, 1967	550 urban wives; France	DM scale: 10 areas	5-item MS scale	Highest MS in egalitarian marriages; lowest in husband-dominant marriage
Osmond & Martin, 1978	561 married, separated and divorced individuals—both males and females; 4 states	1. DM scale: 1 area 2. Frequency of compromise: 1 item	Marital status (married vs. separated/divorced)	1. Intact marriages more egalitarian than broken marriages[c] 2. Intact marriages marked by more compromise[c]
Pond, Ryle, & Hamilton, 1963	86 couples; London, England	1. DM scale: 3 areas 2. Interviewer ratings of domination/submission	Interviewer ratings of marital adjustment	1. Highest MA in egalitarian marriages[c] 2. Highest MA when neither partner dominates; lowest when husband dominates[c]
Sanitos-Rothschild, 1967	133 wives; Athens, Greece	DM scale: 8 areas	4-item MS scale	Highest MS when wife slightly dominant or husband very dominant; lowest when wife very dominant
Scanzoni, 1968	270 urban wives; northern U.S.	1. DM scale: 1 item 2. Amount of conflict and compromise: 22 areas	Marital status (married vs. divorced)	1. Intact marriages more egalitarian than broken marriages 2. Intact marriages marked by less conflict and more compromise
Szinovaca, 1978	1370 wives; Austria	DM scale: 8 areas	1-item MS scale	Highest MS in egalitarian marriages; lowest in wife-dominant and sex-stereotyped marriages[c]
Terman, 1938	1250 suburban couples; California	Amount of conflict and compromise	9-item MS scale	High MS associated with low conflict and high degree of compromise in marriage

Note. From *"Power and Satisfaction in Marriage: A Review and Critique"* by B. Gray-Little and N. Burks, 1983. Psychological Bulletin, *93*, pp. 513–538. Copyright 1983 by the American Psychological Association. Reprinted by permission.

[a]DM = Decision Making.

[b]MS = Marital Satisfaction; MA = Marital Adjustment.

[c]$p \leq .05$

existing data has already been generated. It seems most logical to expect that conflict would be reduced when decision-making power is relatively equal; this way no one need feel disenfranchised. However, the opposite is not inconceivable. Perhaps the many extended decision-making exercises inherent in egalitarian relationships are a source of constant friction, whereas things are more peaceful in relationships where one partner plays a dominant role and the other is accepting of this.

In examining these data, researchers and clinicians can make use of a high-quality narrative review of the literature. *Psychological Bulletin* is the best-known and most prestigious journal that specializes in literature reviews. In 1983 it published a review by Gray-Little and Burks (1983) of 20 empirical explorations of the relation between marital satisfaction and decision-making power; these studies are summarized graphically in Tables 17.1 and 17.2

Inspection of the tables will reveal that sheer quantity indicates that the egalitarian marriage is the more rewarding one. However, despite the pattern indicated in the tables, the opposite position cannot be totally refuted. First of all, one might argue that the self-report studies in Table 17.1 should not be considered at all, because couples may be biased in rating their own decision making. One's objectivity in rating any of one's own personal characteristics has often been criticized (e.g., O'Leary & Turkewitz, 1978; see also Harvey, Hendrick, & Tucker, 1988, for a discussion of the advantages of the self-report). Furthermore, since decision making within a relationship tends to be a private experience, most couples may have few terms of reference for rating their own decision making.

This might indicate that the reviewer should place greater emphasis on observational studies. Observing the process of decision making does permit ready comparison of the decision-making behaviors of different couples. However, one might question whether meaningful decision-making experiences are often accessible to the outside observer. Gray-Little and Burks (1983) point out that the observational studies tend to use simplified, contrived tasks to measure power in marriage and are based on rather simplistic conceptualizations of power.

One might also argue that some of the findings in Table 17.2 should be eliminated because they failed to achieve statistical significance. As well, the significant finding from the Gottman study (1979), which indicated that marital satisfaction was highest in egalitarian couples, is based on a sample of only seven couples and is therefore of limited value.

If one were to summarize this literature based only on observational studies conducted with adequate samples, there would be only two studies with significant findings left. In Gray-Little's (1982) study, wife-dominant and egalitarian marriages were characterized by *lower* satisfaction scores. Only in Sprenkle and Olson's (1978) study did egalitarian couples appear most satisfied with their marriages.

TABLE 17.2. Summary of Observational Studies

Study	Sample	Power measure	Satisfaction measure[a]	Findings
Corrales, 1975	394 couples; Minnesota	Ranking importance of 5 marital issues	Marital Adjustment Balance Scale	Highest MS in egalitarian couples; lowest in wife-dominant couples
Gray-Little, 1982	30 urban black couples; North Carolina	1. SIMFAM: Assertiveness 2. SIMFAM: Effective Control 3. Talking Time 4. Interruptions	10-item MS scale plus measures of positive regard and reciprocity	1. Lowest positive regard in wife-dominant couples[b] 2. Lowest positive regard and reciprocity in wife-dominant couples[b] 3. Lowest MS, reciprocity, and positive regard in egalitarian couples[b] 4. Lowest MS in egalitarian couples[b]
Gottman, 1979	13 clinic and 7 nonclinic rural couples; Indiana	1. Improvisation: Expressive 2. Improvisation: Mood 3. Fun Deck: Expressive 4. Fun Deck: Mood	Locke Marital Relationship Inventory	1. High-satisfaction nonclinic couples more egalitarian[b] 2, 3, 4. No difference between clinic and nonclinic couples
Kolb & Straus, 1974	63 families; Minneapolis	SIMFAM: Effective Control	Child's rating of parents' satisfaction on a 1-item scale	Marriages of high-power husband rated happier than those low-power husbands
Levinger, 1964	15 clinic and 15 nonclinic couples; Cleveland	Ranking two sets of goals, vocabulary and digit-symbol tests	15-item MS scale	No difference in the dominance patterns of satisfied and dissatisfied couple on any measure
Sprenkle & Olson, 1978	25 clinic and 25 nonclinic couples; Minnesota	SIMFAM: Relative Control	Locke-Wallace Marital Adjustment Test	Wife-dominant couples least satisfied; egalitarian couples most satisfied[b]

Note. From "*Power and Satisfaction in Marriage: A Review and Critique*" by B. Gray-Little and N. Burks, 1983. *Psychological Bulletin, 93,* pp. 513–538. Copyright 1983 by the American Psychological Association. Reprinted by permission.

[a]MS = Marital Satisfaction.

[b]$p \le .05$.

SHORTCOMINGS OF THESE "VOTE COUNT" REVIEWS

Variations in Study Quality

In this body of literature, the summary statement that would emerge from a review of only the high-quality studies would not be identical to the conclusion based on all studies in the table. The reviewer's dilemma is once more best solved by looking for associations between the "quality" of studies and their outcomes. It may be possible to accomplish this informally by visually inspecting a summary table or remembering important design dimensions while putting together a review of the literature. However, there are limits to the reviewer's human capabilities of mentally storing and manipulating a number of study variables and their associations with study outcomes (Light & Pillemer, 1984, p. 4). If used properly, quantitative review strategies can accomplish this more efficiently, as will be discussed later.

Strength or Importance of the Findings

There are other limitations to the vote count method. It is apparent that we cannot ascertain the strength or magnitude of the findings beyond the categorical distinctions of "significant" versus "nonsignificant". Knowing the strength of an effect is important in such areas as interpersonal communication where a given behavior probably has multiple causes and multiple correlates. We need to establish not only *whether* one variable is a correlate of another but how important a predictor variable it is when compared with other possible contributing factors. We were sensitized to this issue when considering the articles on marital satisfaction across the stages of a relationship only because Rollins and Cannon (1974) happened to report the statistical strength of their findings, which is relatively unusual in this field.

In a vote count review, where each study gets one "vote," a study with a sample of 30 subjects gets the same weight as a study with 500, and studies with results significant at the .0001 and .05 levels have equal vote. Results that just miss statistical significance bolster the opposition with impact equal to those displaying p values of .90. Hedges and Olkin (1980) have demonstrated that if the "true" impact of a variable (in other words, its impact on an entire population, independent of measurement and sampling error) is equal to one-half a standard deviation, a vote count review of 20 studies with sample sizes of 30 will fail to detect this substantial effect 75% of the time and thus lead researchers and consumers of research to prematurely discard some potentially useful ideas.

Small Sample Research

Besides the fact that many important variables may have only small to moderate "true" effects, researchers in the field of interpersonal relations may often be compelled to work with small samples. This is true for several reasons. First of all, more sophisticated theoretical formulations lead to the use of comprehensive and time-intensive measures (see, e.g. Boland & Follingstad, 1987; Gray-Little & Burks, 1983; Rogers, Millar, & Bavelas, 1985) that cannot be administered to large populations as easily as questionnaire tools. Second, the focus of an individual study may require access to specific populations, such as both husbands and wives in marital therapy or both families at home and their children's peer group at school (who might be asked to rate the social behavior of the children whose parents were interviewed).

Small "True" Effects

The existence of small but potentially important "true" effects may be of particular concern in research on interpersonal relations. Many "true" effects in this area may be "small" to "moderate" in the statistical sense. This is because an individual's behavior in interpersonal situations probably reflects a multitude of influences—heredity, culture, early upbringing, the past history of the particular relationship. Therefore, the effects of a single variable would tend to be smaller in this area of inquiry than in biological research, for example, which often uses identical statistical procedures. Nevertheless, a small effect in interpersonal behavior can be an important one. Rosenthal and Rubin (1982) have demonstrated that, given a therapeutic intervention that accounts for "only" 9% of the variance in an outcome measure, one could expect a success rate of 65% for couples in therapy, compared with 35% for a hypothetical group of untreated controls.

Reviewing Poor Studies

By now, the reader will appreciate the major frustrations of both quantitative and qualitative reviewers of research in the human sciences. The reviewer cannot retroactively improve the quality of the studies reviewed. It is rare to find a review article in which the author ends up satisfied with the studies reviewed. Some may feel that researchers in this area are excessively critical of each other. In any case, the process of reviewing literature can be seen not only as one of summarizing what is known but also of assessing past studies collectively and reflecting on new directions for future research, in terms of improvements in study conceptualization, design, and execution.

Idiosyncratic Dimensions for Structuring a Review Paper

Many nonprofessionals (and, indeed, many professionals) become frustrated when they are unable to determine what research really says about a given issue. In both of the areas discussed above (i.e., stages of satisfaction within a relationship and decision-making roles as a factor in interpersonal conflict), it was not difficult to make some sense of the previous studies, despite the discrepant findings. In many other areas of investigation, ascertaining the conclusions of current research is far more difficult, as discussed in a comprehensive and most readable book by Light and Pillemer (1984).

As an extreme example, Light and Pillemer (1984, p. 5) make reference to two conflicting reviews of research regarding the effects of the environment on the intellectual development of adopted children. Adoption studies of this type have profound influence on theory building in the area of behavior genetics. Munsinger (1974) examined a set of adoption studies and concluded that environmental effects are minimal; Kamin (1978) reviewed the same set of studies and arrived at the opposite conclusion. One specific study from the 1920s was described by Kamin as "large scale and enormously interesting," whereas Munsinger dismissed it because of "methodological and statistical difficulties." Kamin (1978) admonished the public that "readers interested in evaluating the evidence on hereditability of IQ ought not depend on published [review] studies. Those who wish to speak or teach accurately about what is and what is not known have no realistic alternative but to read the literature themselves" (p. 200).

Why do reviewers have so much difficulty agreeing on what the literature says? Light and Pillemer present several reasons. First of all, the traditional review is subjective; there are no rules governing review procedures. Each reviewer brings an idiosyncratic set of assumptions to the process. Some reviewers may search for the most rigorous studies in a data base (though they might well disagree as to which dimensions constitute rigor) whereas others might wish to retain the bulk of the data despite the study's flaws.

Unintended Influences on the Reviewer's Conclusions

In the interpersonal relations literature, most studies gather information from different sources. Each measurement technique has its own advantages and limitations. All too often, different sources of information yield highly discrepant impressions. The reviewer must decide whether data from all sources should be considered and, if so, whether these data should be combined, considered separately, or assigned differential weight in determining the conclusions. Again, the human mind is limited in terms of the numbers of categories and relations it can process. It is easy for a reviewer to overlook important connections between the methods and outcomes of the studies reviewed.

A reviewer reading a study as part of a "vote count" review process will inevitably be influenced by the language of the author more than the data themselves, which the reviewer will probably not re-analyze. While the means and standard deviations are reported in most studies, these may have little impact on a reviewer going over a series of studies using different measures, whereas the authors' narrative sections (the introduction and conclusion) may have greater influence on the outcome of a review than the reviewer realizes.

Combinations of "Apples and Oranges"

An interpersonal relationship is an extremely complex and intricate system. Theorists and researchers conceptualize interpersonal exchanges in a great many ways, including those discussed in other chapters of this volume. The diversity of theoretical and measurement frameworks contributes to the richness of the field but, at the same time, often entails idiosyncratic methods and instruments, which makes studies difficult to categorize and combine for purposes of review. Indeed, many scholars consider research in the social sciences "dilapidated" and "in crisis" because of the failure to achieve consensus regarding standard definitions of research problems and standard research methods (Glass, 1977; Glass, McGaw, & Smith, 1981; Hunter, Schmidt, & Jackson, 1982; Rosenthal, 1984; Wolf, 1986).

In order to attempt a useful synthesis, a reviewer must develop categories of study features, such as observational versus self-report, behavioral versus psychoanalytic intervention. In doing so, some of the individuality of each study is inevitably sacrificed. Some may find that certain studies are billeted with strange bedfellows and may be dissatisfied with the classification. Modern statistical techniques can be of some help here by enabling the reviewer to establish statistically whether certain clusters of studies appear to have consistent effects (see discussion in the following section). However, these procedures cannot resolve the problem that a bit of uniqueness is lost almost every time individual studies are grouped or classified.

NEW STANDARDS IN REVIEWING RESEARCH

There has been increased attention to the art and science of putting together reviews of empirical research. Perhaps more important than any specific technical advance is the growing awareness that increased rigor is necessary in this endeavor. Just as the author of an individual study is responsible for reporting results that would permit another researcher to replicate the study, so the reviewer of a set of studies is responsible for specifying enough information about the sampling and review procedures to permit another reviewer to independently replicate the review and corroborate the conclusions. Of course, there are journals that do not strictly impose these rules on contributors, for either individual studies or review articles, despite the emergence of more stringent requirements in the field in general.

While the procedures for conducting a responsible review are not rigid, several explicit guidelines have been formulated (see Light & Pillemer, 1984, Chap. 6, or Wolf, 1986, pp. 55–56). In general, these standards for review articles parallel what is entailed in conducting sound primary research.

Purpose of the Review

First of all, the purpose of the review must be made explicit. Some may wish to establish whether or not a given proposition is supported by the studies reviewed. The procedures involved in this categorical determination are somewhat different from those involved in establishing the conditions (e.g., type of population, type of study design) under which the given proposition holds.

Description of the Sample

Most guidelines call for clear specification of the procedures for locating and retrieving studies (e.g., computer searches are often used). Reviewers are encouraged to include unpublished studies, such as doctoral dissertations, to correct for the bias in professional journals against nonsignificant findings and/or negative conclusions (Light & Pillemer, 1984).

Judicious Coding and Categorization

Reviewers are encouraged to use their knowledge of the area being reviewed to develop a coding scheme to describe the features of the studies in the sample. This scheme should be as comprehensive and meaningful as possible. Referring to this requirement for an adequate coding scheme and several other aspects of the review process, Wolf (1986) recalls Green and Hall's admonition that "data analysis is an aid to thought, not a substitute" (Green & Hall, 1984, p. 52). Once the studies have been coded, the reviewer must attempt to establish associations between the various features coded and the outcomes of the studies.

There is increasing emphasis on a consideration of quality of research design. Slavin (1987) has taken the position that only studies of high quality should be included in a review (the "best evidence" position) whereas others have adopted broad inclusion criteria in order to consider all available evidence (Glass, McGaw, & Smith, 1981). Probably reflective of majority opinion, Wolf (1986) advocates including quality of design as one of the variables in the review. While ways of implementing this vary, several experts advocate asking a panel of qualified judges to rate the quality of each study. Among the dimensions often considered are degree of experimenter blindness, reliability of measurement, sample size, controls for recording errors, and others (Green & Hall, 1984). By including quality of design as one of the variables of the studies reviewed, the reviewer can avoid discarding large masses of relevant data (from studies that are not of high quality) and can still safeguard the review from erroneous conclusions based on faulty research design in a subset of the original studies.

Reporting the Conclusions

As in primary research, the reviewer is responsible for accurately reporting conclusions based on the data, that is, the studies reviewed. Shortcomings and limitations of the review procedures themselves must be mentioned so that the reader is not misled.

QUANTITATIVE REVIEW PROCEDURES AS FACILITATIVE TOOLS

The implementation of the advances in review techniques discussed in this section often entails the use of quantitative summary statistics for efficiently summarizing the results of studies in the area. Meta-analysis is a well-developed statistical procedure for collectively analyzing the data within the original studies. This "analysis of analyses" (Glass, 1976) yields a statistical estimate of the strength of the combined findings. There are a variety of procedures for calculating this estimate, which is known as "effect size"; the resulting statistics are variously labeled delta (Glass, 1977), r (Rosenthal, 1984), d (Cohen, 1969), g (Hedges, 1981), among others. While the differences among these statistics are not trivial, they are less important than the reviewer's overall rigor in the responsible use of meta-analytic technique (Rosenthal, 1984, Chap. 2).

Meta-analysis is particularly effective in detecting small effects. For example, Rosenthal (1984, pp. 17–18) conducted an experiment in which 41 reviewers were assigned the task of summarizing a given series of seven studies on sex differences in task performance. The participants were randomly assigned to two groups, one of which was directed to use specified quantitative meta-analytic procedures, the other unspecified traditional review techniques. Despite the fact that sex differences were clearly present in the seven studies provided, such differences were detected by only 27% of the group that used traditional methods, compared with 68% of the meta-analysts.

In addition to deriving an overall effect-size estimate, it is also important to establish how consistent the findings are within the studies under review (Hedges & Olkin, 1985; Wolf, 1986). If the results are highly consistent across the data base, subcategories and classifications are not really necessary to explain the data. If the data are not homogeneous, tests for consistency can be used to establish, first, whether the reviewers' subgroupings each display internal consistency and, second, their usefulness in explaining the variance among the study outcomes.

The reader is referred to basic texts by the following authors for a more thorough treatment of meta-analytic procedures, statistical formulae, and so forth: Glass, McGaw, and Smith (1981), Hedges and Olkin (1985), Rosenthal (1984), and Wolf (1986). The following suggestions for the use of meta-analytic procedures illustrate how they might have improved the "vote count" perusal of the *Journal of Marriage and the Family,* discussed earlier, that attempted to review the literature on marital satisfaction across the stages of a relationship:

1. One could calculate and report an overall effect-size estimate for the studies reviewed.

2. One might chart the fluctuations in effect size as a function of the year each study was published (Light & Pillemer, 1984, p. 47). This can help control for fluctuations in cultural norms, values, and common cultural experiences and might clarify the impact of more recent methodological advances.

3. One might mathematically assign greater weight to studies with larger samples (Wolf, 1986).

4. One might report separate effect sizes for observational measures and self-report instruments and test for consistency within each of these subgroupings. One might also ask a panel of experts in the field to rate the quality of measures used in each study; one might then compare separate effect sizes for studies whose measures were rated of low, medium, and high quality.

5. One might contrast the effect sizes for male and female subjects, such as measures of husbands' marital satisfaction at various stages with effect sizes of measures of wives' marital satisfaction at those stages.

6. To assess the relative value of various predictors (say, stage of marriage, decision-making balance, problem-solving techniques, etc. in explaining satisfaction within a relationship), one might consider a multiple regression analysis to determine how well the specific variables of interest contribute to the prediction when analyzed together with other potentially useful variables (Strube & Hartmann, 1983). However, some authorities believe that effect size data rarely satisfy the parametric assumptions of regression analysis (see, e.g., Hedges & Olkin, 1985, pp. 11–12).

7. One might compare the results of studies conducted with different populations (e.g., American minority groups).

The judicious use of meta-analysis would represent a marked advance over early meta-analytic procedures, which were heavily criticized for indiscriminantly lumping together studies of varying quality and dissimilar features. While recent advances in meta-analysis clearly preclude dismissal of these techniques as "mega-silliness" (Eysenck, 1978), it should be recognized that, despite the quantitative nature of meta-analysis, the value of the review is still heavily dependent on the reviewer's judgment in defining its scope and parameters.

Although meta-analysis is a highly useful tool, it is not a panacea for all that is wrong in the area of literature review. As an illustration of this, one might point to a paper by Abrami, Cohen and d'Apollonia (1988) that compared the conclusions of six quantitative reviews on the validity of student ratings of instructional effectiveness. Because of variations in the implementation of meta-analytic procedures, there were marked fluctuations in the final conclusions of the reviews.

How Helpful Is "Help"?

Although meta-analyses are often of particular use in understanding the overall effectiveness of an intervention or therapy technique, intervention research can also be useful for theory building. Rogosa (1988) has pointed out that a causal relationship between variables can be hypothesized if an intervention that successfully improves one variable engenders meaningful change in the other. For example, a theory might indicate that attributions of blame within a relationship cause marital dissatisfaction or dissolution (see the useful vote count review by Bradbury and Fincham, 1990). If treatment studies that focus on improved attributions within relationships (e.g., Baucom & Lester, 1986) demonstrate treatment-related improvement in marital satisfaction, the hypothesized causal relationship between attributions and marital satisfaction is elucidated more clearly than it would be by correlational designs.

Several meta-analytic reviews might be of use to a therapist consulted in the case of Michael and Cathy Stone (see Preface) in determining whether marital therapy has a reasonable chance of helping them overcome their communication problems. Giblin, Sprenkle, and Sheehan (1985) reviewed 85 studies of premarital, marital, and "family enrichment" interventions. The review involves relatively structured intervention packages, rather than the more clinical types of family therapy. The overall effect size estimate was .44 (in standard deviation units), which is significantly different from zero, though small to moderate in size. There were considerable variations among the 23 specific programs studied; Guerney's (1977) Relationship Enhancement Program had the highest effect size. Skill-building interventions were found superior to "insight" approaches. Effect size was unrelated to the cost of the intervention and the leader's experience. Observational measures indicated greater improvement than did self-reports. Additionally, Giblin, Sprenkle, and Sheehan (1985) found that marital enrichment was more effective with highly distressed couples than with those whose functioning was more intact.

Hahlweg and Markman (1988) limited their review to controlled outcome studies of behavioral marital therapy; they reviewed 17 such studies (plus 7 studies of premarital therapy). They found an overall effect size of .95 in standard deviation units. According to Rosenthal and Rubin's (1982) binomial effect-size display formula, this means that one might expect 72% of experimental controls to improve in comparison with 28% of hypothetical controls. Studies in Europe and North America reported similar effects; year of a study's publication was not related to effect size. In contrast with Giblin, Sprenkle, and Sheehan's (1985) conclusions in their review of marital enrichment programs, Hahlweg and Markman (1988) found little difference between observational and self-report measures of outcome for marital interventions (though behavioral measures of *pre*marital interventions had larger effect sizes than self-report measures).

While these meta-analytic reviews are neither complete nor fully consistent, they do enable the researcher, therapist, and even the client to conclude that marital therapy, although not a "miracle cure," is a viable mode of intervention with a clear record of success. Despite their limitations, meta-analytic reviews also give some indication of the relative success rates of various intervention strategies for couples in distress.

RESEARCH AS A GUIDE TO DECISION MAKING

A review of the literature on the impact of an intervention technique is of obvious usefulness for researchers, practitioners, policy-makers, clients, and potential clients. Nevertheless, it should not be assumed that all consumers will attach the same importance to the "track record" that empirical scientists do in making decisions. For example, White and Hatcher (1984) noted that many clinicians are intrigued with the notion that couple complementarity (as opposed to similarity) is associated with marital satisfaction. According to the White and Hatcher review, the preponderance of available data, though limited, suggests that similarity may be more related than complementarity to couple attraction and satisfaction. Nevertheless, the compelling richness of family theory and the charisma of its advocates may have greater impact than a review of research in determining beliefs about marital satisfaction.

Quantitative review techniques should have particular usefulness for scholars of interpersonal communication who are contemplating new studies. A careful and critical inventory of what has already been accomplished, as well as what remains to be learned, can help ensure that the effort involved in conducting new research is a sound investment of time and resources.

References

Abrami, P. C., Cohen, P. A., & d'Apollonia, S. (1988). Implementation problems in meta-analysis. *Review of Educational Research, 58,* 151–179.

Anderson, S. A., Russell, C. S., & Schumm, W. R. (1983). Perceived marital quality and family life-cycle categories: A further analysis. *Journal of Marriage and the Family, 45,* 127–139.

Baucom, D. H., & Lester, G. W. (1986). The usefulness of cognitive restructuring as an adjunct to behavioral marital therapy. *Behavior Therapy, 17,* 385–403.

Boland, J. P., & Follingstad, D. R. (1987). The relationship between communication and marital satisfaction: A review. *Journal of Sex and Marital Therapy, 13,* 286–313.

Bossard, J. H., & Ball, E. S. (1955). Marital unhappiness in the life cycle. *Journal of Marriage and the Family, 17,* 10–14.

Bradbury, T. N., & Fincham, F. D. (1990). Attributions and marriage: Review and critique. *Psychological Bulletin, 107,* 3–33.

Burr, W. R. (1970). Satisfaction with various aspects of marriage over the life cycle sample. *Journal of Marriage and the Family, 32,* 29–37.

Cohen, J. (1969). *Statistical power analysis for the behavioral sciences.* New York: Academic Press.

Deutscher, I. (1964). The quality of post-parental life. *Journal of Marriage and the Family, 26,* 52–59.

Eysenck, H. (1978). An exercise in "mega-silliness". *American Psychologist, 33,* 517.

Giblin, P., Sprenkle, D. H., & Sheehan, R. (1985). Enrichment outcome research: A meta-analysis of premarital, marital, and family interventions. *Journal of Marriage and the Family, 11,* 257–271.

Glass, G. (1976). Primary, secondary, and meta-analysis of research. *Educational Researcher, 5,* 3–8.

Glass, G. (1977). Integrating findings: The meta-analysis of research. *Review of Research in Education, 5,* 351–379.

Glass, G., McGaw, B., & Smith, M. L. (1981). *Meta-analysis in social research.* Beverly Hills: Sage.

Gottman, J. (1979). *Marital interactions: Experimental investigations.* New York: Academic Press.

Gray-Little, B., & Burks, N. (1983). Power and satisfaction in marriage: A review and critique. *Psychological Bulletin, 93,* 513–538.

Green, B., & Hall, J. (1984). Quantitative methods for literature review. *Annual Review of Psychology, 35,* 37–53.

Guerney, B. G. (1977). *Relationship enhancement.* San Francisco: Jossey-Bass.

Hahlweg, K., & Markman, H. J. (1988). Effectiveness of marital therapy: Empirical status of behavioral techniques in preventing and alleviating marital stress. *Journal of Consulting and Clinical Psychology, 56,* 440–447.

Harvey, J. H., Hendrick, S. S., & Tucker, K. (1988). Self-report methods in studying relationships. In S. W. Duck, D. F. Hay, S. E. Hobfoll, W. Ickes, & B. Montgomery (Eds.), *Handbook of personal relationships* (pp. 99–113). New York: Wiley.

Hedges, L. V. (1981). Distribution theory for Glass' estimator of effect size and related estimators. *Journal of Educational Statistics, 6,* 107–128.

Hedges, L. V., & Olkin, I. (1980). Vote-counting methods in research synthesis. *Psychological Bulletin, 88,* 359–369.

Hedges, L. V., & Olkin, I. (1985). *Statistical methods for meta-analysis.* Orlando, FL: Academic Press.

Hunter, J. E., Schmidt, F. L., & Jackson, G. B. (1982). *Meta-analysis: Cumulating research findings across studies.* Beverly Hills, CA: Sage.

Kamin, L. J. (1978). Comment on Munsinger's review of adoption studies. *Psychological Bulletin, 85,* 194–201.

Light, R. J., & Pillemer, D. B. (1984). *Summing up: The science of reviewing research.* Cambridge, MA: Harvard University Press.

Munsinger, H. (1974). The adopted child's IQ: A critical review. *Psychological Bulletin, 82* 623–659.

O'Leary, K. D., & Turkewitz, H. (1978). Methodological errors in marital and child treatment research. *Journal of Consulting and Clinical Psychology, 46,* 247–258.

Rogers, L. E., Millar, F. E., & Bavelas, J. B. (1985). Methods for analyzing marital discourse: Implications of a systems approach. *Family Process, 24,* 175–187.

Rogosa, D. (1988, April). *Casual models do not support scientific conclusions.* Paper presented at the annual meeting of the American Educational Research Association, New Orleans.

Rollins, B., & Cannon, K. L. (1974). Marital satisfaction over the life cycle: A re-evaluation. *Journal of Marriage and the Family, 36,* 271–282.

Rollins, B., & Feldman, H. (1970). Marital satisfaction over the family life cycle. *Journal of Marriage and the Family, 32,* 20–28.

Rosenthal, R. (1984). *Meta-analytic procedures for social research.* Beverly Hills: Sage.

Rosenthal, R., & Rubin, D. B. (1982). A simple, general purpose display of magnitude of experimental effects. *Journal of Educational Psychology, 74,* 166–169.

Slavin, R. E. (1987). Best evidence synthesis: Why less is more. *Educational Researcher, 16,* 15–16.

Sprenkle, D. H., & Olson, D. H. (1978). Circumplex model of marital systems. *Journal of Marriage and Family Counseling, 4,* 59–74.

Strube, M. J., & Hartmann, D. P. (1983). Meta-analysis: Techniques, applications and functions. *Journal of Consulting and Clinical Psychology, 51,* 14–27.

White, S. G., & Hatcher, C. (1984). Couple complementarity and similarity: A review of the literature. *American Journal of Family Therapy, 12,* 15–25.

Wolf, F. M. (1986). *Meta-analysis: Quantitative methods for research synthesis.* Beverly Hills: Sage.

PART IV

CONCLUSION

Chapter 18

Methodology and Open Dialogue

BARBARA M. MONTGOMERY
STEVE DUCK

As much as this book is meant to be about interpersonal interaction in a generic sense, it is also meant to be about the interaction among scholars who study interaction, as noted in Chapter 1. As editors, we had a dual purpose in developing this project. The first was to produce a solid text describing options for doing interaction research and the consequences of choosing various options; the second was to encourage open dialogue about research methods in which the worth of very different—sometimes incommensurate—approaches was acknowledged and confirmed. We feel good about what we have done with regard to both goals. Highly competent researchers wrote the chapters of this text, researchers from a variety of disciplines and with diverse approaches. In the most deliberate of ways, they balanced praise for a technique with criticism of it, and they often offered comparisons between their method and others, contrasting the pros and cons of different ways of studying interaction. Authors also applied their methodological approaches to a sample research problem, illustrating the kinds of questions each method best addresses and the kinds of answers it leads to. Above all else, authors demonstrated a pervasive *reasonableness* in their positions by accepting the viability of other ways of doing interaction research, while still maintaining the worth and integrity of their personal way.

Such openness with regard to methodology occurs infrequently in the study of social interaction, and its rules and techniques are as yet to be formalized. This is not to say that interaction does not occur among scholars subscribing to fundamentally different approaches. In fact, much interaction has taken place of late (e.g., Dervin, Grossberg, O'Keefe, & Wartella 1989; Fisk & Shweder, 1986; *Journal of Communication,* 1983). But often such ventures end up reading more like modern political debates than dialogues. Authors' points seem to pass each other in the dark night of unshared epistemological vocabularies and values. The result is too often a series of ethnocentric monologues and entrenched advocacies rather than a risky openness that could be the basis for true dialogue. We believe that such an approach is inadequate in the face of the current diversity of perspectives about interpersonal interaction. Rather, we choose to empha- size balance and openness, which we have vigorously incorporated into this book's structure and which the authors have bravely endorsed in their writing.

The Challenge of Diverse Ways of Knowing about Interaction

If the treasure of scholarly investigation is manifested by increased un- derstanding, then the field of social interaction inquiry is indeed rich, for understandings—very divergent ones—abound. Until recently, the most prominent differences have been those between the various academic dis- ciplines (due primarily to scholarly disagreement often coupled with firm insistence—even dogma) about the appropriate level of analysis for study- ing interaction. For instance, strong traditions encouraged social psycholo- gists to focus on the individuals in the interaction, attending to their cognitions, attitudes, emotions, and behaviors as distinctly identified per- sons. Communication scholars, on the other hand, have tended to adopt a dyadic focus by centering on the messages of the interaction as they pass from one individual to the other. And sociologists focused more closely on the institutions contextualizing the interaction. We see nothing wrong with the emergence of different traditions and specialties in different disciplines, as long as they are emphases rather than dogmas. Further, we welcome the fact that, as distinct as these differences have been in the past, they appear to be dissipating as interdisciplinary conferences, professional associations, journals (e.g., *Journal of Social and Personal Relationships*), and texts (e.g., Burnett, McGhee, & Clarke, 1987; Duck, Hay, Hobfoll, Ickes, & Montgomery, 1988) bring scholars together to share ideas. It is no longer a foregone conclusion that the level and unit of analysis will signal a research- er's disciplinary identity and vice versa. In fact, there has been movement across disciplines toward encompassing multiple levels of analysis simultaneously (see, e.g., Kenny & Kashy, Chapter 15; McCall & Simmons, Chapter 4; Montgomery, 1984, 1988).

Diversity has not been so readily accommodated with regard to methodological perspectives for studying interaction. Researchers seem less willing to give up their methodological dogmas than their disciplinary ones. At issue is not whether diversity exists; it does. A complete list of current research approaches would challenge the page limitations of this chapter; indeed, the seventeen previous chapters indicate how extensive the research options are. As Shweder (1986) notes, however, the list can be divided into two camps, along a series of dichotomies:

> objective versus subjective, seen versus unseen, outer versus inner, public versus private, controlled versus free, reliable versus unreliable, systematic versus unsystematic, automatic (mechanical) versus willed (purposive), explanation versus understanding, prediction versus understanding, explained-by-reference-to-causal-law versus understood-by-reference-to-intentions, general versus context-specific, regular versus irregular, discovered versus constructed, value-free versus value-saturated, formal versus informal, materialist versus idealist, one versus many, instrumental versus symbolic, motion versus action, science versus humanity. (p. 177)

Many of the authors in this text allude to these same parallel worlds of methodological inquiry. Bochner, Cissna, and Garko (Chapter 2) differentiate between approaches concerned with prediction and control on the one hand and approaches concerned with interpreting meanings on the other. Burnett (Chapter 7) contrasts the assumptions of positivism and the assumptions of interpretivism, and she identifies the gathering of interactants' accounts primarily with the latter. Surra and Ridley (Chapter 3) compare objective with subjective approaches to describing interaction events, and they suggest that the essential differentiating characteristic is the extent of behavioral, affective, and/or cognitive interconnection between observer/reporter and interactants. Other authors (e.g., Metts, Sprecher, & Cupach, Chapter 9; Tracy, Chapter 10; Sillars, Chapter 11; Tardy & Hosman, Chapter 12; Bakeman, Chapter 14; Holmes & Poole, Chapter 16; Schneider, Chapter 17), while sometimes being cautious in drawing the line between the two worlds of the objectivists and the interpretivists, nevertheless refer to similar distinguishing characteristics.

The diversity represented by these two very different approaches to inquiry is, we believe, a sign of a healthy, involving, and evolving field of scholarship. But diversity has its drawbacks. Chief among them is an inattentiveness on the part of each camp to the substantive advances of the other. Scholars seem drawn to the work of those with the same perspective as their own. This is undoubtedly because both the art and the science of competent inquiry rest in presenting rationales and justifications for investigative choices that lead to consensual endorsement among a set of peers. Possession of similar premises is nine-tenths of any consensual agreement. Thus, a conference's programs or a journal's pages are more likely to be occupied by scholars who see the interaction world in the same way (although they might see different things) rather than by scholars who see the same things but look in different ways. The issues then center on how well the research was done, not on why it was done in the first place; on the explanations for the data, not on the nature of the data itself. Such dialogue is usually interesting to the participants, but rarely does it test the limits of the researchers' assumptions. In other words, it is closed and constrained, problems we identified and discussed in Chapter 1.

Seldom is this disregard of alternative approaches the product of outright scorn or contempt. But neither is it entirely innocent. Rather, it seems to stem from a kind of ethnocentric approach to the world of interaction scholarship. Such an approach is characterized by the perception of all who adopt different approaches as "nonnatives"—certainly different and often misguided, uninformed, or crazy—and a reluctance to put one's own approach at risk by engaging these nonnatives in meaningful dialogue (Pearce, 1989). Day-to-day transactions within the ethnocentric world of interaction scholarship are achieved through a script of begrudging pluralism: a kind of "they can do their thing and I can do mine and never the twain shall meet" approach. The long-term script, however, is much less dispassionate. It calls for "revolutions" in which perspectives battle until some are overthrown and others (or, ideally, *one* other) predominate (e.g., Kuhn, 1970). The long and the short of an ethnocentric approach is the kind of mindless but complete allegiance that, as Bochner, Cissna, and Garko (Chapter 2) note, adds "relationalist," "constructivist," and "behaviorist" to the other oppositional sects of modern life.

Toward Coordination through Open Dialogue

A different approach to diversity is possible, one that Pearce (1989) has called "cosmopolitan." Whereas ethnocentric tactics aim primarily for coherence and consistency by promoting one's own perspective in the face of all others, cosmopolitan tactics aim primarily for coordination among different perspectives aimed at accomplishing some task. Coordination refers to the kind of collaboration between participants that produces an interaction that makes sense to both of them. Coordination does *not* require the sharing of the same reality; it requires only that participants be aware of and act with regard to each other's different realities.

Pearce (1989) argues that this is achieved through a kind of

> Social eloquence [that] exploits the potential of symbolic systems to achieve coordination among incommensurate social realities without denying their differences. It consists of a willingness and ability to construct ways of comparing and thus rendering rational the differences among the stories and practices of various social realities. (p. 171)

Ironically, the "willingness and ability to construct ways of comparing" different perspectives is the foundation of communication, of dialogue, and of interaction itself. Prelli (1989) makes a similar point in his analysis of the rhetoric of science, and he concludes that the very notion of "incommensurability" is misleading in that possessing different assumptions about how best to understand something does not preclude reasonable discourse:

> That competing proponents of paradigms choose and work from different conceptions of how to think and to do science does not mean they cannot learn, understand, and assess the reasonableness of each other's paradigms. Interpretive success during interparadigmatic discourse does not require establishing meanings and conceptions that remain the same as we move from one paradigm to another. The ability to understand even a comparatively bizarre culture's conceptions of belief and knowledge is a "hard case" instance of our general abilities to render conceptions different from our own intelligible. (p. 114)

In practice, this means that proponents of different perspectives take not only their own but also others' beliefs and assumptions seriously, recognizing their worth and utility within the context of their respective identifying perspectives. It means that scholars look for the strengths in other perspectives, not just weaknesses. It means that communication between scholars is based on finding ways to *coordinate* research efforts, not necessarily *share* the same interpretations of those efforts.

Participants in this kind of dialogue need to recognize that the "best" arguments for their views—the ones that have been most successful with peers who share their perspective—will be the least successful in dialogue with peers who do not share their perspective. Arguments framed within the logic of one approach are likely to carry very little weight within the logic of another approach. Further, if arguments cannot be framed in terms of other perspectives, their inherent limitations, their narrowness, and incompleteness, become apparent.

Additionally, such dialogue is likely to lead to successful coordination among approaches if it takes place while trying to solve substantive but generalized research problems that have meaning across approaches, like the sample research problem presented in this text. Just as theories and paradigms emerge from exemplary solutions to research puzzles, so too are effective coordination tactics more likely to be realized in the doing of, rather than the stewing about, research. Scholarship progresses through the *testing* of ideas rather than through their mere exposition, and open dialogue promotes testing discussions.

This kind of interaction may or may not result in a participant actually changing his or her approach, but that should not be the point anyway. It is not *sharing* that we seek to promote. Rather, open dialogue is a method through which researchers representing incommensurate schools and approaches might discover new possibilities for *coordinating* their efforts.

Coordination Devices for Engaging in Open Dialogue

Coordination is achieved when the integrity of differing approaches is preserved while proponents interact in the inquiry process. This kind of interaction or dialogue appears to be presently taking place—albeit, in a limited way—in some research circles. One purpose of this section is to present some examples, drawing especially from the chapters presented in this text.

The primary requisite for such dialogue is some vehicle for transporting information back and forth between perspectives. Such vehicles might be termed "perspectival shuttles" in that they link perspectives through information channels. We have identified five such shuttle devices that are being used to connect different viewpoints about interaction processes. These are translations, transformations, enrichments, verifications, and creations. While most of these seem to involve only elemental forms of the open dialogue we have been talking about, their existence is encouraging.

TRANSLATIONS

Translations are attempts to bridge the distinct vocabularies that characterize different perspectives and to find equivalents of the concepts of one perspective in the terms of another. As Shweder (1986) rightly notes, the basic concepts of most schools of inquiry are difficult to translate, and when attempts have been made by one school, the other school usually responds that "something essential has been lost in the translation" (p. 163). The very issue of whether translations can bridge different cultures of thought has been the product of considerable debate (e.g., Derrida, 1985). Yet the goal of translation as it is being used here is not to produce one-to-one correspondence. A translation is not likely to result in the *sharing* of the same meanings for a concept; rather it is merely one device for rendering different experiences of a concept comparable.

Further, translations are usually much more than simple word-for-word interpretations from one perspective's language to another's. Strictly literal translations of any language often miss the point entirely. Rather, coordination can be achieved through translations that creatively find a way to say in one language what has been said in another. As Pearce (1989) notes, "this sometimes requires enriching the language so as to make it possible to say something new" (p. 178).

Just such a translation seems to be serving as a bridge between interpretivists' and objectivists' approaches to the issue of participants' understandings of their own interaction. While traditional objectivists have acknowledged the existence of participants' subjective perceptions, these have been viewed primarily as sources of error in estimating objective reality. Thus, objectivists have attempted to neutralize subject bias with random sampling and scaling techniques or to eliminate it altogether with direct observation. Interpretivists, on the other hand, reject the notion of a singular reality identified by brute facts and unbiased data; instead, they assume that multiple "social realities" are created and recreated in interaction processes and that these realities must be referenced in any explanation of interaction (Berger & Luckman, 1967; Gergen & Davis, 1985).

It is somewhat paradoxical, then, to see the concept of social reality gaining more prominence of late in otherwise traditionally objectivist literatures. This trend is illustrated by the arguments that Poole and Folger (1981) make for establishing the "representational validity" of behavioral coding schemes (see also Baxter, Chapter 13, and Surra & Ridley, Chapter 3). Poole and Folger contend that researchers who use various behavior coding schemes regularly reference participants' understanding of their interactions to explain their findings. Therefore, these researchers are obligated to demonstrate that, in addition to predictive validity, the coding schemes represent well the interactants' meanings for utterances and behaviors. Of late, methods for establishing representational validity have been incorporated in a number of studies relying on coding schemes (see, e.g., Baxter & Dindia, 1990; Folger & Poole, 1982; Planalp, Rutherford, & Honeycutt, 1988).

The point is that the more objectivists reference the concept of "representational validity" in their own research, the more closely they will move toward an understanding of the meaning of "social realities" as it is used in interpretivist research, and vice versa. This kind of conceptual cross-pollination through translation is not aimed at producing some type of hybrid perspective so much as it is aimed at simply increasing understanding for and appreciation of different ways of knowing.

Baxter makes a similar argument in Chapter 13 of this book, suggesting that both objectivist and interpretivist approaches to content analysis could gain much from each other's work by concentrating on issues of translation, especially as they affect the coding process. In particular, her discussion of how interpretive analyses might be more systematized translates the objectivist notions of measurement reliability and validity into concepts and ideas available within an interpretivist view.

Cappella (Chapter 6) is even more direct in his urging researchers to find direct links between results gained from different approaches to interaction assessment. He calls for research projects that would create a "mapping" between objective and subjective measurement forms and between participant and observer perspectives. In effect, Cappella is calling for research aimed at translation, and he enumerates both practical and theoretical advantages, all of which could be organized under the general goal of coordination, that would result from such efforts.

TRANSFORMATIONS

Transformations are attempts to change the information gained from one perspective into a form more useful for a different perspective. As with other kinds of transformations, the "before" and the "after" usually appear quite different, yet they share a common, underlying essence.

Transformations can bridge some gaps between different schools of inquiry. Research projects are frequently designed to include an "exploratory" phase marked by qualitative methods and a "confirmatory" phase marked by quantitative methods (See, e.g., Bakeman, Chapter 14, and Tardy & Hosman, Chapter 12). A few projects carry through with a final "interpretive" phase, marked by another transformation back to qualitative methods. Tracy (Chapter 10), for example, notes that interpretivist, qualitative approaches to discourse analysis are "invaluable to traditional researchers [i.e., objectivists] in the theory invention and hypothesis formulation phases."

Purists have argued that much is forfeited with such transformations, that the richness of qualitative data is lost when it is quantified, and that the precision of quantitative data is lost when it is qualified. But that is really the point of a transformation, for it must preserve the integrity of each perspective involved in the transaction. To do so requires suspending the evaluative criteria of one perspective when moving to another.

The potential gains of transformations outweigh the costs. Bakeman (Chapter 14), for instance, talks about the advantages of moving between an interpretivist and an objectivist vantage point in the same study. He notes that the interpretivist view gives the researcher a sense or a feel for the phenomenon of interest, which is essential, for instance, for developing and refining a viable coding scheme or for illustrating typical patterns in the data. The objectivist view provides a way to insulate data, at least partly, from personal bias and to allow for greater generalization. As Bakeman notes, "At their best, quantitative studies stand as a bulwark against bias, but qualitative studies can greatly enrich numeric understanding."

ENRICHMENTS

Enrichments attempt to enhance understanding by presenting two different and distinct perspectives within the same research. While these are similar to transformations, enrichments differ in that perspectives are not presented sequentially but, rather, side by side. Enrichments proceed with the simultaneous development of different understandings of the same phenomenon.

The challenge of using enrichments is to keep the demarcation line between perspectives clear and sharp. Letting the assumptions of one perspective spill over into another violates the latter's integrity, which the cosmopolitan approach is dedicated to preserving.

As difficult as it may seem to construct effective enrichments, some few have made laudable attempts. For instance, Blumstein & Schwartz (1983) in their book *American Couples* present a detailed, qualitative account of married and cohabiting couples' interaction relative to the issues of money, work, and sex. Interspersed (especially in the extensive notes) is a complementary quantitative analysis of the same issues. Having both analyses available simultaneously enhances and broadens the emerging understanding of the relationship dynamics under study. The precision of the objectivist approach is evident, but so is the richness and depth of information characteristic of interpretivist approaches.

Duck's (Chapter 8) account of diary and log methods illustrates one way that both types of information can be gathered in the same study. Respondents to the Iowa Communication Record (ICR) provide both qualitative information about their interactions (in terms of when, where, and with whom they occurred, how they ended, who started them, and so on) and also quantitative information (in terms of the openness of the conversation, the degree to which it seemed to create change in the relationship, and so forth). From such a technique not only are the subjects' perceptions of the qualitative material available for analysis as subjective contributors to the overall features of the interaction, but also their quantitative assessment of those same interactions are likewise available. Using this technique, Duck, Rutt, Hurst & Strejc (in press) were able to show not only that friends, best friends, and lovers do not have the "qualitative" relationship to each other that they have been traditionally assumed to have, but neither do they have the "quantitative" one. That is, lovers are the only dyads who were shown to meet predominantly for the sake of the relationship, whereas friends and best friends were shown to meet merely for the sake of talk. Nonetheless, best friends, rather than lovers, are the most satisfied with their interactions. From these and similar studies it has been possible to start building up a picture not only of the "facts" about interactions with associates but also of the ways people feel about those facts.

The outcome of building such enrichments into the same study is two distinct understandings of the same phenomenon. Warner (Chapter 5) provides a vivid illustration of the dynamic potential for coordination between these two understandings with dialogue from Woody Allen's film *Annie Hall*. Juxtaposing the main characters' responses to how often they make love (He: "Almost never—three or four times a week"; She: "Constantly—three or four times a week") presents a picture of the place of love making in this couple's relational interaction that is very different—and decidedly richer—from what either the objective answers to the questions alone or the subjective answers alone would have given.

VERIFICATIONS

Verifications are attempts to substantiate conclusions reached within one perspective with evidence gained from another. As stated earlier, a cosmopolitan approach does not assume that different perspectives will always, or even regularly, lead to the same conclusions. In fact, the predominant trend is likely to be just the opposite. But, as proponents of triangulation and multimethod techniques argue, scholars should sit up and take notice in those instances in which similar conclusions *are* realized through decidedly different methods. Rosengren (1989, p. 33) goes so far as to call it "the triumph of science and scholarship" when scholars reach the same conclusions despite their different backgrounds and views.

Consider the literature regarding self-disclosure. One of the reasons self-disclosure and openness enjoy intense attention as interaction characteristics is the verification of their relationship effects across a variety of research paradigms (see, e.g., Derlega & Berg, 1987). Information coming from both therapy case studies and laboratory experiments has been relatively consistent in describing major patterns; and when results have differed, researchers from both sides of the methodological fence have been motivated to go back to their respective paradigms to produce additional information.

In a sense, such ideas lie behind the themes in the chapters by Warner (Chapter 5) and by Holmes and Poole (Chapter 16), who urge verification of findings observed in settings decontextualized from time and process. By attempting to find ways in which such isolated findings fit into and are modified by the general flow of experience, such approaches invite us to ask new questions about the phenomena and their origins.

Verification has also been used in work on nonverbal communication. From studies of single instances of nonverbal communication in isolation from the flow of everyday life have developed many different applications of the work to settings usually studied from entirely different paradigms. One example is the verification of certain nonverbal communication patterns in the specific context of loneliness, a research topic covered in the volume edited by Peplau and Perlman (1982). Findings from fields as diverse as clinical psychology, gerontology, and communication (and from other approaches equally as diverse) now support the general claim that lonely individuals have disrupted and unrewarding nonverbal communication patterns. Such a proposal was first made in the Peplau and Perlman volume, and its verification by workers in different fields and with different approaches helps to develop dialogue between researchers and to produce practical applications of techniques valuable in relieving the problem itself.

Finally, behavioral observation of the type discussed by Sillars in Chapter 11 has now confirmed that distressed marriages also show disturbed nonverbal communication patterns in the everyday conduct of the marital relationship. Further, this approach has shown that the individual patterns of disrupted nonverbal communication shown in isolation by individuals studied in the lab are not simple mechanical difficulties but have distressing effects on partners and lead to lowered enjoyment of interaction. Such verifications are produced by scholars attempting to stretch the findings of other workers to apply to new settings or circumstances and, in so doing, to find the consistencies that emerge from repeated testing.

CREATIONS

Creations are attempts to modify established perspectives and procedures or to devise new ones in light of our knowledge about existing ones. Ways of knowing are not static; rather, they are the dynamic, evolving creations of their proponents and their constructive critics. Further, proponents of different perspectives who interact in the kind of open dialogue described here are likely to be affected by that interaction in the ways they think about and study questions of interest.

Productive creations will be few and far between if scholars representing different perspectives restrict their dialogue to abstract, metaperspectival discussions. Such discussions tend to foster the kind of oppositional and authoritarian pronouncements that impede, rather than encourage, the embracing of new ideas. As Delia (1977) stresses, new perspectives are never adopted by taking a vote after an argument. A similar claim was made earlier by Clore and Byrne (1974), who noted that there are essentially three ways to develop a research program: (1) create your own, even if there are other flourishing paradigms out there already; (2) throw your hand in with one or another of the existing paradigms and attempt to annihilate the influence of the other paradigm(s); or (3) try to find the commonalities in existing (and your own) paradigms and bring them together. Those of us who see the research enterprise as essentially a collaborative endeavor, rather than an imperialistic one, will normally choose to develop the third line of approach, but insofar as the first would require a researcher to assess the strengths of other approaches, it would be a satisfactory road to take as well. An interesting example of the third means of developing scholarship is presented by Pierce, Sarason, and Sarason (1990) in their attempt to reconcile different approaches to the study of social support and to relate its dynamics to the processes of personal relationships as a whole.

As these examples suggest, scholars are more likely to develop new ideas as they interact about common research interests, much as the authors in this text have in expressing their approaches, questions, and concerns about studying the conflict between Cathy and Michael Stone. Berger (1989) calls this a "bottom-up" process of change that occurs "with the realization that a particular research approach is not leading one where one wishes to go" (p. 131). This realization encourages the search for better solutions to the conceptual and methodological problems involved in a particular research project. As Kenny and Kashy (Chapter 15) effectively argue, a key to arriving at such a realization is to view research roadblocks not as problems to be avoided but as opportunities to learn. The number of avenues along which to encounter such opportunities are increased to the extent that one has had meaningful contact with scholars representing different research traditions.

Changes that have occurred over the past few decades in applying the traditional empirical perspective in the social sciences illustrate the point. There has been a softening of the goal to achieve an objective understanding of a stable reality that is lawfully ordered. In practice—and sometimes in print (see, e.g., Fisk & Shweder, 1986)—most interaction researchers are content to describe probabilistic regularities rather than deterministic laws. Most also acknowledge the influence of the culture and the times as qualifiers of their objectivity and of the stability of their findings. Tardy and Hosman (Chapter 12) note further that traditional experimentalists recently have made attempts to decrease the artificiality of research settings and to view subjects as active participants in the interaction process, participants who construct meanings and interpret situations. These modifications are due, at least in part, to the influence of alternative perspectives.

We are not suggesting here that the creation of new perspectives or the modification of old ones should stem from a search for a single, all-encompassing point of view. In the first place, a grand paradigm does not appear to be lurking on the horizon of social scientific thought. More to the point, the search for an overarching perspective smacks of ethnocentrism in its implication that there exists a correct, singularly valid perspective that needs only to be discovered. A cosmopolitan approach, in contrast, acknowledges the inherent differences among perspectives and attempts to bridge them only for the sake of coordinating research efforts.

Conclusion

Admittedly, the descriptions of these various coordination devices seem a bit thin in places. The cosmopolitan approach does not as yet enjoy a widespread following in the social sciences, rendering examples relatively few and far between. This is not terribly surprising: the prevailing ethnocentrism encourages the belief that the willingness to engage in open dialogue with translations, transformations, and so forth signals a deficiency in commitment and understanding of the principles represented in one's own perspective. We, on the other hand, believe that the cosmopolitan approach offers a rich promise of interesting and enlightening dialogue among scholars of social interaction. It is a risk we hope researchers will take more frequently.

References

Baxter, L., & Dindia, K. (1990). Marital partners' perceptions of marital maintenance strategies. *Journal of Social and Personal Relationships, 7*, pp. 187–208.

Berger, C. (1989). Back to the future: Paradigm monologues revisited. In B. Dervin, L. Grossberg, B. O'Keefe & E. Wartella (Eds.), *Rethinking Communication* (pp. 130–134). Newbury Park, CA: Sage.

Berger, P., & Luckman, T. (1967). *The social construction of reality*. New York: Anchor.

Blumstein, P. & Schwartz, P. (1983). *American couples: Money, work, sex*. New York: Morrow.

Burnett, R., McGhee, P. & Clarke, O. (1987). *Accounting for relationships: Explanation, representation, and knowledge*. London: Methuen.

Clore, G. L., & Byrne, D. (1974). A reinforcement affect model of attraction. In T. L. Huston (Ed.), *Foundations of Interpersonal Attraction* (pp. 143–170). New York: Academic Press.

Derlega, V., & Berg, J. (1987). *Self-disclosure: Theory, research, and therapy*. New York: Plenum.

Derrida, J. (1985). *The ear of the other: Otobiography, transference, translation*. New York: Schocken.

Dervin, B., Grossberg, L., O'Keefe, B., & Wartella, E. (1989). *Rethinking communication: Vol. 1. Paradigm issues*. Newbury Park, CA: Sage.

Duck, S. W., Hay, D., Hobfoll, S., Ickes, W., & Montgomery, B. (Eds.). (1988). *Handbook of personal relationships: Theory, research and interventions*. Chichester, UK: Wiley.

Duck, S. W., Rutt, D. J., Hurst, M., & Strejc, H. (in press). Some evident truths about communication in everyday relationships: All communication is not created equal. *Human Communication Research*.

Fisk, D., & Shweder, R. (1986). *Metatheory in social science: Pluralisms and subjectivities*. Chicago: University of Chicago Press.

Folger, J. P., & Poole, M. S. (1982). Relational coding schemes: The question of validity. In M. Burgoon (Ed.), *Communication yearbook 5* (pp. 235–247). New Brunswick, NJ: Transaction.

Gergen, K., & Davis, K. E. (1985). *The social construction of the person.* New York: Springer.

Journal of Communication. (1983). Vol. 33.

Kuhn, T. (1970). *The structure of scientific revolutions.* Chicago, IL: University of Chicago Press.

Montgomery, B. (1984). Individual differences and relational interdependencies in social interaction. *Human Communication Research, 11,* 33–60.

Montgomery, B. (1988). Quality communication in personal relationships. In S. Duck, D. Hay, S. Hobfoll, W. Ickes, & B. Montgomery (Eds.), *Handbook of personal relationships: Theory, research and interventions* (pp. 343–359). Chichester, UK: Wiley.

Pearce, W. B. (1989). *Communication and the human condition.* Carbondale, IL: Southern Illinois University Press.

Peplau, L. A., & Perlman, D. (1982). *Loneliness: A sourcebook of theory, research, and therapy.* New York: Wiley.

Pierce, G., Sarason, B. R., & Sarason, I. G. (1990). Integrating social support perspectives: Working models, personal relationships, and situational factors. In S. W. Duck, *Personal relationships and social support.* (R. Cohen Silver, Ed.; pp. 173–189). London: Sage.

Planalp, S., Rutherford, D., & Honeycutt, J. (1988). Relative and absolute judgments of speech rate from masked and content-standard stimuli. *Human Communication Research, 14,* 516–547.

Poole, M. S., & Folger, J. (1981). A method for establishing the representational validity of interaction coding systems: Do we see what they see? *Human Communication Research, 8,* 26–42.

Prelli, L. (1989). *A rhetoric of science: Inventing scientific discourse.* Columbia, SC: University of South Carolina Press.

Rosengren, K. (1989). Paradigms lost and regained. In B. Dervin, L. Grossberg, B. O'Keefe, & E. Wartella (Eds.), *Rethinking communication: Vol. 1. Paradigm issues* (pp. 21–39). Newbury Park, CA: Sage.

Shweder, R. A. (1986). Divergent rationalities. In D. Fiske & R. Shweder (Eds.), *Metatheory in social science: Pluralisms and subjectivities* (pp. 163–196). Chicago, IL: University of Chicago Press.

Author Index

Subject Index